DISCARDED

THE
UNIVERSITY OF WINNIPEG
PORTAGE & BALMORAL
WINNIPEG, MAN.   R3B 2E9
CANADA

HANDEL'S MESSIAH

From a Portrait by Thomas Hudson (1748)
in the Bodleian Library, Oxford

HANDEL'S MESSIAH

A Touchstone of Taste

by

Robert Manson Myers

> . . . Some to Church repair
> Not for the doctrine, but the music there.
> —ALEXANDER POPE

1971

OCTAGON BOOKS
New York

Copyright, 1948, by The Macmillan Company

Reprinted 1971
by special arrangement with Robert Manson Myers

OCTAGON BOOKS
A DIVISION OF FARRAR, STRAUS & GIROUX, INC.
19 Union Square West
New York, N.Y. 10003

LIBRARY OF CONGRESS CATALOG CARD NUMBER: 72-159747

ISBN 0-374-96035-6

Printed in U.S.A. by
NOBLE OFFSET PRINTERS, INC.
NEW YORK 3, N. Y.

IN MEMORIAM

WILLIETTE RUTH MYERS

(25 January 1889—15 July 1944)

But let my due feet never fail,
To walk the studious Cloysters pale,
And love the high embowed Roof,
With antick Pillars massy proof,
And storied Windows richly dight,
Casting a dimm religious light.
There let the pealing Organ blow,
To the full voic'd Quire below,
In Service high, and Anthems cleer,
As may with sweetnes, through mine ear,
Dissolve me into extasies,
And bring all Heav'n before mine eyes.

Acknowledgments

IN WRITING THIS VOLUME and preparing it for the press I have incurred various obligations which I acknowledge with pleasure. It was my good fortune to pursue the study of Handel's *Messiah* at Columbia University under the scholarly and sympathetic guidance of Professor Marjorie Hope Nicolson, Professor Ernest Hunter Wright, and Professor Paul Henry Lang, whose keen interest and sound judgment provided inspiration and counsel over the course of many months. Of those with whom I enjoyed the privilege of personal conference at Columbia, I should like also to mention Professor Oscar James Campbell, Professor James Lowry Clifford, and Professor Elliot Van Kirk Dobbie. At Yale University Professor Maynard Mack and Professor William K. Wimsatt, Jr., undertook the laborious task of reading portions of the manuscript and offered judicious criticisms. Professor George W. Sherburn of Harvard University read an early draft of this volume with his characteristic generosity and acumen. Miss Nan Cooke Carpenter reviewed and criticized the work at several stages of its development and in its final form. For critical comments upon the manuscript I am also indebted to Professor Seth Bingham, Professor H. C. Hatfield, Professor Douglas Moore, and Professor Norman L. Torrey, all of Columbia University.

I am especially grateful to Mary Countess Howe for permission to reproduce the "Gopsall Portrait" of Handel, to Edward Viscount Curzon for permission to reproduce the portrait of Charles Jennens, to Sir Newman Flower for prompt response to my queries, and to Sir Owen Morshead, Librarian of Windor Castle, for securing for me His Majesty's gracious permission to publish a facsimile of the final page of Handel's autograph score of *Messiah*. In assembling my materials I received courteous consideration from the authorities of the Columbia University Library, the Harvard University Library, the Library of Congress, the New York Public Library, the Yale University Library, and the British Museum. For special assistance I should like to record my debt of gratitude to Miss Jacqueline Castles, Miss A. M. Fielding, Miss Jean Macalister, Miss Eva J. O'Meara, Miss Anne Pratt, Miss Marjorie Gray Wynne, and Mr. Frederic G. Ludwig. Professor Henri Peyre and Professor Curt von Faber du Faur of Yale University kindly consented to check my translations from the French and the German. To George Bernard Shaw I am obligated for permission to quote excerpts from his musical criticism in the London *Star* and *World;* to E. P. Dutton & Co., Inc., of New York, for permission to quote material from the Shrewsbury Edition of Samuel Butler's *Works;* and to Professor Arthur D. Nock of Harvard University for permission to quote short passages from my article, "Fifty Sermons on Handel's *Messiah*," which appeared in *The Harvard Theological Review* for October 1946. Finally I wish to thank the editors of The Macmillan Company for their steady cooperation and imperturbable patience.

ROBERT MANSON MYERS

College of William and Mary
14 September 1947

Contents

A TOUCHSTONE OF TASTE xix

CHAPTER
I. SOME ARE BORN GREAT (1711–1741) 3
I Handel's *Rinaldo* (1711)—Aaron Hill—Giacomo Rossi—Hill's elaborate "machines and decorations"—A cast exclusively Italian—Handel's sudden vogue—Alarm at Drury Lane and York Buildings—Addison and Steele—Hostile criticism in *Spectator* 5—Handel's "Sparrows and Chaffinches"—*The Cruelty of Atreus*—*Spectator* 18—Addison's history of Italian opera in England (1705-1710)—*Arsinoe*—*Camilla*—Bilingual opera—*Rosamond*—*Thomyris*—*Pyrrhus and Demetrius*—*Almahide*—*Hydaspes*—Toby Rentfree—*Etearco*—Lord Chesterfield. II Rigid conventions of eighteenth-century Italian opera—Five standard aria-types—Augustan England's persistent aversion to Italian opera—Vain singers—John Gay—Foreign texts—Addison—John Hughes—Anti-British implications—James Miller—John Dennis—London's desire for *English* music. III *The Beggar's Opera* (1728)—Consequent failure of Italian opera—John Gay—*The Craftsman*—Mrs. Delany—*Haman and Mordecai*—*Esther* (1732)—Birth of concert oratorio—Its impact upon satirical literature—*See and Seem Blind*—*The Manners of the Age*—*The Man of Taste*—William Hogarth—*The Woman of Taste*—Handel's shift from opera to oratorio—Aaron Hill's letter—Handel's motives practical rather than artistic or religious. IV Eighteenth-century definitions of Handelian oratorio—Spiritual concert music—Handel's peculiar qualifications for oratorio—*Messiah* chiefly lyric—Handel's music essentially vocal—His arias—His choruses—His choral technique—His debt to England—Goldsmith—John Potter. V From *Esther* to *Messiah* (1732–1741)—Prohibitive oratorio prices—*Deborah* (1733)—*The Craftsman*—Handel's Oxford excursion—*Athaliah* (1733)—*The Oxford Act*—*The Oxford Act: A Ballad Opera*—Repeated objections to Handel's "noise"—Effect of Handelian oratorio on contemporary verse—*Polymnia*—*Saul*

CONTENTS

CHAPTER

I. SOME ARE BORN GREAT (1711–1741) *(Continued)*
(1739)—*Israel in Egypt* (1739)—Handel's disastrous situation in 1741.

II. THE LORD GAVE THE WORD (1741) 52

I Handel's librettos—Milton, Dryden, Gay, Pope, Congreve—Contemptible trash of Handel's oratorio texts—Humphreys, Miller, Broughton, Morell—Charles Jennens—*Il Moderato*—His eccentric life and character—His conceit—His work on *Messiah*—Handel's share in compiling the text—George Kelly. II "Messiah" theme in eighteenth-century English verse—Pope's *Messiah*—Alsop's *Messiah*—Klopstock's *Messias*—Evaluation of Jennens' text of *Messiah*—A work of art—An epic poem—Specifically contemplative and lyric—Not basically dramatic—A balanced piece of musical architecture—Its universal appeal and influence. III Handel's actual composition of *Messiah* (1741)—Twenty-four days—His autograph score—Its turbulent state—Its implications—Remarkable speed of its transcription—*Messiah* the result of months of rumination—Preliminary sketches in the Fitzwilliam Museum. IV Handel's "plagiarisms"—His self-borrowings in *Messiah*—"And He shall purify"—"His yoke is easy"—"For unto us a Child is born"—"All we like sheep"—"O death, where is thy sting?"—Explanation of Handel's "plagiarisms"—A common eighteenth-century practice—Mozart—Sebastian Bach—Handel's clumsy declamation—His essentially Italian vocal technique—Jennens' dissatisfaction with *Messiah*—Handel's constant alteration of the score. V Traditions regarding Handel's piety—James Beattie—Sir John Hawkins—Handel's "heroic" religion—Handel versus Bach—*Messiah* versus *Saint Matthew Passion*—Essentially "secular" character of *Messiah*—A theatrical "entertainment"—Handel's "paganism"—Edward FitzGerald—Samuel Butler—Handel's purpose artistic rather than didactic—A triumph of human genius.

III. "A SACRED ORATORIO" (1741–1749) 88

I Handel's visit to Dublin (1741–1742)—His departure from London—His delay at Chester—Burney's boyhood recollections—Handel's arrival in Ireland—Music in mid-eighteenth-century Dublin—Matthew Dubourg—The Charitable Musical Society—Neal's Musick Hall—Handel's two series of subscription concerts—The Governors of Mercer's Hospital—Swift and the choir of St. Patrick's

CONTENTS

| CHAPTER | | PAGE |

III. "A SACRED ORATORIO" (1741–1749) (*Continued*)
Cathedral—The choir of Christ Church—Preliminary rehearsals of *Messiah*—First public rehearsal. II First public performance of *Messiah* (13 April 1742)—Dubourg's State Band—Handel's chorus of twenty men—Signora Avolio and Mrs. Cibber—Thomas Sheridan—Patrick Delany—Account in *Faulkner's Journal*—Laurence Whyte—Second performance of *Messiah* (3 June 1742)—Original wordbook—Its complex implications—Handel's farewell to Swift—*Messiah* in Dublin (1742–1752)—The Charitable Musical Society—Mrs. Delany—Benjamin Victor. III Handel's return to London—Pope's *Dunciad*—Success of *Samson* (1743)—Lady Hertford—Horace Walpole—Clerical objections to *Messiah*—First London performance of *A Sacred Oratorio* (23 March 1743)—George II and the "Hallelujah Chorus"—Frigid reception—Explanation—London's deficient musical taste—George Hogarth—Lord Shaftesbury—Sir John Hawkins—Bigotry and misplaced zeal—John Lockman—Catherine Talbot—William Hanbury—Mrs. Delany—"Letter to a Friend, on going to hear the MESSIAH at the Play-House." IV Favorable reception of *Messiah* by *The Daily Advertiser*—*The London Daily Post*—Eliza Heywood—Catherine Talbot—Ann Granville Dewes—John Wesley—Resentment of fashionable patrons —Explanation—Their organized efforts to ruin Handel—Lady Brown—Fielding's *Tom Jones*—Horace Walpole—Lord Chesterfield—*Semele* (1744)—Handel's temporary bankruptcy—*An Ode to Mr. Handel*—Corrupt social and moral state of Georgian England.

IV. THE GLASS OF FASHION (1749–1784) 135
I The London Foundling Hospital—Its chapel—Handel's patronage—First performance of *Messiah* at the Foundling Hospital Chapel (1 May 1750)—Subsequent annual renditions (1750–1759)—Charitable performances of *Messiah* throughout England—Handel as philanthropist. II *Messiah* at Covent Garden Theatre (1749–1759)—A universal favorite—Handel's unquestioned authority in 1750—Elizabeth Carter—James Harris—David Garrick—Charles Avison—William Hayes—William Hughes—Manner of eighteenth-century oratorio performance—Fielding's *Amelia*—Spurious wordbooks—Madame du Boccage —Handel's organ concertos—His blindness—His small orchestra and chorus—Termination of subscription performances of oratorio—Francesca Cuzzoni—Handel's final

CONTENTS

CHAPTER | PAGE

IV. THE GLASS OF FASHION (1749–1784) (*Continued*)
performance of *Messiah*—His death and burial—Poetical tributes. III Handelian idolatry after 1759—Smollett—John Potter—John Lockman—John Langhorne—John Mainwaring—Handel's monument in Westminster Abbey—Spread of *Messiah* throughout England—Salisbury—Bristol—Bath—Church-Langton—Leicester—Oxford—Cambridge—Halifax—Liverpool—Norwich—Birmingham—The Three Choirs—*Messiah* at Gloucester (1757)—At Worcester (1758)—William Shenstone—First cathedral performance at Hereford (1759)—Francis Hopkinson—Elizabeth Ann Linley—Maria Linley—*Messiah* in London (1759–1784)—Covent Garden versus Drury Lane—Reduction of admission prices—Dr. Johnson and *Messiah*—Mrs. Thrale—Boswell—*Messiah* in aesthetic treatises—Dr. John Brown's *Dissertation*—*An Examination of the Oratorios*. IV Publication of *Messiah* in eighteenth-century England—Rare appearance of its title in print—Absence of *Messiah* in Walsh's catalogue—*Handel's Songs Selected from His Oratorios*—*Songs in Messiah*—Its uncertain date—First full-score edition (1767)—Proposals for subscription—List of subscribers—Inaccurate score—Possible explanations for delayed publication.

V. ALL THE KING'S MEN (1784–1791) 187
I George III's passion for Handel—His patronage of the Handel Commemoration of 1784—Commemoration plans announced in *The European Magazine*—Architectural preparations at Westminster Abbey—First performance on May 26—Concert at the Pantheon on May 27—*Messiah* on May 29—Joah Bates—His "band" of 525 performers—Madame Mara—Repetition of first performance on June 3—Repetition of *Messiah* on June 5—Charles Burney—James Boswell—Sir Joshua Reynolds—Mary Palmer—Mary Hamilton—Mrs. Delany—Favorable comment in current periodicals—Clerical condemnation. II Cowper's objections to *Messiah* at Westminster Abbey—John Newton—His fifty sermons on *Messiah*—Purpose of his discourses—His famous fourth sermon—Subsequent sermons—Handel's music versus Jennens' text—"Hallelujah Chorus"—Recapitulation—Sermons privately published in 1786—Mixed critical reaction. III Cowper's melancholy introspection—His criticism of *Messiah* in *The Task*—Anna Seward's disapproval—Her "Remonstrance"—Sir Walter Scott—Nineteenth-century response to New-

CONTENTS

CHAPTER	PAGE

V. ALL THE KING'S MEN (1784–1791) *(Continued)*

ton's *Messiah*—*A Series of Reflections*—Robert Hall—John Jebb—"An English Churchman"—Dean Ramsay. IV Subsequent Abbey Commemorations (1785–1791)—Court Dewes—Horace Walpole—Mrs. Delany—Burney's *Account of the Commemoration*—George III's critical note on *Messiah*—Dr. Johnson's dedication to the King—Poetical tributes to *Messiah* (1784–1790)—Pollingrove Robinson—Thomas Maurice—Thomas Scott—John Ring—Edward Jones—*The Progress of Music*—James Hurdis—Two-year suspension of Handel Commemorations—*Sense Against Sound*—Celebration of 1790—Fanny Burney—William Johnston Temple—Celebration of 1791—Franz Joseph Haydn—Anna Seward—Her excursions to hear *Messiah* at Birmingham—Sheffield—Manchester—London—Handel's *Messiah* versus Haydn's *Creation*—British musical taste in 1802. V Handel's universal dominance of English music throughout the Georgian period—Why is *Messiah* England's favorite oratorio?—Fashion and habit—Its "heavenly" and "sublime" music—Its appeal to all classes—Its sacred text—Its universal theme—Its nonsectarian character—Its peculiar charm for Bible-loving Britons—Its robust assurance—Its authentic expression of England's "religious" spirit.

VI. OPUS OPTIMUM 232

I *Messiah* in Victorian England—Handelian idolatry—Samuel Butler—*Erewhon*—*The Way of All Flesh*—Handel's adoption by the Church of England—His profanity—His "plagiarisms"—His secular music adapted to sacred texts—Phenomenal vogue of *Messiah*—*The Edinburgh Review*—Victor Schoelcher—*Messiah* a divine revelation—Its music "above criticism"—Steady performances in London and throughout England—The Caecilian Society—The Sacred Harmonic Society—Lowell Mason—Vincent Novello—George Bernard Shaw—Birmingham Festival (1852)—*Messiah* at Westminster Abbey (1834)—Charles Greville—Preliminary Handel Festival (1857)—First Great Handel Festival (1859)—Subsequent Triennial Festivals (1859–1926)—Fallacy of Victorian Festivals—Reaction—Jane Welsh Carlyle—Edward FitzGerald—George Bernard Shaw—*Messiah* in Victorian literature—Samuel Butler—George Eliot—John East—Thomas Grinfield—Elizabeth Cheney—A bourgeois institution by 1900. II *Messiah* in America—New York City (16 January 1770)

CONTENTS

CHAPTER

PAGE

VI. OPUS OPTIMUM (*Continued*)
—American musical taste decidedly English—Subsequent performances in New York (1780–1820)—First vocal score of *Messiah* published in America (1803)—*Messiah* in Charleston—Norfolk—Baltimore—Bethlehem—Philadelphia (1772–1810)—First Uranian Concert (1787)—Annotated "Remarks" on the "Hallelujah Chorus"—*Messiah* at University of Pennsylvania (1790–1801)—*Messiah* in Boston (1773–1816)—W. S. Morgan—Josiah Flagg—William Selby—First American imprint of the "Hallelujah Chorus" (1786)—The Musical Society of Boston—The Massachusetts Musical Society—The Handel and Haydn Society—Initial concert—First complete performance of *Messiah* in America (25 December 1818)—First complete performance in New York (18 November 1831)—Jenny Lind—Christine Nilsson—Leopold Damrosch— Spread of *Messiah* throughout the United States—Chicago—Lowell Mason—Ralph Waldo Emerson—Julia Ward Howe—*Messiah* in Lindsborg, Kansas. III *Messiah* on the continent—A feeble exotic in Latin countries—Paris—Ernest David—Hector Berlioz—Edouard Lalo—*Messiah* in France (1784–1873)—Mara—Alexandre Choron—François Fétis—François Castil-Blaze—Ferdinand Gasse—First complete performance of *Messiah* in France (19 December 1873)—Charles Lamoureux—Arthur Pougin—Henri Lavoix—Eugène d'Harcourt—La Société G. F. Haendel—Eugène Borrel—Félix Raugel—*Messiah* at the Trocadéro (23 April 1910)—Subsequent renditions in Paris—*Messiah* in Germany—First performance in Hamburg (15 April 1772)—Michael Arne—C. P. E. Bach—In Mannheim—Abbé Vogler—Mozart—At Weimar—Goethe—Herder—Zelter—*Messiah* in Berlin (19 May 1786)—Johann Adam Hiller—Leipzig—Breslau—Baron van Swieten—Mozart's "additional accompaniments"—His enthusiasm for *Messiah*—Gluck — Haydn — Beethoven — Edward Schulz — Johann A. Stumpff—"Das ist das Wahre!"—Herder's *Adrastea*—Goethe and Zelter—Rochlitz—*Für Freunde der Tonkunst*—Goethe's review—Slow progress of *Messiah* in Germany—Berlin Singakademie—Rhenish Festival —Frankfort Cäcilienverein—Liszt—Wagner—Friedrich Chrysander—*Georg Friedrich Händels Werke*—German revival of Handel following World War I—Adolf Hitler's "Aryanization" of *Israel in Egypt* and *Judas Maccabeus*. IV Mozart's "additional accompaniments"—Criticism in Germany—Rochlitz — Zelter — Hauptmann — First per-

CHAPTER

VI. OPUS OPTIMUM (*Continued*)
formance in London (29 March 1805)—Unfavorable response—*The Sun*—James Bartleman—Sir George Smart—J. Carter—*The Quarterly Musical Magazine*—"A Querist"—Later vogue of Mozart's adaptation—Subsequent "arrangements"—Thomas Pitt—W. H. Birch—J. F. Burrowes—A. L. Tamplin—Mendelssohn—Ignaz von Mosel—Sir Michael Costa—Sir George A. Macfarren—E. F. Rimbault—Sir Arthur Sullivan—New editions—Robert Franz—Friedrich Chrysander—Ebenezer Prout—Corrupt state of *Messiah* score—J. M. Coopersmith—Unfortunate neglect of Handel's other works—A "one-work" composer?

APPENDIX A: TEXT OF HANDEL'S *Messiah* 291

APPENDIX B: A LIST OF SUBSCRIBERS TO THE ORIGINAL FULL-SCORE EDITION OF HANDEL'S *Messiah* (1767) 299

SELECT BIBLIOGRAPHY 303

INDEX 321

Illustrations

GEORGE FRIDERIC HANDEL . . . . *Frontispiece*
    From a Portrait by Thomas Hudson (1748) in the Bodleian Library, Oxford

THE CHORUS 28
    From an Etching by William Hogarth (1732)

CHARLES JENNENS . . . . *facing* 42
    From an Anonymous Portrait in the Possession of Edward Viscount Curzon

FINAL PAGE OF HANDEL'S AUTOGRAPH SCORE OF *Messiah* (1741) 65
    From the Original in the King's Musick Library of the British Museum

GEORGE FRIDERIC HANDEL . . . . *facing* 74
    From the "Gopsall Portrait" by Thomas Hudson (1756) in the Possession of Mary Countess Howe

TITLE PAGE OF THE WORDBOOK OF *Messiah* AS PERFORMED AT NEAL'S MUSICK HALL, DUBLIN (1742) . . 104
    From the Copy in the British Museum

SOUTH VIEW OF THE LONDON FOUNDLING HOSPITAL (1748) 137
    From an Engraving in *The Gentleman's Magazine* (September 1748)

TITLE PAGE OF THE WORDBOOK OF *Messiah* AS PERFORMED AT COVENT GARDEN THEATRE, LONDON (1749) 154
    From the Copy in the Yale University Library

ELIZABETH ANN LINLEY (MRS. RICHARD BRINSLEY SHERIDAN) . . . . *facing* 170
    From a Portrait by Thomas Gainsborough (1785) in the Mellon Collection of the National Gallery of Art, Washington, D. C.

TITLE PAGE OF THE ORIGINAL FULL-SCORE EDITION OF *Messiah* (1767) 184
    From the Copy in the Library of Congress

VIEW OF WESTMINSTER ABBEY DURING THE COMMEMORATION OF HANDEL (1784) . . . . *facing* 202
    From an Engraving by Edward F. Burney in Charles Burney's *Account of the Commemoration* (1785)

VIEW OF THE CRYSTAL PALACE DURING THE GREAT HANDEL FESTIVAL (1859) . . . . *facing* 234
    From an Engraving in *The Illustrated London News* (2 July 1859)

VIEW OF HANDEL'S MONUMENT IN WESTMINSTER ABBEY (1762) . . . . *facing* 266
    From an Engraving by Edward F. Burney in Charles Burney's *Account of the Commemoration* (1785)

A Touchstone of Taste

EACH YEAR AT CHRISTMASTIDE a great chain of harmony encircles the globe, binding village chapel and metropolitan cathedral in solemn exaltation as Handel's *Messiah* once again offers its message of comfort and hope to a festive world. From London to Melbourne, from Boston to Gopher Prairie, thousands of musicians unite in church choirs, concert halls, and broadcasting stations to perform Handel's rendition of the great Christmas narrative, while millions of listeners find their holiday season brightened by its irresistible pathos and triumph. No Christmas would be complete without the annual rite of Handel's *Messiah*. Throughout December musical folk expect its performance as confidently as children await the arrival of Santa Claus. In Boston its faithful rendition by the Handel and Haydn Society is so inextricably interwoven with New England's social fabric that solid Back Bay families would dispense as readily with plum-pudding and mistletoe as with attendance upon Handel's masterpiece in Symphony Hall. With commendable persistence the Oratorio Society of New York repeats *Messiah* in Carnegie Hall each season before an appreciative suburban audience, while in Chicago the employees of Marshall Field annually inspire hundreds of shoppers with Handel's vigorous strains. Popular radio programs feature its less ponderous selections; phonograph shops advertise recordings of its best-loved arias and choruses; motion pictures reenact sentimental stories of Handel's miraculous composition in twenty-four days. Scarcely a church choir of any Protestant denomination fails to sing at least the Christmas portions of *Messiah*, and every college glee club climaxes its annual Yuletide concert by shouting the "Hallelujah Chorus" with pride and confidence. Handel has indeed made Christmastide his own. Each returning season accentuates with peculiar emphasis his grasp upon the musical affections of the Anglo-Saxon world.

Since its first appearance on 13 April 1742 Handel's *Messiah* has been performed more steadily in English-speaking countries than any other choral work in existence. Its muscular Christianity has thrilled thousands to whom *Hamlet* and *Macbeth* are little more than names. Even the familiar symphonies of Mozart and Beethoven demand facilities beyond the scope of most small towns, whereas *Messiah* remains the *cheval de bataille* of every provincial chorus in Great Britain and the United States. Zealous Christians who take no serious interest in music and hear no other musical performance piously avow that this solemn ritual exalts their religious devotion. Generations have lived and died in the firm faith that *Messiah* embraces all that is good and great in music, and though it has passed its bicentennial, its popularity continues unabated with thousands who cannot hum one of its great themes nor in the least comprehend the plan upon which its noblest choruses are constructed.

Throughout England the name of George Frideric Handel has been held in absolute veneration for almost two hundred years. No other composer has so truly touched the heart of John Bull. In his magnificent pomp and militant self-assurance Handel gave England a national music of her own, and Englishmen have unanimously adopted the naturalized German as their national hero in music. His bones lie buried in Westminster Abbey, and numerous landmarks in London remind Englishmen of his long residence there. For forty-nine years "the Shakespeare of music" drew his inspiration from the great people whom he labored to please. It is therefore not inappropriate to claim Handel as the greatest composer England has produced. But if Handel's name is a household word, the household seldom inquires further than the one work by which he is universally known. To the bourgeois

Briton *Messiah* represents the cornerstone of Handel's fame. In his stubborn devotion the orthodox Englishman criticizes its music no more than he criticizes its words. If one could attend a nineteenth-century Handel Festival at the Crystal Palace to hear *Messiah* thundered by a host of four thousand stalwart voices before an audience of tens of thousands (including the Queen and Prince Consort), he would undoubtedly feel that he had discovered the musical soul of England.

In this account of the fortunes and misfortunes of *Messiah* the author seeks to present a biography of Handel's masterpiece, a chapter in the history of English taste. Actually *Messiah* is Handel's least representative (because least dramatic) choral work, but in its phenomenal vogue through two centuries it has dictated the style and conception of subsequent oratorio to the present day. In courses of sermons, in volumes of history and criticism, in scores of poetical tributes *Messiah* has been treated from almost every conceivable religious and artistic point of view. If the reader of literature is impressed with the importance of Handel's music in English social life for two centuries, perhaps the musician will be surprised at Handel's impact upon the subject-matter of English prose and verse. Of the making of books about Handel there is no end. In his flowing full-bottomed wig and magnificent ruffles and gorgeous velvet coat, quick-tempered Mr. Handel might have made gruff remarks on that score. But the author's own feeling is best expressed by the Reverend William Hughes in his disarming preface to a sermon on *The Efficacy and Importance of Musick* in 1749:

As every one must be sensible, that it requires a great Share of Knowledge to add any thing of real Consequence to the REPUBLICK OF LETTERS, (especially in the present curious and discerning Age) it may possibly carry with it an Air of Presumption, to pretend to obtrude the following mean Performance upon the Publick, when Men of the most approv'd Parts and Learning, have already done known justice, to this, as well as other Topicks. But, instead of tiring the Reader with any further Apology, I shall only desire him to peruse it with a proper degree of Candour. If there are no very material Mistakes, it is possible, that some few Inaccuracies may be pass'd over with a favourable, and friendly Eye.

HANDEL'S MESSIAH

OUR LANGUAGE has received innumerable Elegancies and Improvements, from that Infusion of *Hebraisms,* which are derived to it out of the Poetical Passages in Holy Writ. They give a Force and Energy to our Expressions, warm and animate our Language, and convey our Thoughts in more ardent and intense Phrases, than any that are to be met with in our own Tongue. . . .

Since we have therefore such a Treasury of Words, so beautiful in themselves, and so proper for the Airs of Musick, I cannot but wonder that Persons of Distinction should give so little Attention and Encouragement to that kind of Musick, which would have its Foundations in Reason, and which would improve our Virtue in proportion as it raised our Delight. . . . I might shew, from innumerable Passages in Ancient Writers, not only that Vocal and Instrumental Musick were made use of in their Religious Worship, but that their most favourite Diversions were filled with Songs and Hymns to their respective Deities. Had we frequent Entertainments of this Nature among us, they wou'd not a little purifie and exalt our Passions, give our Thoughts a proper Turn, and cherish those Divine Impulses in the Soul, which every one feels that has not stifled them by sensual and immoderate Pleasures.

Musick, when thus applied, raises noble Hints in the Mind of the Hearer, and fills it with great Conceptions. It strengthens Devotion, and advances Praise into Rapture. It lengthens out every act of Worship, and produces more lasting and permanent Impressions in the Mind, than those which accompany any transient Form of Words that are uttered in the ordinary Method of Religious Worship.

—JOSEPH ADDISON, *Spectator* 405

I

Some Are Born Great

> There *Hendel* strikes the strings, the melting strain
> Transports the soul, and thrills through ev'ry vein.
> —John Gay, *Trivia* (1716)

I

ON SATURDAY EVENING, 24 February 1711, London's elegant world flocked to the Queen's Theatre in the Haymarket to hear George Frideric Handel's first Italian opera in England. Yesterday the celebrated composer had spent his twenty-sixth birthday rehearsing for his British debut, and tonight London listened with pleasant anticipation for the opening strains of *Rinaldo*. Late in the preceding autumn the young German had reached London after four triumphant years in Florence and Venice and Rome. Bewildered by the strange bustle of a foreign capital, he had searched out Aaron Hill, Director of the Haymarket Theatre, and this enterprising producer had engaged him at once to compose an opera based on an episode in Tasso's *Jerusalem Delivered*. In his hasty enthusiasm the Director himself had drafted a rough sketch in English, and this outline had been speedily expanded into an Italian libretto by Giacomo Rossi. But the librettist had found himself unable to keep pace with Handel's energetic powers. In his grandiloquent preface Rossi confessed that "The Signor Hendel, the Orpheus of our Age, in setting to musick this lay from Parnassus, had scarcely given me time enough to write it, and I have beheld, to my great astonishment, an entire opera *harmonized* to the last degree of perfection in the short space of a fortnight, by this sublime genius."

On that cold February night the denizens of Mayfair braved the dangers of narrow, muddy, ill-lit streets to attend the *première* of Mr. Handel's magnificent new opera *Rinaldo*. Aaron Hill's expectant audience was not disappointed. On his lavish "machines and decorations" the shrewd director had spared neither pains nor expense, and his rich production combined the bombastic violence of heroic tragedy with all the elaborate theatrical apparatus of Italian baroque opera. Besides profuse thunder and lightning Hill provided his polite audience with spectacular fireworks and fantastic illuminations, while two painted dragons spat fire and smoke amid a grove of fabricated orange trees, and the King of Jerusalem, clad in ermine robes, ventured upon a sea of pasteboard in an open boat. During the performance of Almirena's exquisite *aria d'imitazione* flights of living birds were introduced upon the stage to the tender accompaniment of flutes and flageolets. Meanwhile Italy's choice singers invested Handel's elegant arias with all the grace of Italian vocal art. The title rôle of Rinaldo was created by the renowned Cavaliere Nicolini Grimaldi, an extraordinarily talented male soprano of whom Sir Richard Steele once wrote:

> Nonsense grew pleasing by his *Syren* Arts,
> And stole from *Shakespear*'s self our easie Hearts.

Joseph Addison found Nicolini "the greatest Performer in Dramatick Musick that is now living, or that perhaps ever appeared upon a Stage," and in *Spectator* 405 he sarcastically declared that "The Town is highly obliged to that Excellent Artist, for having shown us the *Italian* Musick in its Perfection." In *Rinaldo* the rôle of Argante was performed by Signor Giuseppe Boschi, the most celebrated basso of his day, who boasted a compass of two and a half octaves and enjoyed great reputation for manliness and vigor. Boschi and Nicolini were supported by a cast exclusively Italian. Eustazio was sung by Signor Valentini Urbani, Goffredo by Signora Francesca Vanini, Armida by Signora Elisabetta Pilotti Schiavonetti, and Almirena by Signora Isabella Girardeau.

Under such favorable auspices *Rinaldo* caught in a night. Composed by a master, heightened by sensational scenic devices, performed by a company of superb Italian singers, Handel's glorious spectacle rose superior to any music yet heard in England and established his British reputation at once. A radiant new star had risen in the harmonic firmament. Fashionable circles greedily sought the composer's company, and Mr. Handel's pudgy fingers improvised on the finest harpsichords in London. *Rinaldo* was sung and danced and paraphrased; its tunes invaded church choirs and drawing-rooms and drinking-dens; years later John Gay filched some of its songs for *The Beggar's Opera*. In the first season it swept London with an unprecedented run of fifteen nights, and during the following year it enjoyed a similar run of nine performances. It was revived with success in 1715 and 1717, and as late as 1731 its vogue was not spent. Even on the continent it won enthusiastic acclaim in Hamburg and Naples.

Meanwhile the coaches and chairs of England's noblest society crowded the Haymarket as the "quality" of London returned again and again to hear Mr. Handel's ravishing Italian strains. With its paltry entertainment Drury Lane became suddenly obscured, and its audiences began steadily drifting to the grand spectacle at the Queen's Theatre. Inevitably all advocates of the English lyric stage grew apprehensive. Two of their spokesmen determined to crush *Rinaldo* at all costs. Sir Richard Steele was a patentee of Old Drury, and only recently he had acquired the concert rooms in York Buildings. But his thin musical offering gained patronage only from those who found no better diversion elsewhere, and now he could scarcely hope to compete with the finest music London had ever heard. Joseph Addison was also acutely alarmed at Handel's good fortune. Still smarting from the recollection of three solitary performances of his own ill-fated English opera *Rosamond* in 1707, Addison withdrew into his corner awaiting a chance to strike, and in *The Spectator* the two essayists joined forces to render *Rinaldo* absurd and odious in the eyes (and ears) of London's musical public. In his attempt to "banish Vice and Ignorance out of the Territories of *Great Britain*" Addison proposed "to enliven Morality with Wit and to temper Wit with Morality." But actually his satirical strokes against Italian music aimed chiefly to avenge his own wretched failure in *Rosamond*, and in several *Tatler* and *Spectator* papers Addison and Steele expended much wit upon this ungrateful theme.

As early as 2 March 1711 Addison hurled his first shaft of abuse at Handel's *Rinaldo*. After fulminating a host of invectives against Italian opera in *Spectator* 5, he grew jocular over Handel's "Sparrows" and derided his painted dragons as fatuous and puerile:

As I was walking the Streets about a Fortnight ago, I saw an ordinary Fellow carrying a Cage full of little Birds upon his Shoulder; and, as I was wondering with my self what Use he would put them to, he was met very luckily by an Acquaintance, who had the same Curiosity. Upon his asking him what he had upon his Shoulder, he told him, that he had been buying Sparrows for the Opera. Sparrows for the Opera, says his Friend, licking his Lips, what are they to be roasted? No, no, says the other, they are to enter towards the end of the first Act, and to fly about the Stage.

This strange Dialogue awakened my Curiosity so far that I immediately bought the Opera, by which means I perceived that the Sparrows were to act the part of Singing Birds in a delightful Grove: though upon a nearer Enquiry I found the Sparrows put the same Trick upon the Audience, that Sir *Martin Mar-all* practised upon his Mistress; for, though they flew in Sight, the Musick proceeded from a Consort of Flagellets and Bird-calls which was planted behind the Scenes. At the same time I made this Discovery, I found by the Discourse of the Actors, that there were great Designs on foot for the Improvement of the Opera; that it had been proposed to break down a part of the Wall, and to surprize the Audience with a Party of an hundred Horse, that there was actually a Project of bringing the *New-River* into the House, to be employed in Jetteaus and Water-works. This Project, as I have since heard, is post-poned 'till the Summer-Season; when it is thought the Coolness that proceeds from Fountains and Cascades will be more acceptable and refreshing to People of Quality. In the mean time, to find out a more agreeable Entertainment for the Winter-Season, the Opera of *Rinaldo* is filled with Thunder and Lightning, Illuminations, and Fireworks; which the Audience may look upon without catching Cold, and indeed without much Danger of being burnt; for there are several Engines filled with Water, and ready to play at a Minute's Warning, in case any such Accident should happen. However, as I have a very great Friendship for the Owner of this Theater, I hope that he has been wise enough to *insure* his House before he would let this Opera be acted in it.

Of the "Sparrows" Addison proceeded to lament that "there have been so many Flights of them let loose in this Opera, that it is feared the House will never get rid of them; and that in other Plays, they may make their Entrance in very wrong and improper Scenes, so as to be seen flying in a Lady's Bed-Chamber, or pearching upon a King's Throne; besides the Inconveniences which the Heads of the Audience may sometimes suffer from them." Addison terminated his essay by informing his readers that "there is a Treaty on Foot with *London* and *Wise,* who will be appointed Gardiners of the Play-House, to furnish the Opera of *Rinaldo* and *Armida* with an Orange-Grove; and that the next time it is Acted, the Singing Birds will be Personated by Tom-Tits: The Undertakers being resolved to spare neither Pains nor Mony, for the Gratification of the Audience."

Late in the following week Addison printed in *Spectator* 14 a witty letter from an imaginary correspondent complaining that "the Undertakers of the *Hay-Market,* having raised too great an Expectation in their printed Opera, very much disappoint their Audience on the Stage." The writer regretted that "The Sparrows and Chaffinches at the *Hay-Market* fly as yet very irregularly over the Stage; and instead of perching on the Trees and performing their Parts, these young Actors either get into the Galleries or put out the Candles." Disregarding the cruelty of exposing these little songsters to cremation among the footlights, the correspondent proceeded to ridicule the "Mechanism and Scenary" of *Rinaldo:* "The Undertakers forgetting to change their Side-Scenes, we were presented with a Prospect of the Ocean in the midst of a delightful Grove; and tho' the Gentlemen on the Stage had very much contributed to the Beauty of the Grove by walking up and down between the Trees, I must own I was not a little astonish'd to see a well-dress'd young Fellow in a full-bottom'd Wigg, appear in the Midst of the Sea, and without any visible Concern taking Snuff." In performance *Rinaldo* evidently failed to fulfill the high expectations excited by the printed version:

> The King of *Jerusalem* is obliged to come from the City on foot, instead of being drawn in a triumphant Chariot by white Horses, as my Opera-Book had promised me; and thus while I expected *Armida's* Dragons should rush forward towards *Argantes,* I found the Hero was obliged to go to *Armida,* and hand her out of her Coach. We had also but a very short Allowance of Thunder and Lightning; tho' I cannot in this Place omit doing Justice to the Boy who had the Direction of the Two painted Dragons, and made them spit Fire and Smoke: He flash'd out his Rosin in such just Proportions and in such due Time, that I could not forbear conceiving Hopes of his being one Day a most excellent Player. I saw indeed but Two things wanting to render his whole Action compleat, I mean the keeping his Head a little lower, and hiding his Candle.

Addison closed *Spectator* 14 with a burlesque "advertisement" of a forthcoming opera: "On the first of *April* will be performed at the Play-house in the *Hay-market* an Opera call'd *The Cruelty of Atreus.* N.B. The Scene wherein *Thyestes* eats his own Children, is to be performed by the famous Mr *Psalmanazar,* lately arrived from *Formosa:* The whole Supper set to Kettle-drums."

Not content with this assault upon the tasteless spectacle of Handel's *Rinaldo,* Addison proceeded in *Spectator* 18 to "deliver down to Posterity a faithful Account of the Italian Opera, and of the gradual Progress which it has made upon the English Stage." Throughout this diverting history of foreign music in London Addison redoubled his attack upon the Italian rage and reinforced his defense of national opera in English. In 1710 Handel came to London as a master of Italian opera, but this fashionable exotic was then of recent growth. Five years earlier London had turned with strange partiality to the musical traditions of Italy, and on 16 January 1705 *Arsinoe* had been performed entirely in English "after the *Italian* Manner, all sung" at Drury Lane Theatre. In this crude performance dialogue and narrative were set to recitative for the first time in England, and the music was adapted from nondescript Italian songs by Thomas Clayton, a musical pretender who with all his conceit exhibited few graces of his art. Quickly the virus of Italian affectation poisoned English taste:

Arsinoe was the first Opera that gave us a Taste of Italian Musick. The great Success which this Opera met with, produced some Attempts of forming Pieces upon Italian Plans, that should give a more natural and reasonable Entertainment than what can be met with in the elaborate Trifles of that Nation. This alarm'd the Poetasters and Fidlers of the Town, who were used to deal in a more ordinary Kind of Ware; and therefore laid down an establish'd Rule, which is receiv'd as such to this very Day, *That nothing is capable of being well set to Musick, that is not Nonsense.*

Of Italian libretto Addison entertained no high opinion. "The finest Writers among the Modern *Italians,*" he declared in *Spectator* 5, "express themselves in such a florid form of Words, and such tedious Circumlocutions, as are used by none but Pedants in our own Country; and at the same time, fill their Writings with such poor Imaginations and Conceits, as our Youths are ashamed of, before they have been Two Years at the University."

In their mania for Italian music Englishmen "immediately fell to translating the Italian Operas; and as there was no great Danger of hurting the Sense of those extraordinary Pieces, our Authors would often make Words of their own that were entirely foreign to the Meaning of the Passages which they pretended to translate; their chief Care being to make the Numbers of the English Verse answer to those of the Italian, that both of them might go to the same Tune." With wry humor Addison showed how the famous song in *Camilla,* "Barbara si t'intendo," designed to express the resentments of an angry lover and translated literally "Barbarous Woman, yes, I know your Meaning," was actually rendered on the English stage as "Frail are a Lover's Hopes." Addison found it "pleasant enough to see the most refined Persons of the British Nation dying away and languishing to Notes that were filled with a Spirit of Rage and Indignation." In such absurd adaptations he found peculiar merriment:

It oftentimes happen'd likewise, that the finest Notes in the Air fell upon the most insignificant words in the Sentence. I have known the Word *And* pursu'd through the whole Gamut, have been entertain'd with many a melodious *The,* and have heard the most beautiful Graces Quavers and Divisions bestow'd upon *Then, For,* and *From;* to the eternal Honour of our English Particles.

But the foreign device most open to ridicule was recitative. In *Spectator* 29 Addison described the "startled" reaction of London audiences when Italian recitative was first introduced upon the English stage:

People were wonderfully surprized to hear Generals singing the Word of Command, and Ladies delivering Messages in Musick. Our Country-men could not forbear laughing when they heard a Lover chanting out a Billet-doux, and even the Superscription of a Letter set to a Tune. The Famous Blunder in an old Play of *Enter a King and two Fidlers Solus,* was now no longer an Absurdity, when it was impossible for a Hero in a Desart, or a Princess in her Closet, to speak any thing unaccompanied with Musical Instruments.

A year after *Arsinoe* Marc Antonio Bononcini, a younger brother of the more famous Giovanni Bononcini, produced *Camilla* on 30 April 1706. Originally this opera was rendered in English by native singers, but at a bilingual performance on 6 December 1707 three vocalists sang in Italian while the rest sang in English. Addison recorded that in this barbarous confusion of tongues Italian singers

> sung their Parts in their own Language, at the same Time that our Countrymen perform'd theirs in our native Tongue. The King or Hero of the Play generally spoke in Italian, and his Slaves answer'd him in English: The Lover frequently made his Court, and gain'd the Heart of his Princess in a Language which she did not understand. One would have thought it very difficult to have carry'd on Dialogues after this Manner, without an Interpreter between the Persons that convers'd together; but this was the State of the English Stage for about three Years.

In the face of such heterogeneous monstrosities strict nationalists sought to stem the Italian tide with a handful of feeble English productions. But even the harmonious verses of Addison's *Rosamond* failed to redeem Thomas Clayton's inadequate musical setting when first performed at Drury Lane on 4 March 1707. In his miserable effusion Clayton not only violated the rudiments of harmony and counterpoint but ignored the fundamental rules of prosody and accent, and his perpetration of noise irritated London ears for only three nights before it sank into permanent oblivion. Early in 1708 a pasticcio entitled *Thomyris,* selected by Marc Antonio Bononcini and Alessandro Scarlatti, furthered the tradition of bilingual performances at the Queen's Theatre. On December 14 of the same year Scarlatti's *Pyrrhus and Demetrius* introduced Nicolini and Valentini in a similarly incongruous spectacle. "We are here nine times madder after operas than ever," wrote Jonathan Swift on 18 January 1709; "and have got a new castrato from Italy, called Nicolini, who exceeds Valentini, I know not how many bars length." On March 15 Swift complained to Ambrose Philips that "The town is run mad after a new opera. Poetry and good sense are dwindling like echo with repetition and voice. Critic [John] Dennis vows to G[od] these operas will be the ruin of the nation, and brings examples from antiquity to prove it. A good old lady five miles out of town asked me the other day what those *uproars* were that her daughter was always going to."

Apparently Englishmen had no desire for Italian itself. Only the superior skill of Italian singers ultimately outlawed the English tongue from London's operatic stage. But the fashion set by excellent performers who knew no language but Italian soon became too strong to resist. "At length," Addison drily declared, "the Audience grew tir'd of understanding Half the Opera, and therefore to ease themselves intirely of the Fatigue of Thinking, have so order'd it at Present that the whole Opera is perform'd in an unknown Tongue." The first purely Italian opera in England was *Almahide,* an anonymous work of considerable merit, first performed at the Haymarket in January 1710. Francesco Mancini's *Hydaspes* appeared on 3 May 1710, but in order to put its London audience at ease, national music was offered between the acts. In this opera Hydaspes was thrown into an amphitheatre to be devoured by a lion, but the sight of his mistress among the spectators inspired him with courage sufficient to strangle the beast. Mancini's lion was much ridiculed in current periodicals. Toby Rentfree devoted a charming epistle to "that terrible Monster" in *Spectator* 314:

You are to know that I am naturally brave, and love Fighting as well as any Man in *England*. This gallant Temper of mine makes me extremely delighted with Battles on the Stage. I give you this Trouble to complain to you, that *Nicolini* refused to gratify me in that Part of the Opera for which I have most Taste. I observe its become a Custom, that whenever any Gentlemen are particularly pleased with a Song, at their crying out *Encore* or *Altro Volto,* the Performer is so obliging as to sing it over again. I was at the Opera the last time *Hydaspes* was performed. At that Part of it where the Heroe engages with the Lion, the graceful Manner with which he put that terrible Monster to Death gave me so great a Pleasure, and at the same time so just a Sense of that Gentleman's Intrepidity and Conduct, that I could not forbear desiring a Repetition of it, by crying out *Altro Volto* in a very audible Voice; and my Friends flatter me that I pronounced those Words with a tollerable good Accent, considering that was but the third Opera I had ever seen in my Life. Yet, notwithstanding all this, there was so little Regard had to me, that the Lion was carried off, and went to Bed, without being kill'd any more that Night. Now, Sir, pray consider that I did not understand a Word of what Mr. *Nicolini* said to this cruel Creature; besides, I have no Ear for Musick; so that during the long Dispute between 'em, the whole Entertainment I had was from my Eye: Why then have not I as much Right to have a graceful Action repeated as another has a pleasing Sound, since he only hears as I only see, and we neither of us know that there is any reasonable thing a doing?

Marc Antonio Bononcini's *Etearco* was the last of three entirely non-English operas performed in London before Handel's arrival in the late autumn of 1710. Without Handel's support Anglo-Italian opera would probably have perished in its infancy, for even in 1710 its vitality was precarious. "At present," declared Addison in *Spectator* 18, "our Notions of Musick are so very uncertain, that we do not know what it is like, only, in general, that we are transported with any thing that is not English: So it be of a foreign Growth, let it be Italian, French, or High-Dutch, it is the same thing. In short, our English Musick is quite rooted out, and nothing yet planted in its stead."

Throughout his delightful censure upon bad taste in scenic decorations and Italian libretto Addison proclaimed no original doctrine. His *Spectator* essays sought frankly to mirror the opinion of coffee-house gossips and Queen Anne wits, and his operatic criticism therefore reflects the current judgment of musically untrained Englishmen. Addison spoke of music as an amateur. Like many Augustan writers he possessed slight feeling for music himself, and his technical incompetence appears in his ignorance of musical terminology and in his lack of familiarity with musical history. But Addison's animadversions are all the more valuable for being characteristic and conventional. His attack on Italian music was provoked by self-interest and national prejudice, but his hostile criticisms indicate clearly that the average eighteenth-century Londoner also failed to appreciate Italian opera. Augustan literature abounds with censure of the foolish craze. Few chances to satirize the exotic species were lost. In a letter to his son on 23 January 1753 Lord Chesterfield summarized English opinion by declaring operas "too absurd and extravagant to mention. I look upon them as a magic scene, contrived to please the eyes and the ears, at the expense of the understanding. . . . Whenever I go to an Opera, I leave my sense and reason at the door with my half-guinea, and deliver myself up to my eyes and my ears."

II

In reading operatic criticism in eighteenth-century English prose and verse one should recall that Italian opera was a highly formalized medium embracing rigid conventions. Strict rule demanded only six principal characters: three women and three men. The "first woman" or *prima donna* was always a high soprano; the "second woman" and the "third woman" were contraltos. The "first man" or *primo uomo* was an artificial soprano, and this *castrato* appeared as hero even if his rôle were that of Ajax or Achilles. The "second man," if not a soprano, must be an artificial contralto. The "third man" was either another contralto or (more rarely) a tenor. If a "fourth man" were required, this additional rôle was generally assigned to a tenor or a bass.

But it was by no means uncommon to employ only artificial sopranos and contraltos for all male rôles. Each principal character sang at least one aria in each of the three acts. Anything like dramatic characterization was rare, for all arias consisted of two parts followed by the indispensable *da capo*. As a general rule all characters, however virtuous or vicious and of whatever age or race, sang the same sort of music according to the same rigid classification of five standard aria-types. The *aria cantabile* was confined to flowing melody supported by slight accompaniment and offering frequent opportunity for extempore embellishment. The *aria di portamento* was equally melodious but substituted sustained swelling notes for lighter ornaments. In its fuller development and richer accompaniment the *aria di mezzo carattere* afforded greater variety in dramatic treatment. The *aria parlante* expressed even deeper feeling and more intense emotion. The favorite *aria di bravura* or *aria d'agilità* involved great executive difficulty and was universally accepted as the natural and legitimate vehicle for displaying a singer's power to the greatest advantage. To these five primary types were added certain subsidiary forms, all of which were employed according to strict patterns of sequence. An aria was introduced to close each scene. One aria must never follow another of the same class, and no singer could claim two arias of any kind in succession. Important arias appeared at the close of the first and second acts. In the second and third acts hero and heroine might perform a grand *scena* consisting of an accompanied recitative followed by an *aria di bravura*. The *prima donna* and *primo uomo* sang together at least one grand duet, and the third act always terminated with an ensemble in which all principal singers participated. From such bounds Handel occasionally parted with the bravest disorder. Instead of chafing under the tyranny of pedantic operatic laws he sometimes cast them to the winds and snatched his grace beyond the reach of Italian musical art.

When one observes the artificial restrictions of baroque operatic construction he is not astonished that free-born Englishmen denounced foreign affectation as effeminate, irrational, and anti-British. Especially repulsive was that disgraceful anomaly, the male soprano. The degeneracy with which warbling *castrati* were caressed and idolized by British nobility is incredible and revolting. When one reads that Cuzzoni and Faustina resorted to physical blows on a London stage, he is perhaps mildly amused; but when he learns that an English noblewoman (upon hearing Farinelli sing) exclaimed with rapture, "One God, one Farinelli!" he is shocked at the extravagance. In London's refined drawing-rooms Italian performers were adored as superior divinities. For years polite society was torn with frenzied violence over the respective merits of Cuzzoni and Faustina, Farinelli and Senesino, Handel and Bononcini.

As for the reigning amusement of the town [wrote John Gay to Dean Swift on 3 February 1723], it is entirely music. . . . There is nobody allowed to say, "I sing," but an eunuch, or an Italian woman. Everybody is grown now as great a judge of music, as they were in your time of poetry, and folks that could not distinguish one tune from another, now daily dispute about the different styles of Handel, Bononcini, and Attilio. . . . In London and Westminster, in all polite conversations, Senesino is daily voted to be the greatest man that ever lived.

In 1720 fifty thousand pounds were subscribed by the Royal Academy of Music for exhibiting Italian operas, but within a decade quarrels of rival managers and contentious singers had overturned the Academy to its foundation. Sober Englishmen found fault chiefly with the extravagant "show'rs of gold" lavished upon capricious Italian performers. Contemporary periodicals directed frequent sarcastic comment at the riches accumulated by foreign singers. A frank complaint in *Grub-Street Journal* 284 may be regarded as representative:

> Whilst *Britain*, destitute of aid,
> Weeps taxes and decaying trade;

> Sees want approach with nimble pace,
> And ruin stare her in the face;
> Charm'd by the sweet *Italian*'s tongue
> In show'rs of gold she pays each song.

With their ridiculous vanity and full-blown conceit the *prima donna* and *primo uomo* of Handel's day were unique in the history of music. Even composers were fettered by the necessity of conciliating rebellious singers, and Handel was sometimes forced to design arias for the particular voices of performers who sought only varied opportunities for personal vocal display. In minimizing jealousies and placating sensitive vocalists Handel frequently sacrificed his freedom to provide dramatic characterization. Neapolitan operas were often mere strings of stereotyped arias tied by the thinnest threads, and Englishmen looked upon Italian performances only as elaborate concerts with scenery and costume, in which singers competed strenuously for the approval of fickle patrons.

"There is no Question," declared Addison in *Spectator* 18, "but our Grand-children will be very curious to know the Reason why their Forefathers used to sit together like an Audience of Foreigners in their own Country, and to hear whole Plays acted before them in a Tongue which they did not understand." Perhaps the most universal objection to Italian opera was its incomprehensibility to English ears. Londoners found the words of Italian music drama meaningless. In *Spectator* 18 Addison pointed his sharpest satire at England's taste for unintelligible squeaking in a foreign tongue:

We no longer understand the Language of our own Stage; insomuch that I have often been afraid, when I have seen our Italian Performers chattering in the Vehemence of Action, that they have been calling us Names, and abusing us among themselves; but I hope, since we do put such an entire Confidence in them, they will not talk against us before our Faces, though they may do it with the same Safety as if it was behind our Backs. In the mean

Time I cannot forbear thinking how naturally an Historian, who writes Two or Three hundred Years hence, and does not know the Taste of his wise Fore-fathers, will make the following Reflection, *In the Beginning of the Eighteenth Century the Italian Tongue was so well understood in* England, *that Opera's were acted on the publick Stage in that Language.*

Italian opera was "exotick," however, not so much because Englishmen could not comprehend Italian as because London's aristocracy remained strangely convinced that no other language was artistically suitable for opera. Modish ladies (whose limited musical sensibilities were scarcely enhanced by their total ignorance of Italian) attended foreign performances with persistent regularity, and their failure to understand Italian libretto afforded satirists ample merriment. Most Englishmen agreed with John Hughes that "Dramatick Entertainments" should be "perform'd in a Language understood by the Audience," since "The great Pleasure in hearing Vocal Musick, arrives from the Association of the Ideas rais'd at the same time by the Expression and the Sounds." Hughes, like Addison, could not endorse the "late Opinion among some, that *English* Words are not proper for Musick." In his preface to *Calypso and Telemachus* (1712) he granted that "the *English* Language is not so soft and full of Vowels as the *Italian,*" but "this does not prove," he insisted, "that it is therefore incapable of Harmony." With mounting protest Englishmen demanded music sung in a language they could understand. "Those who are affectedly partial to the *Italian* Tongue will scarce allow Musick to speak in any other," Hughes continued; "but if Reason may be admitted to have any share in these Entertainments, nothing is more necessary than that the Words shou'd be understood, without which the End of *Vocal Musick* is lost."

Beneath this criticism of Italian music lurked England's intense distrust of everything foreign. Already British insularity had grown sensitive to implications of uncouthness, and to the average Englishman Italian singers and Italian music constituted an unpleasant reflection upon British musical taste. Addison's operatic criticism was political as well as literary and musical. In an amusing poem entitled *Harlequin-Horace; or, The Art of Modern Poetry* (1731) James Miller deplored the Italianization of his countrymen and longed for the "Days of Old when *Englishmen* were *Men*," when "Their Musick like themselves, was grave, and plain." Two years later an anonymous "moral satire" upon *The Manners of the Age* (1733) reinforced Miller's nationalistic prejudice against foreign debauchery:

> 'Twas once fair *Britain's* glory and her praise
> To bind her heroes brows with foreign bayes;
> Victorious wreaths from vanquish'd realms to bring,
> She cannot conquer now—but she can sing;
> And while her warriors on the stage look gay,
> Gentle or eager, just as fiddlers play;
> Made soft or fierce by *Handel's* potent lyre;
> Their rage and love both weakned by the wire;
> Of *Latian* eunuchs, and sweet tunes possest,
> The opera is safe—and *England* blest.

As early as 1706 John Dennis has directed *An Essay on the Operas* against "that soft and effeminate Musick which abounds in the *Italian Opera*." In denouncing Italian affectation as popish and passionately lascivious Dennis had called opera "a Diversion of more pernicious Consequence, than the most licentious Play that ever has appear'd upon the Stage." His central objection to Italian music lay in his wildly illogical concern over England's progress in the War of the Spanish Succession: "At a time when we are contending with our Enemies for our very Being, we are aukwardly aping their Luxuries and Vices, which we neglected or contemn'd while we were at full Peace with them; as if by a certain foreboding Delusion we were preparing our selves for Slavery, and endeavouring to make our selves agreeable to our new Masters."

True-born Englishmen did not want Italian opera. Constantly the foreign species was derided and assailed for its supposed lack of dramatic power, its grotesque extravagance, its effeminate nonsense, its anti-British implications. From the beginning Italian opera in England was, as Dr. Johnson declared in his *Life of Hughes*, "an exotick and irrational entertainment which has been always combated and always has prevailed." Even with excellent music, skilled performers, and magnificent decorations, such entertainments could never become the favorite amusement of an English audience. Foreign opera was a fad, and as such it enjoyed only transient vogue in eighteenth-century London. It never deeply touched the English heart, for any nation with a highly developed spoken drama tends naturally to reject music drama and to tolerate stage music only incidentally. For three decades Handel sought to flatter a whimsical clique of autocratic dilettanti. Polite society heard *Rinaldo* and *Teseo, Radamisto* and *Floridante, Guilio Cesare* and *Muzio Scevola. Tamerlano* was succeeded by *Rodelinda, Scipione* by *Alessandro, Admeto* by *Riccardo Primo,* and so on through that steady stream which finally ceased with *Deidamia* in 1741. In his Italian operas Handel surpassed all predecessors and contemporaries, and some of his familiar operatic arias still give exquisite delight. But after cultivating opera for more than thirty years he left it still fettered by tyrannous conventions which even his eminent genius could not transcend. Opera never fully expressed Handel's nature; it provided no theme commensurate with the grandeur of his conceptions. And in his operatic music he failed to touch the English pulse, for Englishmen hungered and thirsted after *English* music set to *English* words and performed by *English* singers. London learned to know the true Handel only when the German composer abandoned opera and commenced that series of gigantic choral works which spoke directly to the great English middle class and ultimately placed him at the head of "English" composers.

III

On Monday evening, 29 January 1728, London's polite world flocked to the Theatre Royal in Lincoln's-Inn Fields to hear John Rich's production of *The Beggar's Opera,* a "Newgate pastoral" which became the first popular success of the modern English stage. John Gay's enchanting pasticcio was filled with tuneful songs adapted to popular English and Scottish airs by Dr. John Christopher Pepusch. Spoken in dialogue and interspersed with engaging melodies, this sprightly parent of modern musical comedy proved at once a sharp satire on Walpole's administration and a vivacious parody on Italian opera, with its accompanied recitative, its aria *da capo,* its farewell duets, and its heroic prison scenes. In selecting his airs Gay boldly commandeered from Handel and Purcell. At the moment when Handel faced bankruptcy and bitter disputes of recalcitrant singers at the Royal Academy of Music, he found his Crusader's March in *Rinaldo* purloined and adapted to the bawling of highwaymen in "Let us take the road." *The Beggar's Opera* stormed London. Pepusch and Gay had devised the very entertainment for which "the town" languished. Its immediate success continued unabated for sixty-two nights during the first season, and its vogue later assumed the character of a national manifestation. It made "Gay rich and Rich gay." Pepusch's arrangement of familiar old tunes captivated all hearts, and even Mrs. Delany, who deplored Handel's empty houses at the Haymarket, found Gay's witty ballad opera "very comical and full of humour."

It remained for *The Beggar's Opera* to give Italian opera in England its *coup de grâce.* Undoubtedly Gay's charming burlesque became a potent rival of foreign opera even during its first season. On 15 February 1728 Gay wrote to Swift with ill-disguised triumph: "Lord Cobham says that I should have printed it in Italian over against the English, that the ladies might have understood what they read. The outlandish, as they now call it, opera has been so thin of late that some have called that the Beggar's Opera, and if the run continues, I fear I shall have remonstrances drawn up against me by the Royal Academy of Music." Two days later *The Craftsman* ignored Handel's first performance of *Siroe* by heralding Gay's success: "We hear that the *British Opera,* commonly called the *Beggar's Opera,* continues to be acted, at the Theatre in Lincoln's-Inn Fields with general Applause, to the great Mortification of the Performers and Admirers of the *Outlandish Opera* in the Haymarket." Following a "delightful" performance of *Siroe* Handel's staunch friend Mrs. Delany lamented that "the taste of the town is so depraved, that nothing will be approved of but the burlesque." On February 29 she complained that "the English have *no real taste for musick;* for if they had, they could not neglect an entertainment so perfect in its kind for a parcel of ballad singers." During the following season Englishmen still preferred the bewitching burlesque melodies of Gay's opera, but Mrs. Delany remained a steadfast champion of Handel's "charming" operas and a severe critic of London's "vile taste" for "minuets and ballads."

The Beggar's Opera ruined Handel. His operatic enterprise suffered far more than Walpole's administration from Gay's irresistible satire. At heart Britons had always preferred ballad opera in English with spoken dialogue and native tunes, and popular common sense had finally reacted against the affectation of Italian singers performing in an unknown tongue or in a mixture of Italian and English. Handel was a stubborn proponent of Italian opera, but he was first of all an opportunist, and he began to realize that if he would hold his ground against "the *British Opera*" he must take decided measures. Gay's "parcel of ballad singers" convinced him that Londoners would still throng any theatre offering the entertainment they demanded. He observed that mediocre English performers singing English songs in English brought

Gay substantial profits, while Italian singers of superior merit drove managers of opera to debt. *The Beggar's Opera* caused him to consider seriously whether English singers should not be introduced into his own productions. Unlike those feeble creatures who die when their summer of fashion is over, Handel commenced his great work only when he had lost favor with the fickle world of fashion. It was not too late to seek a newer world.

From his despair Handel was suddenly roused by an unexpected revival of a former composition. On 23 February 1732 Bernard Gates, Master of the Children of the Chapel Royal, honored the composer's forty-seventh birthday with a private rendition of *Haman and Mordecai*. Twelve years earlier Handel had composed this charming English masque for a small audience at Canons (the fabulous estate of the Duke of Chandos), but after its initial performance on 29 August 1720 he had shelved it as a *pièce d'occasion* which had served its day. Now the boys of the Chapel Royal captivated Gates' invited guests with a surprise performance of this forgotten masterpiece, adapted from Racine's *Esther* by Alexander Pope and adorned with some of Handel's freshest choral music. "From dinner I went to the Music Club," the Earl of Egmont wrote in his *Diary* for Wednesday, 23 February 1732, "where the King's Chapel boys acted the *History of Hester*, writ by Pope and composed by Hendel; this oratoria or religious opera is exceeding fine, and the company was highly pleased, some of the parts being well performed." A repetition of *Haman and Mordecai* was demanded at once, and within a few weeks the Academy of Ancient Music sponsored two private performances at the Crown and Anchor Tavern in the Strand.

In her indiscreet enthusiasm for Handel's "oratoria" Princess Anne proposed an elaborate public performance of *Haman and Mordecai* at the King's Theatre in the Haymarket. But Dr. Edmund Gibson, Bishop of London, was scandalized at the notion of performing a religious drama in a place of worldly amusement. In his wrath Dr. Gibson sternly prohibited action and scenery in any work treating a Biblical theme, and as Dean of the Chapel Royal he solemnly forbade his choristers to assist in any such performance within his diocese. Meanwhile an unscrupulous speculator announced in *The Daily Journal* on April 17 that Handel's *Esther,* "an Oratorio or sacred Drama," as it was originally composed "for The Most Noble James, Duke of Chandos," would be performed at "the Great Room in Villar's-street, York-buildings" on April 20. At such brazen piracy Handel was indignant. Ignoring England's nebulous copyright laws, he replied at once with a counteradvertisement in *The Daily Journal* on April 19, announcing that "By His Majesty's command" *Esther,* "an Oratorio in English, formerly composed by Mr. Handel, and now revised by him with several Additions," would be performed at the King's Theatre on May 2 "by a great number of the best Voices and Instruments." Significant was a note appended to Handel's advertisement: "There will be no acting on the Stage, but the House will be fitted up in a decent Manner for the Audience. The Musick to be disposed after the Manner of the Coronation Service."

Finding it impossible to produce *Haman and Mordecai* with dramatic representation, Handel wisely resolved to perform his oratorio with singers clad in ordinary dress and seated on a plain stage. Dr. Gibson's interdict could never outlaw non-dramatic performances of sacred music. Since Pope's original masque had crowded six scenes into one act, Handel commissioned Samuel Humphreys to expand *Haman and Mordecai* into a three-act oratorio entitled *Esther.* Within a few weeks the work was substantially revised and enlarged. Handel added several choruses, borrowed material from his former works, and rewrote certain original portions. In reducing Racine's drama to a minimum Humphreys gave additional importance to the chorus and thereby unconsciously accentuated the epic character which was eventually to distinguish oratorio from opera and masque. With its preponderance of choral element *Esther* could scarcely have been effective as drama, and its true merit became apparent only when it was performed as oratorio. Handel's forced decision against stage accessories thus proved an unexpected blessing. Suddenly free from confining theatrical limitations, he could appeal to popular imagination solely through his music. Quite by chance he stumbled from the stage to the concert platform, but his acute artistic sense seized the natural possibilities of his new position.

Handel's first public performance of *Esther* on 2 May 1732 marked the birth of concert oratorio. On the first night crowds were so great that numerous ticket-holders were unable to gain admittance, and Handel's success was assured when the Royal Family arrived in state. That season *Esther* was performed six times with great applause. Hitherto oratorio had been absolutely unknown in England, and London was curious to hear Mr. Handel's novel concoction at the Haymarket. In striking out a new course the composer immediately appealed to human nature's keen desire for novelty. Oratorio became the rage, much as Italian opera had become the rage twenty-five years before. London thronged the Haymarket, not so much for spiritual edification as for Mr. Handel's strange new delights. In a saucy pamphlet entitled *See and Seem Blind; or, A Critical Dissertation on the Publick Diversions* (1732?) an anonymous satirist expressed rare amusement at the current craze for Handel's new "*Oratorio,* or Religious *Farce."* Like most of his contemporaries this witty pamphleteer was puzzled over the meaning of *oratorio,* and he called Handel's new "Sacred *Drama"* a "Religious *Farce"* because "the duce take me if I can make any other Construction of the Word, but he has made a very good *Farce* of it, and put near 4000*l* in his Pocket, of which I am very glad, for I love the Man for his Musick's sake." The author then proceeded to satirize the English vogue for oratorio:

This being a new Thing set the whole World a Madding; Han't you been at the *Oratorio,* says one? Oh! If you don't see the *Oratorio* you see nothing, says t'other; so away goes I to the *Oratorio,* where I saw indeed the finest Assembly of People I ever beheld in my Life, but, to my great Surprize, found this Sacred *Drama* a mere Consort, no Scenary, Dress or Action, so necessary to a *Drama;* but H[ande]l was plac'd in a Pulpit (I suppose they call that their Oratory), by him sate *Senesino, Strada, Bertolli,* and *Turner Robinson,* in their own Habits; before him stood sundry sweet Singers of this our *Israel,* and *Strada* gave us a *Hallelujah* of half an Hour long; *Senesino* and *Bertolli* made rare work with the *English* Tongue you would have sworn it had been *Welch;* I would have wish'd it *Italian,* that they might have sang with more ease to themselves, since, but for the Name of *English,* it might as well have been *Hebrew.*

Literary London was struck by *Esther.* In a day when *decorum* was a shibboleth penny-a-liners inundated Handel with acrostics, couplets, quatrains, and doggerel verses of every description. Scores of intolerable effusions upon "our British *Orpheus*" flooded London bookstalls and graced the pages of England's polite journals. When required at short notice to produce grandiloquent tributes to Handel's genius, London versifiers of the Augustan century were at no loss for a simile. Orpheus, who charmed beasts into civility and inspired stones with animation, hung on a peg (as it were) ready for use, and in eighteenth-century periodicals Handel was repeatedly associated with his distinguished predecessor.

As early as 23 December 1731 Alexander Pope had declared in *The Daily Journal* that "Mr. *Hendel*'s Noble *Oratories*" were "the best composed in the Nation." A few liberal Englishmen found oratorio at once a delightful diversion and a deep inspiration. To Mrs. Delany *Esther* represented "the highest entertainment." In Dublin Mrs. Letitia Pilkington, who "always delighted in Church-Music," was so "charmed" by "the Oratorio of Queen *Esther*" that "at the Conclusion of the Music" she voiced her rapture in twelve "Lines" of pedestrian verse. But *Esther* was not without detractors. Bishops stigmatized Handel's "sacred opera" as profanation, and solemn clergymen denounced the "religious farce" at the Haymarket as unspeakable sacrilege. Even laymen feared the pernicious consequence of making every church a potential concert hall. An anonymous satire on *The Manners of the Age* (1733) ironically declared

> The realm in doubt, till sages shall ordain,
> If *Paul* henceforth, or *H[ei]deg[ge]r*, shall reign.
> If *Moses* for great *Burnet* we must quit,
> And revelation be dethron'd by wit;
> If sacred opera's shall instruct us still,
> And churches empty, as *ridotto*'s fill;
> The *Hebrew* or the *German* leave the field,
> And *David*'s lyre to *Handel*'s spinnet yield.

In lighter vein James Bramston sarcastically proclaimed Handel's spiritual innovation in *The Man of Taste* (1733):

> The Stage should yield the solemn Organ's note,
> And Scripture tremble in the Eunuch's throat.
> Let *Senesino* sing, what *David* writ,
> And *Hallelujahs* charm the pious pit.
> Eager in throngs the town to *Hester* came,
> And *Oratorio* was a lucky name.
> Thou, *Heeideggre!* the *English* taste has found,
> And rul'st the mob of quality with sound.
> In *Lent,* if Masquerades displease the town,
> Call 'em *Ridotto*'s, and they still go down:
> Go on, Prince *Phyz!* to please the British nation,
> Call thy next *Masquerade* a *Convocation.*

Satirists missed few opportunities to ridicule the pious fad. Even Hogarth's familiar etching of *The Chorus* (1732) shows a trace of ribald jealousy at Handel's strange manner of addressing God in recitative and chorus. In *The Woman of Taste* (1733) the anonymous poetaster rose to expansive mirth at the delicious ironies of Handel's *Esther:*

> The joy of young and old, of maid and wife,
> Ne'er miss the *Oratorio* for your life;

THE CHORUS

From an Etching by William Hogarth (1732)

Singing the bait, devotion the pretence,
By music drawn, that modern foe to sense!
Where lofty airs, and humble wit, are found,
The charge quite small—five duets for a pound;
As much each winter sunk, to please your ear,
As wou'd your landlord pay, and sempstress clear.
  To make her triumphs and his art the greater,
Here *Handell* kills fair *Hester's* foes in metre;
Flutes keep due measure with the victim's pangs,
Faustina quav'ring just as *Haman* hangs:

Now warbling baudry—in a holier post,
Now chanting anthems to *the Lord of Host*.
To make the service to each master even,
By *Satan* now employ'd, and now by *heaven;*
And either to displease exceeding loath,
Receives two honest fees to serve 'em both:
The beauteous *Hebrew* pensive for a time,
Married by *Humphreys* to the king in rhime.
Each pulpit scorn'd, the good reforming age
More fond of morals taught 'em by the stage;
(Which though they may some prelates hearts perplex,
Hit you and I, and all our modish sex,)
A vicious town and court not half so soon,
Made vertuous by a sermon as a tune;
Whose melting notes the souls of sinners sooth,
Who fly from *Gibs[o]n* to be sav'd by *Booth;*
In pit or box perform their Maker's will,
Made saints by maxims taught 'em at quadrille:
From *Rich's* hands who absolution take,
Pardon'd by *Cibber* though condemn'd by *W[a]ke.*

Those without strict religious scruples nevertheless protested against non-dramatic oratorio. One journal asked why a singer who could not dress and act as Esther should be allowed to sing the part of Esther, and another journal wrily declared that singing as Biblical characters in ancient costume was less irreverent than singing in décolleté ballroom finery.

Notwithstanding such demands for dramatic performance, however, *Esther* assured Handel that London was ready to hear great choral works without the extraneous attraction of scenery, costume, and dramatization. His success encouraged him to try oratorio once more, but he did not take immediate advantage of his new experience. From 1732 to 1741 he continued to produce Italian operas, but between *Esther* and *Messiah* he wrote four oratorios which determined him ultimately to abandon opera altogether for the new form. On 5 December 1732 a letter from Handel's old friend Aaron Hill expressed his desire to place the composer "at the head of a design, as solid, and imperishable, as your musick and memory." Just as the composer was shifting from opera to oratorio Hill urged Handel to experiment once again with a libretto in English:

I cannot forbear to tell you the earnestness of my wishes, that, as you have made such considerable steps toward it, already, you would let us owe to your inimitable genius, the establishment of *musick,* upon a foundation of good poetry; where the excellence of the *sound* should be no longer dishonour'd, by the poorness of the *sense* it is chain'd to.

My meaning is, that you would be resolute enough, to deliver us from our *Italian bondage;* and demonstrate, that *English* is soft enough for Opera, when compos'd by poets, who know how to distinguish the *sweetness* of our tongue, from the *strength* of it, where the last is less necessary.

I am of opinion, that male and female voices may be found in this kingdom, capable of every thing, that is quite requisite; and, I am sure, a species of dramatic Opera might be invented, that, by reconciling reason and dignity, with musick and fine machinery, would charm the *ear,* and hold fast the *heart,* together.

Such an improvement must, at once, be lasting, and profitable, to a very great degree; and would, infallibly, attract an universal regard, and encouragement.

Such prophetic words recall Addison's pregnant remark in *Spectator* 405: "I could heartily wish there was the same Application and Endeavour to cultivate and improve our Church-Musick, as have been lately bestowed on that of the Stage. Our Composers have one very great Incitement to it: they are sure to meet with Excellent Words, and, at the same time, a wonderful Variety of them. There is no Passion that is not finely expressed in those parts of Inspired Writing, which are proper for Divine Songs and Anthems."

Perhaps Handel's principal reason for turning to oratorio was his astute observation that the British public was better acquainted with the English Bible than with Tasso and Homer and Virgil. In his Italian operas he had exploited the theatrical intrigues of heathen mythology known only to erudite students of Latin and Greek, but in his "sacred" oratorios he drew his themes exclusively from Holy Writ. Such material readily appealed to Englishmen lately revitalized by John Wesley's Methodist revival. Sir John Hawkins recorded that Handel "was well acquainted with the Holy Scriptures, and was sensible that the sublime sentiments with which they abound would give opportunities of displaying his greatest talents." In turning to oratorio "Handel gave another direction to his studies, better suited, as he himself used to declare, to the circumstances of a man in advancing years, than that of adapting music to such vain and trivial poetry as the musical drama is generally made to consist of." But in selecting texts from sacred sources Handel was actually impelled more by practical considerations than by exalted motives of religious fervor. He was a sincere Lutheran, and in his later years he attended church with laudable regularity, but there is little evidence to support the threadbare legend that he was a saint dedicating his art solely to the service of God. In composing oratorios he was fired with worldly ambitions. He laid no embargo upon secular themes, and his purely secular oratorios are among his finest creations. But on the whole heroic Biblical stories best served Handel's purpose in his epic oratorios, for epics appeal by celebrating the familiar, and no literature was more familiar to Englishmen than the Hebrew stories of the Old Testament. Christian religion foundered lamentably under the sleepy church of the Hanoverian kings, but eighteenth-century Anglicans nevertheless knew their Bible as they knew scarcely any other single volume.

In emphasizing the epic character of his oratorios Handel no longer attempted to gratify the frivolous ear of aristocracy. Italian opera had been fashioned to please a fickle and dissipated upper class, but in his oratorios he sought the support of England's sound and receptive middle class. *Esther* was far more palatable to English taste than *Rinaldo*. Oratorio was sung in English; its Biblical theme touched the English heart; its epic nature appealed directly to the British national temperament. By 1732 musical patrons were bored with Italian opera, and their zeal for Handel's "sacred" dramas encouraged the composer to follow the new direction of British taste. Without a shift in fashion he would never have forsaken opera, for he sought always to satisfy his public's demands, and he never consciously composed music which had no chance of winning immediate popularity.

Handel's motive in abandoning opera for oratorio was therefore neither religious nor artistic. Nothing in his career warrants the assumption that he was actuated by any motive nobler than desire for monetary reward. Despite his occasional bankruptcies he was a keen businessman, and in his thirst for financial gain (as well as for musical prestige) he aspired to convert his art into a means of accumulating a fortune. Handel was not satisfied with munificent pensions and permanent royal patronage. Like Shakespeare and Scott he combined the trader and speculator with the poet. Unlike Mozart and Schubert he died in affluence. When *Esther* proved successful he shrewdly observed that oratorio could be produced at much less expense than Italian opera. No costumes and scenery were required; lack of dramatic action resulted in fewer rehearsals; English singers demanded smaller salaries than vain Italian *castrati*. Whereas operatic performances were strictly forbidden on Wednesdays and Fridays during Lent, oratorio was supposedly consistent with the solemnity of the season and could be performed without serious clerical objection. Through this incidental advantage oratorio was able to compete successfully with its gaudy Italian rival. Actually Handel introduced into England a kind of Lenten Biblical opera which took its present form from the lofty English sentiment permitting no suggestion of the theatre in matters of religion.

Thus at forty-seven Handel discovered himself quite by accident. He was reserved for less ephemeral work than contemporary Neapolitan opera, but he would never have dropped opera for oratorio if his schemes had not miserably failed. Without his operatic miscarriage there would have been no *Messiah,* and the "divine Saxon" would probably be known today chiefly to musical historians. If unscrupulous speculators had not pirated *Esther,* Handel might never have experimented with oratorio. If the Bishop of London had not banned scenery and action in religious works, oratorios might have become elaborate sacred operas in English. Handel missed oblivion by chance, and that chance depended upon the peculiar bias of British taste. England's claim to the honor of having encouraged Handelian oratorio is indeed the rather negative claim of having declined to listen to further Italian opera, but Englishmen were nevertheless responsible for the welcome change in Handel's sphere of composition. It is remarkable that in the face of repeated opposition from British aristocracy Handel induced London audiences to hear works not molded for the casual pleasure-seeker. But it is no less remarkable that the worldly society of Horace Walpole's day ultimately encouraged compositions of such spiritual import as *Judas Maccabeus* and *Messiah.* Augustan England was no nest of singing birds, but the Age of Prose and Reason produced one of the world's great monuments of "sacred" choral art.

IV

In eighteenth-century England *oratorio* signified a narrative poem treating a Biblical or legendary theme in a lyric-dramatic-epic form, set to elaborate music for solo and chorus, performed with organ and orchestral accompaniment, and produced in a concert hall or theatre without costume, scenery, or dramatic action. At its first appearance in London oratorio bewildered dramatists and musicians alike. As late as 1763 the author of *An Examination of the Oratorios which have been Performed this Season at Covent-Garden Theatre* smiled at England's recurrent confusion over Handel's novel dramatic form:

I never was more puzzled in my life, than to tell what it is, there are so many discordant opinions about it. At *one end* of the *town,* an *Oratorio* is a sort of sober, solemn entertainment; which, by way of *mortification* in *Lent,* is served up to the public on *fish* and *soup days;* and so the admirers of *Acis and Galatea,* and *Alexander's Feast,* have slyly slipped them in under the names of *Oratorios,* just as a good catholic friend of mine, who was a great lover of *Pork* and *Pease,* used to call it *Sturgeon* whenever he eat it in Lent. On the contrary, at the *other end* of the *Town,* an Oratorio is a bundle of diverting songs and choirs, tied together, with a little solemn nonsense, during which, you may talk, sleep, or stare, without any interruption, either to your own, or the audience's entertainment. Now, for my part, I have a very different idea of a genuine Oratorio, and here I present it to the reader, under the dry form of a definition.

An *Oratorio* then is a *Poem,* accompanied with *music,* where, unincumbered with the absurdity of a *dramatic exhibition,* they jointly affect the mind, by a representation of some great and interesting subject, impressed with all the force of their combined powers. I say, unincumbered with a *dramatic* exhibition, because an *Oratorio,* if *acted,* becomes immediately an *Opera,* with the additional impropriety of a *continued chorus,* and an almost unavoidable want of *unity,* both in *time* and *place.*

Oratorio is not strictly church music. It is rather spiritual concert music, an indefinite form occupying a position midway between secular and liturgical art. Like church music oratorio seeks (without depicting actual events) to arouse a vivid sense of the emotional realities of religion. Like opera it often embodies its purpose in a story and portrays particular characters under the stress of particular emotions. But oratorio is not necessarily religious: there are secular oratorios just as there are religious operas. Among the various modes in which music is wedded to dramatic poetry oratorio occupies a unique position, for it gives the musician considerable latitude in his choice of subject and in his mode of development. It requires neither the subtlety of pure ecclesiastical music nor the dramatic effectiveness of opera. Instead it demands in a composer the power to delineate without great finesse such elemental emotions as joy, grief, fear, and hope, as well as the musical skill to display the chorus in simple and persuasive masses.

In temperament and training Handel was singularly fitted to compose such music. Already his long connection with the operatic stage had stimulated his innate dramatic genius and perfected his inexhaustible flow of melody. With such talents he combined exceptional powers of choral composition. Actually his oratorios are only extensions of his Italian operas upon an imaginary stage. In turning from opera to oratorio he did not forsake his fundamental passion for dramatic music, but merely relinquished its theatrical aspect. Handelian oratorio is therefore operatic in origin and semioperatic in form and method, and it has no historical connection with contemporary German Passion music. Oratorio offered the composer a convenient medium between church music and theatrical music; its novelty lay in its grandiose conception, which was neither suitable for the church nor readily accessible to the theatre. In his preface to *Samson* (1743) Newburgh Hamilton explained that Handel had introduced "a musical Drama, whose Subject must be Scriptural, and in which the Solemnity of Church-Musick is agreeably united with the most pleasing Airs of the Stage." With a firm hand Handel grasped the peculiar powers of oratorio, and he fixed its limits for all time.

Whereas *Messiah* is chiefly lyric, *Israel in Egypt* is conspicuously epic, and *Samson* implies so much dramatic movement that it might well be performed with scenery and action. Fundamentally Handelian oratorio is epic in character, but throughout Handel's thirty-two epic poems dramatic and lyric methods may also be clearly distinguished. In some oratorios the operatic method is so definite that arias and recitatives became utterances of characters in the story while choruses represent a crowd of Babylonians, Romans, or Israelites. Other oratorios retain dramatic rôles both in solos and in choruses but also employ the chorus as the voice of universal Christendom. But such works as *Messiah* and *Israel in Egypt* are utterly beyond the scope of drama, for their arias and choruses are based entirely upon Scriptural texts selected not from narrative but from prophecy and psalm. *Messiah* at once embodies all Handelian methods and typifies none. From the opening announcement of Christ's Advent until His final words before the Ascension, *Messiah* is generally epic and occasionally dramatic as well as predominantly lyric.

Few composers before or since Handel have employed with equal dramatic power the different forms of the human voice. Guided by long operatic experience, he instinctively assumed a more direct and intimate form of musical speech than that adopted by Sebastian Bach. His dominant purpose was to express himself exuberantly through the human voice, and in his firm devotion to that ideal he developed an essentially vocal conception of music. For two centuries Handel has remained unsurpassed in his sure knowledge of range and compass, in his skilful adaptation of difficult melodies to varying vocal registers, in his emphatic display of singers' most brilliant tones, in his dexterous art of according singers appropriate points of relief. Two salient features of his best oratorio style are his deeply expressive and sometimes highly complex arias and his massively organized and often elaborately constructed choruses. In melody Handel rivalled the greatest Italian composers of his time. His solo songs represent most effectively the old Italian *bel canto*, with its lyric grace, its elegant refinement of detail, its noble pathos, and its brilliant coloratura. For hundreds of amazingly varied characters he found convincing emotional expression. His telling and direct solos go straight to the heart.

But the great glory and distinguishing feature of Handelian oratorio is the chorus. Some musicians give chief praise to Handel's arias, but his musical fame rests indisputably upon his skill in writing for bodies of voices. The emancipation of Handel's chorus from theatrical limitations marked the crisis of his career. After *Esther* he more and more differentiated oratorio from opera by exalting the chorus as his most effective and characteristic utterance of epic conceptions. As he gradually gained musical freedom through the disappearance of stage necessities, his chorus became more powerful as a means of dramatic expression as opposed to dramatic action. Even in *Deborah* (1733) his choral emphasis was notable, and in *Athaliah* (1733) his eight-part double choruses appeared for the first time. *Saul* (1739) substantially enlarged the share of chorus, and *Israel in Egypt* (1739) was almost purely choral. Generally Handel's chorus supplies the place of scenery and action: it sets forth the basic mood from which moods of single characters are drawn, and it sustains the emotional keynote and ethical purpose of the composition. Sometimes it depicts the feeling of supposed participants in the imaginary action; sometimes it serves a didactic purpose in propounding moral lessons; frequently it describes thrilling actions for which the voice of a narrator would have proved futile. In his free application of chorus to every dramatic purpose Handel rendered countless shades of human feeling with immediate and unmistakable directness.

No other composer has excelled Handel in his graceful mastery of choral technique. Not one of his choruses fails to exhibit evidence of musical scholarship, yet none presents insuperable difficulties, for Handel's sure command of technical resource makes every choral problem seem easy and proves that severely plain harmony can conceal the richest modulation. His firm knowledge of voices enabled him to gain the maximum effect with the least effort. When one observes the appropriateness of his choral themes, the flexibility of his form under the steady control of vast conceptions, the smoothness of his part writing, the ingenuity of his structural elaboration, and the facility with which his transitions are effected, he is not astonished that Handel's choral counterpoint has won the admiration of almost every great musician. Despite his advanced contrapuntal science, however, Handel depended far more than Bach upon solid chord-movement, and his general choral style represents a felicitous union of homophonic and polyphonic principles. In eighteenth-century London his choral versatility must have aroused wonder and admiration among Englishmen to whom the miracles of Sebastian Bach were still unknown.

But with all their breadth and variety Handel's choruses are economical, simple, and clear. Seizing a few basic harmonies and familiar sequences, the composer employed his unerring sense of proportion to construct choruses which for sheer effectiveness have proved the despair of all imitators. In their massive eloquence Handel's choruses are as elemental as the forces of nature, elevating all before them to the highest pitch of sublimity. "When he chooses," said Mozart, "he strikes like a thunderbolt." Heedless of intricate detail, Handel strove always for the obvious and the grand, but when one finds the appropriate ear-focus he realizes that in his few powerful strokes the composer grasped every essential. Those who let him speak in his own bluff fashion discover in his music a perfect fusion of manner and matter. Handel's skill in choral technique was acquired and developed in England. In an essay "On the Different Schools of Music" (1760) Oliver Goldsmith placed the composer "at the head of the *English* school" and insisted that he "may be said as justly as any man, not *Pergolese* excepted, to have founded a new school of music." In his oratorios, "by steering between the manners of *Italy* and *England,* he has struck out new harmonies, and formed a species of music different from all others." Reared in the atmosphere of the German chorale, Handel was thoroughly equipped to evolve a grand choral form from the English anthem. In masterly fashion he fused the strength of the strict German style with the grace of Italian *bel canto,* blending them with the English flavor of Henry Purcell. It is Handel's indebtedness to the English School rather than his mere residence in London that entitles Englishmen to place the "divine Saxon" in the line of British composers. He is predominant and original by

reason of his eclecticism. Only three years after his death a paragraph in John Potter's *Observations on the Present State of Music and Musicians* (1762) provided significant remarks upon the composer's highly composite technique:

> The ENGLISH music, at this period, is a composition of GERMAN and ITALIAN, in conjunction with the old ancient *English* music: For this agreeable union we are principally beholden to Mr. HANDEL: He not only laid the foundation, but liv'd long enough to compleat it. So that the *English* music may with justness be called *Handel*'s music, and every musician the son of *Handel;* for whatever delicacies, or improvements have been made by others, they are all owing to, and took their rise from, a perusal of his works. What had we to boast of, before he settled in *England*, and new-modell'd our music? Nothing, but some good church music. He has join'd the fulness and majesty of the *German* music, the delicacy and elegance of the *Italian*, to the solidity of the *English;* constituting in the end a magnificence of stile superior to any other nation.

Unquestionably Handel was guided by the taste of genuinely English audiences to produce choruses and declamatory solos exhibiting a decidedly English character. With the eye of genius the shrewd London impresario studiously observed his public and adapted his works to their most obvious tastes. If he had settled in Moscow he would probably have composed Russian music.

In London, however, Handel was content to produce oratorios expressing the English national spirit on its noblest heroic side. Fortunately the epic character of choral oratorio invited themes relating not the fate of single individuals but the weal and woe of whole peoples. Appropriate subjects of the most heroic type Handel found in the history of the Hebrew race and in the plain gospel narratives of the New Testament, for the Hebrew people conveniently symbolize any group united as one nation. But Handel interpreted his sacred texts in no narrow or literal sense. He treated his Biblical record in a broad spirit, glorifying no ecclesiastical dogma but teaching always the ethical dignity of man and the universal efficacy of God's moral law.

So Handel planted oratorio in England's congenial soil, where it quickly took root, eventually sprang forth, and finally flowered luxuriantly. In the field of oratorio everything accomplished for two centuries is profoundly indebted to his achievement. The sustained power of his oratorio style, the expressive nobility of his melody, and the breadth and clarity of his harmonic structure unite to form a wonderful and unsurpassed whole. As the Reverend William Hughes declared in his sermon on *The Efficacy and Importance of Musick* (1749): "To do justice in all respects to the Character of Mr. *Handel,* who has open'd such uncommon Scenes of Delight, who in the greatest Variety of Instances has long since prov'd himself the most perfect Master of Harmony that any Age ever produc'd, would rather require a Volume, than this poor, and imperfect Sketch."

V

Handel's shift from opera to oratorio was not sudden. For nine years he ran the two in double harness. Following the success of *Esther* in 1732 he composed one more Italian opera before proceeding with oratorio during Lent of 1733. On Saturday evening, 17 March 1733, he performed his second English oratorio at the King's Theatre in the Haymarket. That morning *The Daily Journal* announced *Deborah,* "an Oratorio or sacred Drama, in English, composed by Mr. Handel. The House to be fitted up and illuminated in a new and particular Manner; and to be performed by a great number of the best Voices and Instruments." With all her novel features, however, *Deborah* failed to share her older sister's fate. In order to finance his splendid illuminations Handel doubled his prices of admission, so that despite the presence of George II, Queen Caroline, the Prince of Wales, and the three eldest Princesses, Handel's audience was meagre and his reception cold. "Handel thought, encouraged by the Princess Royal, it had merit enough to deserve a guinea," Lady Irwin explained on March 31; "and the first time it was performed at that price, exclusive of subscriber's tickets, there was but a 120 people in the House. The subscribers being refused unless they would pay a guinea, they, insisting upon the right of their silver tickets, forced into the House, and carried their point."

In popularizing English oratorio among eighteenth-century opera-goers Handel faced a delicate task, for his oratorio prices were exorbitant in comparison with prices for operas, plays, and masquerades. Opera prices were usually: Boxes half a guinea, Pit five shillings, First Gallery three shillings, and Second Gallery two shillings. Sometimes Pit and Boxes were combined at half a guinea, with First Gallery five shillings and Second Gallery three shillings and sixpence. When cheaper seats were thus removed, it was customary to apologize in the press, and from the tone of these notices one concludes that the practice met widespread opposition. Playhouse prices were usually: Boxes five shillings, Pit three shillings, First Gallery two shillings, and Second Gallery one shilling. But during Handel's lifetime oratorio prices remained prohibitive. As late as 1756 Mrs. Delany's niece spent her highly-prized guinea "in two plays *instead* of *one oratorio*," and only in 1768 were oratorios performed at playhouse prices for the first time. Doubtless Handel at half a guinea was superior to Colley Cibber at five shillings, but art does not always prevail over questions of cost. A sarcastic letter in *Common Sense* on 13 May 1738 summarized popular complaint: "In our days the celebrated Mr. *Handell* has often exhibited his Oratorios to the Town without any Prohibition, but every Body knows his Entertainments are calculated for the Quality only, and that People of moderate Fortunes cannot pretend to them, although, as Free *Britons*, they have as good a Right to be entertained with what they do not understand as their Betters."

Handel's admission charges at *Deborah* aroused a bitter public. In March 1733 rising prices and exorbitant taxes were favorite themes of conversation, and Prime Minister Robert Walpole, having revived the Salt Tax in 1732, now contemplated a new tax on tobacco and wine. Already the people were furious, and Handel's blunder added fuel to the blaze. England could not do without salt, tobacco, and wine, but she could do without Handel's music. Suddenly London was full of rumors, and her journals were full of impudent squibs. A fierce diatribe against Handel's "tyrannical Schemes and Insolencies to our Town" appeared in *The Craftsman* on 7 April 1733, and this venomous lampoon offers a representative specimen of the gross sarcasms levelled at oratorio during the first decade. Although it bears the signature of Paoli Rolli (one of Handel's librettists), the letter is now attributed to Bolingbroke, who wrote to praise "the noble Stand, lately made by the polite Part of the World, in Defence of their *Liberties* and *Properties,* against the open Attacks and Attempts of Mr. H[ande]l upon both." Actually the letter is a skilfully veiled attack upon Walpole's unpopular Excise Bill, but its virulent assault upon Handel's *Deborah* suggests the coarse personal abuse to which the composer of oratorio was frequently exposed:

The Rise and Progress of Mr. H[ande]l's Power and Fortune are too well known for Me now to relate. Let it suffice to say that He was grown so insolent upon the sudden and undeserved Increase of both, that He thought nothing ought to oppose his imperious and extravagant Will. He had, for some Time, govern'd the *Operas,* and modell'd the *Orchestre,* without the least Controul. No *Voices,* no *Instruments* were admitted, but such as flatter'd his Ears, though They shock'd those of the Audience. *Wretched Scrapers* were put above the *best Hands* in the *Orchestre.* No Musick but *his own* was to be allow'd, though every Body was weary of it; and He had the Impudence to assert, *that there was no Composer in* England *but Himself.* . . . This Excess and Abuse of Power soon disgusted the Town; his Government grew odious; and his *Opera*'s grew empty. However this Degree of Unpopularity and general Hatred, instead of humbling Him, only made Him more furious and desperate.

CHARLES JENNENS
From an Anonymous Portrait
in the Possession of Edward Viscount Curzon

He resolved to make one last Effort to establish his Power and Fortune by Force, since He found it now impossible to hope for it from the good Will of Mankind. In order to This, He form'd a *Plan,* without consulting any of his *Friends,* (if He has any) and declared that at a proper Season He would communicate it to the Publick; assuring us, at the same Time, that it would be very much for the Advantage of the Publick in general, and of *Opera*'s in particular. . . . His *Scheme* set forth in Substance, that the late Decay of *Opera*'s was owing to their *Cheapness,* and to the great *Frauds* committed by the *Door-keepers;* that the *annual Subscribers* were a Parcel of *Rogues,* and made an ill Use of their Tickets, by often *running* two into the Gallery; that to obviate these Abuses He had contrived a Thing, that was better than an *Opera,* call'd an *Oratorio;* to which none should be admitted, but by *printed Permits,* or Tickets of one Guinea each, which should be distributed out of *Warehouses of his own,* and by *Officers of his own naming;* which *Officers* could not so reasonably be supposed to cheat in the Collection of *Guineas,* as the *Door-keepers* in the Collection of *half Guineas;* and lastly, that as the very Being of *Opera*'s depended upon *Him singly,* it was just that the Profit arising from hence should be for his *own Benefit.* . . .

The Absurdity, Extravagancy, and Oppression of *this Scheme* disgusted the whole Town. Many of the most constant Attenders of the *Opera*'s resolved absolutely to renounce them, rather than go to them under such Extortion and Vexation. They exclaim'd against the *insolent and rapacious Projector of this Plan.* The King's old and sworn Servants, of the two Theatres of *Drury-Lane* and *Covent-Garden,* reap'd the Benefit of this general Discontent, and were resorted to in Crowds, by way of Opposition to the *Oratorio.* Even the fairest Breasts were fired with Indignation against this *new Imposition.* Assemblies, Cards, Tea, Coffee, and all other Female Batteries were vigorously employ'd to defeat the *Project,* and destroy the *Projector.* These joint Endeavours of all Ranks and Sexes succeeded so well, that the *Projector* had the Mortification to see but a very thin Audience at his *Oratorio;* and of about two hundred and sixty odd, that it consisted of, it is notorious that not ten paid for their *Permits,* but, on the contrary, had them given Them, and Money into the Bargain, for coming to keep Him in Countenance.

On 6 April 1733 Henry Fielding added to *The Miser* a slight afterpiece called *Deborah; or, A Wife for You All.* Although this trifle was never published and is known today only from a stray playbill, it probably burlesqued Samuel Humphreys' libretto to Handel's *Deborah*.

Amid the furor caused by *Deborah* Handel accepted an invitation to conduct a series of oratorios in the Sheldonian Theatre of Oxford University upon the occasion of the annual Public Act in July 1733. For this celebration he composed his third English oratorio *Athaliah*, adapted by Samuel Humphreys from Racine's tragedy of the same name. At Oxford *Esther* and *Deborah* and *Athaliah* won triumphant acclaim, but the grave dons seemed perplexed by Handel's unwonted departure from recognized University tradition. Jacobite Oxford looked askance at any Whig composer patronized by an unpopular Hanoverian king. On 5 July 1733 Thomas Hearne, whose devotion to "rare monkish manuscripts" was sung by Pope, recorded in coarse terms that "One Handel, a foreigner, (who, they say, was born at Hanover,) being desired to come to Oxford, to perform in musick this Act, in which he hath great skill, is come down, the Vice-Chancellor (Dr. Holmes) having requested him so to do, and, as an encouragement, to allow him the benefit of the Theater both before the Act begins and after it." For this "innovation" Vice-Chancellor Holmes was "much blamed," for Oxford undergraduates and "many gownsmen" found "Handell and (his lowsy crew) a great number of forreign fidlers" considerably less appealing than a company of strolling players who had been "denied coming to Oxford by the Vice-Chancellor." At one performance by "Handel and his company" Hearne complained that "His book (not worth 1d.) he sells for 1s." Shrewd Mr. Handel did not take his "lowsy crew" of "forreign fidlers" to Oxford for nothing. Although he refused to pay one hundred pounds for an honorary doctor's degree in music, he won "vast Applause" with his oratorios and returned to London with several thousand pounds in his purse.

Two amusing pamphlets commemorate Handel's excursion

into oratorio at Oxford. In an anonymous "Letter to a Friend in Town" entitled *The Oxford Act* (1735) the author gave "a particular and exact Account of that Solemnity" and offered witty remarks upon the fortunes of "our old Friend *Handel,* and his Retinue." On Thursday, 5 July 1733, "the great Mr. *Handel* shew'd away with his *Esther,* an Oratorio, or sacred Drama, to a very numerous Audience, at five Shillings a Ticket." Two days later

The Chevalier *Handel* very judiciously, forsooth, ordered out Tickets for his *Esther* this Evening again. Some of the Company, that had found themselves but very scambingly entertained at our dry Disputations, took it into their Heads, to try how a little Fiddling would sit upon them. Such as cou'dn't attend before, squeezed in with as much Alacrity as others strove to get out; so that e're his Myrmidons cou'd gain their Posts, he found that he had little likelihood to be at such a Loss for a House, as once upon a time, Folks say, he was. However, in this Confusion, one of the good-natur'd *Cantab's,* coud'nt help suggesting to him, that his only Way now wou'd be, to carry it off with an Air, and e'en be contented with what he coud'n't help. So that notwithstanding the barbarous and inhuman Combination of such a Parcel of unconscionable Chaps, he disposed, it seems, of most of his Tickets, and had, as you may guess, a pretty mottley Appearance into the Bargain.

On the following Tuesday "The Company in the Evening were entertained with a spick and span new *Oratorio,* called *Athalia.* One of the Royal and Ample had been saying, that truly, 'twas his Opinion, that the Theater was erected for other-guise Purposes, than to be prostituted to a Company of squeeking, bawling, out-landish Singsters, let the Agreement be what it wou'd." On the morning of July 11 "there was luckily enough, for the Benefit of some of *Handel's* People, a *Serenata* in their Grand Hall. After 'twas over, the Person was soon met with, and immediately 'twas down to the very Ground." Apparently Handel was delighted with the success of *Acis and Galatea:* "Oh!— Your Servant—Mr. —! Sir, your very humble Servant! Your Servant Sir!— Well

—but after all—your College Hall isn't half so bad a Room for Musick, it seems, as People fancied—Didn't it sound excellently well?—They say there was a deal of good company." That evening *Athaliah* was "served up again," and on "the next Night he concluded with his *Oratorio* of *Deborah*."

In *The Oxford Act* (1733), "a new ballad-opera, as it was perform'd by a company of students at Oxford," the anonymous satirist provided sprightly comment upon the musical tastes of undergraduates at eighteenth-century Oxford. Apparently Handel's oratorio prices offended dons and undergraduates alike, for in this piece of buffoonery several scholars, accompanied by young ladies, complain that the Public Act has reduced them to desperate straits, with the tragic result that Flippant (an Oxford-Toast) offers to sell her old pair of stays so that she and Thoughtless (a Merton "blood") may proceed to London. In a bombastic soliloquy Thoughtless bewails his misfortunes at having "squander'd away all my ready Rhino" in order "to make a gaudy Appearance for four or five Days this Public Act." Reviewing his expenditures for the past fortnight, the Oxford scholar lays "his Right Hand on his Breast" and tearfully confides that "the Furniture of my Room procur'd me some Tickets to hear that bewitching Musick, that cursed *Handel,* with his confounded *Oratio*'s [!]; I wish him and his company had been yelling in the infernal Shades below." His friend Haughty is in a similar plight:

Our Cases run in a Parallel; nay, 'tis worse with me, for I question whether my gaping Herd of Creditors won't be for sequestring my Fellowship or not. I don't see what Occasion we had for this Act, unless it was to ruin us all: It would have been much more prudent, I think, had it pass'd in the Negative; for I am sure it has done more Harm than Good amongst us; no one has gain'd any thing by it but Mr. *Handel* and his Crew.

To be ruined Haughty and Thoughtless must have accompanied a great many young ladies to *Esther* and *Athaliah* and *Deborah,* for Mr. Handel's tickets were sold at five shillings.

Even the Vice-Chancellor, however, agreed that "if the Truth was known, most of your Money was spent in Tickets to hear the *Oratorio's*; I must confess a Crown each was rather too much; but had you been contented with a single one, without treating all your Acquaintance, that could never have hurt you."

If oratorio was occasionally criticized as inordinately expensive, it was generally condemned as excessively noisy. Eighteenth-century Englishmen frequently censured Handel's love of noise for its own sake. In 1711 Addison complained that *Rinaldo* was "filled with Thunder and Lightning," and when oratorios became fashionable, conservative connoisseurs deplored the tumultuous effects of "Handel's *huge* choruses" and harsh brass instruments. Within a few years oratorio became a symbol for thunderous noise. In 1733 Lady Irwin found *Deborah* "excessive noisy" with "a vast number of instruments and voices, who all perform at a time, and is in music what I fancy a French ordinary in conversation." As early as 18 January 1737 Lady Lucy Wentworth regretted that "a vast deal of musick at Church" had "spoilt every body's devotion, for there was drums and Trumpits as loud as an Oritoria." On 13 January 1739 Lady Strafford reported that for a performance of *Saul* "Mr. Handell has borrow'd of the Duke of Argyll a pair of the largest kettle-drums in the Tower, so to be sure it will be most excessive noisy with a bad set of singers." In *The Dunciad* (1742) Alexander Pope referred to the "Thunders" of "Giant Handel" and in a note circulated the tale that at times Handel actually employed cannon in his orchestra: "Mr. *Handel* had introduced a great number of Hands, and more variety of Instruments into the Orchestra, and employed even Drums and Cannon to make a fuller Chorus; which prov'd so much too manly for the fine Gentlemen of his age, that he was obliged to remove his Music into *Ireland*." Miss Catherine Talbot reported on 18 April 1747 that in *Judas Maccabeus* Handel "has literally introduced guns, and they have a good effect." John Armstrong found Handel "a noisy overbearing bully in Music." In a clever satire entitled *The Art of Composing Music by a Method Entirely New, Suited to the Meanest Capacity* (1751) William Hayes ironically denounced the "manly Strokes of *Handel*" and confessed his preference for "the pathetic Tenderness which breathes in every Strain" of Italian music:

> There was a Time when the Man-Mountain, *Handel,* had got the Superiority, notwithstanding many Attempts had been made to keep him down; and might have maintained it probably, had he been content to have pleased People in their own Way; but his evil Genius would not suffer it: For he, imagining forsooth that nothing could obstruct him in his Career, whilst at the Zenith of his Greatness, broached another Kind of Music; more full, more grand (as his Admirers are pleased to call it, because crouded with Parts) and, to make the Noise the greater, caused it to be performed, by at least double the Number of Voices and Instruments than ever were heard in a Theatre before: In this, he not only thought to rival our Patron God, but others also; particularly *Æolus, Neptune,* and *Jupiter:* For at one Time, I have expected the House to be blown down with his artificial Wind; at another Time, that the Sea would have overflowed its Banks and swallowed us up: But beyond every thing, his Thunder was most intolerable—I shall never get the horrid Rumbling of it out of my Head—This was (literally you will say) taking us by Storm; hah! hah! but mark the Consequence—By this Attempt to personate *Apollo,* he shared the Fate of *Phaëton; Heidegger* revolted, and with him most of the prime Nobility and Gentry.

Common ears found Handel's oratorios full of sound and fury signifying nothing. In an early sketch of Sheridan's *Critic* (1779) the author whose play is being rehearsed directs that a pistol be fired behind the scenes, observing in a stage whisper that "this hint I took from Handel."

No student of eighteenth-century English literature can doubt the impact of Handel's oratorios upon the subject-matter of Augustan prose and verse. When one observes the frequency with which the "Saxon giant" appears in eighteenth-century poems, novels, and letters he cannot fail to remark the absolute dominance of "Mr. *Handel's* musick" among persons of taste and fashion in Georgian England. Never before in the history of art did fashionable amateurs exert such influence as did the modish contemporaries of Horace Walpole. Even in such technical fields as architecture and landscape gardening the non-professional gentleman did not hesitate to dabble in design. Music engendered a similar spirit, and this intimate relation between music and letters accounts for numerous allusions to musical art in eighteenth-century English prose and verse. Witticism and encomium were much admired in Handel's England, but Addisons and Arbuthnots did not abound. A characteristic tribute to Handel's genius may be found in *Polymnia; or, The Charms of Musick* (1733), in which "a Gentleman of Cambridge" offered his readers "an Hymn or Ode, Sacred to Harmony; Occasion'd by Mr. Handel's Oratorio, and the Harmonia Sacra, Perform'd at Whitehall, by the Gentlemen of the Chappel-Royal." For his feeble dedication "To Mr. Handel" this "artless Muse" manufactured nine pedestrian couplets, the dullness of which amply justifies the author's refuge in anonymity:

> I raise my Voice, but you can raise it high'r,
> And to bold Notes, can bolder string my Lyre:
> Tun'd by thy Art, my artless Muse may live,
> And from thy pleasing Strains may Pleasure give.
> Deep hid in Thought may buried Raptures roll,
> Light up the Bard, and fire his kind'ling Soul.
> If genial Beams, on Earth, th' Almighty spreads,
> To ripen Metals, sleeping in their Beds,
> Hence lively Brilliants into Being strive,
> From waking Seeds, yet doubtful if alive.
> Hence, may your Song, my rougher Song, refine;
> To pierce, like Diamonds, and like Diamonds, shine.
> When melting Solo's steal th' attentive Ear,
> Dead is my Sorrow, and extinct my **Fear**.
> But when the full-mouth'd Chorus wounds the Sky,
> The Dead with Fear awake, the Living die.

> So with the rising Musick, Passions rise,
> As with the dying Musick Passion dies.

This is not poetry, but prose run mad. Though its loyal sentiment is highly commendable, its merit is more than dubious, and it is unfortunate that most eighteenth-century effusions upon "the Raptures of bold *Handel's* Strain" are equally indifferent in quality. During the Georgian century few masters spirits sacrificed their precious lifeblood upon the altar of St. Cecilia. But a flourishing tribe of lesser spirits worshipped at her inner shrine, and in their turgid odes and tumid stanzas Handel was repeatedly likened unto Arion, Amphion, and Orpheus.

Despite such encomiums, however, it is clear that relatively few Englishmen received Handel's early oratorios with spontaneous enthusiasm. For twenty-five years his Italian operas inspired ecstatic poetical tributes from British nobility, but his English oratorios, though essentially popular, failed at first to captivate the general mind. Middle-class Englishmen were not yet sufficiently educated to appreciate oratorio, and polite circles regarded Handel's bourgeois innovation as somewhat beneath their patrician taste. Handel was scarcely annoyed at such blunted pin-pricks as *See and Seem Blind* and *The Woman of Taste,* but the more brutal satires provoked by *Esther* and *Deborah* and *Athaliah* positively discouraged his venture into oratorio. Furthermore, he had aroused the hostility of fashionable patrons as early as 1733 by refusing to caress their favorite doll Senesino. Thenceforth those who professed to regulate musical taste vindictively derided the overbearing "foreign" upstart and persistently supported the operatic schemes of his Italian rivals. Patronage from an unpopular court gave Handel's music little additional favor, and the King and Queen incurred no small ridicule for their faithful attendance upon his oratorios. Repeated failures dragged him steadily deeper into debt. In 1737 he became bankrupt, and during his mental distress he was suddenly stricken with paralysis. Late in the same year Queen Caroline's death deprived him of his warmest patron. When he finally produced *Saul* on 16 January 1739, the oratorio made no remarkable impression, and *Israel in Egypt* suffered a similar fate at its first performance on April 4. Mrs. Delany explained that *Israel in Egypt* "did not take" because "it is too solemn for common ears." A simple announcement that the oratorio would be "shorten'd and intermix'd with songs" speaks volumes regarding current taste. London believed that Handel had certainly failed. Rumor declared that the penniless German composer had vanished into his own country. In 1711 Handel was "the Orpheus of our Age"; after thirty years of unmitigated toil he was a ruined and broken man.

But all was not lost. From his dark valley of personal grief Handel emerged into the light of freedom and independence. Defeated in his unprosperous struggle with aristocratic cabals, weary with the heartbreak of fluctuating success and failure, exhausted by the infinite vexations of theatrical management, disgusted by the petty intrigues of obstinate *castrati,* Handel at last shook the dust of Italian opera from his feet and with indomitable courage resolutely "turned to the Gentiles" for inspiration and hope. At fifty-six he commenced his greatest creative period, not (like the great blind poet of Puritanism) "long choosing and beginning late," but driven reluctantly from the scene of his former triumphs. Handel's *Messiah* was born of failure and affliction. With unconquerable will the Saxon composer rose, majestic though in ruin, to create the masterpiece which has consoled the English world for two hundred years. Even the luster of *Israel in Egypt* pales before Handel's glorious *Messiah,* as the grand vestibule is forgotten when we stand at last before the shrine of the inner temple.

II

The Lord Gave The Word

> Again shall Handel raise his laurell'd brow,
> Again shall harmony with rapture glow;
> The spells dissolve, the combination breaks,
> And Punch no longer Frasi's rival squeaks.
> —TOBIAS SMOLLETT, *Advice* (1746)

I

IN HIS ORATORIO TEXTS Handel was associated with the most distinguished literary figures of the Age of Dryden and Pope. During his long residence in England he married his music to the verse of Milton, Dryden, Gay, Pope, and Congreve. "I often regret that Milton and Handel were not contemporaries," Anna Seward once wrote; "that the former knew not the delight of hearing his own poetry heightened as Handel has heightened it." In his *Essay on the Genius and Writings of Pope* (1756) Joseph Warton contended that Milton's *L'Allegro* and *Il Penseroso* "by a strange fatality lay in a sort of obscurity, the private enjoyment of a few curious readers, till they were set to admirable music by Mr. Handel" in 1740. Nowhere did the composer reveal his invigorating love of nature more frankly than in his romantic and picturesque series of genre pictures based upon Milton's companion poems. Handel's favorite oratorio was *Samson* (1743), based upon Newburgh Hamilton's multilated version of *Samson Agonistes* and enhanced by contributions from Milton's ode on "The Passion," "On the Morning of Christs Nativity,"

"On Time," "At a Solemn Musick," "An Epitaph on the Marchioness of Winchester," and Milton's translations of the Psalms. Two of Handel's most popular performances were *Alexander's Feast* (1736) and *An Ode for St. Cecilia's Day* (1739). In these glittering pageants his adroit craftsmanship and inexhaustible vigor provide an admirable counterpart for the ringing rhetoric of Dryden's spirited odes. John Gay's *Acis and Galatea* (1720) inspired Handel to compose delicate strains through which breathe the pastoral spirit of Theocritus and the sunny life of ancient Greece. "It is of Handel's best," declared Edward FitzGerald; "and as classical as any man who wore a full-bottomed wig could write." The libretto of *Haman and Mordecai* (1720) is generally ascribed to Alexander Pope, while the text of *Semele* (1744) was "alter'd from the *Semele* of Mr. William Congreve," written for operatic performance in 1707.

From the exalted heights of Milton and Dryden and Pope it is a dangerously sharp descent to the prosaic plain of Samuel Humphreys and James Miller and Thomas Broughton. Most of Handel's oratorio texts bear the heavy stamp of the amateur. In his grand carelessness he condescended to lift the dead weight of contemptible trash, celebrating futile (and apocryphal) love affairs with all the rhapsodic bathos of contemporary Grub Street hacks. Some of his oratorios are deformed by the crudest absurdities ever tagged by a hungry drudge. Obviously neo-classical libretto was not held in high regard. In 1747 the Reverend Thomas Morell excused deficiencies in his libretto of *Judas Maccabeus* with the startling confession that his verses were "design'd not as a finish'd Poem, but merely as an Oratorio." When one peruses in cold blood the feeble couplets of Handel's oratorio texts he marvels that the composer was inspired to write music around them at all. But Handel marched dauntlessly through the absurdities of his librettos and seized whatever sentiment appeared beneath them. Given the slighest spark of human feeling in his text, he seldom failed to fan it into flame and light up the dark places. In supplying a certain number of incidents described in a certain quantity of doggerel verse Handel's plodding librettists wisely left all inspiration and genius to the composer, so that actually they produced not unsuccessful librettos when superior wits might have succeeded in creating not unsuccessful poems.[1]

Of Handel's many librettists none surpassed Charles Jennens in the art of sinking in poetry. As early as 28 July 1735 Handel thanked his pompous friend for his "very agreeable Letter with the inclosed Oratorio" of *Saul,* which gave the composer "a great deal of Satisfaction" and prompted him "to read it with all the Attention it deserves." Four years later Handel produced Jennens' *Saul* (1739), and during the following season the two friends collaborated on a bowdlerized version of *L'Allegro* and *Il Penseroso* (1740). To reconcile the conflicting tastes of Milton's two poems Jennens concocted a brazen adjunct entitled *Il Moderato.* Here he celebrated the virtues of moderation in numbers which would sound awkward in any company, but which seem doubly pedestrian beside the sonorous verses of Milton. Having amalgamated *L'Allegro* and *Il Penseroso* into alternate strophes and antistrophes, Jennens adorned the combined result with fifty octosyllabic verses from his own pen. His prosaic muse cut a poor figure in Milton's august company, but his ponderous verses were partially redeemed by the skill with which his libretto was assembled.

After the incongruities of *Il Moderato* it is extraordinary that Handel turned to this eccentric millionaire for his libretto of *Messiah.*[2] Certainly Jennens would seem the

---

[1] For a full discussion of eighteenth-century English libretto see my article, "Neo-Classical Criticism of the Ode for Music," *Publications of the Modern Language Association,* LXII, 399–421 (June 1947).

[2] For bibliographical and historical reasons it is not strictly correct to refer to Handel's oratorio as *The Messiah.* The autograph manuscript is styled *Messiah,* and this form appears on all eighteenth-century wordbooks and early printed editions of the score. Both Handel and Jennens generally referred to the oratorio as *Messiah.*

gentleman least likely to accomplish such an excellent performance, for in his vain opulence he had acquired a reputation for ridiculous display. It is strange that an age of decorum and conformity could produce such grotesque originals as Charles Jennens. Born at Gopsall Hall in Leicestershire in 1700, this literary amateur was educated at Balliol College, Oxford. Upon succeeding to the family estate in 1747 he built thereon a Brobdingnagian mansion in which he resided in princely style, remarkable for the number of his servants, the splendor of his equipages, and the profusion of his table. For landscaping his park he spent no less than eighty thousand pounds. A contemporary county historian recorded that "the fine chapel is most elegantly pewed and wainscoted with cedar, and an eagle of burnished gold supports the desk which holds the books." It was Jennens' custom to surround himself with a retinue of sycophants who contrived to keep him ignorant of current opinion by extolling his literary talents and musical skill. Nowhere did he reveal his love of display more strikingly than in his fastidious wardrobe. From his town house in Great Ormond Street, Bloomsbury, he sometimes drove to his publisher's office in Red Lion Court (a distance of five minutes' walk) in a magnificent chariot drawn by four horses with plumes, attended by four lackeys who swept the pavement free of oyster shells before the Gopsall squire descended.

Jennens seems to have entertained no small opinion of his own powers. In his correspondence he revealed his firm conviction that he knew more than Handel about composing oratorios. While Handel was engaged on *Saul* during the autumn of 1738 his librettist disclosed in a letter of September 19 that "Mr. Handel's head is more full of Maggots than ever." Having described two of Handel's "Maggots," Jennens proceeded to enumerate a third reason for his striking assertion:

His third Maggot is a Hallelujah which he has trump'd up at the end of his Oratorio since I went into the Country, because he thought the conclusion of the Oratorio not Grand enough; tho' if that were the case 'twas his own fault, for the words would have bore as Grand Musick as he could have set 'em to: but this Hallelujah, Grand as it is, comes in very nonsensically, having no manner of relation to what goes before. And this is the more extraordinary, because he refused to set a Hallelujah at the end of the first Chorus in the Oratorio, where I had plac'd one & where it was to be introduced with the utmost propriety, upon a pretence that it would make the Entertainment too long. I could tell you more of his Maggots; but it grows late & I must defer the rest till I write next, by which time, I doubt not, more new ones will breed in his Brain.

Fortunately posterity has reversed Jennens' strange decree. Today Handelians find it difficult to credit the haughty squire with sole responsibility for so grand a conception as the Scriptural text of Handel's *Messiah*.³ Certainly the mediocre level of Jennens' literary performances would cast considerable doubt upon his claim to having constructed such a text without assistance. Handel's devotees would doubtless be pleased to gather some shred of evidence that the composer himself had a voice in compiling his altogether excellent libretto.

It seems curious that Handel did not choose the texts of *Messiah* for himself. With no assistance he had compiled a purely Scriptural libretto for *Israel in Egypt* in 1738, and eleven years earlier he had indignantly refused aid from the Bishop of London in selecting appropriate words for George II's Coronation Anthems. "I have read my Bible very well," he said, "and I shall choose for myself." Why,

---

³ William Hone, *The Every-Day Book: and Table Book*, London, 1827, vol. III, part 2, column 651, declared that Charles Jennens never compiled the words of Handel's *Messiah* at all: "It has been said that he put together the words of Handel's 'Messiah': that he had something to do with them is true; but he had a secretary of the name of Pooley, a poor clergyman, who executed the principal part of the work, and, till now, has obtained no part of the credit." It is regrettable that both Newman Flower (*George Frideric Handel*, p. 269) and Herbert Weinstock (*Handel*, pp. 223, 232) repeat this legend as historical fact and enlarge upon Hone's unsupported assertion with great relish.

then, did he not choose the words for *Messiah?* History provides no answer, and speculation is vain. Did Jennens prepare the libretto without consultation and afterwards submit it to Handel complete? Or did Handel show his satisfaction with *Saul* and *Il Moderato* by requesting another text? Probably Handel himself originated the plan of composing an oratorio on the subject of *Messiah.* Certainly he must have controlled the choice of passages selected, for besides the profound judgment evinced in so complete an epitome of Christian history, great skill is shown in the choice of sentences and words peculiarly susceptible of smooth musical declamation. Only an experienced composer capable of executing such a comprehensive and powerful work could easily have arranged so vital a part of his material as the plan upon which his great ideas were to be developed. But all is pure conjecture, for the genesis of *Messiah* remains obscure. According to Handel's own letters Charles Jennens alone selected and organized the Scriptural passages upon which *Messiah* is based. That Jennens possessed some talent is probable; that he was well versed in Scripture is certain. In a special funeral sermon preached upon Jennens at Twycross on 2 January 1774 the Reverend George Kelly eulogized in rhetorical terms the librettist's contribution to Handel's *Messiah:*

As long as the Love of Taste and genuine Harmony prevail, so long should his Memory meet with a due Regard for that judicious Arrangement of Words we find in the sacred Performance of the MESSIAH: to this if we add the Abilities of an inimitable Master of the Science, we cannot sufficiently applaud; a Performance in which the Mind exerts its highest Faculties, and soars aloft beyond this Scene of Things; in which all the irregular Passions and Disquietudes of the human Breast are hushed and softened into Peace, since it reanimates the true Spirit of Devotion, and bids the Soul be wrapped up in the Praises and Contemplations of its God.

II

"Let no pious Christian be offended," wrote Dr. Johnson in his *Life of Watts,* "if I presume to say that religion is not the most desirable subject for poetry." It is unfortunate that so few Augustan versifiers heeded the good doctor's advice. During the Georgian century paltry rhymes upon every conceivable religious theme crowded the columns of London's literary reviews, and quantities of "sacred poems" and "divine odes" on "The Nativity of Christ," on "The Nativity of the Messiah," and on "The Birth of the Messiah" may be extracted from the files of *The Gentleman's Magazine* and *The Monthly Review* as ample testimony to the universal vogue of the "Messiah" theme in eighteenth-century English verse. Pope's *Messiah* (1717) established the tradition: his familiar poem proved so popular that no fewer than seven Latin translations were perpetrated upon London readers within the eighteenth century.[4]

In compiling texts for Handel's *Messiah* Charles Jennens thus adopted a familiar contemporary theme. Even in his own field he was not original, for an Oxford student named Antony Alsop had already written the libretto for a short cantata entitled *Messiah* twenty-five years before.[5] Whether Klopstock's *Messias* (1748-1773) owed its origin to the stimulus of Handel's *Messiah* remains uncertain. Spiritually the "German Milton" was closer akin to the composer of *Messiah* than to the poet of *Paradise Lost,* for Klopstock's gifts were predominantly lyric, and his stilted *Messias* is actually neither Miltonic nor epic. *Messias* manifests German

---

[4] By Dr. Samuel Johnson (1728), Usher Gahagan (1748), Richard Onely (1749), James Kirkpatrick (1750?), Thomas Tyrwhitt (1753), William Bermingham (1760), and Joseph Reeves (second edition, 1794).

[5] See C. H. Kitson, "Musical 'Depreciation,'" *Music and Letters,* XII, 184-193 (April 1931). The cantata was probably composed by James Heseltine, organist of Durham Cathedral from 1710 to 1763; it was presented to Durham Cathedral Library by the Reverend Thomas Drake in 1720. The score was published by Breitkopf & Härtel in 1912.

religious idealism much as *Messiah* expresses the militant faith of the Anglican Church. Like Handelian oratorio *Messias* contains epic, dramatic, and lyric elements. But in oratorio the narrative element is clearly distinguished from sentiment and reflection, whereas in Klopstock narrative and reflection are hopelessly confused, so that only in his lyric passages does he reveal the full splendor of his genius.

What Klopstock sought to accomplish in *Messias* stands achieved in Handel's *Messiah*. With all his pomp Charles Jennens displayed remarkable judgment and skill in selecting his texts strictly from Holy Writ. It is fortunate that *Messiah* is based upon the wondrous poetry of the English Bible rather than upon some chain of rhymed nonsense pitched in a sanctimonious key. Happily for Handel and for *Messiah* Jennens realized that pregnant passages from the Prophets, the Gospel story, St. Paul's Epistles, and the Revelation of St. John would prove superior to any pedestrian versifying of his own, and one is therefore spared the miserable task of keeping his temper and restraining his guffaws at the well-intentioned absurdities of the usual Handelian libretto. Posterity has agreed that Jennens' masterly selection of texts constitutes a work of art in itself. Its rich imagery and concrete symbolism create a felicitous combination of the grand, the poetic, and the passionate upon a plane of almost prophetic elevation.[6]

For the first time in musical history the mighty drama of human redemption was treated as an epic poem in Handel's *Messiah*. Jennens' libretto is an epitome of Christian faith. It portrays in succession every shade of devotional sentiment from piety, resignation, and repentance to hope, faith, and exultation. While Handel's predecessors and contemporaries presented the mystery of Christ in human terms, Jennens translated the facts of Christ's life into exalted symbols of human destiny and produced a Christian epic unfolding the

---

[6] For the complete text of Handel's *Messiah* see Appendix A.

moral autobiography of man. In displaying the character of Messiah he provided a comprehensive view of the divine scheme of Christian redemption through the Incarnation, Passion, and Resurrection, emphasizing the intense aspiration of each human soul, the promise and accomplishment of God's mercy, the apparent triumph of evil and destruction, and the final salvation of mankind through Christ's victory over Sin and Death. When viewed only as an historical fact the Crucifixion remains a tragic incident without deep significance, but Jennens transformed Christ's death into a universal experience occurring for the sake of the individual soul. Logically Handel's masterpiece should be called *Redemption,* for its author celebrates the *idea* of Redemption rather than the *personality* of Christ.

Hence *Messiah* is epic in content and theme, and since its appearance oratorios have hovered doubtfully between the epic and the dramatic. "Though that grand Musical Entertainment is called an *Oratorio*," wrote Dr. John Brown in 1763, "yet it is not *dramatic;* but properly a Collection of *Hymns* or *Anthems* drawn from the sacred Scriptures." Whereas *Samson* might conceivably become an effective sacred opera with scenery, costume, and action, *Messiah* could never be adapted to the stage without distortion. Its incidents are related by implication rather than by narration or dialogue, and Jennens offered a description of events only in the scene wherein angels appear before the shepherds of Bethlehem. While the text of *L'Allegro* is descriptive and that of *Israel in Egypt* is narrative, the text of *Messiah* simply *indicates* events through a series of contemplative recitatives, arias, and choruses upon the "Messiah" theme. Undoubtedly Handel's pulsating dramatic sense guided his choice of subject and directed his striking effects, but in *Messiah* he largely abandoned theatrical means of expression and depicted his scenes with a degree of reserve generally suited to his theme.

Because *Messiah* has become much the best known and

most frequently performed of Handel's works, musicians tend to forget that his masterpiece is the unique exception among Handelian oratorios in being specifically lyric in method. Following its masterly libretto *Messiah* is almost wholly reflective in tone and purpose. Perhaps from wisdom in selection, perhaps from the calm spirit born of personal affliction, perhaps from enforced conformity with English habits of reverence, Handel dwelt upon the deep emotional meaning of *Messiah* rather than upon its external features, so that even in its most passionate moments a note of philosophic calm precludes that mawkishness which the subject might have engendered in less virile minds. In Handel's dramatic oratorios the hero appears surrounded by other characters and sings in person, but throughout *Messiah* both solo voice and chorus simply meditate upon events implied in the text, and consequently recitative, the usual medium for relating incidents, is reduced to a minimum. It is notable that such an entirely *contemplative* work as *Messiah* has won enduring fame. Perhaps its early failure in London was due to its lack of "dramatic interest." Eighteenth-century English audiences generally found little pleasure in mere "consorts" of music, and Handel realized that a semblance of plot or fable was necessary to keep his listeners attentive throughout a four-hour performance. It was not entirely accident that after the austere abstractions of *Messiah* Handel clung to the dramatic style of *Saul* for the rest of his life. Always eminently practical, he recognized the wisdom of consulting current taste, and he probably observed that human emotions provide far more intriguing texts for musical treatment than abstract discussions of theological dogma.

It is as a whole that the libretto of *Messiah* is most remarkable. Its theme is evolved from one central thought, and if there is little dramatic connection between the numbers there is an unbroken sequence of idea and event. Jennens made skilful use of the contrast between aria, recitative, and chorus, so that the three divisions of the oratorio proceed with the inevitable impulse presupposed of good drama. Part I begins with the Old Testament prophecy of Christ's Advent; the Pastoral Symphony links prophecy and fulfillment; the celestial announcements heralding Christ's birth introduce the Nativity. Part II commences with Christ's actual appearance upon earth as the Redeemer and Saviour of mankind; the contemplative Passion music introduces the Resurrection and Atonement; the spread and ultimate triumph of the Gospel reaches its climax in the "Hallelujah Chorus." Part III becomes more doctrinal: in turning from social to personal results of the Messianic visitation it provides a concluding *credo,* expressing faith in the existence of Christ the Redeemer, in the surety of immortal life, and in the attainment of eternal happiness. *Messiah* is thus a balanced piece of musical architecture. Although nearly twenty Biblical writers are represented in its fifty-six numbers, the general effect is cumulative and the oratorio stands essentially as a unity. Its text is well-nigh ideal in the solid continuity with which the Saviour's life is gradually unfolded from prophecy to the last things.

In Charles Jennens' *Messiah* truth had issued from the pen of a moderately gifted man. Handel's knowledge of English was faulty, but after setting the uncouth rhymes of *Il Moderato* and *Saul* he could scarcely fail to appreciate texts drawn from the English Bible. Like Shakespeare he could cast the light of his genius without scruple or misgiving upon whatever object he pleased, but like Shakespeare he also towered in proportion to the height of his theme. Undoubtedly Handel was powerfully stirred by the words of *Messiah*. In general significance and unity of conception Jennens' text excelled all that the composer had yet attempted, and he rose to the height of his great argument. Handel expressed the spirit of his text with such force that thousands who have heard *Messiah* from childhood inevitably associate the Biblical words with his music. For successive generations of Christians his familiar Scriptural passages have acquired deeper meaning and greater force through the strains with which his art has inseparably associated them.

III

With Jennens' Biblical excerpts before him Handel commenced the task of composition on Saturday, 22 August 1741. For twenty-four days the composer remained in the little front room on the first floor of his residence at 57 Lower Brook Street, Hanover Square, until on Monday, 14 September 1741, he brought the final chorus of *Messiah* to a triumphant close with the signature *S. D. G. Fine dell oratorio. G. F. Handel. Septembr 12 1741. ausgefüllt den 14 Septembr.*[7] What happened to Handel during those twenty-four days no man can say. "Whether I was in my body or out of my body as I wrote it I know not," Handel is supposed to have declared afterwards in the words of St. Paul. At regular intervals his manservant brought him food, but when the servant returned he often found the platter untouched and the giant in his den staring into space. Legend declares that sometimes the servant stood in silent astonishment to see his master's tears drop on his page and mingle with the ink as he penned his "divine" notes. While Handel was composing "He was despised" a visitor is reported to have found the trembling composer sobbing with intense emotion, and after the "Hallelujah Chorus" his servant is said to have seen tears streaming from his eyes. "I did think I did see all Heaven before me," Handel later confessed, "and the great God Himself."

From the turbulent state of the autograph score it is clear that Handel composed *Messiah* so quickly that the motion of his pen was sometimes unable to keep pace with the flow of his imagination. With its habit of employing too much ink Handel's goose-quill flew across the page so rapidly that it

---

[7] S. D. G. was a common abbreviation for *Soli Deo Gloria* (To God alone the glory).

reached the bottom before the ink at the top was dry, and the rude appearance of the original score suggests that in several numbers Handel could scarcely commit his inspirations to paper with sufficient speed. Mendelssohn called Handel's untidy pages "coarse scores." So few sheets of his stormy manuscript are free from blots and smears that one is driven to suppose that Handel scattered his ink with the frenzy of distraction. In his passionate artistic irritability he dashed through mistakes with a relentless stab of his quill or swallowed them up in the black mass of an explosive blot. Finding no time for trivial erasures, he drew his pen through errors with such impetuous fury that his quill frequently scratched across bars entirely innocent of music. On at least one page he seems to have upset the inkpot in his vehement energy. Sometimes it is plain that he labored hard: in his uncertainty and hesitation he grew fiercely impatient and smeared huge ink-strokes with his pudgy thumb. On many pages his hasty concentration appears in the slope of note stems, in frequent smudges, and in passages of part-writing displaying note heads without stems. His calmer pages present his nearest approach to neatness, but like Mozart he worked best at white heat.

Through such tempestuous pages it is easy to gain insight into the character and genius of the man who composed *Messiah*. In Handel's autograph score one is brought so close to the composer that he looks over Handel's shoulder as he writes, traces the current of his thoughts, and marks the guise in which his conceptions first took shape. By following Handel step by step through his hundred visions and revisions one observes that even with a great genius the easy flow of ideas springs from the agony of earnest decision and intensive thought. No tranquil, self-contained musician could have transcribed the manuscript of *Messiah*. It is evidently the work of one quick to feel and hardly scrupulous to conceal his fiery temper. And it suggests a man of careless habits, of intense virility, of violently changeable moods. When one

By gracious permission of His Majesty the King

FINAL PAGE OF HANDEL'S AUTOGRAPH SCORE OF *MESSIAH* (1741)
From the Original in the King's Musick Library
of the British Museum

examines *Messiah* as it first sprang from Handel's brain he is astonished at the slight alteration the composer felt it necessary to make in his score. Without the testimony of his manuscript the completeness of his first draft would be incredible.

In its original form *Messiah* occupies 275 oblong folio pages.[8] Two leaves containing the conclusion of the overture

---

[8] Nine and three-fourths inches by twelve inches. The autograph score of *Messiah* was included in the 87 volumes of Handel's original manuscripts bequeathed to his amanuensis, John Christopher Smith, who in turn presented them to George III and Queen Charlotte about 1780. They were preserved with additional purchases and presentations in the Royal Collection of the King's Musick Library at Buckingham Palace until 1911, when George V deposited the entire King's Musick Library in the British Museum on permanent loan. An imperfect facsimile edition of the original

and the opening of "Comfort ye" are missing. On the first page Handel inscribed *Messiah. An Oratorio. Part the first angefangen den 22 August 1741.* At the end of Part I the manuscript is dated "August 28, 1741." On Sunday, "September 6 1741," Handel concluded Part II by composing the "Hallelujah Chorus." Part III was finished on the following Saturday, and during the two succeeding days Handel "filled up" the skeleton score by completing his instrumental accompaniments. Nothing in the range of musical art parallels the speed with which Handel's feat was accomplished. It is characteristic of the composer's almost superhuman capacity for concentration that at the age of fifty-six he completed his *magnum opus* in less than four weeks. John Keats died in his twenty-sixth year; Shelley drowned before he was thirty. Amongst the composers Schubert died at thirty-one, Mozart at thirty-five, and Mendelssohn at thirty-eight. But Handel is best known for works composed after his half-century.

When one considers the originality of Handel's design, the magnitude of its dimensions, the profundity and elaboration of his colossal choruses, and the excellent adaptation of separate parts to the general conception, he finds it difficult to accept the notion that a work so evidently the result of deep thought and rich genius was a hasty, unpremeditated production. Undoubtedly Handel possessed the power of throwing off music with amazing rapidity, but twenty-four days affords little scope for careful consideration and revision of fifty-six elaborate numbers. If *Messiah* was brought into realized form in less than four weeks, its actual composition was probably the result of rumination for months in advance. But when did *Messiah* originate in Handel's mind? And what was the manner of its *creation*? With mysterious suddenness it burst forth, fully organized and alive, but to this day a mist obscures its immediate origin. Of Handel's first designs history offers little evidence, and no gossiping Pepys,

---

score was issued by the Sacred Harmonic Society in 1868. A more satisfactory facsimile was published by Friedrich Chrysander in 1892.

no painstaking Boswell atones for the official chronicler's neglect.

From personal recollection Dr. Burney declared that Handel "spent so studious and sedentary a life, as seldom allowed him to mix in society, or partake of public amusements." Each autumn he generally composed two works in less than ninety days, leaving no trace of composition throughout the succeeding nine months. How did Handel pass those long intervals of seclusion between his various compositions? Is it not logical to suppose that during his apparent idleness he was actually sketching themes for future oratorios? When he commenced the score of *Messiah* on 22 August 1741 nine months had elapsed since the completion of his last Italian opera *Deidamia* on 20 November 1740. After terminating his disastrous operatic career with a final performance of *Deidamia* on 8 April 1741 he had withdrawn into extreme solitude at his residence on Lower Brook Street. History is silent regarding Handel's movements during those months from April 8 to August 22, but throughout the summer of 1741 he was evidently making preparations for actual composition. In the Fitzwilliam Museum at Cambridge one may inspect several careful preliminary sketches of elaborate choral movements in *Messiah*. When the oratorio was completed Handel probably destroyed most of his sketches as so much waste paper, and possibly the few extant studies of *Messiah* escaped his notice only by chance. Beautiful to the imagination is the ideal that for months Handel carried about in his head independent parts of *Messiah,* until in one glowing hour of genius he fused them all into that harmonious whole which surprised even the composer and has delighted the world for two centuries. Handel's manuscript dates do not militate against this notion, for they refer clearly to the transcription of his ideas and not to the moment of their conception. In any case Handel's achievement is striking, and one's amazement only grows when he recalls that the composer finished *Samson* on 29 October 1741.

IV

In his headlong haste Handel frequently followed the not uncommon contemporary practice of borrowing material from former works of his own composition. When one of his ephemeral creations had faded he often plucked out the finest blossoms and arranged them into a fresh bouquet. Nor was' he scrupulous about stealing flowers from other men's gardens. Without acknowledgment he made free and extensive use of foreign sources, and some of his most familiar compositions are now known to have been drawn almost wholly from other musicians. But in *Messiah* not a single instance has been found of the unacknowledged introduction of music not composed by Handel himself. It is to be hoped that this immunity is inherent in *Messiah* through the deliberate will of that man whose tears mingled with his ink as he composed "He was despised," and who "did think" he saw "all Heaven" before him "and the great God Himself" as he penned his immortal "Hallelujah Chorus." But if the originality of Handel's *magnum opus* has never been seriously impugned, there is no escape from the fact that several familiar choruses in *Messiah* are taken partly or wholly from Handel's secular Italian *duetti di camera,* composed in July 1741 for the pleasure and practice of Princess Caroline of Hanover. Handel's *Messiah* is not a homogeneous inspiration. Curious as the truth may sound to pious transcendental ears, choruses which for a century were hallowed as divine utterances are actually adaptations of lively themes originally set to the Arcadian texts of Handel's Italian chamber duets. Sometimes the composer merely reset his discarded works with slight modification; sometimes he excised, amplified, or altered his original with absolute freedom. An investigation of Handel's adaptations in *Messiah* indicates the slight degree to which he adjusted his borrowed melodies as well as the striking variance between the sentiments of the texts involved.[9]

The two Italian duets which paid largest tribute to Handel's masterpiece were written in London less than two months before the composition of *Messiah*. From a duet dated "a Londra, a 1 di Luglio, 1741" Handel derived melodies for two choruses, "And He shall purify" and "His yoke is easy." Although not amorous, the words are far removed in sentiment from those to which the music was finally set in *Messiah*:

> Quel fior che all' alba ride,
> [His yoke is easy,]
> Il sole poi l'uccide,
> [His burthen is light,]
> E tomba ha nella sera.
> [His burthen, His burthen is light].

With its curious opening phrases this jocular fugal chorus in *Messiah* puzzled orthodox Handelians for years, but a glance at the text to which the music was originally composed fully explains Handel's roulade of sixteenth notes upon the first syllable of *easy*: "The flower that laughs in the rosy dawn withers in the sunlight and sinks into the grave at evening." Handel's word-painting on *ride* (laughs) is admirably suited to flowers laughing at dawn, but in *Messiah* the same buoyant *fioriture* seem less appropriate to the easy yoke which Christ has laid upon His people. Evidently Handel himself felt that something remained wanting after these tortuous convolutions, for he ended his chorus with a grand passage in which dignity and beauty are wondrously blended. From the same duet Handel extracted music for his florid vocal fugue "And He shall purify the sons of Levi" in *Messiah*:

---

[9] Musical quotations illustrating Handel's adaptation of his own chamber duets to choruses in *Messiah* may be found in Sedley Taylor, *The Indebtedness of Handel to Works of Other Composers*, Cambridge, 1906, pp. 36–46. For a thorough discussion of Handel's "plagiarisms" consult Percy Robinson, *Handel and His Orbit*, London, 1908.

> È un fior la vita ancora:
> L'occaso ha nell' aurora,
> [And He shall purify]
> E perde in un sol dì la primavera,
> [And He shall purify the sons]
> La primavera.
> [The sons of Levi].

This blithe Italian text may be translated: "Life too is a flower; it comes with the morning and dies with the spring of a single day." In Handel's original music the riot of semiquavers upon *primavera* (spring) is highly commendable, but in *Messiah* the same brisk ornamentation seems scarcely adapted to the triumphs of Levitical purification. Possibly Handel designed these spirited embellishments to impress upon his audience the necessity for a thorough cleansing of the Levites, but even if one concedes that some of the sons of Levi were unworthy of their priestly office Handel's elaborate insistence upon their purification appears somewhat overdone. His difficult roulades of sixteenth notes upon the word *purify* possess little inherent dramatic significance, and whatever religious depth the chorus breathes must be projected into its lighthearted rhythms by the listener himself. But even here Handel applied his stroke of genius and closed his chorus with an inspired episode expressing the words "That they may offer unto the Lord an offering in righteousness." When inspiration *did* come Handel proved himself a giant—the man upon whose grave even Beethoven declared he would kneel bareheaded.

From a second Italian duet, signed and dated "a Londra . . . July ye 3, 1741," Handel adapted the bulk of one of the most celebrated choruses in *Messiah*. In the first half of "For unto us a Child is born" the composer offered extravagant roulades originally composed for a madrigal denouncing blind Love and cruel Beauty for their lying cajoleries:

Nò, di voi non vo' fidarmi,
[For unto us a Child is born,]
Cieco Amor, crudel beltà!
[Unto us a Son is given,]
Troppo siete menzognere,
[And the government shall be up-]
Lusinghiere Deità!
[-on his shoulder].

Music which Handel composed to the words, "No, I will not trust you, blind Love, cruel Beauty! You are too treacherous, too charming a deity!" later emerged in *Messiah* without change of key or melody as a jolly chorus expressing the world's consummate joy at the nativity of Christ. With its breezy rigmarole of fifty-seven sixteenth notes upon the word *born* this much-belauded "sacred" chorus may strike the uninitiated ear as almost impertinent, but when it assumes its proper position within Handel's lucid architectonic scheme, it becomes justified in the musical design by its grand outcome. In addition to material drawn from his Italian duet Handel introduced those powerful choral shouts declaring the names of Messiah: "Wonderful, Counsellor, The Mighty God, The Everlasting Father, The Prince of Peace." Even the stirring movement with which he approaches this magnificent proclamation is derived from the duet, but the colossal bursts of sound on the epithets themselves were original inspirations drawn from the sacred text. In these strokes of genius Handel went straight to the point. Seeing in his secular theme potentialities for majestic interpretation, he wisely endured inconveniences in his opening theme for the sake of a spacious general structure which could be readily expanded to embrace new material.

One need scarcely dilate upon the sportive strain of Handel's rendition of "All we like sheep have gone astray; we have turned every one to his own way." Surely more affecting words were never penned, but Handel invested his heartbreaking text with all the rollicking exuberance of a Gilbert and Sullivan comic opera. His *allegro moderato* was built wholly upon subjects derived from the same Italian duet from which he had already drawn the energetic theme of "For unto us":

> Sò per prova i vostri inganni
> [All we like sheep have gone astray;]
> Due tiranni
> [We have turned]
> Due tiranni siete ogn' or.
> [Every one to his own way].

Here Handel's sound scarcely seems an echo to his sense. His sprightly Italian text roundly defies the tyranny and deceits of *crudel beltà* and *cieco Amor,* but such cheerful animation seems hardly suited to the pathetic announcement that humanity has erred and strayed like lost sheep. In Handel's famous chorus sin glories in its shame with almost alcoholic exhilaration. His lost sheep meander hopelessly through a wealth of intricate semiquavers, stumbling over decorous roulades and falling into mazes of counterpoint that prove inextricable. A less dramatic composer than Handel would scarcely have rendered his solemn English text with such defiance, for the discrepancy between his self-accusing words and his vivacious music is patent to any listener emancipated from the lethargy of custom. It is indeed singular that Handel's chorus should contain in itself such merry proof of the tragic statement it has made. But all this furor quickly subsides into reflection when the profoundly moving strains of Handel's closing *adagio* proclaim the fatal retribution in a mighty hymn which is significantly British in character and truly Handelian in harmony. Having exhausted the secular material before him, this wonderful man escaped the influence of his chamber duet by making the very audacity with which he had treated his text supply him with means for creating a tremendous effect of contrast. Suddenly Handel shifted his tempo to *adagio* and passed into minor harmony, leading his chorus into a solemn sequence upon the words "The Lord hath laid on Him the iniquity of us all." Here Handel combined moral grandeur with a depth of expression commensurate with his theme. In rising to a proper appreciation of his text he thus demonstrated how a Jupiter can rouse himself from the doze which has brought disgrace to his cause.

Besides his recent Italian *duetti di camera* Handel had composed several amorous madrigals as early as 1712. From one of these forgotten songs he selected music for a tragic duet and chorus in *Messiah*:

> Se tu non lasci amore,
> Mio cor, ti pentirai, lo so ben io;
> Lontano dal tuo bene,
> Tu non avrai che pene!
> Ma, con chi parlo, oh Dio!
> Quando non ho più core,
> O il core che pur ho non è più mio!

A prose translation of this text discloses a trifling exhortation to abandon love: "If you do not let love alone, my heart, you will regret it, that is certain. Separated from the one you love, you will endure only suffering. But to whom do I speak, oh God? Since I no longer have a heart, or having one it is no longer mine!" Music originally composed to these ardent words Handel introduced into *Messiah* to express the following sentiments: "O death, where is thy sting? O grave, where is thy victory? The sting of death is sin, and the strength of sin is the law. But thanks be to God, who giveth us the victory through our Lord Jesus Christ."

Such are the foreign sources to which Handel resorted when composing his most "inspired" oratorio. In English essays much rhetorical nonsense has been perpetuated upon the subject of Handel's indebtedness to his own works and to those of other composers. Actually his "plagiarisms" vary greatly in importance. Certainly his use of his own chamber duets in *Messiah* cannot be considered parallel to his wholesale adaptations from Erba's *Magnificat* in *Israel in Egypt*. Sometimes his appropriation of old materials consists merely in the adoption of fugal themes which had stimulated the imagination of composers for two hundred years, such as the series of four ascending and descending notes employed in the "Hallelujah Chorus" in *Messiah*. In similar fashion Handel built his chorus "And with His stripes" upon a subject which has been reckoned common property for so long that the original thief is unknown. Discovery that the same theme appears in Bach's *Well-Tempered Clavier* and in the Kyrie of Mozart's *Requiem* proves nothing beyond the plain fact of resemblance, for the similarity extends in no case to the treatment, and during the eighteenth century fugal themes were generally considered public property. It has been suggested without proof that Handel converted a theme of Bononcini into the overture to *Messiah*. It is quite true that the Pastoral Symphony (in which Victorian pietists saw angels hovering over the plains of Bethlehem) is based upon a bagpipe tune played at Christmas by the *pifferari* of Naples and Rome, but this indebtedness is acknowledged in Handel's autograph score by the abbreviation *pifa* at the beginning of the movement.

In 1762 John Potter voiced the musical ethics of his day when he declared that a composer "should examine every thing he can meet with and like *the curious bee, suck sweets from every flower*." Musical pasticcios were common in eighteenth-century London, and Handel's oratorios were seldom performed during his lifetime without the substitution and addition of favorite arias from other works. Later even Mozart's operas were sometimes adorned with arias derived from foreign sources. Music was in the same state as architecture and literature: just as Shakespeare adapted whole passages from Plutarch and Holinshed for use in his own plays, so Wren was indebted to Palladian architects and Handel appropriated the works of Erba, Urio, and Stradella. Handel's greatest contemporary perpetrated equally daring perform-

GEORGE FRIDERIC HANDEL

From the "Gopsall Portrait" by Thomas Hudson (1756) in the Possession of Mary Countess Howe

ances of "sacred" music adapted from secular sources. In *The Choice of Hercules* Sebastian Bach produced a song in which "Pleasure" soothes Hercules to sleep with suggestions to "follow the allurements of raging desire, revel in enjoyment and recognize no bounds." Later Bach introduced the same music, substantially unaltered, into his celebrated cradle song in *The Christmas Oratorio*. It should be recalled that many pages of Bach's *Mass in B Minor* are drawn from secular sources, while some of the finest Lutheran chorales (including "O sacred Head now wounded") were originally secular songs.

One clumsy feature of Handelian oratorio is the composer's appalling ignorance of English accentuation and his consequent awkwardness in English declamation. Handel's imperfect familiarity with the delicacies of English pronunciation frequently produced in his music false accents which sometimes actually violate the sense of his text. As a foreigner he not only rendered long syllables short and short syllables long but also assigned long notes and accents to syllables and words pronounced rapidly in normal speech. In the first recitative of *Messiah* he made a monosyllable of *crieth;* in the first chorus he allowed only one accent to *glory;* and in the second chorus of Part II he made *surely* a trisyllable. Minor inaccuracies may be gracefully altered by skilful singers, but to correct faulty accentuation the music itself must sometimes be distorted. Handel's autograph score requires "the first fruits *of* them that sleep"; "the dead shall be raised in*corr*up*ti*ble"; "If *God* be for *us*." Many errors actually obscure the sense of Handel's text and remain extremely difficult to regulate: "the chas*tise*ment of our peace"; "*For* unto us a Child is born"; "He *was* despised"; "He *shall* feed His flock"; "Come *unto* Him." Few persons know Purcell's English songs and anthems well enough to appreciate the truly un-English nature of Handel's verbal declamation. Despite its awkward mannerisms *Messiah* has penetrated so deeply into the flesh and blood of Anglican religion that

Englishmen consider Handel's clumsy settings natural and normal. It is not generally known that some of his more egregious declamatory faults have been expurgated by subsequent editors. The "divine Saxon" was an assiduous churchgoer and studied his Scriptures with laudable enthusiasm, but the noble language of the English Bible could hardly affect a German musician as it affects those for whom Shakespeare and the Bible provide the elements of everyday speech. Handel's vocal technique remained always Italian, and although English speech-rhythms eventually helped to shape his themes, he never succeeded in writing genuinely English recitative.

It is not astonishing that Charles Jennens was but partially satisfied with Handel's treatment of his excellent Biblical text. From the beginning that pompous amateur appears to have been fully aware of his own achievement in *Messiah*. In a letter to an unknown friend he registered his complaints on 30 August 1745:

I shall shew you a collection I gave Handel, call'd Messiah, which I value highly, and he has made a fine Entertainment of it, tho' not near so good as he might and ought to have done. I have with great difficulty made him correct some of the grossest faults in the composition, but he retain'd his Overture obstinately, in which there are some passages far unworthy of Handel, but much more unworthy of the Messiah.

In characteristic fashion the superior Gopsall squire deplored "faults" in the "fine Entertainment" that has satisfied and delighted the English-speaking world for two hundred years. Jennens' unique strictures on Handel's interpretation of *Messiah* shed light upon his own conceited nature as well as upon the composer's firm independence. From this letter alone it would be impossible to determine Jennens' true evaluation of Handel's "unworthy" music, but one cannot gainsay his deliberate criticisms *au pied de la lettre*. In speaking of "a fine Entertainment" Jennens implied no sacrilege, and his complaints of "faults in the composition" hardly referred to awkward declamation or forbidden progressions in Handel's music. When he offered the composer a "collection" which he "valued highly" it was but natural that Jennens should entertain strong personal sentiments regarding its proper musical interpretation. And it is unfortunately true that parts of Handel's *Messiah* are indeed "not near so good as he might and ought to have done." But in charging Handel with gross faults and obstinacy Jennens faced the delicate task of interfering with the conceptions of a great artist. Already he had apprised Handel of his dissatisfaction with *Messiah,* for on 19 July 1744 the exasperated composer had written to Jennens humbly begging him to "Be pleased to point out these passages in the Messiah which you think require altering," since "you do me the Honour to encourage my Messiah undertakings, and even to promote them with a particular kindness." More than two years after *Messiah* had commenced its career of public performance Jennens proposed correction of "the grossest faults" in the oratorio! It would be curious today to study Jennens' memorandum of suggested alterations. Possibly his proposals were embodied in Handel's "additional Alterations" appended to Randall & Abell's first full-score edition in 1767. The propriety of Jennens' dogmatic criticisms remains to be determined by those who can ascertain which of Handel's alterations in *Messiah* were instigated by his grandiose patron.

Evidently Handel set high value upon the musical judgment of his haughty friend. Perhaps many adjustments in *Messiah* were prompted by Jennens' suggestions. Although Handel drafted his original score with unprecedented speed he ultimately devoted more time and thought to *Messiah* than to any other single composition. Conscious of its special importance, he touched and retouched *Messiah* with painstaking self-criticism, rewriting or deleting inappropriate passages and amending or expanding whole numbers. Nearly one-third of *Messiah* underwent some revision before the oratorio reached its final form.[10] Notwithstanding the censures of Charles Jennens, however, Handel steadily retained his overture and failed ever to reconsider his secular adaptations. He deemed no setting final. It was his custom constantly to rewrite portions of his work, sometimes providing entirely new settings for his words, sometimes developing original music into superior movements with fresh orchestration, sometimes adapting himself to momentary limitations by inserting whole pages torn from previous scores. With all his grand conceptions Handel was emphatically a man of resource. Under adverse conditions he was content to make the most effective use of all available means. To accommodate the capabilities of his singers he even substituted recitatives for arias or converted choruses into solos, and in the absence of special soloists he sometimes transposed or rewrote arias to suit the caprices of inferior substitutes. From various scores of *Messiah* it is plain that Handel executed whatever change helped to produce an *effective* performance. When one observes how setting after setting was tried and abandoned until satisfaction was finally attained, he learns in some measure to gauge the manner and strength of the man whose patience and skill elevated *Messiah* to immortality. Guided by that gigantic sense of proportion which had already produced *Israel in Egypt,* Handel composed a work which, despite its faults, remains unsurpassed in musical art for sustained vigor and boldness of design.

V

For two centuries *Messiah* has been celebrated as a preeminently "sacred" composition voicing Handel's private

---

[10] Considerations of space forbid discussion of questions raised by comparison of various *Messiah* manuscripts. Several versions of most arias exist, and a study of Handel's alterations in *Messiah* is fascinating and instructive. For technical details students should consult W. G. Cusins, *Handel's Messiah: An Examination of the Original and of Some Contemporary MSS,* London, 1874.

religious convictions and hymning the spiritual emotions of the Protestant world. Unthinking rhapsodists have insisted that every note in *Messiah* shows evidence of divine inspiration, and popular musical historians, living largely on apocryphal anecdote, have perpetuated this sentimentalism by picturing the "divine Saxon" in numerous touching situations and by quoting pious phrases supposedly uttered by Handel himself in the warmth of religious exaltation. English biographers never tire of the hackneyed tale that while composing the "Hallelujah Chorus" Handel imagined he "did see all Heaven" before his eyes and "the great God Himself" seated on His throne. A few days before his death he is reported to have expressed a desire to breathe his last on Good Friday, "in hopes of meeting his good God, his sweet Lord and Saviour, on the day of His Resurrection." Few such affecting anecdotes could bear close examination, but good people with *Messiah* in their heads still seek to convert Handel into a saint:

> Several days after the first exhibition of the same divine oratorio [wrote Dr. James Beattie], Mr. Handel came to pay his respects to Lord Kinnoul, with whom he was particularly acquainted. His lordship, as was natural, paid him some compliments on the noble entertainment which he had lately given the town. "My lord," said Handel, "I should be sorry if I only entertained them, I wish to make them better."

In 1780 Dr. Beattie declared that this anecdote "tends to confirm my theory that Handel, in spite of all that has been said to the contrary, must have been a pious man." Apparently even Handel's contemporaries were not unanimously agreed upon his devotional inclinations. From personal acquaintance, however, Sir John Hawkins believed the composer to be a sincere if somewhat easy-going Christian:

> He was a man of blameless morals, and throughout his life manifested a deep sense of religion. In conversation he would frequently declare the pleasure he felt in setting the Scriptures to music: and how much the contemplating the many sublime pas-

sages in the Psalms had contributed to his edification; and now that he found himself near his end, these sentiments were improved into solid and rational piety, attended with a calm and even temper of mind. For the last two or three years of his life he was used to attend divine service in his own parish church of St. George, Hanover-square, where, during the prayers, the eyes that at this instant are employed in a faint portrait of his excellencies, have seen him on his knees, expressing by his looks and gesticulations the utmost fervor of devotion. . . . In his religion he was of the Lutheran profession; in which he was not such a bigot as to decline a general conformity with that of the country which he had chosen for his residence; at the same time that he entertained very serious notions touching its importance. These he would frequently express in his remarks on the constitution of the English government; and he would often speak of it as one of the great felicities of his life that he was settled in a country where no man suffers any molestation or inconvenience on account of his religious principles.

Not a breath of suspicion has ever been cast upon Handel's moral character. He was never married, and he courted no female but the Muse. "His social affections," Hawkins continued, "were not very strong; and to this it may be imputed that he spent his whole life in a state of celibacy; that he had no female attachment of another kind may be ascribed to a better reason."

Undoubtedly Handel was a good man. He was brought up in the bosom of the Lutheran Church, and he lived an intense inner life. But in his balanced strength he was neither morbid nor excessive. He was no introspective Rousseau, proclaiming his sorrows and inward struggles in self-accusing *Confessions*. Throughout his long career no love-passage broke the solid continuity of his works; no trembling in his bold handwriting betrayed the presence of secret disturbances or transcendent religious ecstacies. With simple sincerity he accepted the tolerant theology of his time as sufficient explanation of human existence. To him the persons of the Trinity were entities as solid as a hearty dinner, a well-stocked wine cellar, and a bulging purse. If Handel wished to die on Good Friday he fully intended to enter Heaven clad in his richest full-bottomed wig and finest scarlet coat, with gorgeous ruffles at his neck, ample gold lace at each sleeve, and a gleaming sword at his side. At the proper moment he would make his stately bow to the assembled angels and perhaps offer a few pungent remarks upon the proper method of tuning harps. No matter how high Handel's inspiration soared, he always kept his feet planted firmly on the good earth. When composing the "Hallelujah Chorus" he "did think" he "did see" God seated on His throne, just as when he composed *Semele* he probably imagined he saw Jupiter on his throne, and the fact only proves his intense imaginative powers and his relative freedom from the genuinely devotional mood.

Whatever Handel's religious beliefs may have been, they were certainly of the sort which sensible men entertain but do not discuss. The composer evinced heroic moral qualities, but he was never the aggressive sectarian eulogized by Victorian clergymen in fulsome sermons upon the "efficacy" of "sacred" music. As a man he was exceedingly vigorous, proud, self-willed, independent, and egoistic; his temper was frank, generous, honest, straightforward, and cheerful. When irritated he was violent; when opposed he was indomitable. His profound emotion when composing *Messiah* sprang not from a disordered mental state, but rather from militant faith in a God of splendid power. In 1741 he was defeated and disillusioned, and his unfortunate struggles drove him inevitably to the real and the earnest in art. As a strong man of the earth who bravely faced his trials and failures he appeals to twentieth-century minds no less forcibly than as a musician of conviction and eloquence.

Handel's true nature emerges most clearly when he is compared with Sebastian Bach. It is singular that the two most gifted masters of Protestant music during the period of the Late Baroque were born in the same country less than a month apart. Bach and Handel shared the sterling qualities of the German middle class of their day. Both employed with incomparable effect all the musical science of their time; both had quick tempers, and both became blind in old age. But in character and method they were radically opposed. Whereas Bach led the retired life of a German cantor, Handel was ordained to delight the fashionable courts of Rome and London. Whereas Bach remained indifferent to the applause of the crowd, Handel found it his very breath of life. Handel devoted himself chiefly to the epic; Bach was content to develop the lyric. Handel's music is predominantly vocal in line and color; Bach's music is definitely instrumental in character. Handel designed his works for performance on festal state occasions; Bach demands serious application, and he is thus adored chiefly by a select thinking public.

Actually the two composers evinced little spiritual kinship. Handel's sunny serenity and lordly splendor stand in bold contrast to the pious mysticism of Bach and the German chorale. Where Bach was abased in the dust Handel was bright, shining, and confident, troubled by no sense of sin and free from all melancholy introspection. Bach was the intensive psychologist of the soul. In the contemplative mood of the cloister he delved into the obscure recesses of the heart and fathomed the unknown depths of the spirit. His claustral strains immortalized the German Lutheran's inner fervor and sturdy love of God. But Handel was an orthodox Protestant moving in a cosmopolitan world, a man of action with little time for morbid illusions, an energetic impresario swift to record external impressions in terms of solid, muscular music. Thomas Hudson's familiar portraits show Handel gorgeous in flowing wig and fine raiment, a man of strong intellect and abounding self-reliance, a grandiose figure destined to prophesy before kings. What a contrast to the modest choirmaster of Leipzig with his humble introspection and his secret raptures! If Bach is sensation, Handel is perception. If Bach is contemplation, Handel is action. Bach's idealism becomes Handel's realism. And if Bach's humble searchings are pervasively Lutheran, Handel's positive assertions are gloriously Anglican.

It is not surprising that Handel's *Messiah* is utterly unlike Bach's *Saint Matthew Passion* (1729) in both style and poetic conception. A comparison of the two works reveals in most convincing manner the sharp temperamental differences between the two composers. One composition is a piece of Lutheran church music; the other is a brilliant English concert oratorio of Italian ancestry. In *Messiah* Handel's colorful choruses are perhaps less satisfying to pious ears than the deeply religious choruses of Bach, but in dramatic effect Handel's choruses are of broader character than the fanatical Hebrew exclamations of Bach's *Passion*. In the latter work the Saviour Himself speaks, and a chorus of Jews and apostles emphasizes events narrated by an "Evangelist." But Handel's soloists are impersonal, and his chorus develops the narrative by means of Scriptural passages commenting on the story. Bach's congregation participates in his music; Handel's audience takes no part. Like all ecclesiastical music Bach's *Passion* seeks to heighten the religious feelings of individual believers engaged in a common act of worship. But worship is in no sense the object of *Messiah*. Handel's vivid work is a drama (however unique in its kind), and like all drama it seeks to win public applause by blending external facts into an artistic and organic whole. *Messiah* is not, however, an historical drama, and it touches upon such historical events as the Nativity only in their most generalized and symbolic form. Bach's narrative, on the other hand, is chronological. With the calm inner spirit of the New Testament he recreated the personality and acts of Christ in human terms, ignoring all anticipation of His ultimate triumph, and thus remaining faithful to the original conception of the office proper to Good Friday. Handel, however, avoided the human element in Christ and treated His triumph and glorification in nonliturgical terms. Whereas Bach emphasized the physical side of Christ's Passion, Handel stressed the spiritual. Bach gave the facts; Handel gave their meaning. Bach's *Passion* is a church service; Handel's *Messiah* is a poem. If Bach touches deeper religious feelings, Handel's independent dramatic standpoint is equally true art. Each work is a triumph of genius, and both stand near the apex of human achievement. They are as different as the artists who composed them, and a knowledge of one only enhances respect for the other.

If Bach's choral works suggest the cathedral, Handel's oratorios display all the freedom of the concert platform. Bach's Passions and cantatas were designed to be rendered in church, and his austere ecclesiasticism accordingly rouses a vague disquiet. Handel's oratorios were composed for performance in the concert room, and his dramatic variety excites eager applause. Although the cultivation of oratorio sprang from the Church, Handelian oratorios are in no sense genuinely religious functions. Handel was never a church musician, and he seldom wrote music for the Church. He was always a composer for the theatre and the concert hall, and his oratorios, though often Biblical in theme, illustrate his pervasive theatricalism as forcibly as his finest Italian operas. From long operatic experience he developed a keen sense for stunning dramatic situations, and whenever his theme afforded him scope he invariably responded with directly theatrical music. Thus his "sacred" oratorios are neither liturgical nor ecclesiastical in tone, and even *Messiah* owes much of its charm and effectiveness to its theatrical garnish. Its musical structure and even its text have no connection with any liturgy. Its first performance took place in a Dublin music hall, and for decades it was regularly performed during Lent at Covent Garden Theatre. In Handel's day *Messiah* was a public "entertainment," just as *Rinaldo* and *Alexander's Feast* were entertainments, and the composer never once conducted his "sacred oratorio" in church or cathedral. Throughout the eighteenth century the line of demarcation between sacred and secular music was slender and ill-defined. On the continent opera was allowed to take subjects from Holy Writ, and even in England divine service often admitted bourées and jigs without scandalizing London congregations. Alexander Pope was probably not alone when, in a note to *The Dunciad,* he denounced the "false Taste in *Music,* improper to the subjects, as of light arias in churches, often practised by the organists." Eighteenth-century Anglicans would have found Bach's German Lutheranism dull and impertinent. Consequently English "church" composers resorted to a musical style essentially the same whether the words were secular or sacred. Not the slightest stylistic feature distinguishes Handel's "sacred" music from his secular. He boasted no two styles, and his operatic manner is identical with his oratorian.

As an operatic composer Handel sought never to reveal his own personality, but always to depict some object or to render some dramatic scene. Never did he cling with greater resolution to this laudable intention than in *Messiah.* Never therefore did he compose a work more fundamentally secular in spirit. Despite its theological subject *Messiah* is as much a hymn to joy as the Ninth Symphony, and into its buoyant strains Handel poured an infinitely contagious delight in living that somehow suggests the fresh pagan world of old Greece. Edward FitzGerald believed that the composer permitted himself to be "tied down to Orthodoxy" only with great reluctance:

He (Handel) was a good old Pagan at heart, and (till he had to yield to the fashionable Piety of England) stuck to Opera, and Cantatas, such as Acis and Galatea, Milton's Penseroso, Alexander's Feast, etc., where he could revel and plunge without being tied down to Orthodoxy. And these are (to my mind) his really great works: these, and his Coronation Anthems, where Human Pomp is to be accompanied and illustrated.

Handel devoted his greatest art to no other temple than the free sky and the broad earth. Religion is merely a background for his gorgeous musical dramas. Even in *Messiah* the celebrated "Hallelujah Chorus" might serve with equal propriety as a grand coronation march for some pagan potentate. In his broad conception of Christianity Handel was, as FitzGerald observed, a true child of the Enlightenment:

> I think Handel never gets out of his wig: that is, out of his age: his Hallelujah chorus is a chorus not of angels, but of well-fed earthly choristers, ranged tier above tier in a Gothic cathedral, with princes for audience, and their military trumpets flourishing over the full volume of the organ. Handel's gods are like Homer's, and his sublime never reaches beyond the region of the clouds.

It is notable that Handel's artistic fire burned more steadily in his so-called "non-religious" works than in those through which misguided devotees observe signs of "sacred" inspiration. Actually he exhibited a most subtle appreciation for the manner of pagan rites. His portraits of heroic pagans are splendid and original. Samuel Butler declared with affectionate candor that Handel "had not only a sympathy for paganism, but for the shades and gradations of paganism." He who saw Heaven open as he penned his "Hallelujah Chorus" was equally at home in the high places of heathendom.

Stolid Victorian tradition unfortunately reduced Handel's masterpiece to the level of an edifying Christmas digestive, and thousands still delude themselves with the belief that in listening to *Messiah* they are performing an act of solemn devotion. Ironically enough, Handel is still generally regarded as a church composer *par excellence*. But only once in his long career did he compose an oratorio which may with the slightest propriety be termed Christian in spirit, and even *Messiah* is by no means an exposition of the Christian faith nor a dissertation upon the merits and rewards of godliness. To assert that *Messiah* is a record of Handel's private emotions or a product of exceptional religious exaltation is arrant nonsense and deliberate artistic deception. Though imbued with deep personal conviction Handel was no rapt pietist preaching musical sermons, and those who pretend to discern in *Mes-*

siah an evangelical purpose do so only through wilful distortion of an immortal work of art. If Handel's aim had been didactic he would scarcely have painted his heathen in such glowing colors or depicted his pagans so vividly that they frequently outshine his Christians. With its noble theme *Messiah* is indeed edifying, but whatever spiritual virtues it may possess are wholly adventitious. If, as Victorians declared, a performance of *Messiah* "converts even a holiday audience into a devout congregation," such an overwhelming devotional effect can hardly be credited to the music alone. Edification, however excellent in itself, has nothing to do with art, though art is frequently compelled to be its handmaiden.

But *Messiah* must not be dismissed with deprecating remarks upon its secular character. If it evinces no didactic purpose it still possesses all the poetry and vivid imagination of an artistic triumph. If it fails as a sermon it succeeds as a song, a magnificent effort of human genius devoted to the grandest of all possible themes. Handel's all-embracing sympathy for every manifestation of human energy elevates *Messiah* far above dogmatic creeds and makes it the common property of all mankind. It is eminently human, suffused with the vigor of an impulsive nature bold to utter its feelings in robust, picturesque music. Those who seek to glorify *Messiah* with the halo of ecclesiastical fervor inevitably rob Handel's positively monumental work of its great musical force. No one wants artifice in the place of art. And no sensitive musician wants shoddy sentimentality in the place of critical Handelian enthusiasm.

III

"A Sacred Oratorio"

> Strong in new Arms, lo! Giant HANDEL stands,
> Like bold Briareus, with a hundred hands;
> To stir, to rouze, to shake the Soul he comes,
> And Jove's own Thunders follow Mars's Drums.
> —ALEXANDER POPE, *The Dunciad* (1742)

I

LATE IN THE SUMMER of 1741 Handel received an invitation from William Cavendish, fourth Duke of Devonshire, then Lord Lieutenant of Ireland, to visit Dublin and perform his oratorios for the pleasure of "that generous and polite Nation." The composer was complimented and delighted. For several years fashionable London autocrats had derided his music as Hanoverian and dull, and in 1741 his fortunes had reached their lowest ebb after repeated failures both in opera and in oratorio. Warned by bitter experience, Handel determined at once to appeal from the indifference of England to the friendly enthusiasm of her sister nation across the Irish Sea. Whether he commenced *Messiah* with the intention of a Dublin performance remains uncertain, for the date and terms of the Duke's invitation have not been preserved, but when he completed his oratorio on September 14 he was naturally reluctant to submit such music to the capricious taste of aristocratic London. Perhaps a signal success in Dublin would effect a permanent change in his fortunes at home. Furthermore, his friend Matthew Dubourg was then resident in Ireland as Conductor of the State Band, and an influential society of amateurs had recently erected a new music hall in the Irish capital. After preliminary inquiries of several Irish friends Handel speedily began preparations for his long journey from London to Dublin. During September and October communications passed between Handel and the Governors of three benevolent institutions in Ireland (the Charitable Infirmary, Mercer's Hospital, and the Charitable Musical Society for the Relief of Imprisoned Debtors). With his usual liberality the composer agreed to contribute a portion of his profits to Dublin charities, and he also promised to perform some *special* oratorio solely "for the Benefit and Enlargement of poor and distressed Prisoners for Debt in the several Marshalseas of the city of Dublin."

During the first week of November 1741 Handel put *Messiah* into his bag and set out for Dublin with Susannah Maria Cibber, distinguished tragedienne and one of England's favorite singers. At Chester he was detained by adverse winds. Years later Dr. Burney recorded his amusing recollections of Handel at this time:

When HANDEL went through Chester, in his way to Ireland, this year, 1741, I was at the Public-School in that city, and very well remember seeing him smoke a pipe, over a dish of coffee, at the Exchange-Coffee-house; for being extremely curious to see so extraordinary a man, I watched him narrowly as long as he remained in Chester; which, on account of the wind being unfavourable for his embarking at Parkgate, was several days. During this time, he applied to Mr. [Edmund] Baker, the Organist, my first music-master, to know whether there were any choirmen in the cathedral who could sing *at sight;* as he wished to prove some books that had been hastily transcribed, by trying the choruses which he intended to perform in Ireland. Mr. Baker mentioned some of the most likely singers then in Chester, and, among the rest, a printer of the name of Janson, who had a good base [!] voice, and was one of the best musicians in the choir. . . . A time was fixed for this private rehearsal at the *Golden Falcon,* where HANDEL was quartered; but, alas! on trial of the chorus in the Messiah, *"And with his stripes we are healed,"*—Poor Janson, after repeated attempts, failed so egregiously, that HANDEL let loose his great bear upon him; and after swearing in four or five languages, cried out in broken English: "You shcauntrell tit not you dell me dat you could sing at soite?"—"Yes, sir, says the printer, and so I can; but not at *first sight*."

After many delays Mr. Handel and Mrs. Cibber reached Dublin on November 18. Three days later *Faulkner's Journal* announced the arrival of "the celebrated Dr. Handell," a "Gentleman universally known by his excellent Compositions in all kinds of Musick, and particularly for his *Te Deum, Jubilate, Anthems,* and other Compositions in Church Musick." On November 24 Signora Avolio, "an excellent Singer, who comes to this Kingdom to perform in Mr. Handel's Musical Entertainment," reached Dublin "in the Yatcht from Park-gate." Meanwhile Handel had settled in his rooms in Abbey Street. From the minute-book of Mercer's Hospital it appears that on November 21 three trustees were "desired to wait on Mr. Handel to ask the favour of him to play on the Organ at the Musical Performance in St. Andrew's Church" on December 10. Handel graciously complied, and two days later Mrs. Cibber appeared at the Theatre Royal in Aungier Street as Indiana in Steele's *Conscious Lovers,* "being the first time of her performance in this kingdom."

Mid-eighteenth-century Dublin was a prosperous city of over one hundred thousand persons. In its flourishing artistic and intellectual atmosphere musicians and actors enjoyed high social position. David Garrick played in Dublin as early as 1742, and many prominent eighteenth-century dramatists and actors were born in the Irish metropolis. The city that welcomed Handel with all possible marks of esteem was also the birthplace of Jonathan Swift and Richard Brinsley Sheridan as well as the training ground of Oliver Goldsmith. Dublin's taste for literature and drama was surpassed only by her strong enthusiasm for music. A public garden for musical entertainments followed the model of London's Vauxhall Gardens; a thriving musical academy was established in 1755 by Lord Mornington; and a considerable society of polite amateurs frequently sang in charity concerts to benefit inmates of Dublin prisons. Foreign artists were warmly welcomed, and Matthew Dubourg, an eminent violinist and the favorite pupil of Geminiani, made Dublin his residence from 1728 to 1767. Ballad operas were heard there shortly after their London production, and some pieces were performed in Ireland for the first time. Skill in music was a fashionable attainment. Many elite Dubliners belonged to the Charitable Musical Society, one of five prominent musical groups organized to raise sums for charitable causes. Revelation of frightful abuses in Irish debtors' prisons had left a deep impression upon the public conscience, and Dublin's musical societies had been formed to relieve prisoners by compounding with their creditors and discharging as many as possible from confinement. In 1740 the Charitable Musical Society alone had liberated 188 "miserable persons of both sexes" from extreme affliction in the Marshalsea. During the year of Handel's first performance of *Messiah* the same organization released 142 languishing debtors at an expenditure of no less than £1225.[1]

So flourishing was the Charitable Musical Society that its members resolved in 1740 to erect an elegant new hall for their meetings, rehearsals, and performances. On 2 October 1741 the "New Musick Hall in Fishamble Street" was first opened to the public with great *éclat* under the ownership and presidency of a Dublin music-publisher named Neal. This hall was designated "New" to distinguish it from the Crow-Street Music Hall (also known as Mr. Johnson's Hall) built by the Anacreontic Society ten years before. "The Great Musick-Hall" in Fishamble Street was "finished in the genteelest manner" and provided the finest public apartment

---

[1] Handel's visit to Dublin has been investigated in complete detail by Horatio Townsend, *An Account of the Visit of Handel to Dublin,* Dublin, 1852. All quotations from *Faulkner's Journal* in this volume are drawn from Townsend's admirable work.

Dublin had ever seen. It seated six hundred persons "with full ease." For years it was Ireland's principal rendezvous for public concerts and brilliant assemblies, and throughout the eighteenth century it remained the chief festive resort of wealthy and refined Dubliners. Information concerning Neal's Musick Hall probably helped to attract Handel to Dublin. At his first public concert the composer found the hall a "charming Room" in which "the Musick sounds delightfully."

Handel's cordial reception in Ireland compensated greatly for his previous disasters. His house became the resort of professionals and amateurs alike, and little time was lost in producing selections from the splendid music which he had brought from England. A series of subscription concerts was announced in *Faulkner's Journal* on December 12, and the first of Handel's "Six Musical Entertainments" took place on December 23, when *L'Allegro, Il Penseroso, ed Il Moderato* was performed in Neal's Musick Hall before "a more numerous and polite Audience than ever was seen upon the like Occasion." A glowing account of Handel's first public concert in Dublin appeared in *Faulkner's Journal* on December 29: "The Performance was superior to any thing of the kind in the Kingdom before; and our Nobility and Gentry, to shew their Taste for all kinds of Genius, expressed their great Satisfaction, and have already given all imaginable Encouragement to this grand Musick." On the same day Handel wrote Charles Jennens a touching letter describing his initial success. The haughty Gopsall squire must have been pleased to learn that his barbarous mutilation of Milton had given "great Satisfaction" to such a "numerous and polite" audience!

I am emboldened, Sir, by the generous Concern You please to take in relation to my affairs, to give you an account to the Success I have met here. The Nobility did me the Honour to make amongst themselves a Subscription for 6 Nights, which did fill a Room of 600 Persons. so that I needed not sell one single Ticket at the Door. and without Vanity the Performance was received with a general Approbation. Sig^(ra) Avolio, which I brought with me from London pleases extraordinary. I have formed an other Tenor Voice which gives great satisfaction, the Basses and Counter Tenors are very good, and the rest of the Chorus Singers (by my Direction) do exceeding well, as for the Instruments they are really excellent. Mr. Dubourgh being at the Head of them, and the Musick sounds delightfully in this charming Room, which puts me in such spirits (and my Health being so good) that I exert my self on my Organ with more than usual success. I opened with the Allegro, Penseroso, & Moderato, and I assure you that the Words of the Moderato are vastly admired. The Audience being composed (besides the Flower of Ladyes of Distinction and other People of the greatest quality) of so many Bishops, Deans, Heads of the Colledge, the most eminent People in the Law as the Chancellor, Auditor General, &ct. all which are very much taken with the Poetry. So that I am desired to perform it again the next time. I cannot sufficiently express the kind treatment I receive here, but the Politness of this generous Nation can not be unknown to You, so I let you judge of the satisfaction I enjoy, passing my time with Honnour, profit and pleasure. They propose already to have some more Performances when the 6 Nights of the Subscription are over, and My Lord Duc the Lord Lieutenant (who is always present with all His Family on those Nights) will easily obtain a longer Permission for me by His Majesty, so that I shall be obliged to make my stay here longer than I thought.

By command of the Duke and Duchess of Devonshire *L'Allegro* was repeated on 13 January 1742. A week later Handel's third "Entertainment" featured *Acis and Galatea* and *An Ode for St. Cecilia's Day,* and at the fourth concert on January 27 the program was repeated by special Viceregal command. *Esther* was heard on February 3 and February 10 as the fifth and sixth concerts in Handel's first subscription series. A second series commenced on February 17 with a performance of *Alexander's Feast.* Subscribers heard the same work on March 2, *L'Allegro* on March 17, *Hymen* on March 24 and March 31, and *Esther* on April 3, "being the last time of Mr. Handel's Subscription Performance."

Meanwhile the Governors of Mercer's Hospital had applied to the Deans and Chapters of Dublin's two cathedral churches (Christ Church and St. Patrick's Cathedral) for the assistance of the two choirs at certain benefit performances of the Philharmonick Society. Such arrangements involved some difficulty, for at this time Jonathan Swift was still Dean of St. Patrick's, and despite his approaching insanity he had not relaxed his despotic discipline of the Cathedral singers. Notwithstanding his inherent antipathy toward music Swift labored long and hard to perfect his choir. His correspondence with Dr. Arbuthnot repeatedly emphasized the Dean's concern over his vicars-choral and their behavior. As early as 4 January 1742 the Governors of Mercer's Hospital ordered that John Rochfort, John Putland, and Richard Baldwin apply to the Dean and Chapter of St. Patrick's "for their leave that such of the choir as shall be willing may assist at the Philharmonick Society Performances, which are principally intended for the benefit of the sd. Hospital." At a subsequent meeting of the Governors on January 23 the delegates reported that

The Dean and Chapter of St. Patricks are ready to concur with the Dean and Chapter of Christ Church, in permitting the Choir to assist at the Musical Performance of the Philharmonick Society,—if the Dean and Chapter of Christ Church will concur with them in permitting the Choir to assist at Mr. Handel's. They think that every argument in favour of the one, may be urged with equal strength at least in favour of the other. Particularly that which with them is of greatest weight, the advantage of Mercer's Hospital. Mr. Handel having offer'd, and being still ready, in return for such a favour, to give the Governors some of his choicest Musick, and to direct and assist at the performance of it for the benefit of the hospital, which will in one night raise a considerable sum for their use, without lessening the annual Contribution of the Philharmonick Society, or any of their other funds.

Evidently Handel had previously "offer'd" to "direct and assist at the performance" of "some of his choicest Musick" for the benefit of Mercer's Hospital. Now he was "still ready" to fulfill his promise provided that the two choirs should agree to "assist" in his forthcoming performance of *Messiah*. From the minutes of a subsequent meeting of the Governors on January 27 it appears that Dean Swift (perhaps through Sub-Dean John Wynne) granted his license to six vicars-choral and two choristers of St. Patrick's Cathedral to assist at weekly performances of the Philharmonick Society, "upon account of their being chiefly intended for the benefit of this Hospital." Dean Swift's opposition had been substantially overcome. At once plans moved forward to produce *Messiah* with the assistance of both cathedral choirs and the best talent in Dublin.

Several weeks later Handel commenced preliminary rehearsals of *Messiah* in the ancient church of St. Werburgh. Singers and instrumentalists were rigorously trained by the irascible German, and Dublin eagerly awaited announcement of public rehearsals. Finally on 27 March 1742 the title of Handel's oratorio appeared in print for the first time:

For Relief of the Prisoners in the several Gaols, and for the Support of Mercer's Hospital in Stephen's street, and of the Charitable Infirmary on the Inn's Quay, on Monday the 12th of April, will be performed at the Musick Hall in Fishamble street, *Mr. Handel's new Grand Oratorio, called the* MESSIAH, in which the Gentlemen of the Choirs of both Cathedrals will assist, with some Concertos on the Organ, by Mr. Handell. Tickets to be had at the Musick Hall, and at Mr. Neal's in Christ Church-yard, at half a Guinea each. N.B. No Person will be admitted to the Rehearsal without a Rehearsal Ticket, which will be given gratis with the Ticket for the Performance when payed for.

On April 3 *Faulkner's Journal* announced a public rehearsal of *Messiah* for the following Thursday:

On Thursday next, being the 8th Inst., at the Musick Hall in Fishamble-street, will be the Rehearsal of Mr. Handel's new Grand Sacred Oratorio, called *The* MESSIAH, in which the **Gentlemen of both Choirs will assist**: with some Concertos on the Organ by Mr. Handel. The Doors will be opened at Eleven, and no Person to be admitted without a Rehearsal Ticket, which is given gratis with the Tickets for the Performance, when paid for. Tickets to be had at the Musick Hall, and at Mr. Neal's in Christ-Church-yard, at Half a Guinea each.

In advertisements of Handel's former subscription concerts the composer was never mentioned specifically as a performer of "Concertos on the Organ," but notices of the first rendition of *Messiah* refer expressly to "Concertos on the Organ by Mr. Handel." Perhaps at previous concerts Handel had left the organ entirely to Maclaine (an excellent musician whom the composer had imported from England), but apparently he deemed it proper to distinguish his initial production of *Messiah* with an organ performance of his own. Whereas in former notices tickets were advertised as available at "Mr. Handel's house in Abbey-street," tickets for *Messiah* were "to be had at the Musick Hall, and at Mr. Neal's in Christ-Church-yard." In directing *Messiah* Handel was evidently relieved of all business responsibilities. He had formerly agreed "to give the Governors some of his choicest Musick, and to direct and assist at the performance of it for the benefit of the hospital," and having secured the assistance of both choirs, he could now produce his masterpiece in a style otherwise impracticable. At the rehearsal on 8 April 1742 Handel's *Messiah* was heard for the first time by a public audience, and two days later its reception was described by *Faulkner's Journal*:

Yesterday, Mr. Handel's new Grand Sacred Oratorio, called The MESSIAH, was rehearsed at the Musick Hall in Fishamble-street, to a most Grand, Polite, and Crowded Audience; and was performed so well, that it gave universal Satisfaction to all present; and was allowed by the greatest Judges, to be the finest Composition of Musick that ever was heard, and the sacred Words as properly adapted for the occasion.

N.B. At the desire of several persons of Distinction, the above Performance is put off to Tuesday next. The doors will be opened at Eleven, and the Performance begin at Twelve.

Many Ladies and Gentlemen who are well-wishers to this Noble and Grand Charity, for which this Oratorio was composed, request it as a Favour, that the Ladies who honour this Performance with their Presence, would be pleased to come without Hoops, as it will greatly encrease the Charity, by making Room for more company.

A similar notice of the first public rehearsal appeared in *The Dublin News-Letter* on April 10:

Yesterday Morning, at the Musick Hall in Fishamble-street, there was a public Rehearsal of the Messiah, Mr. Handel's new sacred Oratorio, which in the opinion of the best Judges, far surpasses anything of that Nature, which has been performed in this or any other Kingdom. This elegant Entertainment was conducted in the most regular Manner, and to the entire satisfaction of the most crowded and polite Assembly.

For the benefit of three very important public Charities, there will be a grand Performance of this Oratorio on Tuesday next in the forenoon, the doors will be opened at Eleven, and the Performance begins at Twelve a clock.

N.B. At the desire of several persons of Distinction, Monday being Cathedral Day, the Performance is put off till Tuesday.

II

On Tuesday morning, 13 April 1742, Dublin's fashionable world flocked to Neal's Musick Hall in Fishamble Street to hear Mr. Handel's "new Grand Sacred Oratorio" performed publicly for the first time.[2] At midday the brilliant assemblage sat tense with anticipation as prominent dignitaries in church and state waited amid the gay throng of aristocratic patrons for the appearance of Mr. Handel and the commencement of his "elegant Entertainment." That morning *Faulk-*

---

[2] For over a century contrary tales circulated as to the manner, time, and place of Handel's first performance of *Messiah*. Finally Horatio Townsend resolved this confusion in his *Account of the Visit of Handel to Dublin*, pp. 71–79. Townsend concluded "with perfect certainty" that "no performance of the *Messiah* took place in London till after Handel's return from Ireland, and that Dublin may rightfully claim the honour of being first to witness and applaud this sublime and immortal work."

ner's Journal had once more besought the ladies to discard their hoops:

> This day will be performed Mr. Handell's new Grand Sacred Oratorio, called the MESSIAH. The doors will be opened at Eleven, and the performance begin at Twelve.
>
> The Stewards of the Charitable Musical Society request the Favour of the ladies not to come with hoops this day to the Musick Hall in Fishamble Street. The Gentlemen are desired to come without their swords.

In a day when fashion dictated hoopskirts boasting a circumference of nine yards such a notice must have created general consternation in the female world. But apparently no discordant voice broke the universal enthusiasm for Handel's masterpiece, and fine wardrobes were accordingly overhauled with haste to meet the strange demands of the Charitable Musical Society. On that April morning Fishamble Street afforded a magnificent spectacle of ladies in bright gowns, gentlemen in decorated uniforms, white-gloved beaux in full-bottomed wigs, and various degrees of nobility in all the splendor of the Viceregal *cortège*. Scores of liveried footmen assisted ladies from handsome chariots, while pages waited to fetch sedan chairs or darted to and fro shouting after family coaches. Inside the hall Handel's "polite" audience comprised "Bishops, Deans, Heads of the Colledge," and "the most eminent People in the Law," as well as "the Flower of Ladyes of Distinction and other People of the greatest quality." On that historic occasion seven hundred discriminating connoisseurs crowded into the small concert room, while hundreds more stood in the street hoping to hear some portion of the music within.

Finally Mr. Handel appeared on the platform and the overture began. For four hours "the admiring crowded Audience" sat transfixed with rapture as the pathos of Handel's melodies and the grandeur of his choruses "conspired to transport and charm the ravished Heart and Ear." During the stately overture the hall was gloomy and still, but when the "full-mouth'd" choruses burst upon the room and encompassed Handel's audience in a sea of splendid sound the effect was instantaneous and remarkable. For that performance Matthew Dubourg was chief violinist and leader of a "most celebrated Band of Vocal and Instrumental Musick." His State Band probably formed the nucleus of what Dr. Burney called "a very respectable orchestre." After Handel's twelve subscription concerts these performers undoubtedly displayed all the marks of the composer's rigid discipline. Maclaine presided at the organ, and Handel performed his concertos between the parts of the oratorio. His chorus was composed entirely of boys and men from Dublin's two cathedral choirs, for female voices never sang in Handel's choruses during his lifetime. His choir (like his orchestra) was always relatively small, and at the first performance of *Messiah* the chorus presumably numbered no more than twenty voices. But Handel's fourteen men and six boys were probably superior to several times their number of ordinary singers to be found in the ranks of modern oratorio societies, for Handel was a strict disciplinarian with a firm knowledge of voices, and during the past three months the exacting drillmaster had brought his forces to an exceptional degree of efficiency.

Of the soloists Dr. Burney recorded that Mrs. Cibber and Signora Avolio were "the principal performers," and both ladies followed Handel's generous example in giving their services gratuitously. Already Signora Avolio had sung with great applause in Dublin. As early as 29 December 1741 Handel had written that she "pleases extraordinary," and *Faulkner's Journal* had declared the Italian soprano "an excellent Singer." But it was Mrs. Cibber who won the tears of the audience at the first performance of *Messiah*. Her mezzo-soprano voice was of slight compass, and Horace Walpole once declared in derision that she possessed "no voice at all," but in *Messiah* the so-called "nightingale of the stage" entranced her hearers with that incomparable pathos which was later to establish her reputation as London's most accomplished tragic actress. Mrs. Cibber's emotional intensity seems to have produced an indescribable sadness in her singing. As late as 1756 Thomas Sheridan recalled her "wonderful" rendition of Handel's contralto arias at the initial performance of *Messiah*:

No person of sensibility, who has had the good fortune to hear Mrs Cibber sing in the oratorio of the Messiah, will find it very difficult to give credit to accounts of the most wonderful effects produced from so powerful an union. And yet it was not to any extraordinary powers of voice (whereof she has but a very moderate share) nor to a greater degree of skill in musick (wherein many of the Italians must be allowed to exceed her) that she owed her excellence, but to expression only; her acknowledged superiority in which could proceed from nothing but skill in her profession.

Handel is said to have composed "He was despised" expressly to suit the limited range of Mrs. Cibber's voice. From the depths of her tragic (and notorious) life she sang this famous aria with such tender grief that during the first performance the Reverend Patrick Delany found himself enthralled beyond his usual discretion by the pathetic beauty of her voice. Despite his old-fashioned prejudice against public singers, that worthy divine so far forgot himself (and his Bible) that at the close of Mrs. Cibber's aria he rose in his place and in an audible voice solemnly addressed that not altogether immaculate lady: "Woman, for this be all thy sins forgiven thee!"

On the first day *Messiah* was received with transports of wonder and delight. The Irish heart was touched, and the Irish capital was fervid with excitement. Fine ladies exhausted every trope and figure in praise of the new oratorio, while gentlemen of fashion tore rhetoric to tatters in their admiration for Handel's masterpiece. *Faulkner's Journal* was not addicted to superlatives, but on the following Saturday, 17 April 1742, its pages featured a full account of the first performance of *Messiah*:

"A SACRED ORATORIO" 101

On Tuesday last, Mr. Handel's Sacred Grand Oratorio, the MESSIAH, was performed in the New Musick Hall in Fishamble-street; the best Judges allowed it to be the most finished piece of Musick. Words are wanting to express the exquisite Delight it afforded to the admiring crowded Audience. The Sublime, the Grand, and the Tender, adapted to the most elevated, majestick and moving Words, conspired to transport and charm the ravished Heart and Ear. It is but Justice to Mr. Handel that the World should know he generously gave the Money arising from this Grand Performance, to be equally shared by the Society for relieving Prisoners, the Charitable Infirmary, and Mercer's Hospital, for which they will ever gratefully remember his Name: and that the Gentlemen of the two Choirs, Mr. Dubourg, Mrs. Avolio, and Mrs. Cibber, who all performed their Parts to Admiration, acted also on the same disinterested Principle, satisfied with the deserved Applause of the Publick, and the conscious Pleasure of promoting such useful and extensive Charity. There were above 700 People in the Room, and the Sum collected for that Noble and Pious Charity, amounted to about £400, out of which £127 goes to each of the three great and pious Charities.

On April 20 a certain Laurence Whyte published in *Faulkner's Journal* a pious rhapsody distinguished more for benevolent zeal than for poetic fire:

On Mr. Handel's performance of his *Oratorio*, call'd the *Messiah*, for the support of Hospitals and other pious Uses, at the Musick Hall in Fishamble-street, on Tuesday, April 13th, 1742, before the Lords Justices, and a vast Assembly of the Nobility and Gentry of both sexes. By Mr. L. Whyte.

> What can we offer more in *Handel's* praise?
> Since his *Messiah* gain'd him groves of bays;
> Groves that can never wither nor decay,
> Whose *Vistos* his Ability display:
> Here *Nature* smiles, when grac'd with Handel's art,
> Transports the ear, and ravishes the heart;
> To all the nobler *Passions* we are mov'd,
> When various strains repeated and improv'd,
> Express each different Circumstance and State,
> As if each sound became articulate.
>   None but the great Messiah could inflame,
> And raise his Soul to so Sublime a Theme,

> Profound the Thoughts, the subject all divine,
> Not like the tales of *Pindus* and the *Nine:*
> Or Heathen Deities, those Sons of Fiction,
> Sprung from old Fables, stuff'd with contradiction;
> But our Messiah, blessed be his name!
> Both Heaven and Earth his *Miracles* proclaim.
> His birth, his Passion, and his Resurrection,
> With his ascension have a strong connection;
> What Prophets spoke, or Sybils could relate,
> In him were all their Prophecies compleat.
> The *Word* made Flesh, both God and Man became,
> Then let all nations glorify his name!
> Let Halleluiahs round the Globe be sung,
> To our Messiah, from a virgin sprung.

Notwithstanding its metaphorical incongruity this uninspired memorial is remarkable for its good sense and aesthetic justice, and its provides a typical specimen of the sort of versification admitted into public journals in teacup times of hood and hoop.

Such were the sentiments of Handel's contemporaries at the first performance of its masterpiece in Dublin. It had been reserved for the Irish people to set their seal of enthusiastic approval upon *Messiah,* and the citizens of Dublin seem to have been worthy of their honor. With characteristic humanity the composer performed his masterpiece solely for the benefit of wretched persons imprisoned for debt. By an appropriate coincidence Handel's supreme tribute to Him who came to break the bonds and set the prisoner free literally proclaimed deliverance to the captive at its first performance. "There was," wrote the Reverend John Mainwaring, "a peculiar propriety in this design from the subject of the Oratorio itself; and there was a peculiar grace in it from the situation of HANDEL's affairs." *Messiah* created so profound an impression that a repetition was demanded within a few weeks. Following a successful performance of *Saul* on May 25 the composer issued his last public announcement in Ireland on 29 May 1742:

At the Particular Desire of several of the Nobility and Gentry.

On Thursday next, being the 3d day of June, at the new Musick Hall in Fishamble-street, will be performed Mr. Handel's new Grand Sacred Oratorio, called MESSIAH, with Concertos on the Organ. Tickets will be delivered at Mr. Handel's house in Abbey-street, and at Mr. Neal's in Christ-church-yard, at Half a guinea each. A Rehearsal Ticket will be given with the ticket for the Performance. The Rehearsal will be on Tuesday the 1st of June, at Twelve, and the Performance at Seven in the Evening. In order to keep the Room as cool as possible, a Pane of Glass will be removed from the top of each of the Windows.

N.B. This will be the last Performance of Mr. Handel's during his stay in this Kingdom.

With this second audition of *Messiah* Handel's public career in Dublin came to a close. Lest any "persons of Quality" should be frightened away from his final performance by Dublin's stifling heat, shrewd Mr. Handel took precautions "to keep the Room as cool as possible." But such steps were unnecessary, for Handel's Irish audience were prepared to endure any extremes of temperature and precipitation to hear the composer's "most finished piece of Musick."

During 1891 Handelians were stirred by the announcement that a copy of the original wordbook of *Messiah* had been discovered in Dublin. An advertisement of *Messiah* in *The Dublin News-Letter* of 27 March 1742 had stated that "Books are also to be had at a British sixpence each," but for a century historians had sought in vain for such a treasure, until by 1891 its very existence was doubtful. One day Professor Edward Dowden was rummaging through the stores of a secondhand Dublin bookshop when he discovered a small quarto volume bound in old calf and marked "J.M." Upon inspection Dowden observed that the volume contained the missing wordbook of Handel's *Messiah* bound with a libretto of *Acis and Galatea*. A motto on the title page contained the "Lines" which Charles Jennens had sent to Handel in Dublin

MESSIAH.

AN

ORATORIO

Compos'd by Mr. *HANDEL.*

MAJORA CANAMUS.

And without Controversy, great is the Mystery of Godliness: God was manifested in the Flesh, justified by the Spirit, seen of Angels, preached among the Gentiles, believed on in the World, received up in Glory.
In whom are hid all the Treasures of Wisdom and Knowledge.

DUBLIN: Printed by GEORGE FAULKNER, 1742.

(Price a British Six-pence.)

TITLE PAGE OF THE WORDBOOK OF *MESSIAH*
AS PERFORMED AT NEAL'S MUSICK HALL, DUBLIN (1742)
From the Copy in the British Museum

"in order to be prefixed to Your Oratorio Messiah."[3] At once Professor Dowden handed the volume to Dr. James C. Culwick, organist of the Chapel Royal in Dublin, who after patient scrutiny analyzed the wordbook in a pamphlet published in the autumn of 1891.[4] Later the volume was purchased by the trustees of the British Museum.[5]

Until Professor Dowden's signal discovery little was known of the precise form of *Messiah* at its first rendition. Beyond the fact that Mrs. Cibber and Signora Avolio were "the principal performers" even Townsend was forced to be vague and incomplete. But the original wordbook partially dispels the mystery of 13 April 1742, for on its pages an auditor presumably of the original performance scribbled with a blunt pencil the names of the singers of nearly all the solo items. With an uncertainty of spelling that suggests intense preoccupation a member of Handel's Dublin audience incorporated the soloists' names in the margin of his wordbook beside the songs they sang. Unfortunately some of the writing was cut away by the binder, but every word can be ascertained with assistance from Handel's Dublin score. An examination of the wordbook in connection with various known manuscripts of *Messiah* yields several facts suggestive to the musician and fascinating to the layman. From the pencilled notations it emerges that Handel employed five male

---

[3] On 29 December 1741 Handel wrote to Jennens: "It was with the greatest Pleasure I saw the continuation of Your kindness by the Lines you was pleased to send me, in order to be prefixed to Your Oratorio Messiah, which I set to Musick before I left England."

[4] James C. Culwick, *Handel's Messiah: Discovery of the Original Word-Book*, Dublin, 1891. Neither the overture nor the Pastoral Symphony is mentioned in the original wordbook. At first glance the absence of these two numbers suggests that they were not performed on 13 April 1742, but actually Handel seldom (if ever) mentioned an overture in his oratorio wordbooks, and this habit was followed until much later times. It is also notable that while all songs and choruses and the duet are printed in italics, recitatives are distinguished by roman type.

[5] In September 1891 a second copy of the original wordbook of *Messiah* was found buried among some manuscripts in the library of Trinity College in Dublin. This volume proved an imperfect copy with no pencilled notes, and it is therefore of little historical value.

soloists for the original performance of *Messiah*: James Bailey (tenor), William Lambe (counter-tenor), Joseph Ward (alto), John Hill (bass), and John Mason (bass). Nothing is known of these five singers beyond the fact that the first four were members of both cathedral choirs, and that Mason was a vicar-choral of Christ Church alone.

Regarding Handel's female vocalists, however, the original wordbook creates more problems than it solves. According to *Faulkner's Journal* Signora Avolio and Mrs. Cibber sang in the first performance of *Messiah*, but in the wordbook the name of Signora Avolio does not appear, and several soprano numbers are marked "M'clean" (referring presumably to the wife of Handel's organist, who is known to have accompanied her husband to Ireland). Apparently Mrs. Maclaine did not sing every soprano solo, for no name is pencilled against "Rejoice greatly," "Come unto Him," and "How beautiful are the feet." Perhaps Signora Avolio does not appear because the original owner was unable to spell her name, but it is more probable that she did not participate in the performance. With good reason it has been suggested that the notes pencilled in this wordbook refer to Handel's second performance on 3 June 1742, since the "Dublin score," from which Handel conducted the first performance, provides a list of names which do not agree entirely with those mentioned in the wordbook. It is also notable that the original libretto omitted the recitative "Unto which of the angels," and a slip of paper containing the words of this number and the words of the succeeding chorus has been pasted into its correct place. Was this insertion an afterthought intended to separate two choruses? Or was the omission simply a printer's error? Unfortunately no record of Handel's second *Messiah* performance has survived. Perhaps at the first rendition Signora Avolio found her burden too heavy and arranged to share her soprano solos with Mrs. Maclaine at the second performance. All is conjecture. The notes were probably pencilled in haste, and they cannot be regarded as final evidence.

Details of Handel's initial performance of *Messiah* remain obscure, and the wordbook by no means thoroughly solves the mystery.[6]

Following his *Messiah* performance of 3 June 1742 Handel remained in Dublin till late August, reluctant to leave the Irish friends he had made during his delightful visit in "that generous and polite Nation." But after attending David Garrick's *Hamlet* performance in Smock-Alley Theatre on August 12, he packed his bag and set out for London the next day. Just before his departure he waited on Dean Swift, whose rage by that time had become absolute madness. In her *Memoirs*

---

[6] From the wordbook it is clear that Handel found his music beyond the powers of his soloists and that he was forced to modify his original intentions considerably in several recitatives and arias. James Bailey seems to have been scarcely equal to the demands of the tenor solos, and John Mason was apparently Handel's only capable male soloist for the occasion. "Comfort ye" and "Every valley" were sung by Bailey; "Thus saith the Lord" and "But who may abide" (in recitative) were sung by Mason. Lambe rendered "Behold, a virgin shall conceive" and "O thou that tellest," and Mason returned in "For behold, darkness shall cover the earth" and "The people that walked in darkness." Mrs. Maclaine sang "There were shepherds" and the three succeeding recitatives. "Rejoice greatly" was probably rendered by Signora Avolio in the 12/8 version, although no name is penciled in the wordbook here. Mrs. Cibber sang "Then shall the eyes" and "He shall feed His flock" (in the key of F), and Signora Avolio probably followed with "Come unto Him." At the first performance "He was despised" fell to Mrs. Cibber. Bailey sang "All they that see Him." Curiously enough, Mrs. Maclaine rendered "Thy Rebuke," "Behold and see," "He was cut off," and "But Thou didst not leave." According to the wordbook "Unto which of the angels" was omitted at the initial performance. Mason sang "Thou art gone up" probably in the D minor version for bass. "How beautiful are the feet" was sung as an alto duet, probably by Mrs. Cibber and Signora Avolio (singing the second alto modified and chiefly an octave higher). This duet was followed by the chorus "Break forth into joy" (later discarded), and the present chorus "Their sound is gone out" had no place in the first performance. Hill sang "Why do the nations" in a version partly rewritten as recitative. Apparently Bailey was not equal to "He that dwelleth" and "Thou shalt break them," for the recitative was lengthened and sung by Lambe in a version transposed a minor third higher to fit between "Let us break" in C and "Hallelujah" in D. Mrs. Maclaine was the first interpreter of "I know that my Redeemer liveth." Hill sang "Behold, I tell you a mystery" and "The trumpet shall sound"; Ward performed "Then shall be brought to pass"; Ward and Bailey united in an abbreviated form of the duet "O death, where is thy sting?" Mrs. Cibber sang "If God be for us" in a version transposed for alto in C minor.

Mrs. Letitia Pilkington recorded that Handel found the Dean almost totally insensible:

> I was told the last sensible Words he uttered, were on this Occasion: Mr. *Handel,* when about to quit *Ireland,* went to take his leave of him: The Servant was a considerable Time, E'er he could make the Dean understand him; which, when he did, he cryed, "O! A *German,* and a Genius! A Prodigy! admit him." The Servant did so, just to let Mr. *Handel* behold the Ruins of the greatest Wit that ever lived along the Tide of Time, where all at length are lost.

So the two great men met. Perhaps Handel's compliments upon the vicars-choral of St. Patrick's Cathedral once again roused the wretched Dean from his stupor. Perhaps for one moment Jonathan Swift glowed with fresh pride in that choir for which he had so diligently labored.

Handel's visit to Dublin constitutes a pleasing episode in the history of eighteenth-century Ireland. It was not soon forgotten. On 19 November 1743 *Faulkner's Journal* stated that a third performance of Handel's *Messiah* would take place in Neal's Musick Hall on the evening of December 16 following a preliminary rehearsal at noon on December 12. After several weeks of advertisements, however, the Charitable Musical Society was obliged to postpone its performance for reasons announced in *Faulkner's Journal* on December 6:

> From the Charitable Musical Society. The said society having obtained from the celebrated Mr. Handell, a copy of the Score of the Grand Musical Entertainment, called the MESSIAH, they intended to have it rehearsed on the 12th, and performed on the 16th of December, Inst. for the Benefit and Enlargement of Prisoners confined for Debt, pursuant to their advertisements; and in order to have it executed in the best Manner, they had prevailed on Mr. Dubourg to give them his Assistance, and also applyed by a Deputation of the Society to the members of the Choirs of the two Cathedrals to assist therein, (the necessary approbation of their so doing being first obtained on due Application) which several of them promised, and at a Meeting for that Purpose, chose and received their Parts; but after Prepara-

tions had been made, at considerable Expence, to the Surprise of the Society, several of the Members of the said Choirs, (some of whom had engaged as before mentioned) thought fit to decline performing, and returned their Parts, for Reasons that no way related to or concerned the said Society; they are therefore obliged to postpone that Entertainment until Friday the 3rd day of February next, to the great Detriment and Delay of their Charitable Intentions, the good Effects whereof have been manifested for several years past. By that time the Society will provide such Performers as will do justice to that Sublime Composition, and for the future will take such measures as shall effectually free them from Apprehension of a second Disappointment to the Publick or themselves.

On 28 January 1744 *Faulkner's Journal* advertised the long-delayed rehearsal in strange terms suggesting the rival claims of music and a *cause célèbre* upon public interest: "The Rehearsal of Mr. Handel's sacred Oratorio called the MESSIAH will certainly be on Wednesday the 1st day of February, . . . and if Lord Netterville's trial should come on the Friday following, the Performance will be postponed to a further Day." Later *Faulkner's Journal* recorded a private rehearsal of Handel's "Grand Musical Entertainment" on January 30:

We hear that the Oratorio called the MESSIAH was privately rehearsed last Night in the Presence of some of the best Judges, who expressed the utmost satisfaction on the Occasion. This fine piece is to be publicly rehearsed on Wednesday next at Noon, for the Benefit and Enlargement of Prisoners confined for Debt; and as the audience will be very numerous, we hear the Ladies have resolved to come without Hoops, as when the same was performed by Mr. Handel.

It is amusing to note the urgency with which eighteenth-century journals implored ladies to attend public performances of oratorios "without Hoops." Apparently the awkward fashion struck even contemporaries as obnoxious and absurd, for at every important performance of *Messiah* during Handel's lifetime newspaper advertisements besought "the Favour of the Ladies" to "lay aside their Hoops" in order to accommodate "an hundred Persons more with full ease." As late as 1790 Directors of the Handel Festival in Westminster Abbey decreed that "no ladies will be admitted with hats, and they are particularly requested to come without feathers, and very small hoops, if any." A quaint comment upon contemporary fashion appeared in *Faulkner's Journal* on 4 February 1744:

From the Charitable Musical Society for the Relief of poor Prisoners.

The Society beg leave respectfully to address themselves to the Ladies, and to appeal to such of them as were at the public Rehearsal last Wednesday, for the necessity of this their Request, that had the Ladies laid aside their Hoops, the Musick Hall would contain an hundred Persons more with full ease. As this Entertainment is exhibited for a very Charitable Account, and that the chief intent of the Assembly is Charity, they humbly hope the Ladies will not take amiss to be requested to lay aside a *Mode,* (for one evening) however Ornamental on other Occasions. N.B. On Account of Lord Netterville's Tryal, the Grand Performance of the sacred Oratorio of the Messiah is put off to Tuesday the 7th inst. to begin at 6 o'clock in the Evening precisely.

We hear from all hands of the great satisfaction given last Wednesday to a crowded Audience, at the Rehearsal of the sacred Oratorio of the Messiah; nothing can come up to the choice of the subject, the Words are those of the sacred Text, the Musick extremely well adapted, and the execution, under Mr. Dubourg's Direction, by the most celebrated Band of Vocal and Instrumental Musick, was carried on through all the Parts with universal applause.

A repetition of *Messiah* was heard in Neal's Musick Hall on 27 February 1744. When the Charitable Musical Society ceased to exist its "copy of the Score of the Grand Musical Entertainment, called the MESSIAH" passed into the possession of Mercer's Hospital.

In the decade following Handel's engagement in Dublin the composer's music enjoyed great vogue in the Irish capital. To the Dublin concert-goer of 1750 Handel's oratorios were both familiar and fashionable. From the correspondence of Mrs. Delany it is clear that *Esther* and *Deborah* and *Saul* and *Joshua* won greater applause in mid-eighteenth-century Dublin than even *Samson* and *Judas Maccabeus* received in London.[7] But from the beginning the Irish favorite was *Messiah*. As early as 21 December 1745 Mrs. Delany recorded a satisfactory performance of "that Sublime Composition" by the Charitable Musical Society of Dublin. "It was very well performed," she wrote, "and I much delighted. You know how much I delight in music, and that piece is very charming." Five years later she expressed her joy at the prospect of "a feast of music" during the Christmas season of 1750:

On Tuesday morning next, the rehearsal of the Messiah is to be for the benefit of debtors—on Thursday evening it will be performed. I hope to go to both; our new, and *therefore* favourite performer Morella is to play the first fiddle, and conduct the whole. I am afraid *his French taste* will prevail; I shall *not be able to endure* his introducing *froth and nonsense* in that sublime and awful piece of music. What makes me fear this will be the case, is, that in the closing of the eighth concerto of Corelli, instead of playing it *clear and distinct,* he filled it up with *frippery and graces which quite destroyed the effect* of the sweet notes, and solemn pauses that conclude it.

Later she reported that *Messiah* had been "very tolerably performed," although "*voices* and *hands* were wanting to do it justice." Her "great pleasure" in its "heavenly" strains had been "greatly heightened by considering how many poor prisoners would be released by it." Morella had "conducted the Messiah very well—*surprizingly so,* considering he was *not before acquainted* with such sublime music." Before the performance she had "thought it would be impossible for his wild fancy and fingers to have kept within bounds; but Handel's music inspired and *awed him,*" and "he came off with great applause." Most amusing was Mrs. Delany's ac-

---

[7] For details see my article, "Mrs. Delany: An Eighteenth-Century Handelian," *The Musical Quarterly*, XXXII, 12–36 (January 1946).

count of a Dublin performance of *Messiah* on 14 December 1752:

Yesterday morning we went to the rehearsal of the "Messiah," it was very tolerably performed. I was a little afraid of it, as I think the music *very affecting*, and I found it so—but am glad I went, as I felt great comfort from it, and I had the good fortune to have Mrs. Bernard sit by me, the Primate's sister, a most worthy sensible woman, of an exalted mind; it adds greatly to the satisfaction of such an entertainment to be seated by those who have the same relish for it we have ourselves. *The babblers* of my acquaintance were at a distance, indeed I took care to place myself *as far from them as I could.*

Following this rehearsal of *Messiah* the oratorio was "exhibited" several times during the Christmas season. After a performance on 27 December 1752 Benjamin Victor recorded his exhilaration in a letter to the Reverend William Rothery of Chelsea:

You must be a lover of music—If *Handel's Messiah* should be performed in London, as it undoubtedly will in the lent season, I beg it as a favour to me, that you will go early, and take your wife with you, your time and money cannot be so well employed; take care to get a book of the oratorio some days before, that you may well digest the subject, there you will hear *glad tidings* and truly divine rejoicings at the birth of *Christ,* and feel real sorrows for his sufferings—but, oh! when those sufferings are over, what a transporting full chorus! where all the instruments, and three sets of voices are employed to express the following passages, which I must quote—
    Lift up your heads, O ye gates! and be ye lift up ye Everlasting doors, and the king of glory shall come in.
    Who is the king of glory? The Lord strong and mighty, The Lord mighty in battle, the Lord of Hosts;
    He is the king of glory!
    And he shall reign for ever, King of Kings, Lord of Lords.
How truly poetical is the diction of the Oriental writers.
    Mr. Handel, when he was here, composed this excellent oratorio, and gave it to a charitable musical society; by whom it is annually performed for the relief of poor debtors, and very well,

as we have good cathedral singers, to whom this music is chiefly adapted—the performance is just over, and you will conclude I am never absent. As much as I detest fatigue and inconvenience, I would ride forty miles in the wind and rain to be present at a performance of the Messiah in London, under the conduct of Handel—I remember it there—He had an hundred instruments, and fifty voices! O how magnificent the full chorusses.

III

When Handel returned to London late in August 1742 he found the hostility of English aristocracy but little diminished. During his absence no less a bard than Alexander Pope had sung his praises in *The Dunciad,* but the opposition of Handel's enemies did not thoroughly subside for some years to come. Pope is reputed to have known little and cared less about music, but when Dr. Arbuthnot praised Handel in extravagant terms Pope laid the words to heart and later satirized Handel's enemies in a brilliant attack upon Italian opera in the fourth book of *The Dunciad.* Once Pope explained to John Christopher Smith (Handel's amanuensis) that "merit in every branch or science ought to be encouraged; that the extreme illiberality with which many persons had joined to ruin Handel, in opposing his Operas, called forth his indignation; and though nature had denied his being gratified by Handel's uncommon talents in the musical line, yet when his powers were generally acknowledged, he thought it incumbent upon him to pay a tribute due to genius." But Pope's generous praise of Handel's "uncommon talents" did not substantially improve the composer's position in London. After his return from "th' Hibernian shore" Handel was still uncertain whether or not he should "do something in the Oratorio way," and on 9 September 1742 he wrote Jennens contradicting a report that he was to direct London opera during the following season:

It was indeed Your humble servant which intended You a visit in my way from Ireland to London. for I certainly could have given you a better account by word of mouth, as by writing, how well Your Messiah was received in that country, yet as a Noble Lord, and no less than the Bishop of Elphim (A Nobleman very learned in musick) has given his observations in writing of this Oratorio, I send you here annexed the contents of it in his own words—

I shall send the printed Book of the Messiah to Mr Sted for you. As for my success in general in that generous and polite Nation, I reserve the account of it till I have the Honour to see you in London. . . . Whether I shall do something in the Oratorio way (as several of my friend desire) i can not determine as yet. Certain it is that this time 12 month I shall continue my Oratorio's in Ireland, where they are agoing to make a large subscription allready for that Purpose.

In this letter Handel enclosed the critical observations of Dr. Edward Synge, Bishop of Elphin, upon the first performance of *Messiah,* as well as a copy of the original wordbook issued by George Faulkner on 13 April 1742. In September Handel was evidently projecting a second series of oratorio concerts in Dublin for the following year, but subsequent events prove that any such scheme came to naught.

At first Handel made no effort to produce *Messiah* in London. On 17 February 1743 a notice in *The Daily Advertiser* announced a series of six subscription concerts at Covent Garden, opening the next day with the oratorio which he had composed immediately before his departure for Ireland. *Samson* was an instantaneous and permanent success. With a distinguished cast including Susannah Cibber, Kitty Clive, and John Beard it pursued a popular run of six nights. On February 26 Lady Hertford reported that the "new oratorio called *Sampson*" was "filled with all the people of quality in town; and they say Handel has exerted himself to make it the finest piece of music he ever composed, and say he has not failed in his attempt." Even Horace Walpole was compelled to agree that *Samson* was a public favorite. "The oratorios thrive abundantly," he wrote on March 3; "for my part they give me an idea of heaven, where everybody is to sing, whether they have voices or not." For *Samson* Handel "has hired all the goddesses from farces and the singers of *Roast Beef* from between the acts at both theatres." At Covent Garden these motley performers "sing, and make brave hallelujahs," while "the good company encore the recitative, if it happens to have any cadence like what they call a tune."

London was so pleased with *Samson* that Handel was induced to extend his subscription series to twelve concerts, including two more performances of *Samson*, one of *L'Allegro* and *An Ode for St. Cecilia's Day*, and three of *Messiah*. At last London was to hear Handel's masterpiece. But before the composer could advertise *Messiah* the cries of desecration which had blocked *Haman and Mordecai* eleven years before broke out afresh. Handel's fashionable enemies raised hypocritical protests against the profanation of any such "sacred" performance in a London playhouse. Pious devotees were scandalized at the sacrilege of converting the Life and Passion of Christ into a theatrical entertainment, and strict clergymen even denounced the blasphemy of printing *Messiah* on a playbill. In the face of such powerful prejudice Handel resolved to advertise his work simply as *A Sacred Oratorio*. On Saturday, 19 March 1743, *The London Daily Post* announced Handel's first London performance of *Messiah* as "The Ninth Night" in his subscription series:

At the Theatre-Royal in Covent-Garden, Wednesday next, will be perform'd A NEW SACRED ORATORIO. A CONCERTO on the ORGAN, And a Solo on the Violin by Mr. DUBOURG. Tickets well be deliver'd to Subscribers on Tuesday next, at Mr. Handel's House in Brook-street. Pit and Boxes to be put together, and no Person to be admitted without Tickets, which will be deliver'd that Day, at the Office in Covent-Garden Theatre, at Half a Guinea each. First Gallery 5s. Upper Gallery 3s. 6d. The Galleries will be open'd at Four o'clock. Pit and Boxes at Five.

Already ecclesiastical authorities were on the alert. When *A Sacred Oratorio* was advertised they sought to obtain injunctions preventing its performance, on the ground that Covent Garden Theatre was a place of worldly amusement and that in any case public entertainments during Lent were sacrilegious and therefore censurable.

Notwithstanding the objections of misguided religiosity Handel proceeded to perform *A Sacred Oratorio* for the first time in London on Wednesday, 23 March 1743. Two days later a second rendition followed, and on March 29 the oratorio was heard for the last time during that season. For the first performance Handel's alterations were considerable. Mrs. Cibber shared the female solos with Mrs. Clive and Signora Avolio; John Beard, Thomas Reinhold, and Thomas Lowe were the male soloists. Handel himself directed the performance, and Matthew Dubourg led the orchestra. As the glorious strains of the "Hallelujah Chorus" burst upon the awed assemblage, thick-witted George II found himself so deeply affected by Handel's music (or so eager to shift his position) that he started to his feet with all the spontaneous verve a sixty-year-old gout-ridden monarch could muster. Instantly his phlegmatic courtiers also rose, and since no Englishman may remain seated while his King is standing, the audience at once followed suit, thus inaugurating a custom which persists to the present day. Actually the King's gesture was more a tribute to Handel's impressive music than an instance of exceptional religious devotion, for such words had often been set to music before, but such elevated strains had seldom (if ever) been previously heard at Covent Garden Theatre. Nineteenth-century devotionists preferred to attribute the custom of standing during the "Hallelujah Chorus" to "the decency of a reverent people," but even during the eighteenth century Dr. James Beattie observed more truly that the "fashion" was due rather to George II's sudden impulse at the first London performance:

When Handel's Messiah was first performed [in London], the audience were exceedingly struck and affected by the music in general; but when that chorus struck up, For the Lord God

Omnipotent reigneth, they were so transported, that they all, together with the King (who happened to be present), started up, and remained standing till the chorus ended; and hence it became the fashion in England for the audience to stand while that part of the music is performing.[8]

It is a curious indication of public taste that this casual eighteenth-century "fashion" has remained for two centuries an inviolable tradition both in England and in America. Even today thousands who can scarcely distinguish F sharp from middle C punctiliously observe a custom established by a stupid Hanoverian king and his worldly court two hundred years ago.

Despite the King's presence, however, *Messiah* fell so flat that Handel was forced after three performances to withdraw his "sacred oratorio" amid a storm of disapprobation. The masterpiece that fills every concert hall and every church at which it is now performed was heard with chilling apathy and stolid indifference during its first season in England. Genuine lovers of music could scarcely have failed to mark its beauties, but those few Handelians were powerless to withstand the combined forces of bigotry and frivolity. Noblemen censured *A Sacred Oratorio* as dull, and clergymen condemned it as

---

[8] Sir William Forbes, *An Account of the Life and Writings of James Beattie, LL.D.*, London, 1824, II, 61–62. James Cradock, *Literary and Miscellaneous Memoirs*, London, 1828, I, 124, perpetuated an absurd legend concerning the first London performance of *Messiah:* "The Oratorio was soon afterwards brought out in London, and the grand Hallelujah Chorus was intended for the conclusion, but finding that the second act hung heavily, and that some disappointment began to be expressed, Handel instantly rushed forwards, and commanded the last chorus to be then performed. This was most triumphantly encored, and this expedient completely saved that inspired Oratorio." Cradock's anecdote is sensational and dramatic but little more. Any audience which felt that the "second act" of *Messiah* "hung heavily" would hardly be overwhelmed even by the "Hallelujah Chorus." Furthermore, this "grand chorus" has never occupied any other position in *Messiah* than that which it now holds. Even in the original manuscript the "Hallelujah Chorus" closes Part II, and the "Amen" terminates the oratorio. Cradock was born in 1742 and thus spoke only from oral tradition gathered in "early youth." His preposterous story is characteristic of many apocryphal anecdotes manufactured and disseminated by nineteenth-century Handelians.

irreligious. Most Londoners thought nothing of the matter. In 1743 formal dramatic criticism was still rare, and few notices of *Messiah* appeared in contemporary London journals. The composer is said to have refused indignantly Walsh's derisive offer of twenty guineas for the full score. Clerical opposition proved so strong that the name of Handel's masterpiece first appeared on a London playbill only as late as 1749. For six years he was permitted to advertise and perform *Messiah* under no other title than *A Sacred Oratorio,* and even during that interval the work was but rarely sung.[9] After 1743 *Messiah* was not heard in London again till the spring of 1745, when it was twice performed at Covent Garden before frigid audiences. Thenceforth the oratorio was heard no more till 23 March 1749.

Such prolonged suspension and such infrequent performances indicate incredible coolness on the part of eighteenth-century English audiences. "Nothing can account for a circumstance so discreditable to the musical taste of England," wrote George Hogarth a century later, "but the supposition that the spirit of factious hostility, against which Handel had struggled so long, was still alive." According to Lord Shaftesbury *Messiah* was indifferently relished, "partly from the scruples some persons had entertained against carrying on such a performance in a Play-House, and partly for not entering into the genius of the composition." In 1743 oratorio was

---

[9] Handel's original title was not absolutely unknown during those six years (1743–1749) when *Messiah* was announced simply as *A Sacred Oratorio*. A notice in *The London Daily Post* on 12 December 1743 advertised publication of "Six overtures from the Operas and Oratorio's of Sampson, Messia, Saul, Deidamia, Hymen, Parnasso." On 10 March 1744 Mrs. Delany reported from London that "The oratorios fill very well, notwithstanding the spite of the opera party: nine of the twelve are over. Joseph is to be performed (I hope) once more, then Saul, and the Messiah finishes." On March 14 she heard *Joseph:* " 'Twas the last night, and I think I prefer it to every thing he has made, except the Messiah." But on March 21 "the last night of the oratorio" was "concluded with Saul: I was in hopes of the Messiah." Evidently Mrs. Delany had heard *Messiah* in London in March 1743. On 2 May 1745 *The General Advertiser* announced publication of *An Ode to Mr. Handel,* in which a footnote explained that lines 101–128 allude to "the sacred Oratorio of *Messiah*."

still a comparative novelty; as late as 1760 Mainwaring declared its style "little suited as yet to the apprehensions of the generality." Handel's audience preferred the sonorous dignity of the *Dettingen Te Deum* and the glittering pageantry of *Alexander's Feast* to the more sober attractions of *Messiah*. With its preponderance of choruses *Messiah* failed at first to please patrons accustomed to a much greater proportion of solos. Even *Israel in Egypt* had failed until its magnificent choruses were "intermix'd with songs," and Hawkins believed that *Messiah* won little recognition at first because "it consisted chiefly of chorus, and the airs contained in it were greatly inferior to most in his operas and former oratorios."

But perhaps it would be more just to accuse the bigots of conspiracy than the town of deficient taste. What is more difficult to overcome than the prejudice of ignorance or the spirit of misplaced zeal? During the composer's lifetime clergymen insisted that oratorios taken from sacred history should be performed in church as though they were anthems, and that any display of dramatic feeling in such compositions should be decently draped. No slander was spared. Pietists who eagerly applauded Bononcini's loose operas and thrilled to the coarse obscenities of contemporary drama branded *Messiah* as sacrilege and condemned Handel as a profane fellow to whom not even Holy Writ was sacred. "Notwithstanding the wonderful Sublimity of Mr. Handel's compositions," wrote John Lockman in his preface to *Rosalinda* (1740), "yet the Place in which oratorios are commonly performed among us and some other Circumstances must necessarily lessen the Solemnity of this Entertainment." After hearing *Messiah* at Covent Garden in 1756 Miss Catherine Talbot (an ardent Handelian) reluctantly conceded that "the playhouse is an unfit place for such a solemn performance." In 1763 the Reverend William Hanbury "was very unwilling so sacred a piece of composition as the *Messiah* should be performed in a playhouse; but it could not be avoided, for we had applied for the church, and were denied."

At a time when the ultra-religious were scandalized by association of sacred subjects with the theatre, only such "liberals" as Mrs. Delany could combine spiritual zeal with culture, and even she was at first shocked by a performance of Porpora's oratorio *David and Bathsheba* on 27 March 1734:

It is a fine solemn piece of music, but I confess I think the subject too solemn for a theatre. To have words of piety made use of *only* to introduce good music, is *reversing* what it ought to be, and most of the people that hear the oratorio make no reflection on the meaning of the words, though God is addressed in the most solemn manner.

A decade later Mrs. Delany found Handel's *Semele* "charming," but "it being a profane story D[r]. D[elany] does not think it proper for him to go; but when Joseph or Samson is performed I shall persuade him to go—you know *how much* he delights in music." Such scruples were not uncommon. For years the storm of the Church rolled over Handel's head. As late as 1775 one religious periodical published a "Letter to a Friend, on going to hear the Messiah at the Play-house," and this quaint epistle from an anonymous divine is so little known that quotation in full requires no apology:

I seemed to surprise you the other day, at my hinting to you, that I esteemed it wrong to go to the Messiah at the play-house. After I parted from you, I thought of our very short conversation on this point; and was led to imagine that it might not be unuseful, either to myself or you, if I collected my thoughts upon paper, and sent them to you.

First, I must premise, that my objections do not at all arise from any dislike of, or disapprobation I have to, *music;* it is a noble, may I not say a heavenly science? Rev. xiv. 2, 3. and has been and is, on various occasions made an handmaid to religion; therefore in itself it is not only lawful, but delightful, and one of those helps our gracious God hath afforded us, towards that elevation of soul so exquisitely described Eph. v. 19.

An emblem it is of that blessed state, where all is harmony and love, and where the jarrings of discord shall never disquiet us more: nay, farther yet, I will allow, that music, when used in subordination to the will of God, is one of those gifts which are bestowed for our lawful and innocent amusement and recreation.

Neither do I object to the piece in question, as wanting any one particular to render it the most finished exhibition of the composer's art now extant amongst us.

Where then lies my objection, since I neither object to music itself, nor this particular piece?

Again, Are not the words, the words of inspired prophets and evangelist, of *holy men of old, who spake as they were moved by the Holy Ghost?*

I answer, Yes: and here begins my ground of objection, because these sacred truths are exhibited, in their turn, with the other diversions of the town, performed by the same people, with the same intent, in the same place.

There are a certain quantity of people in the world, and those by no means the fewest, whose whole business is to drive God, and death and judgment, and heaven and hell, out of their thoughts as far as they can; and whether an obscene farce, or a fine piece of music, is going forward at the play-house, all is one to them, being diverted is all they aim at, and you will be sure to find them there. Now is this a footing to put God's word upon? to dress it up for the diversion of its despisers and revilers, to make it take its turn with the lascivious scenes of Congreve and Vanburgh, and thus prostitute its sacred and most important truths, to be the sport of a play-house auditory? Doth not this fall directly within that well-known prohibition of the Son of God, "Give not that which is holy unto the dogs, neither cast ye your pearls before swine," Matt. vii. 6. Now this is one light, as I apprehend, in which we ought to look upon the performance of the Messiah at the play-house; and if so, whoever attends upon it, is guilty of countenancing this grievous dishonour done to the Most High; the more serious and religious any person appears to be in other respects, the more doth his presence aid and abet this foul abuse of sacred things.

"O but (says one) I do not go there with any other mind but as I would go to church; I have been as devout at the Messiah as ever I was in my life." "And for my part (says another) I see no harm in its being performed in a play-house: what signifies the place?" Thus did your once gay and thoughtless friend once argue, thus did he cheat himself, even after those divine truths had in a measure been impressed upon his heart, till he was convinced, by travelling farther in the ways of God, that all this was but the wisdom from beneath, the dictates of a blind heart, inventing plausible excuses for doing its own will. It then occurred to me, that what was sacred to the cause of God, was not to be made use of as a public diversion: that what I had called and fansied to be devotion, was nothing else than my love of music, and my admiration of Mr. Handel's chorusses; that the true devotion of the heart, and the raising the animal spirits, were very different, and owing to different causes; the first is always the work of God's Spirit; the second of the spirit of delusion too often, but always, I doubt not, upon such occasions as these. Then as for the play-house, it is a place dedicated—not to God, to speak as mildly as I can; and if not dedicated to God, to what or whom is it dedicated? Sad experience shews us! One night the Lord Jesus, and his precious salvation, are blasphemed in the Minor, as well as other plays that might be named. Why is this? To get money, and to divert the town. The next night— "Behold the Lamb of God that taketh away the sins of the world," by the help of music, and an assemblage of polite company, I say, Behold the Lamb of God, set forth with just the same success—to get money and divert the town.

I believe nobody is less scrupulous than myself about forms and places; the earth is the Lord's and the fulness thereof; but still let even an heathen teach us:

Publica privatis secernere, sacra profanis.

Suppose we see an advertisement worded thus, "On Tuesday next will be exhibited, in St. Paul's church, a comedy called The Relapse, or Virtue in Danger, to which will be added The Rape of Proserpine, with the Birth and Adventures of Harlequin, with Dancing and other entertainments, as will be expressed in the Bills of the Day," should not we immediately cry out, *Monstrum horrendum!* Why so? Such an exhibition at Covent-garden play-house excites no amazement—It is clear, then, the difference of *place* is *all* in this matter. Well then; suppose we say, that "On Friday next will be exhibited, for the Entertainment of the Town, at the Theatre Royal in Covent-garden, the Birth, Life, Miracles, Sufferings, and Death of Jesus the Son of God, set to Music by Mr. Handel, together with a Solo on the Violin by Signor Giardini, and a Concerto on the Organ by Mr. Stanley;" —*an sunt christianis haec auribus consentanea?* especially if we add "Orange wenches and whores ready as usual;" which is no more than real fact, at every performance of this sacred piece: neither have the concertoes of the above eminent masters any more to do with it than rope-dancing or tumbling. Now can a man say that this is an assembly fit for a christian? or is the theatre any more calculated for the Messiah, than St. Paul's church is for the entertainments above-mentioned? What reason can be given for the impropriety of the one, that does not equally affect the other?

The first thing that made the performance of the Messiah, as a public diversion, strike me as a very wrong thing, and convinced me of the spirit with which people attend it, was, seeing an advertisement of its being performed somewhere (at Gloucester I believe); the tickets were to be five shillings each: and then came this N.B. "The same Ticket will admit one Gentleman or two Ladies to the Ball at night;" so that I perceived the same spirit carried them to both, as well as the same ticket; and that the intent of the performers of the Messiah, and that of the fiddlers at the ball, was just the same; to get money, by diverting so many people.

But to return to the question about the play-house: Suppose king Lear, instead of his solemn prayer to the goddess Nature, should be thought to verge too much upon paganism; and Mr. Garrick, in order to christianize the character, should make him kneel down, and say the Lord's prayer; *Risum teneatis?* would be too ludicrous a question to ask on such an occasion: the utmost abhorrence would surely be excited, and even the world cry out Shame! for which the impropriety of the place would certainly be assigned, as one grand reason: but what would my friend think of a person who attended upon this, and defended his doing so, by saying, He had no notion about place, and that he had as much devotion there as any-where else?

An commota crimine mentis
Absolves hominem?

Again: Let us suppose, by way of diversion, the communion-service set to music, and exhibited at the play-house, and, during Lent, taking its turn with Love-a-la-mode, to fill Mr. Garrick's house; notwithstanding the audience should stand up at the more particular striking parts of it, as they do at some of the chorusses in the Messiah; would not this be reckoned a most unfit entertainment for a theatre? yet is there not one single sentiment throughout the whole, that is not grounded upon the very scriptures of which the Messiah is composed; if so, this proves the representation of the Messiah equally improper. To shew the force of this, I will relate a fact.

A certain lady of fashion went to the Messiah, and, I must tell you, a person too of no sort of real seriousness: she observed the audience stand up at the chorus at the end of the second part. This struck her with what she had not thought of before, that there was something very particular, to be sure, in the words; she took up her book, and looked at them, and upon considering them and the place she was in, together with the purpose of her being there, she was so filled with horror, that she trembled from head to foot, at the thoughts of its being possible for people to make those solemn and awful words a subject-matter for public diversion at a play-house; and I do believe the whole world would not get her there again.

And now let me recommend what has been said to the candour of my amiable and much-loved friend, who knows I can have no view in thus laying my thoughts before him, but an honest and serious endeavour after the glory of our great and holy Messiah; in convincing my friend of a thing so wrong in every point of view, not only in those already observed upon, but many others that might be named.[10]

IV

If rigid churchmen observed in Handel's *Messiah* the taint of blasphemy a few enlightened Englishmen nevertheless hailed the oratorio as a masterpiece in Christian thought. Eighteenth-century religious liberals frequently attacked those false devotees who saw indecorum in the union of a sacred theme with the music of a master. As early as 31 March 1743 several verses in *The Daily Advertiser* came to Handel's defense in reply to hostile strictures against *Messiah* published in *The Universal Spectator* on March 19:

Wrote extempore by a gentleman, on reading the *Universal Spectator,* on Mr. Handel's new Oratorio, perform'd at the Theatre Royal in Covent-Garden.

---

[10] *The Gospel Magazine; or, Treasury of Divine Knowledge,* II, 67–72 (February 1775). The letter is dated 13 March 1761. For a thorough analysis of clerical objections to Handel's oratorios in eighteenth-century England, see my former study, *Early Moral Criticism of Handelian Oratorio,* Williamsburg, 1947.

> Cease, Zealots, cease to blame these Heav'nly Lays,
> For Seraphs fit to sing Messiah's Praise!
> Nor, for your trivial argument, assign,
> "The Theatre not fit for praise Divine,"
> These hallow'd Lays to Musick give new Grace,
> To Virtue Awe, and sanctify the Place.
> To Harmony, like his, Celestial Pow'r is giv'n,
> T' exalt the Soul from Earth, and make, of Hell, a Heav'n.

Perhaps the "gentleman" who "wrote extempore" upon "Mr. Handel's new oratorio" was the composer's loyal friend and librettist Charles Jennens. The rhyme forms part of the notice of Handel's last performance for that season, and probably the composer (who managed his own concerts) inserted the lines as part of his advertisement.

During the next few years other Handelians united to corroborate the "gentleman" who defended the "Heav'nly Lays" of Handel's "hallow'd" *Messiah*. Already an article on *Israel in Egypt* in *The London Daily Post* for 1 April 1740 had emphatically opposed "the stupid senseless *Exceptions* that have been taken to so truly religious Representations as *this,* in particular, and the other *Oratorios*" from the place in which they were performed:

The Theatre, on this Occasion, ought to be enter'd with more solemnity than a Church; inasmuch as the Entertainment you go to is really in itself the noblest Adoration and Homage paid to the Deity that ever was in one. So sublime an Act of Devotion as this *Representation* carries in it, to a Heart and Ear duly tuned for it, would consecrate even Hell itself—It is the Action that is done in it that hallows the Place, and not the Place the Action.

In her *Epistles for the Ladies* (1749) Eliza Heywood devoted her most ponderous phrases to reflections upon "The Power of Divine Music." At a performance of "Mr. *Handel*'s fine Oratorio of *Joshua*" she found herself "transported into the most divine Extasy," even though "the Words were not quite so elegant, nor so well as I could have wished adapted" to the music:

I closed my Eyes, and imagined myself amidst the angelic Choir in the bright Regions of everlasting Day, chanting the Praises of my great Creator, and his ineffable *Messiah*.—I seemed, methought, to have nothing of this gross Earth about me, but was all Soul!—all Spirit!

I cannot help thinking, but that Entertainments of this Nature frequently exhibited, would have an Effect over the most obdurate Minds, and go a great Way in reforming an Age, which seems to be degenerating equally into an Irreverence for the Deity, and a Brutality of Behavior to each other; but as this Depravity of Taste, of Principles, and Manners, has spread itself from *London* even to the remotest Parts of this Island, I should be glad there were *Oratorios* established in every City and great Town throughout the Kingdom; but even then, to be of general Service, they ought to be given *gratis,* and all Degrees of People allowed to partake of them, otherwise it is but an inconsiderable Number, in comparison with the whole, whose Fortunes would admit of their being improved this Way.

Although she admittedly possessed "no ear for music, and no skill in it" Catherine Talbot remained for twenty years one of Handel's staunch supporters, and she frequently heard his oratorios performed both in London and at Oxford. "What in the compass of imagination," she once asked, "can be so fine as cathedral or oratorio music, where every power of harmony is exerted to express sentiments the most exalted, and affections the most just and noble." In speaking of a performance of *Judas Maccabeus* at which Handel had "literally introduced guns" she declared that "Those oratorios of Handel's are certainly (next to the *hooting of owls*) the most solemnly striking music one can hear." On 27 December 1743 she recorded great satisfaction at an Oxford performance of *Samson*:

I will own the having been highly delighted with several songs in Sampson, and especially with the choruses. I heard that oratorio performed this winter in one of the College Halls, and I believe to the full as finely as it ever was in town: and having never heard any oratorio before, I was extremely struck with such a kind of harmony as seems the only language adapted to devotion. I really cannot help thinking this kind of entertainment must necessarily have some effect in correcting or moderating at least the levity of the age; and let an audience be ever so thoughtless, they can scarcely come away, I should think, without being the better for an evening so spent.

Miss Talbot's favorite oratorio was *Messiah*. Her account of a Covent Garden performance in April 1756 proved how sure was the opinion of Handel's faithful minority:

The only public place I have been to this winter was last Friday to hear the Messiah, nor can there be a nobler entertainment. I think it is impossible for the most trifling not to be the better for it. I was wishing all the Jews, Heathens, and Infidels in the world (a pretty full house you'll say) to be present. The Morocco ambassador was there, and if his interpreter could do justice to the divine words (the music any one that has a heart must feel) how must he be affected, when in the grand choruses the whole audience solemnly rose up in joint acknowledgement, that He for our sakes *had been despised and rejected of men*, was, *their Creator, Redeemer, King of kings, Lord of lords!* To be sure, the playhouse is an unfit place for such a solemn performance, but I fear I shall be in Oxfordshire before it is to be heard at the Foundling Hospital, where the benevolent design and the attendance of the little boys and girls, adds a peculiar beauty even to this noblest composition.

Another loyal Handelian was Ann Granville Dewes, whose elder brother (Bernard Granville) was an ardent patron of Handel and apparently one of the composer's most devoted friends. To Mrs. Dewes oratorio represented supreme musical art. Apologizing for being an "enthusiast" in an age of discipline and decorum, she wrote to her brother on 3 December 1750 criticizing "those people who have not felt the pleasure of devotion" at Handel's *Messiah*:

I hope you find Mr. Handel well. I beg my compliments to him: he has not a more real admirer of his great work than myself; his wonderful Messiah will never be out of my head; and I may say *my heart* was raised almost to heaven by it. It is only those people who have not felt the pleasure of devotion that can make any objection to that performance, which is calculated to raise our devotion, and make us truly sensible of the power of the divine words he has chose beyond any human work that ever yet appeared, and I am sure I may venture to say ever will. If anything can give us an idea of the Last Day it must be that part—"The trumpet shall sound, the dead shall be raised." It is few people I can say so much to as this, for they would call me an enthusiast; but when I wish to raise my thoughts above this world and all its trifling concerns, I look over what oratorios I have, and even my poor way of fumbling gives me pleasing recollections, but I have nothing of the Messiah, but *He was despised,* &c.

It is notable that from the beginning John Wesley held Handel's *Messiah* in high respect. On 29 August 1762 he recorded in his *Journal* that the music at Exeter Cathedral even "exceeded the *Messiah* itself." In August 1758 he had heard *Messiah* at Bristol: "I doubt if that congregation was ever so serious at a sermon," he wrote, "as they were during this performance. In many parts, especially several of the choruses, it exceeded my expectation."

Notwithstanding the endorsement of John Wesley and others, however, clerical condemnation seriously delayed the success of *Messiah* for almost a decade. Frequently Fortune is in no hurry to array herself on the side of merit. In Handel's case no master-mind invested with the authority of patronage and fashion pioneered in praising *Messiah* or in proclaiming its worth to a fickle public. Shortsighted British aristocrats had never forgiven Handel for refusing further to indulge the caprices of Senesino:

It would remain a perpetual stigma on the taste of the nation [wrote Dr. Burney], if it should be recorded, that his MESSIAH, that truly noble and sublime work, was not only ill-attended, but ill-received, on its first performance . . . , were its miscarriage not to be wholly ascribed to the resentment of the many great personages whom he had offended, in refusing to compose for Senesino, by whom he thought himself affronted; or even for the Opera, unless that singer were dismissed; which inflexibility being construed into insolence, was the cause of powerful oppositions that were at once oppressive and mortifying.

England's early rejection of *Messiah* may thus be ascribed as much to personal resentment as to shallow musical taste. In Handel's day music was still enslaved by the degrading system of patronage, and most composers languished in a slough of flunkeydom. But Handel flaunted his independence and moved with resolute determination, snapping his fingers in the face of princely patrons and daring to defy the bluest blood in England. What was to be done with this insufferable German upstart, this mere musician, who despite persistent opposition succeeded in discharging his debts to the uttermost farthing? Chosen leaders of British "quality" resolved to crush Handel at once. They devised a systematic campaign to boycott his oratorios, and no scheme proved too petty for the gratification of their spite.

Not content with open competition of theatre against theatre, Handel's opponents stooped to the meanest devices to secure his failure. As early as 1741 the fashionable cabal actually hired little street arabs to tear down advertisements Handel had posted about London. A letter in *The London Daily Post* of 4 April 1741 deplored the ignominious conduct of "those little vermin" who "pull down even his bills as fast as he has put them up, and use a thousand other little acts to injure and distress him." Women led the crusade. In order to rob Handel of his audiences aristocratic ladies carefully scheduled private concerts and balls on oratorio nights, and the composer's known friends did not fail to receive invitations. At Lady Godolphin's town house regular sets were made up to play cards during Handel's performances, and a certain Lady Brown (otherwise unknown to history) was damned to permanent fame by Dr. Burney for having "distinguished herself as a persevering enemy to Handel." That empress of fashion was one of the first "who had the courage, at the risk of her windows, to have concerts of a Sunday Evening," and Mainwaring wrote that she "exerted all her influence to spirit up a new opposition" against the composer. When lovely woman stoops to folly even the sanctity of Lent remains no longer inviolable. In 1745 Lady Brown and her wealthy friends actually subsidized a poor mimic named Russell to set up a puppet-show in opposition to Handel's oratorios, but after that wretch had served their wanton purpose the callous ladies allowed him to be thrown into Newgate for debts contracted in their service. In polite circles it soon became a sign of good taste to ridicule Handel's oratorios, and whoever refused to renounce the composer could expect no favors from the aristocracy. To this foolish mania Fielding alluded in *Tom Jones* (1749):

> It was Mr. *Western*'s Custom every Afternoon, as soon as he was drunk, to hear his Daughter play on the Harpsichord: for he was a great Lover of Music, and perhaps, had he lived in Town, might have passed for a Connoisseur: for he always excepted against the finest Compositions of Mr. *Handel*. He never relished any Music but what was light and airy; and indeed his most favourite Tunes, were *Old Sir* Simon *the King, St.* George *he was for* England, *Bobbing* Joan, and some others.

Although Sophia Western was "a perfect Mistress of Music, and would never willingly have played any but *Handel*'s," she was "so devoted to her Father's Pleasure, that she learnt all those Tunes to oblige him." But if Handel's music pleased the daughter of Squire Western it failed to soothe the savage breast of Horace Walpole. During Handel's bitter struggles over *Messiah* that supercilious dilettante derived keen satisfaction from attending Italian opera on oratorio nights. "I have not only very little music in me," he proudly declared, "but the company I keep are far from Handelians." With characteristic hauteur Walpole recommended his brother in 1745 as "perfectly master of all the quarrels that have been fashionably on foot about Handel." Inability to appreciate the German composer was indeed hardly confined to peers and peeresses. Distinguished men of letters frequently ridiculed him, and even Pope's splendid tribute in *The Dunciad* was not inspired by direct admiration. One evening Horace Walpole is said to have met Lord Chesterfield leaving Covent Garden Theatre at an early hour.

"What, my Lord!" exclaimed Walpole. "Are you dismissed? Is there no oratorio this evening?"

"Yes," Lord Chesterfield replied, "they are still performing. But I thought it best to retire, lest I disturb the King in his privacy."

After a persistent campaign Handel's opponents managed to contrive that his oratorios were performed to empty chairs. From Mrs. Delany's correspondence it is clear that even those few who did attend Handel's performances were not always peacefully disposed. "There was no disturbance at the playhouse," she observed after a performance of *Semele* on 10 February 1744, "and the Goths were not so very absurd as to declare, in a public manner, their disapprobation of such a composer." On February 21 she explained that *Semele* "has a strong party against it, viz. the fine ladies, petit maitres, and *ignoramus's*. All the opera people are enraged at Handel, but Lady Cobham, Lady Westmoreland and Lady Chesterfield never fail it." By systematically organizing brilliant festivities in opposition to Handel's oratorios London's polite world drove the composer into temporary bankruptcy in 1745. His houses grew so "thin" that he was unable to meet expenses, and for the second time in his career he was forced to suspend payment. A few loyal friends, however, induced him to continue the 1744-1745 season long enough to perform sixteen of the proposed twenty-four concerts. *A Sacred Oratorio* was heard on April 9 and 11. On May 2 *The General Advertiser* announced publication of *An Ode to Mr. Handel,* an anonymous poem eulogizing the composer's "sacred" works and offering several stanzas in praise of *Messiah*:

> Tremendous theme of song! the theme of love
> And melting mercy HE, when sung to strains,

> Which from prophetic lips
> Touch'd with ethereal fire,
> Breath'd balmy Peace, yet breathing in the charm
> Of healing sounds; fit prelude to the pomp
> Of choral energy,
> Whose lofty accents rise
>
> To speak MESSIAH's names; the God of Might,
> The Wond'rous and the Wise—the Prince of Peace.
> Him, feeder of the flock
> And leader of the lambs,
>
> The tuneful tenderness of trilling notes
> Symphonious speaks: Him pious pity paints
> In mournful melody
> The man of sorrows; grief
>
> Sits heavy on his soul, and bitterness
> Fills deep his deadly draught——He deigns to die——
> The God who conquers Death,
> When, bursting from the Grave,
>
> Mighty he mounts, and wing'd with rapid winds,
> Thro' Heav'ns wide portals opening to their Lord,
> To boundless realms return'd,
> The King of Glory reigns.
>
> Pow'rs, dominations, thrones resound HE REIGNS,
> High Hallelujahs of empyreal hosts,
> And pealing Praises join
> The thunder of the spheres.

One cannot fully comprehend the fierce conflicts through which Handel was forced to struggle, nor the bitter failure of *Messiah* during its first six years in London, without some knowledge of English social conditions throughout the era of the first two Georges. Among the numerous excellences of England's Augustan period spiritual fervor has never been reckoned. All historians agree that during the second quarter of the eighteenth century the moral tone of English society had sunk to new depths of depravity. If the tiny clique of nobles intimately connected with the court appeared less dissolute than their grandfathers of the Restoration period seventy-five years before, their manners were more vulgar and their tastes were less refined. A sodden coarseness permeated England's "best society." Under its thin veneer of courtly polish London's fashionable world proved haughty, unscrupulous, and even cruel. Stolid George II united the morals of a rake with the manners of a boor, and his sole claim to artistic distinction lay in his steady patronage of Handel's music. Queen Caroline displayed great native force of character, but she made her husband's gross vices the theme of broad jests and seldom remained in her drawing-room half an hour without shocking her ladies. Prime Minister Robert Walpole, whose tastes never rose above the stable and the cockpit, lived in open adultery throughout most of his public career and scandalized even that profligate age by the bacchanalian orgies of his country seat at Houghton. A period of commercial prosperity only reinforced those ostentatious vices which accompany sudden increase in national wealth, and "polite" amusements displayed a flagrant extravagance untempered either by taste or by religion. Cards were the common form of entertainment, and stakes were high. Drama consisted chiefly of gaudy spectacles and lewd farces, while music languished under the patronage of a shallow taste. The audience that rose to its feet to honor the sublime strains of Handel's *Messiah* was the same audience that had guffawed over the jocularities of *The Beggar's Opera* fifteen years before. Public manners were openly lax, and in high places reverence was almost nonexistent. Drunkenness was scarcely a matter of reproach, and profanity issued unabashed from the lips of fine ladies. A fatuous church still awaited the rousing blows of John Wesley and George Whitefield. If religion was preached in the pulpit it was seldom practiced in the parsonage, and sporting Anglican clergymen were sometimes hardly to be distinguished in character from their least devout parishioners. From concurrent testimony of history and literature it is clear that England's "aristocracy" had never before shown less refinement or purity than at just the moment when Handel composed his *Messiah* and John Wesley commenced his epoch-making work of reform. For such an age *A Sacred Oratorio* held little appeal. Handel's inspirations lay outside the rut of mid-eighteenth-century theological comprehension. It is astonishing that during the century of Voltaire and Swift Handel could conceive works whose grandeur has seldom been surpassed. And it is no less amazing that at the moment when Pope was polishing his most finished satires Handel was offering Englishmen music which for sublimity has scarcely been paralleled in literature since *Paradise Lost.*

IV

The Glass of Fashion

And now the Chapel's silver bell you hear
That summons you to all the Pride of Pray'r:
Light quirks of Music, broken and uneven,
Make the soul dance upon a Jig to Heav'n.
— ALEXANDER POPE, *Of Taste* (1731)

I

ON 17 OCTOBER 1739 Captain Thomas Coram, a retired seaman, secured a royal charter incorporating the London Foundling Hospital "for the reception, maintenance, and education of exposed and deserted young children." Less than two years later the "Governors and Guardians" of the Hospital opened a house in Hatton Garden on 25 March 1741. From the beginning this noble charity was entirely free, and all foundlings were admitted indiscriminately. Any person bringing a child rang a bell at the Hospital gate, deposited the foundling in a basket hung at an inner door, and waited to hear whether the infant was accepted at once or returned as diseased. No question whatever was asked about the child's parentage or background. When the full quota of children had been admitted a notice was affixed to the door stating that "The House is Full." Frequently as many as one hundred children were offered when only twenty could be received, and after several serious riots the women were required to ballot for admission by drawing balls from a bag. At length the Foundling Hospital outgrew its temporary home, and donations were accepted to meet its enormously increased expenses. More spacious accommodations were erected on a spot then known as Lamb's-Conduit-Fields, and on 19 January 1750 the new institution was formally opened with six hundred children. By then the Hospital had become a fashionable London charity. Its celebrated patrons numbered eminent painters and musicians as well as the King and the Prince of Wales. One of the earliest "Governors and Guardians" was William Hogarth, whose admirable full-length portrait of his friend Captain Coram remained for years a precious heirloom of the foundation. The Hospital's valuable collection of paintings also included works by Allan Ramsay, Sir Godfrey Kneller, Sir Joshua Reynolds, and Thomas Gainsborough. Public exhibition of these gifts attracted hosts of spectators each day, and a visit to "the Foundling" soon became a popular morning excursion.

In 1747 a Chapel was designed for the Foundling Hospital by Theodore Jacobson, and George II contributed no less than three thousand pounds toward its immediate construction. Two years later Handel himself followed suit by presenting the Chapel with an excellent new organ built by Richard Parker. On 4 May 1749 the composer attended a meeting of the Foundling Hospital Committee and there proposed a concert of "vocal and instrumental musick," offering to apply all proceeds toward completing the Chapel. Handel's generous act was not unwelcome. He was immediately enrolled as one of the Governors and Guardians of the Hospital, and on May 27 the promised performance took place. Expressly for the occasion he composed his excellent Foundling Anthem upon the words "Blessed are they that consider the poor." This concert marked the beginning of Handel's rich patronage of the Foundling Hospital, and at the composer's suggestion musical performances eventually became a source of great profit to the Hospital funds. From the Minutes of the institution it emerges that the Foundling Committee resolved on 7 February 1750 "That the Secretary do wait upon Mr. Handel to propose a performance of

SOUTH VIEW OF THE LONDON FOUNDLING HOSPITAL (1748)
From an Engraving in *The Gentleman's Magazine* (September 1748)

musick and voices on Tuesday, the first of May next." Evidently Handel agreed to the proposal with characteristic benevolence, for the Minutes of 18 April 1750 contain the following entry:

The Secretary acquainted the Committee that Mr. Handel had agreed to the following Advertizement to be published for his intended Performance.

"Hospital for the Maintenance and Education of Exposed and Deserted Young Children in Lamb's Conduit Fields April 18th, 1750.

"George Frederick Handel Esq. having presented this Hospital with a very fine Organ for the Chapel thereof, and repeated his offer of assistance to promote this Charity; on Tuesday the First Day of May 1750 at Twelve o'clock at noon, Mr. Handel will open the said Organ; and the sacred Oratorio called 'Messiah' will be performed under his direction.

"Tickets for this performance are ready to be delivered by the Steward at the Hospital, at Batson's Coffee-House in Cornhill, and White's Chocolate House in St. James's Street, at half a Guinea each."

Ordered—That the said Advertizement be published in the Daily Advertizer, on Friday next, and every day after to Tuesday the first of May; Twice a week in the General Advertizer, twice a week in the Gazetteer, and twice a week in some evening papers.

On April 20 the "Advertizement" duly appeared with the significant addition that "There will be no collection."

Handel accordingly "opened the Organ" at the Foundling Chapel with a rendition of *Messiah* on 1 May 1750. It was the first popular performance of his "sacred oratorio" in England. During the morning London's polite world, never slow to support fashionable charity, flocked to Lamb's-Conduit-Fields *en masse,* and the Reverend William Stukeley observed "An infinite croud of coaches at our end of the town to hear Handel's music at the opening of the Chapel of the Foundling." Although the Chapel could accommodate a thousand persons "with full ease," the crush was so terrible that dozens of "Nobility and Gentry" were rejected at the doors. Distinguished persons who had failed to purchase tickets in advance drove to the Chapel expecting to secure seats with little difficulty. Could munificent subscribers to the Hospital funds be denied admittance? In haphazard fashion all vacant seats were quickly resold to persons on hand, so that later the original owners were turned away for want of room. Despite this confusion, however, *The Gentleman's Magazine* "computed" that "upwards of 1200 persons of distinction" heard Handel's performance of *Messiah* that day. The net proceeds amounted to no less than £728. "I am glad the Foundling Hospital was so full, and carried on with such decency," wrote Mrs. Delany to her brother on June 17; "I am sure it pleased our friend Handel, and I love to have him pleased." But the composer could scarcely have been pleased with the slipshod manner of collection, for he had never yet issued tickets which he had not sooner or later honored. On the following day he attended a meeting of the Foundling Hospital Committee and offered to give a second performance of *Messiah* two weeks later. Accordingly *The General Advertiser* published a detailed notice on May 4:

A computation was made of what number of persons the Chapel of the Hospital would conveniently hold, and no greater Number of Tickets were delivered to hear the Performance there on the First instant. But so many Persons of Distinction coming unprovided with tickets and pressing to pay for tickets, caused a greater number to be admitted than were expected; and some that had tickets not finding room going away. To prevent disappointment to such persons, and for the further promotion of this charity, this is to give notice that George Frederick Handel, Esq; has generously offered that the sacred oratorio called "Messiah" shall be performed again under his direction, in the chapel of this Hospital, on Tuesday the 15th instant, at twelve of the clock at noon; and the tickets delivered out, and not brought in on the 1st instant, will then be received.

NOTE.—There will be no collection; and it is hoped, that no Person will take it ill, that they cannot be admitted without Tickets.

On May 15 Handel's crowded audience nearly doubled the charitable sum derived from the first performance two weeks before.

After "opening" the organ at the Foundling Chapel Handel continued to give at least one annual performance of *Messiah* for the benefit of the Hospital until his death in 1759. On 18 April 1751 *Messiah* was performed for the third time at the Chapel "under the direction of George Frederick Handel, Esq; who played a voluntary upon the organ" before "a great appearance of persons of distinction." *The London Magazine* reported that tickets were "delivered out" to the sum of £600. Ladies of quality appeared "in small Hoops" and gentlemen of fashion came "without Swords" in order "to make their Seats more convenient to themselves." Handel's success was so great that "at the request of several persons of distinction" he agreed to repeat *Messiah* on May 16, when his "voluntary" upon the organ "met with universal applause" from "a very numerous and splendid audience." According to *The Gentleman's Magazine* "there were above 500 coaches besides chairs, &c. and the tickets amounted to over 700 guineas." For the fifth performance on 9 April 1752 "the number of tickets given out was 1200" (each at half a guinea), and the Minutes of the Hospital Committee reported "a most noble and grand audience, who expressed the greatest satisfaction at the exquisiteness of the composition, the completeness of the performance, and the great benevolence of Mr. Handel." In that "noble and grand audience" sat Miss Catherine Talbot and her mother: "I had vast pleasure," she wrote on April 22, "in carrying my mother this year, for the first time, to hear the Messiah, at the Foundling. She was as much charmed as I expected." At the sixth performance of *Messiah* on 1 May 1753 "the inimitable composer" of "that solemn piece of musick" conducted the oratorio and "play'd himself a voluntary on the fine organ he gave to that chapel." According to *The*

London Magazine, "there were above 800 coaches and chairs, and the tickets amounted to 925 guineas."

Year after year Handel personally superintended the annual performance of *Messiah* for the benefit of the Foundling Hospital. In 1751 his sight began to fail, and by 1753 he had become totally blind, but he still remained faithful to his original intention, and each year he performed an organ concerto according to his usual custom. From 1754 to 1758 he conducted five more performances of *Messiah,* making a total of eleven presentations for the benefit of the Hospital funds. At a *Messiah* performance on 2 May 1754 Mrs. Delany reported that "the music was *too fine,* I never heard it so well performed. The chapel is fine, and the sight of so many poor children brought up (I hope to good purpose), was a pleasant sight." Two years later Miss Talbot regretted that she would be in Oxfordshire before *Messiah* was heard at the Foundling Hospital, "where the benevolent design and the attendance of the little boys and girls, add a peculiar beauty even to this noblest composition." On 7 April 1756 the Foundling Committee scheduled Handel's regular performance of *Messiah* for May 19:

Mr. Handel having renewed his charitable offer of performing the Oratorio "Messiah" at the Chapel of this Hospital,

Resolved—That the said performance be on Wednesday, the 19th of next Month, and that the Secretary do write a letter to Mr. Handel to return him Thanks and acquaint him with the Day fix'd upon, and to desire that he will please to give people Directions to Mr. Smith the Organist of this Hospital, in relation thereto.

Eventually *Messiah* came to be so identified with the Foundling Hospital that the Governors even sought to secure the copyright. In a codicil to Handel's will dated 4 August 1757 the composer bequeathed "a fair copy of the score, and all parts of my oratorio called the *Messiah* to the Foundling

Hospital."[1] Apparently Handel's generous provision became prematurely known, for the Governors misconstrued the nature of his gift and assumed that they were to hold forever the exclusive privilege of performance. With a wonderful degree of ignorance the Foundling Committee promptly prepared a petition by which to secure from Parliament all legal rights in *Messiah*. The document concluded

That in order to raise a further sum for the benefit of the said Charity, George Frederick Handel, Esq; hath been charitably pleased to give to this corporation a composition of music, called "the Oratorio of the Messiah," composed by him the said George Frederick Handel, reserving to himself the liberty only of performing the same for his own benefit during his life: and whereas the said benefaction cannot be secured to the sole use of your petitioners except by the authority of Parliament, your petitioners, therefore, humbly pray, that leave may be given to bring in a bill for the purposes aforesaid.

When one of the Governors submitted this petition to Handel he discovered at once that the Committee had built upon a false foundation, for the choleric composer had scarcely read the document before he burst into rage. "Te Deivel!" he exclaimed in tones worthy of his own Polyphemus. "For vat sal de Foundling put mein oratorio in de Parlement! Te Deivel! mein moosic sal not go to de Parlement!" Instead of recording this explosion of unparliamentary language the Minutes of the Hospital Committee state more temperately that "the same did not seem agreeable to Mr. Handel for the present." Here the matter dropped, never to be revived. With Handel's full concurrence, however, the Governors appointed his factotum, John Christopher Smith, first organist of the Chapel.

---

[1] The Foundling score of *Messiah* has been carefully preserved in three oblong volumes penned by John Christopher Smith. Handel's instrumental parts were forgotten or overlooked until 1894, when H. Davan Wetton (organist of the Foundling Hospital) discovered them by accident in an old cupboard near the organ, where they had probably lain undisturbed and unknown for over a century.

Under Handel's superintendence *Messiah* continued to draw crowded audiences to the Foundling Hospital each year. Since the composer's musicians generally contributed their assistance gratis, considerable profits accrued to the charity with each presentation. Aside from the Foundling Anthem in 1749 Handel's eleven performances of *Messiah* at the Foundling Chapel added £6935 to the Hospital funds, and following his death subsequent renditions of his "sacred oratorio" swelled the composer's total benefaction to £10,299. From 1760 to 1768 John Christopher Smith conducted eight performances of *Messiah*, which benefited the institution to the amount of £1332, and from 1769 to 1777 nine performances under the direction of John Stanley (the celebrated blind organist) brought the Hospital treasury no less a sum than £2032. For several years annual performances of *Messiah* were also heard for the benefit of Westminster Infirmary and Brownlow-Street Lying-in Hospital. All over England Handel's *magnum opus* supported life and relieved suffering through its regular performances for charitable purposes. In 1821 a rendition in Westminster Abbey secured sufficient funds to rebuild Westminster Infirmary, which had been established in 1719 "for the relief of the sick and needy in all parts of the world." Throughout the Victorian period *Messiah* was the favorite composition for public charities of all kinds, and London's Sacred Harmonic Society performed it annually for the benefit of "decayed musicians" and their distressed families. It is singularly appropriate that the composer's greatest triumph was thus dedicated to benevolent causes from its first performance. As if designed to illustrate all of Handel's excellences, *Messiah* has (in the words of Dr. Burney) "fed the hungry, clothed the naked, fostered the orphan, and enriched succeeding managers of Oratorios, more than any single musical production in this or any country."

Like many men whom society considers bears, Handel revealed under his gruff exterior a tender and compassionate heart. All his life he preserved his connection with charitable objects. As early as 1753 William Hayes lauded the composer as the principal benefactor of the Foundling Hospital:

> As a moral, good, and charitable Man, let Infants, not only those who feel the Effects of his Bounty, but even such who are yet unborn, chaunt forth his Praise, whose annual Benefaction to an Hospital for the Maintenance of the *Forsaken, the Fatherless, and those who have none to help them,* will render HIM and his MESSIAH, truly Immortal and crowned with Glory, by the KING of KINGS and LORD of LORDS.

Messiah was heard in London only thirty-four times during the composer's lifetime, and eleven of these performances took place for the benefit of the Foundling Hospital. Handel therefore performed the oratorio only twenty-three times for his own benefit, preferring to diminish his own profits in order that the charitable institution might derive further gain from his most popular work. His act of benevolence appears ever more creditable when one observes that after 1750 *Messiah* was the sole oratorio upon which Handel could confidently depend to attract a great audience. As a permanent memorial to the composer's generosity a forgotten passageway near the Foundling Hospital to this day bears the name of Handel Street.

II

Not until the Foundling Hospital performances of 1750 did *Messiah* win any appreciable measure of acclaim from English connoisseurs. Perhaps its final triumph at Covent Garden and its enormous vogue throughout England were originally due to its close identification with that charitable institution. The composition which for seven years had suffered the scorn of indifference suddenly became London's favorite oratorio, and thenceforth, "to the honour of the public at large, and disgrace of cabal and faction," *Messiah* was heard (according to Dr. Burney) with "universal admiration and applause" by "overflowing audiences" and performed "in all parts of the kingdom with increasing reverence and delight." After 1750 *Messiah* took England by storm. The patronage of nobility and the edict of fashion conspired to make Handel's masterpiece a popular success. "His Messiah," wrote Hawkins, "was frequently performed to such audiences, as he could no otherwise accommodate than by erecting seats on the stage, to such a number as scarcely left room for the performers." Among misguided devotionists a broader spirit began to prevail, and ultimately Handel's "fine entertainment" was endorsed even by the Church. *Messiah* was slow to gain universal favor, but once it had conquered the spirit of opposition it never relaxed its firm hold upon the English heart.

By 1759 the sexagenarian was solidly planted on his feet. Thenceforth his authority in England was seldom questioned, and his fame was established firmly as a rock. To Englishmen Handel epitomized great music. Mrs. Elizabeth Carter spoke for her generation when she confessed in 1746 that "Every body I either love or admire, every conversation that struck me with peculiar pleasure, and every fine passage of a favourite author, the powerful magic of Mr. Handel conjures up to my thoughts." As early as 1744 James Harris (Earl of Malmesbury) placed Handel at the head of the "great Professors" of music, and in his treatise "Concerning Music, Painting, and Poetry" he eulogized the composer "whose Genius, having been cultivated by continued Exercise, and being itself far the sublimest and most universal now known, has justly placed him without an Equal, or a Second." In February 1755 David Garrick won the applause of all London when, in his prologue to John Christopher Smith's opera *The Fairies,* he delivered a rhymed encomium of the composer,

> Whose sacred dramas shake and melt the heart,
> Whose heaven-born strains the coldest breast inspire,
> Whose *chorus-thunder* sets the soul on fire!
> Inflam'd, astonish'd! at those magic airs,
> When *Samson* groans, and frantic *Saul* despairs.

In 1752 Charles Avison published his celebrated *Essay on Musical Expression,* in which he boldly confessed his preference for French and Italian music and frankly depreciated Handel and the Germans. Even Avison, however, was forced to acknowledge the talents of that "illustrious" composer "in whose manly Style we often find the noblest Harmonies; and these enlivened with such a Variety of Modulation, as could hardly have been expected from one who hath supplyed the Town with musical Entertainments of every Kind, for thirty Years together." During the following spring Dr. William Hayes, Professor of Music at Oxford, answered Avison in his anonymous *Remarks on Mr. Avison's Essay on Musical Expression,* in which he asserted that if Geminiani is "the *Titian* in Music" Handel is "undoubtedly the *Rubens.*" In response to Hayes' "Remarks" Avison issued in 1753 a revised and enlarged edition of his *Essay on Musical Expression,* and he proceeded to publish in the same year *A Reply to the Author of Remarks on the Essay on Musical Expression.* Throughout this pamphlet war Hayes advanced excellent arguments in praise of Handel, but Avison's work is held superior as literature.

Even more curious to the student of *Messiah* is an extremely rare volume of *Remarks upon Church Musick; to which are added Several Observations upon Some of Mr. Handel's Oratorio's, and other Parts of His Works* (1758), published in Worcester "by a Lover of Harmony." A second edition issued five years later disclosed that its author was the Reverend William Hughes, minor canon of Worcester Cathedral Church and Vicar of St. Peter's in Worcester. In his somewhat fulsome "Remarks" Hughes insisted that Handel's "Beauties" are "Numerous and Various," and he went on to explain in lavish detail why *Samson* "must always stand foremost" among the works of "that Celebrated Master" of music:

If Mr *Handel* has excell'd this Work in the *Oratorio* of the *Messiah* (as many are inclin'd to think) I must confess that I have neither Judgment or Abilities sufficient to discern it. No one will pretend to say that it is not a great Composition, but then it does not exactly follow that the Oratorio of Samson is not greater.
   Not to pass by some few of the principal Beauties in the Oratorio of the Messiah. *He was despised and rejected of Men,* &c. is a Strain truly mournful. It is almost impossible to hear it without shedding of Tears. The Accompanyments in the Song, viz. *Why do the Nations so furiously rage together,* &c. are kept up with a great Spirit of Invention, *The Lord God Omnipotent reigneth,* &c. is a most elevated Chorus. *The Trumpet shall sound,* &c. has a charming Effect. The Pastoral Strain is truly pleasing. With regard to both these Oratorios, I shall only say, that every One has an undoubted Right to hear and to judge for himself.

It is notable that Hughes (like Handel himself) preferred *Samson* to *Messiah*. Several eighteenth-century critics concurred with Hughes in declining to rank *Messiah* "foremost in the Compositions of that great *Harmonist*." Perhaps it was chiefly Handel's lofty Christian theme that placed *Messiah* above his other works in the hearts of unschooled eighteenth-century Englishmen.
   During his final decade Handel was undoubtedly England's favorite composer. At Covent Garden *Messiah* became the popular rage, much as *Esther* had become the rage twenty years before. An illuminating glimpse of oratorio performance in mid-eighteenth-century London may be found in Fielding's engaging novel *Amelia* (1751). In the chapter "In which Amelia, with her Friend, goes to the Oratorio" Amelia and Mrs. Ellison set out early in order to reach Covent Garden in time to secure seats in the front row of the gallery:

Indeed there was only one Person in the House when they came: for *Amelia*'s Inclinations, when she gave a Loose to them, were pretty eager for this Diversion, she being a great Lover of Music, and particularly of Mr. *Handel*'s Compositions. Mrs. *Ellison* was, I suppose, a great Lover likewise of Music, for she was the more impatient of the two; which was rather the more extraordinary, as these Entertainments were not such Novelties to her as they were to poor *Amelia*.

Tho' our Ladies arrived full two Hours before they saw the Back of Mr. *Handel;* yet this Time of Expectation did not hang extremely heavy on their Hands; for besides their own Chat, they had the Company of the Gentleman, whom they found at their first Arrival in the Galery; and who, though plainly, or rather roughly dressed, very luckily for the Women happened to be not only well-bred, but a Person of a very lively Conversation. The Gentleman on his part seemed highly charmed with *Amelia*, and in fact was so: for, though he restrained himself entirely within the Rules of Good-Breeding, yet was he in the highest Degree officious to catch at every Opportunity of shewing his Respect, and doing her little Services. He procured her a Book and Wax-Candle, and held the Candle for her himself during the whole Entertainment.

At the End of the Oratorio, he declared he would not leave the Ladies till he had seen them safe into their Chairs or Coach; and at the same time very earnestly entreated that he might have the Honour of waiting on them.

For every important performance of *Messiah* Handel issued a printed wordbook of the Scriptural text, "As it is Perform'd at the Theatre-Royal in Covent-Garden." Even during the composer's lifetime, however, spurious and incorrect wordbooks circulated freely, much to the annoyance of Handel's compilers but more to the indignation of his legitimate publishers. On 25 March 1768 an interesting new edition of the words of *Messiah,* "corrected by the compiler," was announced in *The Public Advertiser,* but Charles Jennens' name did not appear. A London newspaper published the following notice on 17 March 1769:

This Day is published, in Quarto, Price 1s., a new Edition, corrected by the Compiler, Messiah, an Oratorio set to Music by Mr. Handel.

Printed (by permission of the Compiler) for E. Johnson, No.

12 in Avemary Lane, Ludgate Street; and for W. Russel: sold also by the Booksellers.

Though editions of Oratorios in a small Letter (too small for the purpose in the huddled manner the readers sit) are sold at the Haymarket House at 6*d.*, none but the large Letter sort of 1*s.* are sold at Covent Garden House. Notwithstanding the Compiler's Injunction against it, a spurious Edition of Messiah is persisted to be printed, and is even sold at Covent Garden Theatre. Those therefore who desire to have the genuine and correct Edition, and would discourage such a contumelious Proceeding, will be pleased to buy before they get to the House, as it is not to be had there (an instance of ill treatment of an author's edition of which there is no example), and that they may do so conveniently, it is planted in various places. This only authorized Edition has E. Johnson's and W. Russel's Names in the Title.[2]

Evidently there was little luxury about *Messiah* performances in a day when audiences sat "huddled" together, seeking to scrutinize their "Book" in the flickering light of a "Wax-Candle." A letter from London written on 15 April 1750 by Madame Anne Marie du Boccage (a once famous but now forgotten French poetess) affords a welcome peep at Handel during one of his oratorio performances at Covent Garden Theatre:

The Oratorio, or pious concert, pleases us highly. English words are sung by Italian performers and accompanied by a variety of instruments. Handel is the soul of it. When he makes his appearance two wax candles are carried before him, which are laid upon his organ. Amidst a loud clapping of hands he seats himself, and the whole band of music strikes up exactly at the same moment. At the interludes he plays concertos of his own composition, either alone or accompanied by the orchestra. These are equally admirable for the harmony and the execution.

Handel never conducted with a baton: in keeping with eighteenth-century custom he always directed his oratorios while seated at the organ. When everything went well at his

---

[2] A clipping from an unidentified newspaper quoted in *Notes and Queries*, 5th Series, III, 105 (6 February 1875).

performances a certain nodding vibration of his enormous white wig was supposed to denote his pleasure and satisfaction. Without this signal nice observers were sure that Handel was out of humor. At the close of an aria the voice with which the composer shouted "Chorus!" was said to be formidable indeed. His performances of *Messiah* were always interspersed with organ concertos, and in them he displayed his unrivalled executive skill. Of Handel's virtuosity at the organ Sir John Hawkins recorded that persons "who, had they been left to themselves, would have interrupted the hearing of others by their talking, were by the performance of Handel not only charmed into silence, but were generally the loudest in their acclamations." Throughout his audience "Silence, the truest applause, succeeded the instant that he addressed himself to the instrument, and that so profound, that it checked respiration, and seemed to controul the functions of nature." After his blindness Handel was unable to conduct oratorios without assistance from his pupil and faithful friend John Christopher Smith, but until his death he continued regularly to perform "an extempore on the organ" at each *Messiah* performance at Covent Garden Theatre. "Noble Handel hath lost an eye," wrote Sir Edward Turner on 14 March 1751, "but I have the Rapture to say that St. Cecilia makes no complaint of any Defect in his Fingers." It is difficult to think without emotion of Beethoven standing deaf amid his orchestra or of Handel turning his sightless eyes to the sun. William Coxe found it "a most affecting spectacle to see the venerable musician, whose efforts had charmed the ear of a discerning public, led by the hand of friendship to the front of the stage, to make an obeisance of acknowledgment to his enraptured audience."

In eighteenth-century literature one finds little concrete information regarding Handel's actual mode of oratorio performance. For two centuries even the extent of his orchestra and the size of his chorus remained vague. Dr. Burney recorded simply that Handel "always employed a very numerous band" and that he "was always aspiring at numbers in his scores and in his orchestra." The historian ventured his own opinion that "nothing can express his grand conceptions but an omnipotent band: the generality of his productions in the hands of a few performers, is like the club of Alcides, or the bow of Ulysses in the hands of a dwarf." In his brilliant satire on *The Art of Composing Music* (1751) William Hayes complained ironically that Handel performed his oratorios with "at least double the Number of Voices and Instruments than ever were heard in a Theatre before." Alexander Pope likened Handel unto "bold Briareus, with a hundred Hands," and Benjamin Victor recorded that "a performance of the Messiah in London, under the conduct of Handel" featured "an hundred instruments, and fifty voices." Such figures are at best approximate. But a unique document in the handwriting of John Christopher Smith, entitled "A list of the Performers in the Oratorio call'd *Messiah* at the Foundling Hospital, May 3rd, 1759" affords concrete evidence concerning a typical *Messiah* performance under Handel's personal direction. Although the composer had died several weeks before, his amanuensis conducted the performance according to schedule, and Smith's bill of expenses is still preserved in the archives of the Foundling Hospital. From his list of performers it is evident that the chorus on that occasion included 6 boys, 12 adult choristers, and 5 soloists. The orchestra consisted of 12 violins, 3 "Tenners" (violas), 4 "hautbois" (oboes), 4 bassoons, 2 violoncellos, 2 contrabasses, 2 trumpets, 2 horns, a pair of kettledrums, an organ, and a harpsichord—making a total of 35 instrumentalists against a choral force of 23. Even if the orchestra were divided into *concertino* and *ripieno* so that its full force was seldom employed, such disproportion between instruments and voices would produce curious effects upon twentieth-century ears.

Evidently Handel considered such a body of performers sufficient to produce all effects required in a chapel seating a thousand persons. Two centuries ago English singing groups were never large. Ambitious choral music was performed by professional soloists connected with churches, theatres, and universities. Volunteer choruses containing hundreds and even thousands of voices emerged only when Victorian England demonstrated her taste for spectacular musical display. Women never sang in Handel's choirs.[3] The composer employed female soloists both in opera and in oratorio, but in his choruses he depended solely on men and boys. The Church had always frowned upon female voices, and the stage had remained equally closed to them for years. Only late in the century did the clear superiority of women's soprano voices enable them to assume their obvious and natural position in a large choir. In general Handel's choristers were experienced soloists, borrowed from superior church and cathedral choirs for occasional performance in theatre or concert room. Even his boys were exceedingly well trained, and the composer frequently engaged some gifted boy soprano to perform important songs. But with all his talented vocalists Handel never heard *Messiah* sung by a chorus as large as any one of five hundred choirs in the United States today. Even at the first great Handel Commemoration of 1784 the chorus for *Messiah* numbered only 275,

---

[3] Women first sang in London oratorio choruses at a performance of Thomas Augustine Arne's *Judith* in 1773. On 27 February 1773 *The Public Advertiser* recorded that "The striking Appearance of the Band and Chorus, which were much more numerous than they have usually been, received a most pleasing addition from the Female Singers, then first introduced." At the Gloucester Music-Meeting of 1772 "the celebrated female chorus-singers, as they were called, from the North of England" were engaged "for the first time, to assist the trebles in the chorusses" [Daniel Lysons, *History of the Origin and Progress of the Meeting of the Three Choirs of Gloucester, Worcester, and Hereford*, Gloucester, 1812, p. 203]. At the second Birmingham Festival (1778) a prominent feature was the appearance of "the celebrated WOMEN CHORUS SINGERS from Lancashire." Conservative England was slow to accept such a daring innovation. Even at the great Handel Commemoration of 1784 a soprano chorus of sixty voices included only twelve women alongside forty-seven boys and one man. On this occasion all forty-eight contraltos were men. Not until 1848 did women sing contralto parts in oratorio choruses.

and that choir was the largest choral force ever gathered for a single performance up to that time.

Following the unequivocal success of *Judas Maccabeus* in 1747 Handel abandoned subscription performances of oratorios and threw his theatre open to all comers. Finding that his aristocratic patrons had failed him, he determined to enter into no further engagement with subscribers for so many performances each season, but rather to seek support from the "generality" by performing oratorios when he chose. England's great middle class had no share in the follies of Handel's luxurious patrons, and if the composer was constantly persecuted by a frivolous clique, he seldom appealed in vain to the general public. At Covent Garden on 23 March 1749 he performed *Messiah* under its original title for the first time in London. Once master of the situation he never again hesitated to advertise his "sacred oratorio" by its correct name. On 11 April 1750 he brought his concert series to an extremely successful conclusion with another performance of *Messiah,* and thereafter he continued to perform his masterpiece each spring both at Covent Garden Theatre and in the Foundling Hospital Chapel. In Dublin *Messiah* was generally performed at Christmas, but London preferred its "sacred" strains during Lent, and every London performance of *Messiah* conducted by Handel took place in the spring.[4]

---

[4] By some curious misconception of Handel's purpose, tradition has declared the music of *Messiah* peculiarly appropriate to the Christmas season. During the eighteenth century the oratorio retained its original Lenten associations, but in 1791 the Caecilian Society of London introduced the custom of annual performances of *Messiah* at Christmastide. Throughout Great Britain and the United States its Christmas performance gradually became an indispensable rite. Till 1861 the Caecilian Society performed *Messiah* regularly on Christmas Eve; from 1836 to 1882 the Sacred Harmonic Society of London sang it annually each December in Exeter Hall. On 25 December 1818 Boston's Handel and Haydn Society gave its first complete performance of *Messiah* in Boylston Hall, and this Yuletide tradition has continued unbroken in Boston to the present day. As early as 1850 *Messiah* became the regular Christmas feature of the Harmonic Society of New York. When that organization dissolved twenty-four years later, the Oratorio Society of New York commenced its annual Christmas performances of

MESSIAH.

AN

ORATORIO.

As it is Perform'd at the

THEATRE-ROYAL

IN

COVENT-GARDEN.

Set to Musick by Mr. HANDEL.

MAJORA CANAMUS.

And without Controversy, great is the Mystery of Godliness: God was manifested in the Flesh, justified by the Spirit, seen of Angels, preached among the Gentiles, believed on in the World, received up into Glory. In whom are hid all the Treasures of Wisdom and Knowledge.

LONDON:

Printed by and for J. WATTS; and Sold by him at the Printing-Office in *Wild-Court* near *Lincoln's-Inn-Fields:*

And by B. DOD at the *Bible* and *Key* in *Ave-Mary-Lane* near *Stationers-Hall.*

[Price One Shilling.]

TITLE PAGE OF THE WORDBOOK OF *MESSIAH*
AS PERFORMED AT COVENT GARDEN THEATRE, LONDON (1749)
From the Copy in the Yale University Library

Early in 1750 Francesca Cuzzoni, glorious heroine of operatic disputes twenty-five years before, returned to the scene of her former triumphs, penniless and broken after two scandalous decades on the continent. Despite her past behavior to him Handel engaged Cuzzoni for one performance of *Messiah*. Dr. Burney heard her sing and reported that her once golden voice had now become leaden: "Her throat was so nearly ossified by age that all the mellifluous qualities, which had made it so enchanting, were nearly annihilated." At Covent Garden *Messiah* was heard twice in 1752, once in 1753, once in 1754, twice in 1755, twice in 1756, twice in 1757, three times in 1758, and three times in 1759. A characteristic entry appeared in John Baker's *Diary* on 10 March 1758: "Went après midi con Uxor in chariot to 'Messiah,' could not get seat in Upper Gallery, sat in lower." From 1743 to his death in 1759 Handel conducted *Messiah* twenty-three times at Covent Garden Theatre, and all but the first six performances won "universal Admiration and Applause."

Toward the close of 1758 Handel's health began to decline. Despite his blindness and loss of appetite, however, he managed to fulfill all his engagements until within several days of his death. He celebrated his seventy-fourth birthday on 23 February 1759. On the following day *The Public Advertiser* scheduled the opening of his oratorio season for March 2. After successful performances of *Solomon, Susanna, Samson,* and *Judas Maccabeus* during March, *The Public Advertiser* announced Handel's "Eleventh Night" on April 6:

At the Theatre Royal in Covent Garden this day will be presented a Sacred Oratorio, call'd THE MESSIAH. Being the last time of performing IT this Season. Pit and Boxes to be laid together, and no person to be admitted without Tickets, which will be delivered this Day at the Office in the Theatre at Half

---

Messiah on 25 December 1874. Today *Messiah* is seldom heard regularly at any other period of the Christian year. Actually, however, less than one-fifth of the entire work has direct bearing on the Nativity, and one can scarcely exaggerate the impropriety of celebrating Christ's Passion during the joyful Christmas season.

Guinea each. First Gallery, 5s. Upper Gallery, 3s. 6d. Galleries to be open'd at Half an Hour after Four o'clock. Pit and Boxes at Five. To begin at Half an Hour after Six.

That evening Handel directed *Messiah* for the last time. In his *Diary* Thomas Green recorded that throughout the performance the composer conducted "apparently in great suffering; but when he came to his concerto he rallied, and kindling as he advanced, descanted extemporaneously with his accustomed ability and force; of a most dignified and awe-inspiring port." At the close of the oratorio Handel was suddenly seized with faintness, and he returned to Lower Brook Street never to rise from his bed again. Curiously enough, London periodicals took no notice of the fact for several days. On April 7 *The Public Advertiser* announced a performance of *Messiah* at the Foundling Chapel on "the 3d of May, at twelve o'clock, under the direction of George Frederick Handel, Esq." Without the slightest allusion to Handel's illness the same journal six days later repeated its advertisement of *Messiah,* to be performed "under the direction of the author" at the Foundling Hospital on May 3. Meanwhile the composer was dying. Somewhat tardily *The Whitehall Evening Post* reported on April 12 that "Mr. Handel, who was in Hopes to have set out for Bath last Saturday, has continued so ill, that he could not undertake the Journey." Early on the morning of April 14, the day before Easter Sunday, Handel breathed his last. On the same day *The Public Advertiser* again announced the twelfth performance of *Messiah* at the Foundling Hospital "under the direction of George Frederick Handel, Esq." Without adding one word of regret the editor repeated his advertisement of *Messiah* on April 19, merely substituting "under the direction of Mr. Smith" for "under the direction of the author." By now several London journals had published obscure notices of Handel's death. On April 17 *The Daily Advertiser* featured a lame poetical obituary "On GEORGE FREDERICK

HANDEL, ESQ. *who performed in his celebrated Oratorio of* Messiah, *on the 6th, and dyed the 14th Instant*":

> To melt the soul, to captivate the ear,
> (Angels his melody might deign to hear)
> T' anticipate on Earth the joys of Heaven,
> Was Handel's task; to him the pow'r was given!
> Ah! when he late attuned Messiah's praise,
> With sounds celestial, and melodious lays;
> A last farewell his languid looks expresst,
> And thus methinks th' enraptured crowd addrest.
> "Adieu, my dearest friends! and also you,
> Joint sons of sacred harmony, adieu!
> Apollo, whisp'ring, prompts me to retire,
> And bids me join the bright seraphic choir!
> O for Elijah's car," great Handel cry'd;
> Messiah heard his voice—and Handel dy'd.

Three days later the composer of *Messiah* was buried in great state in Poet's Corner of Westminster Abbey. "Though he had mention'd being privately interr'd," *The Whitehall Evening Post* declared, "yet from the Respect due to so celebrated a Man, the Bishop, Prebends, and the whole choir attended to pay the last Honours due to his memory." *The Gentleman's Magazine* reported that "there were not fewer than 3000 persons present on this occasion." For half a century Handel had labored to flatter British ears, and now England had paid the composer her highest tribute by placing his remains in her national shrine.

III

"I could not help feeling a damp on my spirits," wrote Mrs. Delany on 5 May 1759, "when I heard that great master of music was no more, and I shall now be *less able* to bear any other music than I used to be." At Handel's death in 1759 the English public quickly rose to a sense of what it had lost. Voguish amateurs who could scarcely distinguish a crotchet from a quaver suddenly professed rapture at

Handel's *Messiah*, while "connoisseurs" devoid of the slightest sensibility refused to patronize musical performances which failed to feature Handel's name on the bills. Portraits of Handel were raked up and hawked about, and engravings of the Saxon composer appeared in every London print shop. Gentlemen of taste wore Handel in their shirt pins, and ladies of fashion rubbed their chins against Handel in their brooches. Coquettes giggled behind Handel's likeness on illustrated fans, and diligent boys and girls strummed Handel's "lessons" on every family spinet in the kingdom. Even card parties broke down before London's infatuation for Handelian oratorio. In his *Continuation of the Complete History of England* (1760) Tobias Smollett declared that "the liberal arts sustained a lamentable loss" in Handel's death, since the composer was "universally admired for his stupendous genius in the sublime parts of musical composition," and had proved himself "the most celebrated master in music which this age had produced." In his *Observations on the Present State of Music and Musicians* (1762) John Potter insisted that Handel "should be stil'd *The prince of musicians,* as he was the greatest *Europe* ever produc'd, both as a composer and player." Handelian memorial verses became common, and John Lockman's tribute *"To the* MANES *of Mr.* HANDEL" was typical:

> To mourn o'er thee, I call not on the nine,
> Nor wait for influence at Apollo's shrine;
> Vain fiction! O for David's sacred string!
> Who but a muse divine of thee should sing?—
>   Fall'n thy slow-wasting tenement of clay,
> Back to the stars thy spirit wing'd her way;
> For heav'n indulgent only lent thee here,
> Our pangs to soften, and our griefs to chear;
> Our jarring passions sweetly to controul,
> And lift to extasy th' aspiring soul.
>   O wondrous, sounds, thine from yon region came,
> And hence, thus strongly, they each breast inflame!

Such strains thou heard'st at thy return to skies,
When the Messiah bless'd thy ravish'd eyes.
Cherubs, in his high praise, thy anthems sung,
And heav'n with thy great hallelujahs rung.

Early in 1760 the Reverend John Langhorne produced *The Tears of Music: A Poem to the Memory of Mr. Handel*. According to *The Gentleman's Magazine* "this harmonious and elegant poem" rose far superior to those "crude rhapsodies" so frequently laid at the feet of St. Cecilia. After praising Handel's *Water Musick, L'Allegro, Samson, Judas Maccabeus,* and *Jephtha* Langhorne devoted an eloquent passage to *Messiah*:

> I feel, I feel the sacred Impulse—hark!
> Wak'd from according Lyres the sweet Strains flow
> In Symphony divine; from Air to Air
> The trembling Numbers fly: swift bursts away
> The Flow of Joy; now swells the Flight of Praise.
> Springs the shrill Trump aloft; the toiling Chords
> Melodious labour thro' the flying Maze;
> And the deep Base his strong Sounds rolls away,
> Majestically sweet—Yet, HANDEL, raise,
> Yet wake to higher Strains thy sacred Lyre:
> The Name of Ages, the Supreme of Things,
> The great MESSIAH asks it; He whose Hand
> Led into Form yon everlasting Orbs,
> The Harmony of Nature—He whose Hand
> Stretch'd o'er the wilds of Space this beauteous Ball,
> Whose Spirit breathes thro' all his smiling Works
> Music and Love—yet HANDEL raise the Strain.
> Hark! what angelic Sounds, what Voice divine
> Breathes thro' the ravisht Air! my rapt Ear feels
> The Harmony of Heaven. Hail sacred Choir!
> Immortal Spirits, hail! If haply those
> That erst in favour'd PALESTINE proclaim'd
> Glory and Peace: her Angel-haunted Groves,
> Her piny Mountains, and her golden Vales
> Re-echo'd Peace—But, Oh! suspend the Strain—
> The swelling Joy's too much for mortal Bounds!
> 'Tis Transport even to Pain. Oh, lead me then,

> Convey me to the sad, the mournful Scene,
> Where trembling Nature saw her GOD expire.
> Flow, stupid Tears! and veil the conscious Eye
> That yet presumes to gaze—
> Flow, stupid Tears! in vain—ye too confess
> That HE alone unequal'd Sorrow bore.

Late in the spring of 1760 the Reverend John Mainwaring published his familiar *Memoirs of the Life of the Late George Frederic Handel,* written (as Dr. Burney declared) not only "with zeal and candour" but also "with science and elegance." It was the first biography of the German composer. In his analysis of the oratorios Mainwaring pointed out that "the sublime strokes" of Handel's choruses "look more like the effects of illumination, than of mere natural genius." From a "multitude of examples that might be produced" he chose "For unto us a Child is born," "Lift up your heads," and the "Hallelujah Chorus" from *Messiah* to illustrate Handel's peculiar excellences in choral composition:

> After these vast efforts of genius, we find him rising still higher in the three concluding Chorusses, each of which surpasses the preceding, till in the winding up of the Amen, the ear is fill'd with such a glow of harmony, as leaves the mind in a kind of heavenly extasy. . . . It is true, that, in the wonderful performance above-mentioned, there are great inequalities, as in most of HANDEL'S: but whoever should examine it throughout, must consider him as a down-right prodigy.

Following Handel's death British journals continued for several years to honor his memory with doubtful poetical tributes, grandiloquent biographical eulogies, and verbose essays analyzing his genius as an "English" composer. On 10 July 1762 the grand monument which now graces the south transept of Westminster Abbey was dedicated and first exhibited in its present position against the western wall. Designed and executed by Louis François Roubiliac, this somewhat theatrical composition was, by an extraordinary coincidence, the sculptor's last important work in England, whereas his statue of Handel in Vauxhall Gardens (1738) had been his first. Roubiliac had taken a cast of Handel's features after the composer's death. In the monument Handel stands at full length, in an erect and noble attitude, with face turned slightly heavenward as if in earnest thought. He leans against a table covered with musical instruments. His right hand holds a pen and rests lightly upon an unfinished score of *Messiah,* on which the opening words and music of "I know that my Redeemer liveth" are distinctly legible. An organ occupies the background of the monument, and in the upper part of the enclosed arch an angel is seated on a cloud, playing upon a harp as Handel listens. An appropriately simple (if somewhat inaccurate) inscription appears at the base of the memorial.

By 1759 Handel's *Messiah* had been heard not only in London but also in scores of cities and towns throughout England. Already it had won a degree of popularity far exceeding that of any other oratorio, and its immense vogue caused it to be adopted for charitable occasions in every shire of the kingdom. From the beginning Englishmen found a universal favorite in "the grand Chorus from Mr. *Handel's* sacred Oratorio call'd *Messiah.*" As early as 1752 the oratorio was heard at a music festival in Salisbury. On 17 May 1755 *Messiah* was first performed at Bath, conducted by Dr. William Hayes at Wiltshire's Rooms on the Walk. On 14 January 1756 "The New Musick Room" at Bristol was "opened" with a performance of *Messiah* at which the "band" was "compos'd of the principal performers, vocal and instrumental, from London, Oxford, Salisbury, Gloucester, Wells, Bath, &c.," and a "concerto" was played on the organ by Robert Broderip. *Messiah* was repeated "at the opening of the new organ" on 3 March 1757, and similar musical festivals were heard in "The New Musick Room" in 1758 and 1759. Following Handel's death in 1759 two days of memorial performances at Bath Abbey and the Lower Rooms "gave universal Satisfaction to the vast number of Gentlemen and

Ladies present on the occasion." On 14 May 1759 *Boddeley's Bath Journal* announced a performance of *Messiah* for May 17:

No Expence has been wanting to engage the best Voices from Salisbury, Gloucester, Bristol and Worcester Cathedrals. . . . There will be a Collection each Day at the Church Door, at going in. It is to be hoped that no Persons, who are Owners of Pews, will take offence at their being laid open these Days, for the Use of the Charity. Gentlemen and Ladies are desired to discharge their Servants at the Church Door. All the profits arising from the Oratorio's will likewise be applied to the Use of Charity.

Handel's death inspired countless commemorative performances throughout the kingdom. Even at Church-Langton (a village community in Leicestershire) *Messiah* was performed with "great eclat" under the direction of William Hayes on 27 September 1759. On this occasion the Reverend William Hanbury was confident of success, since "an oratorio was never heard of in the country" and since "novelty is what always engages the attention of the English." His description of the *Messiah* performance affords curious insight into the profound effects of Handel's "sacred oratorio" upon a rural eighteenth-century audience:

The next day for the sacred oratorio being also a fine day, company of all sorts seemed to flock in with a redoubled force; the foot-roads from every quarter were lined with common people, and the quality and gentry in their different carriages rattled in from every part. All were in full dress, and more than two hundred coaches, chariots, landaus, and post-chaises were counted at Church-Langton; a sight which, I believe I may safely say, hardly ever before graced a country-village; neither perhaps had any church in England so splendid a congregation, that was composed of so many, and such fine women, as well as a proportional number of gentlemen; for the number of beautiful ladies was very great, which occasioned the meeting to be afterwards much talked of on their account.

The time for the beginning of the performance being advanced, the overture was struck off, and then the different parts of that noble oratorio the Messiah succeeded in order. The music, on so solemn a subject, by so good a band, was most affecting; and to see the effect it had on different persons was astonishingly moving and strange. An eye without tears I believe could hardly be found in the whole church, and every one endeavoured to conceal the emotions of his heart: drooping heads, to render the tears unnoticed, became for a while almost general, till by now and then looking about, and finding others affected in the like manner, no concealment in a little time was made. Tears then with unconcern were seen trickling down the faces of many: and then indeed, it was extremely moving to see the pity, compassion, and devotion, that had possessed the greatest part present.

Much company coming too late were disappointed; for the moment the overture was struck off, the doors were barricaded, to frustrate any attempts that should be made by the common people to rush in. The crowd upon that became general and uniform, and rendered it impossible for any fresh-comer to get near the church. A young lady, coming singly on horseback, with one servant only, offered twenty guineas to any person or persons who could procure her admittance; and altho' many attempts were made, it could not be effected. Who this lady was I could never learn.

As soon as the oratorio ended, and the company was out of the church, the doors were set wide open, and part of it performed over again for the entertainment of the common-people; and it was really curious to see what a hurry they were in to get in, and what striving there was immediately to get out again; for they crushed one another to an amazing degree. A boy was fairly squeezed up, and walked upon their heads; and such outcries were made by the fatter part of the rabble, that few could attend to what the band was doing: it pleased them however, and thus ended this day's performance in the church. And altho' very few of the company there had ever heard an oratorio, yet those who had at the Foundling Hospital, Oxford, or the Three Choirs, declared they never knew it at any of those places so well done; and many who have since heard it at some or other of those places, acknowledge, that in the whole it falls short of what they heard at Church-Langton. The disposition of the performers to the greatest advantage, the propriety of the number of voices and instruments, the uniformity, size, and nature of the church, together with the best instruments and voices at each part, contributed to demand the title of EMINENCE before all others yet performed.

A second rendition of *Messiah* was scheduled for 31 July 1760. At this Meeting "the company was equally numerous and polite; every inn was crouded, and beds and lodging let at a great rate; prices of provisions were raised as before, and the different vehicles assembled the company from every part." At the third performance of *Messiah* at Church-Langton on 9 July 1761 "the music went off with the usual eclat." Few persons attended *Judas Maccabeus,* but "the usual number or more filled the church for the Messiah." With some dryness Hanbury observed that "The appearance would have been equally noble, had not some of the ladies made a point of coming in an undress or dishabille. This was indeed more convenient, but the brilliancy of the appearance was thereby eclipsed." At Leicester in 1762 "A general report was industriously propagated, that the Messiah was not to be performed," and Hanbury recorded that "this did us much disservice, for numbers were known to stay away on believing it, tho' so contrary to advertisement." Obviously *Messiah* was the general favorite. When the oratorio was advertised at Nottingham during the following spring "joy seemed to dawn on the whole town, and tickets for the *Messiah* went off at a brisk rate." On 31 May 1763 *Messiah* "went on with great justice, and gained general applause" from a huge audience including "much company who came from distant parts purely to hear the Messiah, and return."

Performances of *Messiah* at Church-Langton may be considered typical of scores of performances throughout England during the third quarter of the eighteenth century. Besides stimulating regularly recurring three-choir festivals, the English Handel cult from 1759 to 1784 launched innumerable isolated celebrations which ultimately established local choruses in every city and town. On 5 July 1759 *Messiah* was heard at Oxford as part of the Public Act, and during the following spring the oratorio was performed at Cambridge on 22 May 1760 under the direction of Dr. John Randall. The first performance of *Messiah* north of the Trent River took place at Halifax in 1766. In Liverpool the oratorio was originally sung at St. Peter's Church on 30 April 1766 under the direction of Dr. William Hayes. A second performance took place at St. Thomas' Church in 1770, and a third at St. Peter's Church in 1778, with the celebrated Giardini as conductor of the band. At the Salisbury Festival of 1770 Mrs. James Harris recorded that *Messiah* "went off divinely." On 31 March 1774 *Messiah* was heard at Bristol Cathedral, when ninety-one musicians united for the benefit of Bristol "Infirmary" and precocious "Master Charles Wesley" rendered "a concerto on the organ." In his *Book of Musical Anecdote* (1878) Frederick J. Crowest recorded that when *Messiah* was originally heard in Norwich, a gentleman named Hardingham was aroused to a violent pitch of emotional tension:

As the oratorio proceeded, the gentleman in question was observed to grow much agitated, standing upon a bench, distorting his face, and contorting his limbs in a very extraordinary manner. At length he dismounted, and with a strange expression of countenance, made his way to the orchestra, and, catching up one of the wax-lights that stood within his reach, he attempted to set fire to the room. On seeing this, several gentlemen rushed upon him, and had him conveyed home; but never to the end of his days did Mr. Hardingham recover his senses.

Music festivals at Birmingham commenced in 1768, when *Messiah* was first performed at St. Philip's Church by a chorus of forty boys and men and an orchestra of twenty-five. For the benefit of the General Hospital each performance was followed by a ball in the evening. A second meeting was held in 1778, and in 1784 the Birmingham Musical Festivals became triennial.

By far the most important eighteenth-century music-meetings were those held triennially by the Three Choirs of Gloucester, Worcester, and Hereford. Following an initial festival at Gloucester in 1724 these three choirs proceeded to meet annually for combined performance. From the beginning the rotation has continued almost unbroken to the present day. In 1737 William Boyce was appointed conductor, and under his guidance the scheme was broadened to include instrumental works and oratorios. Originally performances continued for only two days, but at Gloucester in 1757 the Music-Meeting was extended to a third evening in order to introduce *Messiah* for the first time at the Boothall. After *Judas Maccabeus* and *Acis and Galatea* Handel's masterpiece won "rapturous Applause," and with but one exception it was repeated annually at every subsequent Meeting of the Three Choirs from 1757 to 1932.[5] For the initial performance Dr. Hayes conducted a band of "three trumpets, a pair of kettle-drums, four hautboys, four bassoons, two double basses, violins, violoncellos, and chorus singers in proportion." When *Messiah* was first performed at Worcester in 1758, admission prices were raised to five shillings and the Meeting was further extended to include three morning performances. Among the audience at *Messiah* was William Shenstone, to whom Handel had always seemed "a wight of skill and judgment deep." On 25 November 1758 Shenstone recorded his opinion of Handel's masterpiece:

I need not mention what an appearance there was of company at Worcester; dazzling enough, you may suppose, to a person who,

---

[5] At Hereford in 1834 Samuel Wesley sought to introduce variety by rendering only selections from *Messiah* on the same program with Mozart's *Requiem,* but Victorians resented this innovation, and *Messiah* was subsequently performed in the usual fashion. During World War I the Meeting was suspended for six years (1914–1919), but *Messiah* was revived at Worcester in 1920 and performed with renewed success until 1933, when the annual performance was officially replaced by selections. Directors felt that occasional performances of *Messiah* as a whole, with selections during the intervening period, might encourage worthier presentations. A thorough account of the Three Choirs (1722–1811) may be found in Daniel Lysons, *History of the Origin and Progress of the Meeting of the Three Choirs of Gloucester, Worcester, and Hereford, and of the Charity Connected with It,* Gloucester, 1812. Subsequent revisions and additions were published at Gloucester by John Amott (1864), Charles Lee Williams (1894), Harry Godwin Chance (1922), and Theodore Hannam-Clark (1931).

like me, has not seen a public place these ten years. Yet I made a shift to enjoy the splendour, as well as the music that was prepared for us. I presume, nothing in the way of harmony can possibly go further than the Oratorio of The Messiah. It seems the best composer's best composition. Yet I fancied I could observe *some parts* in it, wherein Handel's judgement failed him; where the music was not equal, or was even *opposite,* to what the words required.

Until the close of 1758 Three-Choir Festivals were restricted to theatres, concert rooms, and shire halls. A landmark was therefore passed when *Messiah* was first admitted into the Cathedral at Hereford in 1759. As the Wesleyan Movement gained momentum oratorios were occasionally performed in Methodist chapels, but no oratorio except *Messiah* was heard in an English cathedral until 1787, when *Israel in Egypt* was finally admitted into the Cathedral at Gloucester. At Hereford in 1759 *Messiah* was heard for the first time in the morning, and the same ticket which admitted its bearer to hear Handel's "sacred oratorio" in the Cathedral also introduced "one Gentleman or two Ladies" gratis to the ball that evening. In the following year *Messiah* was performed at the Boothall in Gloucester as a tribute to Handel, "the first musical composer of his time, and, in some respects, of any time or country in Europe." On the second night Dr. Hayes performed his setting of Collins' *Ode on the Passions,* after which he introduced his *Ode to the Memory of Mr. Handel.* On 14 September 1761 William Shenstone reported that he had heard "The Messiah well performed" on his "last digression" to Worcester. Five years later Francis Hopkinson, the American composer, "had the Pleasure of hearing the *Messiah* and other solemn Pieces of Music performed by the best Hands" at Gloucester:

When I was in England, I had an excruciating Boil, which was at the Height of Inflamation & Tension; I went, nevertheless, to a public Place & heard the Oratorio of the Messiah performed to Admiration. I felt no more Pain of the Boil—it even broke whilst

I was there without my perceiving it. Had I been in my Chamber, I should have cried out with Anguish. May not the Firmness of Martyrs be accounted for on the same Principle?

In 1769 *Messiah* was first performed in the Cathedral at Gloucester, after which a ball was given in the evening at the Boothall. At Worcester the oratorio was first heard in the Cathedral in 1770, when sixteen-year-old Elizabeth Linley made her debut at the Three-Choir Festivals.

Of all eighteenth-century English singers none possessed more touching musical powers, none acquired more brilliant public acclaim than Elizabeth Ann Linley, the "Maid of Bath," daughter of Dr. Thomas Linley and wife of Richard Brinsley Sheridan. From early youth Thomas Linley had specialized in Handel's works. In 1752 he had christened his eldest son George Frederick, and after 1768 he had devoted himself almost exclusively to the organization of provincial oratorios designed to popularize the composer's name. Elizabeth inherited her father's affection for Handel. She took particular delight in Handel's arias, and she consecrated her art to his strains both at Bath concerts and in London oratorios. "Miss Linley proved to Handel, what Garrick was to Shakespeare," wrote William Coxe; "and those who recollect her captivating voice, feel the full merit of the great master's mind." Dr. Burney found "the British Cecilia" an "exquisite and darling singer" who with "crystalline clarity" rendered Handel's graceful intricacies "important and attractive" to rapturous audiences. Contemporaries united to praise Elizabeth Linley's character and talents. Bishops declared her the link between mortals and angels; schoolmasters spoke of her as more than human; statesmen sat up half the night to hear her songs. Gainsborough painted her several times and twice modelled her face in clay. Sir Joshua Reynolds depicted her twice as St. Cecilia and employed her as his model for the Virgin in his painting of the Nativity. Miss Linley acquired such favor with the British public that at sixteen she gave popularity to any performance at which she appeared. Her favorite oratorio was *Messiah*. A contemporary journal recorded that while she was singing "I know that my Redeemer liveth" at a musical festival in Salisbury,

a little bullfinch that had found means by some accident or other to secrete itself in the cathedral, was so struck by the inimitable sweetness, and harmonious simplicity of her manner of singing, that mistaking it for the voice of a feathered chorister of the woods, and far from being intimidated by the numerous assemblage of spectators, it perched immediately on the gallery over her head, and accompanied her with the musical warblings of its little throat through a great part of the song.

In August 1771 Miss Linley was "first female singer" in a performance of *Messiah* at Hereford, and at Gloucester in 1772 she shared the female solos in *Messiah* with her younger sister Maria.[6] Shortly thereafter she eloped with Sheridan, and following their marriage she resolved to abandon her musical career. Nearly fourteen hundred persons attended *Messiah* at Worcester in 1773 to hear Mrs. Sheridan's farewell performance in public. "At the close of this Meeting," wrote the Reverend Daniel Lysons, "she took leave of an admiring public, in the full lustre of unrivalled talents, leaving the minds of her enraptured audience impressed with a remembrance, not soon to be eradicated, of her sweet and

---

[6] Maria Linley died of a fever on 5 September 1784. On her deathbed she suddenly rose and began to sing her favorite aria, "I know that my Redeemer liveth" from *Messiah*. According to Alicia Lefanu, she "was attended by Dr. [Henry] Harrington, a gentleman no less celebrated for his medical skill than for his musical abilities. A little time previous to her death, when confined to her bed, she raised herself up, and with unexpected and momentary animation sung a part of the anthem, 'I know that my Redeemer liveth.' The female attendant . . . described [the scene] as the most affecting she had ever witnessed. The pathetic, and almost super-human sweetness of the notes breathed by the young and lovely creature, who was just departing from them, and the awful hope inculcated in the words of the air she had chosen, contributed to give an appearance of inspiration to this last effort of a voice that had delighted every ear. Dr. Harrington was greatly overcome by the scene, and could only exclaim, 'She is an angel!' as he left the room. Exhausted by the effort, she sunk into the arms of the attendant, and shortly afterwards breathed her last."

powerful tones, and charmed with her generosity and benevolence."

Elizabeth Linley was only fifteen when she first sang in London oratorios during the spring of 1769. In the following season eleven-year-old Maria Linley made her theatrical debut in a metropolitan performance of *Messiah*. During 1771 and 1772 the two girls frequently appeared in benefit performances of Handel's masterpiece both in London and in the provinces, and twice in April 1773 they shared the female solos in presentations of *Messiah* at Covent Garden. By now oratorios were firmly rooted in the English heart. Since 1759 there had been no dearth of *Messiah* performances in London, and *Samson, Judas Maccabeus,* and *Messiah* seldom failed to draw crowded houses both at Covent Garden and at Drury Lane. In 1760 *Messiah* had been performed no fewer than seven times at Covent Garden. During the succeeding decade the oratorio had gradually assumed that unrivalled position in English music which it maintains to this day. But if *Messiah* attracted multitudes at each London performance, its audience consisted chiefly of persons from the fashionable world. Until Dr. Samuel Arnold first performed oratorios at playhouse prices in 1768 *Messiah* was too expensive an "entertainment" to prove of vital consequence to the average Englishman. In 1772 *The Theatrical Register* hailed with joy the "reduction of the terms of admission to Oratorios, which before, were too exorbitant to be afforded by the generality of the Frequenters of Playhouses. This reduction," it declared, "has given many an opportunity of enjoying this noble Species of Entertainment, who were heretofore, excluded on account of the great expence." Once admitted to oratorio, the "generality" of London were most enthusiastic:

When the Doctor first performed the *Messiah* [wrote Thomas Busby], the crowd at the doors was so excessive, that when they were opened, the money-takers, unable to resist the pressure, fled from their posts; and, among those who rushed unimpeded

ELIZABETH ANN LINLEY
(MRS. RICHARD BRINSLEY SHERIDAN)

From a Portrait by Thomas Gainsborough (1785)
in the Mellon Collection of the National Gallery of Art,
Washington, D. C.

into the boxes, was a fish-woman in a red cloak. When the curtain rose, the blaze of the illumined orchestra, together with the numerous assemblage of vocal and instrumental performers, so dazzled and astonished her, that in her extacy she exclaimed aloud, "Oh, how fine! which is the Messiah? show me the Messiah?" "That's the Messiah," answered a wag in the pit, pointing at the Doctor.—"Where?"—"The little gentleman at the harpsichord." This excited throughout the house a degree of merriment, which scarcely subsided during the whole evening; and the Doctor's friends long indulged themselves in complimenting him with the appellation with which he had been publicly honoured.

In the spring of 1774 Johann Friedrich Karl Grimm, a German visitor to London, reported that "the Oratorios, usually by Handel, which were to be heard twice a week during Lent, were not remarkable for the voices." A year later Mrs. James Harris conceded that she "could not say much of the voices" at "the oratorio in the Haymarket," but she insisted that "the instrumental parts and the choruses went as well as in the days of Handel."

On 8 March 1771 Dr. Samuel Johnson accompanied Mrs. Thrale to a performance of *Messiah* at Covent Garden Theatre. England's literary dictator was notably deficient in musical taste: he maintained frankly and deliberately that "music is in itself a triviality, occasionally rising to the dignity of a nuisance." It is therefore scarcely surprising that the good doctor composed Latin verses during the singing of Handel's *Messiah*. "He was for the most part an exceedingly bad playhouse companion," Mrs. Thrale wrote in her *Anecdotes* (1786), since "his person drew people's eyes upon the box, and the loudness of his voice made it difficult for me to hear any body but himself." During *Messiah*, however, "he sat surprisingly quiet, and I flattered myself that he was listening to the music." But "the Instant we got home" he repeated a set of Latin verses composed "In Theatro: March 8, 1771," and "he bid me translate them." Oddly enough, eighteenth-century Englishmen frequently associated Handel and Johnson. In his *Journal of a Tour to the Hebrides* (1773) even Boswell sought to explain Johnson's "bow-wow way" by drawing an analogy from Handel's music. "The *Messiah*," he wrote, "played upon the Canterbury organ is more sublime that when played upon an inferior instrument, but very slight music will seem grand when conveyed to the ear through that majestic medium." Later Boswell added that Johnson "might be an ordinary composer at times," but "he was for the most part a Handel." In an essay on "Haendel et L'Angleterre" (1913) George Bernard Shaw wittily observed that "Si le Dr. Johnson avait été compositeur, il aurait certainement composé comme Haendel." Physically and temperamentally the two gentlemen were not dissimilar. Both were "unwieldy from corpulency," both possessed booming voices and gargantuan appetites, both displayed gruff tempers and grotesque manners, both evinced boundless energy and dynamic gusto for living, both exhibited a passion for London, and both disclosed kindly hearts tucked away beneath rather formidable exteriors.

If Boswell considered Handel's *Messiah* "grand" and "sublime," Mrs. Thrale ranked the oratorio alongside Homer's *Iliad*. Later eighteenth-century critics universally regarded *Messiah* as a touchstone of artistic excellence. During the quarter-century following Handel's death numerous aesthetic treatises interpreted his oratorios in dogmatic terms, and although many such tracts speedily sank into well-deserved oblivion, several quaint volumes remain to this day curiously indicative of English musical taste throughout the reign of George III. In 1763 the Reverend John ("Estimate") Brown produced a significant critical work entitled *A Dissertation on the Rise, Union, and Power, the Progressions, Separations, and Corruptions, of Poetry and Music*. Concluding that "upon the whole" Handel's compositions "surpass every thing yet produced in Grandeur and Expression," Brown predicted with perfect orthodoxy that the composer's oratorios "will ever be the richest Fountain for *Imitation* or *Adoption*" and that "even singly taken" they "will justly command the Regard and Admiration of all succeeding Ages." Inspired by Brown's fervor, one nameless Handelian promptly published *An Examination of the Oratorios which have been Performed this Season at Covent-Garden Theatre* (1763). In this thorough analysis of "the present state of music in England" the writer maintained that "the oratorio, either from a partiality to its author, or misapprehension of its nature, has continued unexamined and uncensured, and in consequence remains incomplete, and unimproved." Being "strongly sensible of the wretched state in which the oratorio has, from the first, subsisted in this nation," the author threw in "his mite towards rectifying the public taste, by attempting an examination of such of *Handel's Oratorios* as are at present in performance" in London. After enumerating certain "defects and improprieties" of "the poetical and musical constitution of the oratorio," he offered a "particular examination" and "candid review" of *The Occasional Oratorio, Messiah, Samson, Acis and Galatea, Judas Maccabeus,* and *Alexander's Feast.* His "observations" on "the *musical* composition" of *Messiah* afford rich insight into critical opinion regarding Handel's masterpiece four years after the composer's death.

Without reference to the overture the author proceeded at once to declare that the "opening" of "Comfort ye" is "fine" and that its recitative is "noble" and "affecting." The "second verse" (beginning "The voice of him that crieth in the wilderness") he found to be "something above *Handel's* ordinary stile of recitative," but by no means comparable to the preceding strains.

The first song of *Every valley shall be exalted,* &c. is equally proper and pleasing; the general subject of the air is agreeable to the words, and the incidental imitations of *exalted, made low, the crooked straight,* and *the rough places plain,* contribute greatly to render it more striking. But the succeeding chorus, *And the glory of God shall be revealed,* . . . ought to have followed immediately without the interruption of a symphony, being connected to the preceding song both by the subject and the particle *and*. The part quoted is well expressed by the musician; but the remainder of the words are incapable of expression, at the same time that the chorus, though the music is good, becomes fatiguing by its length. . . . The words *I will shake the heavens, and the earth, and the sea, and the dry land; and I will shake all nations, and the desire of all nations shall come;* would have afforded subject for Mr. *Handel*'s sublimest conceptions in the tremendous style; but in their present form are unaffecting and unheeded. The next song too, of *But who may abide the day of his coming,* had it been properly expressed by music, might have imprinted on the soul the most awful reverence of that great day it alludes to; but, as it stands at present, has little merit or no effect. The concluding words, *He is like a refiner's fire,* afford little room for musical expression; and though the music is in general good in itself, yet the divisions on *appeareth, a, refiner's,* are puerile, and very much debase the rest. The succeeding chorus, *And he shall purify the sons of Levi,* is likewise incapable of expression; but the fugue is good, and the harmony full, except where the continued divisions upon *purify* interrupt it. The song of *O thou that tellest good tidings to Zion,* has not much in it to commend, and only little to blame; the air is joyous and easy, but some of the words are ill accented, such as *Jerusalem* and *Judah* are set precisely to the same notes.

"For, behold, darkness shall cover the earth" was pronounced "good," but "The people that walked in darkness" was found to be "only of the middling stamp, both in music and expression; the author indeed had given little room for the latter, but it is the composer's fault that the former is not more perfect." The writer complained that the "symphony" of "For unto us a Child is born" delays the entrance of the voices, "creates Expectation and Presentiment, destroys Surprize, and thus *lessens* the *Impression* and *Effect.*" His evaluation of this chorus is notable:

The music to the words quoted is too light, and too much allied to a gossiping song at a Christening, instead of that dignity of joy which ought to have hailed the coming of the *prince of peace*. The remaining part however, *And his name shall be called Wonderful,* &c. is greatly set, and every way worthy of the subject and

Handel, except that the ritornello lessens the effect, and is more particularly hurtful in this place, because it makes the contrast between this grand chorus and the pastoral symphony, which immediately follows, less manifest and less affecting. . . . The first part of *Glory be to God in the highest* is fine; the second, *and peace on earth,* is still more noble; but the fugue to the concluding words, *good will towards men,* is equally improper and unnatural. The next song is very ill conducted throughout; the words *Rejoice greatly, O daughter of Sion, shout, O daughter of Jerusalem,* are evidently calculated for the choral expression; the da capo is fatiguing, and the tedious division on *rejoice* is disagreable.

Handel's touching recitative upon the words "Then shall the eyes of the blind be opened" failed to win the writer's applause. Of "He shall feed His flock," however, he declared that "nothing can be more tender than the words, nothing more soothing and pathetic than the music." But "His yoke is easy" sounded "peculiarly absurd and unpleasing." Apparently its jog-trot exuberance was notorious as early as 1763:

The same thought had been nobly expressed in the last verse of the preceding song, *Take his yoke upon you, and learn of him,* &c. and now we have in this chorus, *His yoke is easy, and his burden is light,* but very *differently* expressed. The first is soft and affecting; the second an airy and injudicious imitation of the words *easy* and *burden light,* loaded with an insipid division on *easy* and *burden.* To have finished the act properly it was only necessary to have repeated the last verse of the succeeding song, with the addition of the choral parts to the music; but as it stands at present, I am at a loss to determine whether the *author* was most to blame in inserting the words, or Mr. *Handel* in adapting them so very unworthy of his great abilities.

In his analysis of Part II the author indicated that "Behold the Lamb of God" is a "fine chorus," although "the ritornello prevents our feeling" the "full force" of its pathos:

The song of *He was despised and rejected of men,* is too well known, and too deservedly admired, to need any encomiums here; yet it may not be amiss to give it as one of the strongest instances of the hurtfulness of the da capo, since, by its interventions, even this most exquisite song becomes sensibly tiresome. The next chorus, *Surely he hath born* [!] *our griefs,* &c. has little either pathos or expression; and the fugue, and division upon the conclusion *With his stripes we are healed,* are neither pleasing to the ear nor conformable to nature. The chorus, *All we like sheep have gone astray, we have turned every one to his own way,* is defective. . . . The music is joyous, and an imitation of the *wandering* of sheep, instead of the solemn sorrow of repentance: the divisions upon *have gone astray,* are improper and inexpressive; and though the expression in the conclusion, *The Lord has laid on him the iniquity of us all,* is considerably better, yet it only serves to set the impropriety of the former verse in a more glaring light. In the next recitative *Handel* has attempted the expression, and, what is surprising in him, has failed in it. The words are, *All they that see him laugh him to scorn,* &c. and the accompanyment is an imitation of *laughing,* of *shooting out the lips,* and *shaking the head.* But it is hardly possible to express these by music, so as either to please by the similitude, or affect by the subject. The following chorus, *He trusted in God that he would deliver him, let him deliver him if he delight in him,* is only tolerable at best; and the fugue upon the latter part, and division upon *delight,* are certainly blameable. . . . If the reader will look over the beginning of this act, he will find three long and loud chorus's together without any repose given to the ear, except by a single and trifling recitative; and will be sensible, from what he felt himself at the performance, how necessary it is to afford relaxation in order to give pleasure. The next recitative, *Thy rebuke has broken his heart,* and the song, *Behold and see if there be any sorrow like unto his sorrow,* are noble specimens of Mr. *Handel*'s great abilities. . . . The recitative which follows, *He was cut off from the land of the living,* &c. is of the middling cast, but its merit, and that of the succeeding song, *Thou didst not leave his soul in hell,* &c. are so much eclipsed by the preceding recitative and song, that they please less here than they would probably have done in any other place. The next chorus, *Lift up your heads, O ye gates,* &c. though the music is good, and the conduct of it generally admired; yet certainly it wants magnificence throughout the whole. . . . The chorus of *Let all the angels of God worship him,* is good in point of musical composition; the author had given no opportunity for expression. The recitative of *Thou art gone up on high, thou hast led captivity captive,* &c. is fine in the first part, and as bad in the second. The chorus of *The Lord gave the word, great was the company of the preachers,* is very exceptionable on several accounts. In the first place, the words are incapable of musical expression: secondly, the expression which is attempted is absurd; he endeavours to express the *greatness* of the *company* by the *loudness* of their *roaring*—a thing never heard of among *preachers*. . . . The next song, *How beautiful are the feet of them that preach the gospel,* &c. the chorus, *Their sound is gone out into all lands,* &c. the song, *Why do the nations so furiously rage together,* &c. may all be characterized by the same word middling, as there is little beauty or default in any of them, except the division on *nations* in the last. The succeeding chorus, *Let us break their bonds asunder,* is *too* abrupt in its intervention; it is a total change of subject without the least warning, which, with the outreé expression, renders it very disagreeable: it turns entirely on a forced imitation of *break asunder* and *cast away,* and becomes ridiculous by over-acting. . . . The next song, *Thou shalt break them with a rod of Iron, thou shalt dash them in pieces like a potters vessel,* has little to praise or little to blame, except the division upon *potters*. The concluding chorus, *Hallelahjah* [!], *the Lord God omnipotent reigneth,* is, however, truly striking and sublime, by the most perfect conduct it rises by degrees to the highest pitch of sublimity and pathos, till music exhausts her utmost powers in the noble expression of *King of Kings, and Lord of Lords.*

At the beginning of Part III the writer pronounced the "deservedly admired" aria, "I know that my Redeemer liveth," a "fine and pathetic" song, although most of the words "are not very proper for music" and the "melting flow" of "this angelic song" is "impeded by the untoward construction of the words." In the succeeding chorus,

> *Since by man came death*
> *By man came also the resurrection of the dead;*
> *For as in Adam all die,*
> *Even so in Christ shall all be made alive.*

There is an evident contrast between the 1st and 2d, the 3d and 4th lines, but *Handel* by endeavouring to shew it highest colours, has once again spoiled all by over-labour. Thus the 1st is serious and melancholy to the highest degree; the 2d equally light and jocund; the 3d returns again to the strains of woe, and the 4th is another loud burst of mirth. . . . *The trumpet shall sound, and the dead shall be raised incorruptible and we shall all be changed,* is very faulty and very unworthy of the master-hand which set it. The words would have admitted the full exertion of his strength in instrumental music, and made the most striking and sublime chorus that ever was composed. Instead of that, it is a simple solo song, the accompanyment is a trifling trumpet air, and the whole tenor of the music infinitely beneath the subject. . . . The duet, *O death where is thy sting?* &c. is great, and affecting; and shews plainly, that the errors in the expression of this kind of subject . . . did not arise from an ignorance of them in *Handel,* but from haste or inattention. . . . Had *Handel* never composed another chorus but . . . *Worthy is the lamb that was slain,* &c. he might with justice have been ranked at the head of musical composers; the melody is fine, and the conduct inimitable; the expression perfect, and the harmony has that noble fullness which distinguishes this great master from all his competitors to fame. But the last chorus, *Blessing and honour, glory and power, be unto him,* &c. is . . . rather calculated for the display of the author's skill in a fine fugue, than a natural expression of the subject. The fugue, too, on *Amen,* is entirely absurd, and without reason: at most, *Amen* is only a devout *fiat;* and ought never, therefore, to have been frittered, as it is, by endless divisions upon *A*—and afterwards *men.* If it was capable of expression, or of adding any thing to the force of the whole, it ought to have been set to a few great and slow notes, by way of a solemn close; and thus *Purcell* has managed it, at the end of one of his finest anthems, the effect of which is infinitely superior to what any musical division could produce.

Having analyzed *Messiah* "with the most scrupulous minuteness," the author proceeded to examine *Samson* "with the same degree of accuracy," in order to indicate "how much is wanting to perfection, even in these two most finished performances of Mr. *Handel,* in the sacred and dramatic form." In his conclusion the critic extolled Handel as "the Shakespeare of Music" and suggested that the "striking excellencies" of *Messiah* and *Samson* outweigh the "common defects" of these two "capital" oratorios:

> From this review of the *Messiah,* and *Samson,* every unprejudiced person will see how much is wanting to perfection in these greatest of Mr. *Handel*'s compositions, and what ample room there still remains both for correction and improvement. Perhaps the patrons of genius may think that too great pains have been taken to point out faults, and too small encomiums passed on *beauties.* Yet before they condemn the writer, let them consider, how easy it is to animadvert on common defects, how difficult it is to find words worthy of striking excellencies; let them consider how easy it would be to expose *Shakespear's Puns, his Gibes and Gambols,* how difficult it would be for *panegyric* to follow him in the flight of genius. There is something more in this allusion than bare illustration, and the respective talents of these *heroes* of *Parnassus* bear as strong a resemblance as their errors and successes. They are the darling sons of the sister sciences, poetry and music; they both have faults, but they are the faults of genius; they both abound in *beauties,* but they are beauties which art cannot reach. Criticism may blame both, but taste must admire them equally; and envy must praise their invention, even where she brands their judgment: in a word, tho' these sons of genius sometimes dazzle, sometimes scorch, their light will always be [p]referred to the frigid moon-shine of art and imitation.

IV

It is an extraordinary fact that the complete score of Handel's *Messiah* was never published during the composer's lifetime.[7] In 1742 Handel presented the Dublin Charitable Musical Society with a manuscript of his "sacred oratorio," and fifteen years later he bequeathed another score of *Messiah* to the Governors of the Foundling Hospital. Since Handel

---

[7] Regarding the first publication of *Messiah* William C. Smith has reconciled numerous contradictions and corrected traditional inaccuracies in two excellent articles: "The Earliest Editions of Handel's *Messiah,*" *The Musical Times,* LXVI, 985–990 (November 1925); "Handel's *Messiah*: Recent Discoveries of Early Editions," *The Musical Times,* LXXXII, 427–428 (December 1941).

permitted *Messiah* to be performed in London only under his personal direction, manuscript copies thus easily sufficed for all English and Irish performances until 1759. It is nevertheless remarkable that the masterpiece of England's greatest composer remained unpublished for twenty-five years. To persons familiar with the speed of modern production it seems almost incredible that, despite Handel's enormous popularity, only *one* of his choral works (*Alexander's Feast*) was fully published before his death. John Walsh generally paid Handel twenty guineas for each oratorio which he printed, but in 1743 the composer is said to have refused such a sum for *Messiah*. Handel nevertheless permitted the overture to be engraved at once, and it appeared in a collection advertised in *The London Daily Post* as early as 12 December 1743:

Six Overtures from the Opera and Oratorio's of Sampson, Messia, Saul, Deidamia, Hymen, Parnasso; set for the Harpsichord. Compos'd by Mr. Handel. The 8th Book. These Overtures are also to be had for Violins, in eight Parts.

A similar advertisement in *The Daily Advertiser* of December 14 substituted "The Sacred Oratorio" for "Messia," and this modification likewise appeared on the title page of the instrumental parts of the same overtures. It is significant that on all later sets of instrumental parts (published after 1749) *Messiah* was advertised under its correct title. Between 1730 and 1760 Walsh issued seven volumes of *Sonatas or Chamber Aires for a German Flute, Violin, or Harpsichord,* "Being the most Celebrated Songs and Ariets Collected out of all the Late Oratorios and Operas Compos'd by Mr. Handel." Volume Five of this collection (published in 1744) contains one item from *Messiah*: "He was despised." An index attributes this aria to *Messiah*, but the song itself is designated simply as an "Air by Mr. Handel in the Sacred Oratorio." No item from *Messiah* appears in Volume Six, but Volume Seven (published in 1760) contains nine, and here again each selection is ascribed to *Messiah* in the index, whereas no such acknowledgment appears on the page itself. In 1749 Walsh commenced to publish a series of four hundred of *Handel's Songs Selected from His Oratorios,* and five oblong volumes appeared at irregular intervals during the next ten years. Throughout this collection of "songs" the publisher scattered *all* the vocal solos and the duet from *Messiah,* but it is again striking that all other songs bear the titles of the oratorios from which they are taken, whereas those drawn from *Messiah* are reproduced without identification. Walsh issued several editions of these four hundred "songs." In the index to the volumes containing the instrumental parts all items from *Messiah* are properly identified, and in several of the parts the word *Messiah* also introduces the aria "But who may abide." Perhaps Handel was unable to resist Walsh's entreaties for permission to insert selections from *Messiah,* but if so, the composer probably stipulated that Walsh should not indicate the source from which such arias were drawn.

Meanwhile Walsh had issued several collected editions of the favorite *Songs in Messiah,* originally advertised in 1763 but probably first published some fifteen years before. Regarding the actual date of the first edition of *Songs in Messiah* Handelian biographers have created much confusion and produced little evidence. Even a cursory glance at contemporary newspapers reveals that publication of Handel's works was generally well advertised, and that with few exceptions Walsh announced complete editions of oratorio "songs" immediately following their initial production. Most of these collections of songs contain catalogues of earlier works also "To be had of the Publisher." As Handel continued producing oratorios Walsh's advertised list of their titles lengthened accordingly, but to the present day the most diligent research has failed to locate a single reference to a full-score *Messiah* or even to *Songs in Messiah* in London advertisements before 1763. Definite notice of the publication of *Messiah* first appeared in *The Public Advertiser* on 29 March 1763:

> This Day is published a Second Set of Handel's Grand Songs in Score, introduced in his Oratorios not printed before. Handel's Oratorios in Score of Judas Maccabeus, Samson, Occasional Oratorio, Messiah, Alexander's Feast, Acis and Galatea. Also a complete Set bound, 14 vols.

Since no volume of *Songs in Messiah* was ever advertised during Handel's lifetime, and since the title is not mentioned in Walsh's catalogue of 1760, it has been assumed that *Songs in Messiah* was not printed before 1763 (or 1760 at the earliest). It is, however, highly improbable that a masterpiece which for ten years had enjoyed increasing popularity should have failed to merit at least partial publication during a period when the songs in Handel's other oratorios were all openly published and widely advertised in contemporary London journals. Much internal evidence suggests that *Songs in Messiah* was first published as early as 1749. Several extremely rare folio editions bear Walsh's imprint, and throughout these early collections it is notable that each aria from *Messiah* appears in its original version and contains none of Handel's subsequent alterations and improvements. One cannot easily account for the appearance of "O thou that tellest" and "He was despised" an octave higher in the G clef long after these songs had ceased to be sung by that voice. And why should *Songs in Messiah* contain the original version of "But who may abide" (which Handel had discarded after the London performance of 1743) when a subsequent arrangement containing the *prestissimo* movement had been in use for years? In 1743 Handel composed a special version of "And lo!" for Mrs. Clive, and this alteration appears in *Songs in Messiah,* although Mrs. Clive never sang for Handel after 1746 and the original recitative was restored long before 1760. It is therefore probable that the earliest edition of *Songs in Messiah* appeared without public notice a few years after the first performance of *Messiah* in London. A number of later editions containing slight variations from the original were published throughout the eighteenth century, but not till 1767 did the word *Messiah* appear freely in publications of Handel's works.

As early as 29 June 1751 Walsh announced that "A Complete Set of all Mr. Handel's Oratorios may be had neatly bound in eleven Volumes." Many such advertisements might be quoted to suggest that the publisher was offering *all* of Handel's oratorios to date. Walsh's advertisements were sometimes contradictory and frequently inaccurate, but it is still curious that subsequent to the production of *Messiah* he advertised "A Complete Set of all Mr. Handel's Oratorios." Actually, however, it is certain that *Messiah* was not published in its complete form until 1767. A preliminary announcement of *Messiah* in *The Public Advertiser* of 4 December 1766 was followed nine days later by a fuller advertisement inserted by Randall & Abell (successors to John Walsh) of 13 Catharine Street in the Strand. On 13 December 1766 *The Public Advertiser* announced:

Proposals for Printing by Subscription, The complete Score of the Oratorio called MESSIAH; composed by Mr. Handel, with his additional Alterations. The Price to Subscribers is One Guinea and a Half; One Guinea to be paid at the Time of subscribing, and Half a Guinea more on the Delivery of the Book, which will be in May next. It is desired that those Gentlemen and Ladies who are willing to encourage the Work, will send in their Subscriptions that the Proprietors may be secured of a sufficient Number to answer the Expence of so great an Undertaking.

On 4 July 1767 *The Public Advertiser* declared that copies of *Messiah* would be available "on Tuesday next, the 7th inst." On July 23 the same journal announced that the oratorio was finally ready to be delivered to subscribers. Among those who subscribed to the first complete edition of Handel's *Messiah* it is pleasant to observe (besides George III and

MESSIAH

AN Oratorio

IN SCORE

As it was Originally Perform'd.

Compoſed by

Mr. HANDEL

To which are added

His additional Alterations.

London. Printed by Meſſrs. Randall & Abell Succeſſors to the late Mr. J. Walſh in Catharine Street in the Strand — of whom may be had the compleat Scores of Samson, Alexander's Feast, and Acis & Galatea.

TITLE PAGE OF THE ORIGINAL FULL-SCORE EDITION OF MESSIAH (1767)

From the Copy in the Library of Congress

Queen Charlotte) such familiar names as Charles Burney, Samuel Johnson, William Cowper, Charles Jennens, Thomas Linley, John Randall, Samuel Arnold, and Benjamin Cooke.[8] Only ninety persons (and two musical societies) subscribed, and only 129 copies were reserved in advance. No fewer than nineteen subscribers lived in Cambridge, and Charles Jennens was set down for three copies. It has been noted that in the original full-score version of *Messiah* all arias were printed from the same plates formerly used for *Songs in Messiah* (1763), but the choruses were obviously printed from plates engraved at a subsequent date. Unfortunately the Randall & Abell score of *Messiah* is extremely incorrect, for Handel's autograph manuscript is highly illegible, and Walsh evidently failed to engage an expert musician to correct the printed proofs. Dozens of deplorable mistakes were thus perpetuated, and these errors passed without question into various later editions published in England, America, and Germany. For years it was accepted that Randall & Abell issued only one full-score edition of *Messiah*, but it is now clear that no less than five editions of Handel's masterpiece appeared between 1767 and 1773. Within a decade Handel's oratorios became common property. Following Randall's death Messrs. Wright & Wilkinson secured the premises at 13 Catharine Street and proceeded to reprint from Walsh's plates such of Handel's compositions as were still in demand. By 1784 James Harrison of 18 Paternoster Row was publishing certain of Handel's works in oblong folio volumes, and John Bland of 45 Holborn had begun to issue Handel's single songs and complete oratorios in great quantity.

It is a curious reflection upon eighteenth-century English taste that Handel's *Messiah* remained unpublished till eight years after the composer's death. If *Songs in Messiah* were issued as early as 1749, and if instrumental selections from *Messiah* were published even earlier, why was the oratorio

---

[8] For a complete list of subscribers see Appendix B.

never advertised in the customary manner? Omission of the source of *Messiah* excerpts included in *Handel's Songs Selected from His Oratorios* and in *Songs in Messiah* suggests that some significant fact lay behind the *extremely* occasional use of *Messiah* as title of the oratorio. Perhaps Englishmen had expressed some definite objection to publishing *Messiah* (in whole or in part) under its proper name. Perhaps the same cries of desecration that forced Handel to perform *Messiah* only as *A Sacred Oratorio* also compelled him to suppress the original title even in published excerpts. During Handel's lifetime Walsh doubtless sold *Songs in Messiah* to anyone who requested it, but until a broader spirit prevailed he scrupulously avoided the publicity of advertisement and quietly inserted movements from *Messiah* in miscellaneous collections without indicating their source. After 1750, however, *Messiah* was a fashionable favorite, and thenceforth Handel's refusal to publish his masterpiece must be ascribed to better reasons. Apparently Handel did not wish to print *Messiah*. Despite public indifference the composer seems always to have regarded his masterpiece with peculiar reverence and solicitude. Possibly he wished to retain control of the score for financial purposes. Whatever his motives may have been, there was obviously some potent reason why *Messiah* was treated differently from Handel's other oratorios during the composer's lifetime. Perhaps some obscure eighteenth-century family correspondence or musical publication will ultimately emerge to indicate whether the answer lies in Walsh's avarice, in Handel's special regard for his masterpiece, or in Georgian England's strange prejudice against the union of a Scriptural theme with the music of a master. Beneath occasional certainties and numerous speculations concerning the first publication of *Messiah* a mystery still awaits solution.

V

All the King's Men

> Remember Handel? Who that was not born
> Deaf as the dead to harmony, forgets,
> Or can, the more than Homer of his age?
> —WILLIAM COWPER, *The Task* (1785)

I

IN EARLY CHILDHOOD George III frequently heard Handel conduct morning concerts in the drawing-room of the royal residence at Leicester House. One day the composer was struck by the earnest attention of the four-year-old child. "A good boy, a good boy," cried Handel, "you shall protect my fame when I am dead." No one familiar with the subsequent career of "Farmer George" could deny that Handel's prediction was amply fulfilled during the sixty years of George III's turbulent reign. To the stolid Georgian kings Handel represented the peak of artistic attainment. His music was apparently the sole point upon which that scandalously disunited family could agree. George III spoke French and German with facility, but he knew nothing of classical art and literature, and Handel's music constituted his one elevated taste. His predilection for the German composer amounted almost to a prejudice. He scraped Handel on his violin, pecked Handel on his harpsichord, and whistled Handel on his German flute. At every royal concert he demanded the music of his favorite composer. With his support *Messiah* was first published in 1767, and later he patronized Dr.

Samuel Arnold's famous edition of *The Works of G. F. Handel* (1785–1797). During an interview with George III in Kew Gardens on 2 February 1789 Fanny Burney introduced his "favorite theme, Handel," but when the King "ran over most of his oratorios, attempting to sing the subjects of several airs and choruses," she found him "so dreadfully hoarse that the sound was terrible." From 1799 to 1820 the King was engulfed in total insanity, and during those tragic years of isolation he spent much of his time in a rectangular room lined on both sides with harpsichords. Groping his way about, he stopped here and there to play favorite snatches from Handel's oratorios, especially Dalila's mad love song from *Samson* and Jephtha's lamentation at the loss of his daughter. Certainly no eighteenth-century Handelian was more enthusiastic or more influential than George III. At a time when royal patronage was especially valuable he publicized Handel's works and secured for them the highest place of honor in England's great national functions.

It is therefore not surprising that the King warmly endorsed a plan to commemorate the centenary of Handel's birth by a series of gigantic Handelian performances under the roof that covers the composer's dust. Early in 1783 three musical amateurs (Viscount Fitzwilliam, Sir Watkin Williams Wynne, and Joah Bates) conceived the notion of celebrating Handel's memory by performing his greatest works "on such a scale of magnificence, as could not be equalled in any part of the world." To three such fervent Handelians it occurred that 1784 would be a proper time to inaugurate such a custom, for that year marked the twenty-fifth anniversary of Handel's death and also what was erroneously computed to be the centenary of the composer's birth. Immediately the plan won eager support from the Managers of the Musical Fund and from the Directors of the Concert of Ancient Musick. When the design reached the ears of George III he heartily sanctioned it with his patronage and fixed upon Westminster Abbey as the place most appropriate for such a celebration. Since all proceeds were to be applied to charity, the Bishop of Rochester readily consented to the use of the national shrine, and it was thereupon determined to give two performances in Westminster Abbey on May 26 and 29 and one performance at the Pantheon on May 27. A grandiose "Account of the Life of George-Frederick Handel: with a Description of the Intended Celebrity at Westminster-Abbey and the Pantheon in Commemoration of his Memory" appeared in *The European Magazine* for March 1784:

The English nation have seldom been wanting in gratitude to those who have contributed either to the glory or to the entertainment of the country. In no part of the world have there arisen monuments to eternize the memory of statesmen, legislators, warriors, or benefactors to society, at the public expence, more than in England. In no quarter of the globe have those who have contributed to the amusements of life, been more amply rewarded, or more respectfully noticed. The Jubilee in commemoration of Shakspeare a few years since, though ridiculed by the wits of the time, was not unworthy of a nation's gratitude; and the like mark of respect now in contemplation, under the sanction of Royalty, to do honour to the Shakspeare of musick, GEORGE-FREDERICK HANDEL, will afford another proof that distinguished merit will not be buried in oblivion, and, it may be presumed, will excite a spirit of emulation in others to deserve, and to obtain the like marks of respect and reverence.

In its ecstatic anticipation of *Messiah* on 29 May 1784 *The European Magazine* declared that "The number of voices and instruments which are to unite in the performance of this Oratorio will produce an effect, that those best versed in the power of sounds can have but a very imperfect idea of; and even such as are auditors will never have language to express the sensations they must feel, if they have *music* in their souls!" Throughout the month preceding the Commemoration elaborate architectural preparations at Westminster Abbey were supervised by James Wyatt and approved by George III. According to *The European Magazine*:

The present organ will be taken down, and a grand gallery erected in the room, from a design of [Mr. James Wyatt], for the reception of their Majesties, and all the younger branches of the Royal Family, of an age capable of relishing the performance, together with the Royal attendants. This gallery will be hung with crimson velvet fringed with gold. Over the western door of the Abbey, will be erected a large new organ, built by Mr. [Samuel] Green for Canterbury cathedral, but which is to be fixed up in the Abbey on this occasion. Mr. [Joah] Bates, we are informed, means to play the organ. The base of the orchestra, which will contain a band of about five hundred vocal and instrumental performers, is to be seven feet from the ground. In short, the whole will form a *coup d'oeil,* equally novel, magnificent, and splendid.

During the last week of May London was crowded with families drawn to the capital to attend the Handel Commemoration. "I never remember it so full," wrote Dr. Burney, "not only so late in the year, but at any time in my life, except at the coronation of his present Majesty." Scores of performers came from remote parts of the kingdom at their own expense. *Scots Magazine* reported that "The popular rage for this extraordinary novelty was such, that all the tickets which were issued were bought up with an avidity beyond all expectation; so that the day before the performance not a single ticket was to be gotten through the whole town."

On Wednesday morning, 26 May 1784, the first great Handel Festival commenced in Westminster Abbey with a performance of Handel's *Dettingen Te Deum,* one of the Coronation Anthems, one of the Chandos Anthems, part of the Foundling Anthem, and several other fragments. Long before the appointed hour crowds of well-dressed persons had assembled before the Abbey doors. In his *Account of the Commemoration* Dr. Burney reported that the struggle, though short, was for the time as violent as any ever witnessed at a theatre:

Early in the morning, the weather being very favourable, persons of all ranks quitted their carriages with impatience and apprehension, lest they should not obtain seats, and presented themselves at the several doors of Westminster Abbey, which were advertised to be opened at Nine o'clock; but the doorkeepers not having taken their posts, and the Orchestra not being wholly finished, or, perhaps, the rest of the Abbey quite ready for the reception of the audience, till near Ten o'clock; such a croud of ladies and gentlemen were assembled together as became very formidable and terrific to each other, particularly the female part of the expectants; for some of these being in full dress, and every instant more and more incommoded and alarmed, by the violence of those who pressed forward, in order to get near the door, screamed; others fainted; and all were dismayed and apprehensive of fatal consequences: as many of the most violent, among the gentlemen, threatened to break open the doors; a measure, which if adopted, would, probably, have cost many of the most feeble and helpless their lives; as they must, infallibly, have been thrown down, and trampled on, by the robust and impatient part of the croud.

Inside the Abbey the "Directors" of the Commemoration wore special gold medals appended to white ribbons, and carried white wands tipped with gold. Eight or ten gold medals had been struck expressly for the occasion, and the King himself not only condescended to accept one but actually wore it to all performances "in compliment both to the living and to the dead." Seating of spectators was supervised by "Assistant Directors," who wore silver medals and carried white wands tipped with silver. On the first day four hundred royal footguards graced the avenues of Westminster Abbey, and forty yeomen attended the King and Queen.

Before ten in the morning [wrote *The European Magazine*] the appearance was numerous, and, about half after eleven, the immense space was crowded to overflowing; the number was not short of 4000, the greatest part of which were ladies. By the natural coolness of the Abbey, and the contrivance of the Directors, the place was not so intolerable for heat as might be imagined from the season. Their Majesties arrived about a quarter past twelve o'clock. The King came first into his box, and, on viewing the brilliant spectacle, he started and stood for some moments seemingly in an extasy of astonishment, an extasy which could only be exceeded by the bounding transports of our amiable Queen. The Royal Pair were accompanied by Prince Edward and the Princess Royal, who sat on the King's right, and the Princesses Augusta, Sophia, and Elizabeth, on the Queen's left hand; they were all in one box, which was most elegantly adorned.

Contemporary periodicals found it "scarcely possible" to describe in adequate terms the grandeur of that "sublime" exhibition. "So grand and beautiful a spectacle," continued *The European Magazine,* "with at the same time a feast so rich and perfect, has not been presented to the public eye within our memory." All the "youth, beauty, grandeur, and taste of the nation" were here "grouped in all the natural and easy appearance of the *pêle-mêle.* The Ladies were without diamonds, feathers, or flowers, and thus, in our mind, their charms were embellished." Westminster Abbey was "simple, grand, striking in its contrivance," and "the dispositions of the throne, the orchestra, the ornaments, all so exactly harmonising with the tone of the cathedral, were imagined in a taste at once both curious and correct."

A performance of Handel's works at the Pantheon on the evening of May 27 featured miscellaneous songs and choruses as well as four concertos and one overture. At this concert an audience of almost three thousand persons "presented a most brilliant appearance," although "the general anxiety was such, and the fear of not being present at this solemnity made the company so eager, that the press at the doors was as great, and the entrance as vehemently contested for, as it is at the pit and galleries of the theatre on a night of unusual invitation." *The European Magazine* reported that "Stars and Duchesses disdained not to set their shoulders to the crowd, and jostle for admission to this triumph of art."

On the following day eight hundred persons derived "great satisfaction" from a rehearsal of *Messiah,* and on Saturday, May 29, that "most sublime Oratorio of Handel" was "executed" at Westminster Abbey "in a manner worthy of that great composer." More than four thousand tickets had been issued, and the cathedral was "crowded to excess" with elegant throngs reminiscent of "the splendor and magnificence" of former days.

Though the company which attended this day's performance [wrote Dr. Burney] was considerably more numerous than that of Wednesday, yet, by the experience acquired, and measures pursued, such good order reigned in every department, that it was impossible to enter or quit a public place, of any kind, with more facility, or to be seated more commodiously, when there, than at this magnificent exhibition. And though the chief part of the audience, by coming early, had a long period to fill up, yet, suffering no inconvenience from numbers, heat, or cold; and having a building so venerable, so fitted up, and so filled, to examine, all the languor, lassitude, and tediousness were kept off, which usually seize body and mind in public places, before the long expected pleasure arrives. The very filling the Abbey with such company, and the Orchestra with such performers, was a new, varied, and amusing spectacle, before the arrival of their Majesties and their beautiful offspring crowned the whole, and rendered the *ensemble* as enchanting to the eye, as such sublime Music, so exquisitely performed, must have been to every ear.

At noon the Royal Family and numerous attendants arrived in state. Immediately *Messiah* began, and its performance was in no respect inferior to that of the first day. Joah Bates presided at the organ and conducted the orchestra in a manner which *Scots Magazine* pronounced "above panegyric." According to *The European Magazine* he "appeared to be so agitated and inflamed by the subject during the performance —his mind was so involved and his powers so roused, that his instrument, though immense in its tone, could hardly give utterance to his sentiments." The size and proportion of Bates' orchestra would make any modern conductor gasp. His "band" consisted of 48 first violins, 47 second violins, 26 violas, 21 violoncellos, 15 contrabasses, 6 flutes, 13 first oboes, 13 second oboes, 26 bassoons, 1 double bassoon, 12 horns, 12 trumpets, 6 trombones, 3 pairs of kettledrums, and 1 organ. His singers (including all principals) numbered 60 sopranos

(47 boys, 12 women, and 1 man), 48 altos (all men), 83 tenors, and 84 basses, making a total ensemble of 525 vocal and instrumental performers. Such unprecedented numbers produced effects which eighteenth-century periodicals found difficult to describe.

> It would be presumptive in us to enter into a detail of the performance [declared *The European Magazine*]. It was in so grand, so superior, and so exalted a stile, that it must not be subjected to the rules of pettyfogging criticism. Our readers may imagine better than we can describe, the fulness of a band of more than 500 instruments. They may conceive what must be produced by a combination of all the executive powers in the country, inflamed and actuated by the Muse of Handel. . . . The immense volume and torrent of sound was almost too much for the head or the senses to bear—we were elevated into a species of delirium. . . . No error appeared throughout any of the performance; every person was perfect and regular; no mistakes interrupted the general effect; nor did any accident allay the universal satisfaction which was experienced during the whole of this wonderful exhibition.

At the close of Part II the "Hallelujah Chorus" was repeated at the King's request. "This movement," continued *The Universal Magazine,* "is better calculated to display the power of a full volume of sound, and, in course, to produce a wonderful effect with a large band, than any other composition whatever." A "most respectable list" of soloists that day "acquitted themselves with much credit," and the celebrated Gertrude Elisabeth Mara rendered Handel's soprano arias "in the most exquisite stile." *The London Chronicle* found it "above panegyric" to do justice to Mara's excellence, particularly in the aria, "I know that my Redeemer liveth," in which "her expression and pathos were so powerful, that there were but few eyes that were not moistened with a tear." A little before four o'clock the oratorio ended. According to *The London Chronicle,* Their Majesties took their departure in a "very gracious" manner:

The Royal descendents retired from the audience with every demonstration of politeness; the youngest Princess, not accustomed to such meetings, was prompted by the Princess Royal to make her obeisance; it unfortunately happened, that the front of the State-box was nearly as high as the Princess's chin, so that her head was invisible for a time. The Princess Royal could not restrain the laugh, so much provoked, and every lip wore a smile on the occasion.

Actuated by the prodigious success of the Handel Commemoration, Queen Charlotte at once commanded a repetition of the first day's performance at Westminster Abbey on Thursday morning, June 3, and of *Messiah* at the same place on Saturday morning, June 5. Advertisements of these two additional performances appeared in London newspapers on May 31. A public rehearsal for the fourth concert took place at Westminster Abbey on June 2, and on the following day a vast audience heard a program almost identical with that of the first performance. A proposed rehearsal of *Messiah* on June 4 was cancelled in deference to the King's birthday. In his *Account of the Commemoration* Dr. Burney provided a thorough review of the performance of *Messiah* on June 5:

Those who attended this day's Commemoration at the Abbey were, seemingly, of a higher class than had yet appeared there; so that though the croud was somewhat less than at the preceding performance of the same Oratorio, the exhibition was more splendid. Indeed, as a spectacle, it was so magnificent to the sight, and, as a musical performance, so mellifluous and grateful to the ear, that it will be difficult for the *mind's eye* of those who were absent, to form an adequate idea of the show, or the *mental ear* of the sound, from description. Every one present must have found full employment for the two senses which afford us the most refined pleasure; as it is from the eye and the ear that intellect is fed, and the mind furnished with its best intelligence.

There was a change in the manner of executing the Music to *"Lift up your heads, O ye gates,"* which deserves to be mentioned. On the former occasion, the alternate semi-choruses were performed by *all* the voices belonging to each part; but to-day, in order to heighten the contrast, only by three of the principal singers, till about the thirty-third bar; when the whole Chorus from each side of the Orchestra, joined by all the instruments, burst out, *"He is the king of glory."* This had a most admirable effect, and brought tears into the eyes of several of the performers. Indeed, if we may judge from the plenitude of satisfaction which appeared in the countenance of all present, this effect was not superficial, nor confined to the Orchestra.

Another new and grand effect was produced to-day in the Hallelujah, and last Chorus, *"Worthy is the Lamb,"* by the introduction of the *tromboni*, which were not used in these Choruses, on the former occasion.

At the first performance of the Messiah, his Majesty expressed a desire to the earl of Sandwich of hearing the most truly sublime of all Chorusses: *"Allelujah! for the Lord God omnipotent reigneth,"* a second time; and this gracious wish was conveyed to the Orchestra, by the waving of his lordship's wand. At this second performance of that matchless Oratorio, his Majesty was pleased to make the signal himself, with a gentle motion of his right hand in which was the printed book of the words, not only for the repetition of this, but of the final Chorus, in the last part, to the great gratification of all his happy subjects present; and, perhaps, the subjects of no sovereign prince on the globe were ever before so delighted with the effects of a royal mandate.

It is pleasant to observe that James Boswell attended this performance of *Messiah* in the company of Sir Joshua Reynolds. At Westminster Abbey the two gentlemen joined Dr. Burney, Miss Mary Palmer, and Miss Mary Hamilton at nine o'clock on Saturday morning. After securing "proper seats for hearing the Musick" the five of them engaged "very agreeably in conversation" until the performance commenced at noon. Miss Hamilton was deeply moved by *Messiah,* and her diary provides a charming personal account of the final day of the great Handel Commemoration:

June 5th was the day of the Handel Celebration & performance of the Messiah at the Abbey; Got up at 6,—at a ¼ before 9 Dr. Burney & Miss Palmer came for me in Dr. Burney's Coach; Sir Joshua Reynolds & Mr. Boswell followed in Sir J.'s Chariot. . . .

We got in without any difficulty; the lower part was already filled with people, but Dr. Burney got us the proper seats for hearing the Musick, Sir Joshua introduced me to Mr. Boswell, (the Mr. Boswell who wrote the history of Corsica). From 9 till 12 passed away very agreeably in conversation with Miss Palmer & these 3 sensible Men, & remarking the countenances of the company. . . . Mr. Boswell is one of those people with whom one instantly feels acquainted, we conversed together with as much ease & pleasantry as if we had been intimate a long time.

At 12 their Majesties, the 3 elder Princesses & the 3 younger Princes & their attendants made their appearance & the Concert began.

I was so delighted that I thought myself in the heavenly regions. 513 Performers, the Harmony so unbroken that it was like the fall of Waters from one source, imperceptibly blended. The Spectacle too was sublime, So universal a silence, So great a number of People. Were I to attempt to say all I felt & thought I should fill many pages; it was over at 4 o'clock. I got out easily took leave of my companions & was brought home by Dr. Burney. I felt myself quite exhausted.

Eighty-four-year-old Mrs. Delany was able to attend four of the five concerts of the first Commemoration. It is regrettable that she recorded no details of the performances, for it would be curious to read the comments of Handel's personal friend on that occasion, especially since Mrs. Delany had many years before heard oratorio performances directed by the composer himself.

Perhaps Mrs. Delany was more stunned than entranced by the unwieldy mass of performers mustered to render Handel's *Messiah* at Westminster Abbey. In the composer's lifetime a group of sixty vocal and instrumental performers had been deemed adequate for any oratorio performance, but the centennial celebration of 1784 drafted hundreds of musicians, apparently more with a view to majestic noise than with any particular artistic discrimination. Such an immense ensemble was undoubtedly baroque. Its rigid, stupendous proportions exceeded those of Wagner's utmost demands, and the orchestra alone was four times the size of that normally employed for such purposes today. Despite such disproportion, however, current periodicals exhausted every superlative in praising the Handel Commemoration. "So extraordinary a spectacle, we believe, never before solicited the public notice," wrote *The European Magazine*, "nor was ever conducted with so much propriety on the part of the Managers, or so much satisfaction to the numerous spectators." *Scots Magazine* lauded "what must be a kind of epoch in the art, because it establishes attainments never before experienced, nor indeed thought possible."

Some few periodicals, however, concurred with *Scots Magazine* in entertaining "a vain wish" that "the object" of the Handel Commemoration "had been less fleeting." To *The Universal Magazine* "The situation of the times" seemed to accord "but ill with splendid festivals, and a profusion of expense." As one turns the pages of contemporary records, he is struck by the fact that the ecclesiastical tone of Westminster Abbey failed to redeem the frank worldliness of a brilliant public spectacle. Church officials attempted to control at least the physical appearance of the fashionable audience by announcing that only small hoops would be tolerated and that no ladies wearing hats (particularly hats with feathers) would be admitted. But the audience proved beyond clerical control. On the morning of the first performance persons of all ranks struggled violently to gain admittance to Westminster Abbey, and Dr. Burney recorded that "the female part of the expectants" screamed and fainted with apprehension of "fatal consequences" from being trampled upon by "the robust and impatient part of the croud." Inside the Abbey soloists received storms of applause, while cheap theatrical effects rendered Handel's solemn strains noisy and bombastic, and the thunder of chorus and kettledrums for four hours proved almost deafening. Indeed it is not astonishing that such an incongruous juxtaposition of sacred and secular elements aroused a cry of desecration from conservative churchmen and provoked fierce condemnation from poet and priest alike.

II

Strict devotees were scandalized at the sacrilege of commemorating a composer by singing his own works in the temple of the Lord, even though his works were supposedly dedicated to the glory of God, and even though the poor gained seven thousand pounds from the performance. To William Cowper the Handel Commemoration was nothing less than profanation of a sacred building. Although he entertained high respect for Handel's genius, he was seriously alarmed at the growing prevalence of profane delights. That thousands of persons (all in danger of eternal punishment) should gather in a cathedral to honor a fellow-sinner by singing of their own future damnation, appeared to him the most incredible folly he could conceive. On 20 November 1784 he sent the Reverend William Unwin a "short drama" designed to "set the musical business in so clear a light that you will no longer doubt the propriety of the censure":

Scene opens, and discovers the Abbey filled with Hearers and Performers. An ANGEL *descends into the midst of them.*
Angel. What are you about?
Answer. Commemorating Handel.
Angel. What is a commemoration?
Answer. A ceremony instituted in honour of him whom we commemorate.
Angel. But you sing anthems?
Answer. Yes, because he composed them.
Angel. And Italian airs?
Answer. Yes, and for the same reason.
Angel. So then because Handel set anthems to music, you sing them in honour of Handel; and because he composed the music of Italian songs, you sing them in a church. Truly Handel is much obliged to you, but God is greatly dishonoured.
[*Exit* ANGEL, *and the music proceeds without further impediment.*

Cowper was not alone in his condemnation of the Abbey celebration. Early in June 1784 his intimate associate the

Reverend John Newton expressed a desire to recall his countrymen to a sense of their true situation by preaching a course of fifty sermons on the words of Handel's *Messiah,* and Cowper warmly applauded his intention, although he confessed doubt as to results. On 21 June 1784 Cowper wrote to encourage his friend:

We are much pleased with your designed improvement of the late preposterous celebrity, and have no doubt that, in good hands, the foolish occasion will turn to good account. A religious service, instituted in honour of a musician, and performed in the house of God, is a subject that calls loudly for the animadversion of an enlightened minister; and would be no mean one for a satirist, could a poet of that description be found spiritual enough to feel and resent the profanation. It is reasonable to suppose that in the next year's almanack we shall find the name of Handel among the red-lettered worthies, for it would surely puzzle the Pope to add any thing to his canonisation.

For half a century serious Anglican divines had piously denounced all *playhouse* performances of Handel's *Messiah* as a species of profanation, while other clergymen with equal vehemence had opposed all *cathedral* performances of Handel's "sacred" oratorios as unspeakable sacrilege. To Newton's stern mind oratorios represented evil in a most insidious form, and he determined, like other Evangelicals, to oppose them with solemn denunciation. He never fully escaped the Scriptural fetters of his age. With Cowper he held extreme Calvinistic views, although his evangelical fervor drew him close to the sentiments of Wesleyan Methodism. But the Wesleys, a highly gifted musical family, refused to leave all the best tunes to the Devil, whereas Newton deemed every form of music except simple hymn-singing the exclusive prerogative of Satan.

Of all Newton's sermons the most curious are those preached in 1784 and 1785 upon Handel's *Messiah.*[1] Follow-

---

[1] *Messiah: Fifty Expository Discourses, on the Series of Scriptural Passages, which form the Subject of the Celebrated Oratorio of Handel,* 2 vols., London,

ing the Commemoration *Messiah* aroused general enthusiasm, and it is evident that in adopting a popular theme Newton made use of current fashion to attract further attention to his own work. In his fifty sermons he endeavored "according to the measure of my ability and experience" to indicate "the meaning and importance of the well-chosen series of scriptural passages, which are set to music in the Oratorio of *the Messiah*." He believed that "The arrangement or series of these passages, is so judiciously disposed, so well connected, and so fully comprehends all the principal truths of the gospel, that I should not attempt either to alter, or to enlarge it." In his first sermon he explained the occasion for his discourses:

Conversation in almost every company, for some time past, has much turned upon the commemoration of Handel; the grand musical entertainments, and particularly his Oratorio of the *Messiah*, which have been repeatedly performed on that occasion in Westminster Abbey. If it could be reasonably hoped that the performers and the company assembled to hear the music, or the greater part, or even a considerable part of them, were capable of entering into the spirit of the subject, I will readily allow that the *Messiah*, executed in so masterly a manner, by persons whose hearts, as well as their voices and instruments, were tuned to the Redeemer's praise; accompanied with the grateful emotions of an audience duly affected with a sense of their obligations to his love; might afford one of the highest and noblest gratifications, of which we are capable in the present life. But they who love the Redeemer, and therefore delight to join in his praise, if they did not find it convenient, or think it expedient, to hear the *Messiah* at Westminster, may comfort themselves with the thought, that, in a little time, they shall be still more abundantly gratified. Ere long death shall rend the vail which hides eternal things from their view, and introduce them to that unceasing song and universal chorus, which are even now performing before the throne of God and the Lamb. Till then, I apprehend, that true Christians, without the assistance of either

---

1786. For further details and references see my article, "Fifty Sermons on Handel's *Messiah*," *The Harvard Theological Review*, XXXIX, 217–241 (October 1946).

vocal or instrumental music, may find greater pleasure in a humble contemplation on the *words* of the *Messiah,* than they can derive from the utmost efforts of musical genius. This therefore is the plan I spoke of. I mean to lead your meditations to the language of the Oratorio, and to consider in their order, (if the Lord on whom our breath depends shall be pleased to afford life, ability and opportunity) the several sublime and interesting passages of Scripture which are the basis of that admired composition.

Here Newton revealed no strong sense of impropriety in the *Messiah* performance at Westminster Abbey. Thus far he agreed that such performances were *capable* of inspiring "the highest and noblest gratifications" in "the performers and the company assembled." But in his sermon on "The Angel's Message and Song" he proceeded to more serious criticism:

The gratification of the *Great,* the *Wealthy,* and the *Gay,* was chiefly consulted in the late exhibitions in Westminster-Abbey. But notwithstanding the expence of the preparations, and the splendid appearance of the auditory, I may take it for granted, that the shepherds, who were honoured with the first information of the birth of MESSIAH, enjoyed at free cost, a much more sublime and delightful entertainment. How poor and trivial is the most studied magnificence and brilliancy of an earthly court, compared with that effulgence of glory which surrounded the shepherds? The performers of this Oratorio, if I may be allowed the expression, were a multitude of the heavenly host. And though I do not suppose that the angel delivered his message in the cadence, which we call *Recitative,* I have no doubt but the chorus was a *Song,* sweetly melodious as from blest voices. . . . We have reason to believe, there is, in the world of light and love, something analogous to what we call music, though different in kind, and vastly superior in effect, to any strains that can be produced by the most exquisite voices, or instruments, upon earth.

Newton was convinced that "the sufferings of the Son of God, are, by no means, a proper subject for the amusement of a vacant hour." He complained that at Westminster Abbey the Scriptural message was reduced to the level of a worldly

VIEW OF WESTMINSTER ABBEY DURING THE COMMEMORATION
OF HANDEL (1784)

From an Engraving by Edward F. Burney
in Charles Burney's *Account of the Commemoration* (1785)

entertainment. In his fourth sermon he sharply criticized "the spirit and temper of at least the greater part of the performers, and of the audience" at the Handel Commemoration, and in his famous description of the Abbey celebration he provided material for all subsequent objectors to *Messiah* performances:

> I represent to myself a number of persons of various characters, involved in one common charge of high treason. They are already in a state of confinement, but not yet brought to their trial. The facts, however, are so plain, and the evidence against them so strong and pointed, that there is not the least doubt of their guilt being fully proved, and that nothing but a pardon can preserve them from punishment. In this situation, it should seem their wisdom, to avail themselves of every expedient in their power for obtaining mercy. But they are entirely regardless of their danger, and wholly taken up with contriving methods of amusing themselves, that they may pass away the term of their imprisonment with as much chearfulness as possible. Among other resources, they call in the assistance of music. And amidst a great variety of subjects in this way, they are particularly pleased with one. They chuse to make the solemnities of their impending trial, the character of their judge, the methods of his procedure, and the awful sentence to which they are exposed, the ground-work of a musical entertainment. And, as if they were quite unconcerned in the event, their attention is chiefly fixed upon the skill of the composer, in adapting the style of his music, to the very solemn language and subject with which they are trifling. The king, however, out of his great clemency and compassion towards those who have no pity for themselves, prevents them with his goodness. Undesired by them, he sends them a gracious message. He assures them that he is unwilling they should suffer: he requires, yea, he entreats them to submit. . . . But instead of taking a single step towards a compliance with his goodness, they set his message likewise to music; and this, together with a description of their present state, and of the fearful doom awaiting them if they continue obstinate, is sung for their diversion, accompanied with the sound of cornet, flute, harp, sackbut, psaltery, dulcimer, and all kinds of instruments. Surely, if such a case as I have supposed could be found in real life, though I might admire the musical taste of these people, I should commiserate their insensibility!

Newton terminated this flat rhetoric by coldly censuring the holiday mood of Abbey audiences and by emphasizing "the great impropriety" of "making the fundamental truths of christianity" the theme of public entertainments:

> Mr. Handel . . . has been commemorated and praised, many years after his death, in a place professedly devoted to the praise and worship of God; yea, (if I am not mis-informed) the stated worship of God, in that place, was suspended for a considerable time, that it might be duly prepared for the commemoration of Mr. Handel. But, alas! how few are disposed to praise and commemorate MESSIAH himself! The same great truths, divested of the music, when delivered from the pulpit, are heard by many admirers of the oratorio with indifference, too often with contempt.

In strengthening his argument *against* performances of *Messiah* Newton sometimes inadvertently provided excellent arguments in their favor. Apparently he failed to realize that one who refuses to hear the "great truths" of Scripture elsewhere (or one who hears them from the pulpit with "indifference" and "contempt") may hear them at a *Messiah* performance and find himself stirred by Handel's composition to consider the Scriptural texts to which the music is set.

In subsequent sermons Newton proceeded to chastise connoisseurs who attended *Messiah* performances for musical delight rather than for spiritual edification. Speaking of "those who *crucify the Son of God afresh, and put him to open shame*," he condemned "persons who can bear to hear of his passion and his kingdom, when made the subject of a musical entertainment, but upon no other occasion." Frequently he repeated his central conviction that "the great truths of God" were not enhanced by Handel's music but rather buried beneath its impressive grandeur. "If you heard the *Messiah*, you were, perhaps, affected by the music," he said in a characteristic passage; "how much are you to be pitied, if you are hitherto unaffected by the sentiment!" To

Newton the words of *Messiah* were of far greater consequence than Handel's most stunning music:

The music of the *Messiah* is but an ornament of the words, which have a very weighty sense. This sense no music can explain, and when rightly understood, will have such an effect as no music can produce. That the music of the *Messiah* has a great effect in its own kind, I can easily believe. . . . I can allow, that they who heard the *Messiah,* might be greatly impressed during the performance; but when it was ended, I suppose they would retain the very same dispositions they had before it began.

Even the grand "Hallelujah Chorus" was powerless until the hearer absorbed "an abiding sense" of its profound significance for all Englishmen:

The impression, which the performance of this passage in the Oratorio, usually makes upon the audience, is well known. But however great the power of music may be, . . . it cannot soften and change the hard heart, it cannot bend the obdurate will of man. If all the people who successively hear *the Messiah,* who are struck and astonished, for the moment, by this chorus in particular, were to bring away with them an abiding sense of the importance of the sentiment it contains, the nation would soon wear a new face. But do the professed lovers of sacred music in this enlightened age, generally live, as if they really believed that *the Lord God omnipotent reigneth?* Rather, do not the greater part of them live, as they might do, if they were sure of the contrary?

Actually Newton nursed no bitterness towards Handel's "sublime" music. He commended the "great propriety" of the "Hallelujah Chorus" and praised "I know that my Redeemer liveth" as "a beautiful and well chosen introduction to the third part of the *Messiah.*" But in his sermons Newton displayed only a slight acquaintance with Handel's masterpiece. From his frequent use of such phrases as "I have heard" and "I have been informed" it is clear that he knew little about "the celebrated oratorio" upon which he preached fifty sermons! "I have been informed," he declared in a typical quotation, "that the music to which this passage is set, is so well adapted to the idea that it expresses, as, in a manner, to startle those who hear it."

In his final sermon Newton summarized his criticism of the Handel Commemoration and recapitulated the central theme of his fifty discourses:

> It is probable, that those of my hearers, who admire this Oratorio, and are often present when it is performed, may think me harsh and singular in my opinion, that of all our musical compositions this is the most improper for a public entertainment. But while it continues to be equally acceptable, whether performed in a church or in the theatre, and while the greater part of the performers and of the audience, are the same at both places, I can rate it no higher, than as one of the many fashionable amusements, which mark the character of this age of dissipation. Though the subject be serious and sólemn, in the highest sense, yea, for that very reason, and though the music is, in a striking manner, adapted to the subject, yet, if the far greater part of the people who frequent the Oratorio, are evidently unaffected by the Redeemer's love, and uninfluenced by his commands, I am afraid, it is no better, than a profanation of the name and truths of God, a crucifying the Son of God afresh. You must judge for yourselves. If you think differently from me, you will act accordingly.—Yet, permit me to hope and to pray, that the next time you hear *the Messiah,* God may bring something that you have heard in the course of these sermons, nearly connected with the peace and welfare of your souls, effectually to your remembrance.

With this forceful peroration Newton brought his sermons to a close. In the spring of 1785 he delivered his last discourse and promptly made arrangements for private publication. Cowper had followed the series with deep interest, and when Newton asked his help in securing an appropriate motto, he promised to search his library:

> I shall not leave my books unransacked; but there is something so new and peculiar in the occasion that suggested your subject, that I question whether, in all the classics, can be found a sentence suited to it. Our sins and follies, in this country, assume a

shape that Heathen writers had never any opportunity to notice. They deified the dead, indeed, but not in the Temple of Jupiter. The new-made god had an altar of his own; and they conducted the ceremony without sacrilege or confusion.

Cowper declared himself "happy to serve" his friend with whatever "may occur susceptible of accommodating to your purpose," and he expressed his belief that the Bible "will abundantly supply you with applicable passages. All passages, indeed, that animadvert upon the profanation of God's house and worship, seem to present themselves upon the occasion." For his motto Newton finally chose a verse from the Old Testament: "Oh that they were wise, that they understood this!" (*Deuteronomy* 32:29).

Newton's *Messiah* was first published in two enormous octavo volumes early in 1786, and *The Universal Magazine* advertised it as available in May. Critical reaction was mixed. *The Monthly Review* observed that Newton's sermons "contain much real piety, and may be read with profit by all, and, probably, with peculiar pleasure by those who are of the party." In most periodicals, however, Newton was sharply ridiculed for conducting a crusade against Handel's *Messiah*. Certainly he failed to reflect the popular verdict in his objections to that "sacred" oratorio. But his complaints were in strict accord with the tone and spirit of the Evangelical Revival, and when one overlooks a few narrow and uncharitable passages, the sermons still answer a wholesome purpose in emphasizing the solemn words of an oratorio now admired chiefly for its music.

III

In condemning the Handel celebrations Cowper was not content merely to encourage his friend in the progress of his sermons on *Messiah*. Cowper's own convictions were strong. Deeply affected by the religious movements of his day, he rejected the cold impersonality of early eighteenth-century deism and sought comfort in the more subjective and emotional experiences offered by the new evangelical sects. Of the many hymn-writers of eighteenth-century England Cowper was the most gifted and distinguished, and his finely-wrought *Olney Hymns* (1779) express the hope of this new evangelicalism. But the ecstatic poet of the religious revival was by nature introspective, and his constant heart-searching (aroused by fears lest God's grace be withdrawn) proved too much for his already gloomy tendency to self-distrust. He never lost his persuasion that he was irretrievably damned, and his religious despair thereafter appeared in the gentle melancholy and morbid religiosity of much of his verse. In *The Task* (1785) he determined "to have a stroke at vice, vanity, and folly, wherever I find them." Book Six is entitled "The Winter Walk at Noon," and here he deplored the faults of urban civilization and lashed the British aristocracy for its moral deficiencies. Speaking of the late Handel Festival, he directed his sharpest lines at the "Commemoration-mad" who had recently thrilled to *Messiah* at Westminster Abbey:

> Man praises man. Desert in arts or arms
> Wins public honour; and ten thousand sit
> Patiently present at a sacred song,
> Commemoration-mad; content to hear
> (O wonderful effect of music's power!)
> Messiah's eulogy for Handel's sake.
> But less, methinks, than sacrilege might serve—
> (For was it less? What heathen would have dared
> To strip Jove's statue of his oaken wreath,
> And hang it up in honour of a man?)
> Much less might serve, when all that we design
> Is but to gratify an itching ear,
> And give the day to a musician's praise.
> Remember Handel? Who that was not born
> Deaf as the dead to harmony, forgets,
> Or can, the more than Homer of his age?
> Yes—we remember him; and while we praise
> A talent so divine, remember too

> That His most holy book from whom it came
> Was never meant, was never used before,
> To buckram out the memory of a man.

This bitter passage is somewhat incoherent and more than a trifle rash. Intensely pious himself, Cowper was offended that a recognized masterpiece of "sacred" music, based upon purely Scriptural texts and composed by a genius whom he revered, should be performed in a solemn cathedral where, according to the Prayer Book, the entire service is to be chanted or sung to organ accompaniment. Apparently Cowper could not comprehend that a sensitive hearer may find *Messiah* a magnificent hymn. Eventually he dismissed the matter as too foolish to deserve serious consideration:

> But hush!—the Muse perhaps is too severe,
> And, with a gravity beyond the size
> And measures of the offence, rebukes a deed
> Less impious than absurd, and owing more
> To want of judgment than to wrong design.

Cowper's remarks contain no criticism of Handel himself; he even implies that "the more than Homer of his age" is too celebrated a genius to require formal commemoration.

But one writer failed to agree that Cowper's "ill-natured" reproach and "corrosive fires" found just cause in the great Handel Commemoration. To Anna Seward, "The Swan of Lichfield," Cowper was a "vapourish egotist" whose "generally red and angry beams" were by no means "auspicious to human happiness, or to human virtue." In one of her rare visits to London she herself had been "charmed by the Abbey music," and she had quoted lines from *Paradise Lost* to convey her satisfaction during the performance:

People universally assert, that the world never produced any thing of equal effect in the art. Indeed, I believe, that at these festivals, music touched her ne-plus ultra of excellence; for though, perhaps, every solo song has, from the impossibility of any single voice filling completely so immense a space, been heard in smaller scenes to greater advantage; yet, the sublimity of the harmonies, so full and complete in all those *great* effects which Handel's matchless genius conceived, though, from the comparative nothingness of the best band *those* days could afford him, he heard them not complete with his *mortal* ears; the exclusion of every thing harsh, and disagreeably noisy, by the care taken that no order of instruments, or of voices, should preponderate; the exquisite delicacy with which the songs were accompanied, and the picturesque power of several of the chorusses, that endued the ear with the powers of the eye;—all these admirables produced one grand result, that completely satisfied my imagination, high as report had taught me to set its claims.

Anna Seward was delighted at the appearance of Cowper's masterpiece, but she was outraged when she read his fiery censures upon the Abbey celebrations. Deploring Cowper's "ungenerous sentiments" and the "harsh asperity" of his "satiric scourge," she granted that "But for the illiberal protest of this author against the generosity of encomium, against the gratitude of tributary praise, I should have read his poetry with pleasure unallayed, as I confess it was exquisite." Three years later she expressed her reactions in a blank verse "Remonstrance addressed to William Cowper, Esq. in 1788, on the sarcasms levelled at national gratitude in *The Task*." Because of "the reported depression on his spirits" she graciously refused either to send the lines to Cowper or to publish them during his lifetime:

> Lo! in a strain
> Fanatic and illiberal as the lay
> Maligning Avon's festival, thou scorn'st
> Thy country, marshalling in holy shrines
> The harmonic strength of Europe, to fulfil
> The great designs Briarean Handel plann'd;
> That mighty, matchless German, who attun'd
> His lyre seraphic to thy native tongue!—
> Thou heard'st with grudging and disgusted ear
> Those great designs attain'd, when, thro' the aisles
> Of the vast ancient fane, in torrents burst
> Those floods of harmony, that lift the soul

Upon their swelling and tumultuous waves
Up to the Throne of God.—O! what is Virtue,
If praise of those, who thus their talents ten
Ardent improv'd, is folly, or is vice?

To Anna Seward there could be no "nobler virtue," no greater "tributary praise," than "the prodigious *éclat* of our Handelian commemorations, when the musical strength of this whole kingdom, and perhaps the flower of the science through Europe, were assembled together by the royal wish, hinted, yet not amounting to either command or desire; so that the assistance of every individual was voluntary, and met no golden fee of reward." In an editorial note to Miss Seward's "Remonstrance" Sir Walter Scott remarked that the charitable purpose of the Abbey performances "places the injustice of Cowper's sarcasm upon a level with its absurdity, accusing them, as it does, of a profane and idolatrous tendency."

Newton's fifty sermons on Handel's *Messiah* and Cowper's strictures on Handel Festivals were not soon forgotten. Long after both men lay in their graves pious ladies and reverend clergymen mused upon those curious offshoots of eighteenth-century English evangelicalism. In 1812 appeared a quaint volume entitled *A Series of Reflections on the Sacred Oratorio of the Messiah,* by "a Lady," in which the author "ingenuously" confessed that her work was "chiefly compiled from a larger work on the same subject" by John Newton. "Care has been observed," she wrote, "to avoid any peculiarities respecting certain controverted points of doctrine; and the liberty has been also used of altering any expressions that occurred, so as to adapt them to the purpose in view." A lengthy preface explained the author's motive in making her "Reflections" public:

The following *Reflections* on this celebrated composition, are offered to elucidate the *sense,* and to impart a taste for the *words* of the Oratorio, by briefly commenting on the series of sublime and well-selected passages of Scripture, of which it consists. In this respect, as well as in the pre-eminent excellence of the music, THE MESSIAH bears a character to which no other production of a similar kind has equal pretensions.

It is then, humbly, hoped, that the admirers of Sacred Music may derive benefit, as well as pleasure, from a perusal of these *Reflections;* not only bearing them in mind, during the performance of this noblest production of Musical Science, but even after the *sounds* of the orchestra have ceased.

A pleasing expectation is, also, entertained, that they who do not feel the inclination, or who have not the opportunity, thus to gratify themselves, as *hearers* of the performance, may yet derive a very high degree of enjoyment from mediating on the *sense* of the composition, and from pursuing, in that happy and judicious arrangement which it presents to the reader, a train of suitable reflections on the most important and affecting subjects which can occupy the attention of a rational being.

In its review of the fifth edition (1831) *The Christian Remembrancer* recommended *A Series of Reflections* "to the favour of all parents who would wish their children to be *edified,* as well as *delighted,* by the momentous words, and the captivating sounds, of the SACRED ORATORIO OF THE MESSIAH." The reviewer was certain that "Every contemplative Christian, who has been charmed with the sublime melodies of Handel, as adapted by that great master of music to the sublimer words of the sacred oratorio of the Messiah, will be gratified by the 'Reflections' of this amiable lady." Her "useful and pleasing work" received official sanction from the Lord Bishop of Durham and reached its seventh edition in 1836.

Throughout the Victorian period Newton's sermons stimulated constant discussion among theologians as well as musicians. That eloquent English noncomformist Robert Hall failed to share Newton's repugnance to performances of Handel's *Messiah,* for he had found himself deeply affected by the grandeur of the first great Handel Commemoration in 1784. When the King and his subjects rose for the "Hallelujah Chorus" Hall was ineffably moved by what struck him as "a great act of national assent to the fundamental truths of religion." In one of his *Three Lectures on the Cathedral Service of the Church of England* (1843) the Reverend John Jebb was also "thoroughly persuaded" that "it was by the direction and blessing of Divine Providence that the works of this first of musicians were produced and have been suffered to maintain their place in our sanctuaries." During the same year a volume of *Remarks upon the Use and Abuse of Musical Festivals* (1843) announced the conviction of "An English Churchman" that "If the compositions of any living being can claim an hearing in God's House, from the fact of their being dedicated to God's service, most surely those of the immortal Handel will claim first place." In answering those who insisted that "God's House must necessarily be desecrated" by oratorio performances, the writer declared it "very like a profanation" that such "sublime productions" as *Messiah* and *Israel in Egypt* should be performed "in a common concert room" with "no outward sanctity of place" and "no sort of controul over persons' feelings."

Most detailed of all replies to Newton's *Messiah* was Dean Edward B. Ramsay's thoroughgoing response in his *Two Lectures on the Genius of Handel,* delivered in January 1862. In his rather pious discussion of the "distinctive character" of Handel's "sacred compositions" Ramsay regretted that "well meaning, conscientious persons have felt it their duty to protest against oratorios, forbidding their families to attend on such performances as they would forbid their attendance on scenes of mere earthly gaiety, on the opera, and on theatrical entertainments." Ramsay found it difficult to impute sincerity to such "unadvised and party traditionary assertions." He maintained that "Handel's music is oftentimes of a salutary nature," that "it is capable of elevating the thoughts," and that "it adds a charm and interest to the sublime passages of Scripture." He pointed out that when anyone already familiar with *Messiah* reads or hears such Scriptural passages as "For unto us a Child is born" and "He was despised and rejected of men," he usually associates the Biblical texts with Handel's music. "They seem indissoluble," Ramsay declared, "and I suppose I should so connect them were I hearing them on the bed of death." Thus he expressed his conviction that Handel's *Messiah,* founded on the life of Christ and based on Scriptural texts, could be performed nowhere else so fitly as in a solemn cathedral. He doubted the piety of those who felt no devotion on hearing *Messiah* within *any* building, but he believed that the oratorio realized its highest expression only within the ancient and consecrated walls of Westminster Abbey:

> I can hardly believe that those good persons who object to attendance upon the performance of oratorios are in reality quite sincere, or that they have deeply and seriously considered the subject in all its bearings upon the religious sensibilities of our nature. The appreciation of the great works of Handel, and other great masters, is spreading throughout the land, and now extends from the highest to the lowest in the social scale. The Handel commemorations have become identified with national feelings. Surely it were better to direct such a movement, and give it the full religious character of which it is capable, than make the vain attempt of putting it down as evil.

IV

After the gigantic Handel Commemoration of 1784 "Grand Musical Festivals" of even vaster proportions were heard in Westminster Abbey in 1785, 1786, 1787, 1790, and 1791. For several years the number of performers and the skill of their execution steadily increased, until by 1791 the Abbey Commemorations had benefited metropolitan charities to the sum of fifty thousand pounds. From 1784 Handel's *Messiah* became the standard feature of all Festivals both in London and throughout the provinces. In 1785 four "grand performances of sacred music from the works of Handel" drew "full and fashionable" audiences to Westminster Abbey, and on 2 June 1785 Court Dewes (nephew of Mrs. Delany) described the first performance in rapturous terms:

I was this morning at the music in the Abby, which was by far *the finest thing* both for *sight* or *sound* I *ever saw or heard;* I think you and Bernard would have been full *as well* entertained with it as with the best day's fly-fishing you ever had! . . . Mrs. Delany tolerably well, and *she was at the Abby this morning!*

At the 1785 Festival 616 performers rendered *Messiah,* and in the following year "the vocal and instrumental band" rose to 640. In 1786 the first of three performances at Westminster Abbey was rendered on May 31. At the rehearsal on May 29 sixty-eight-year-old Horace Walpole shared the Bishop of Rochester's gallery with Princess Amelia. "The sight was really fine," he wrote, "and the performance magnificent; but the chorus and kettle-drums for four hours were so thunderful, that they gave me the headache, to which I am not at all subject." Magazine accounts of the 1786 Festival echoed the rhapsodic extravagance of Commemoration enthusiasts two years before. "There was heaven in the eye, and heaven in the mind," declared *The Town and Country Magazine.* "Devotion, love, reverence, and admiration pervaded every heart, and inspired every soul with the sweet sympathy of mental enjoyment." An ensemble of 806 musicians performed *Messiah* in the Handel Festival of 1787. "Mrs. Delany did *not* go to the meeting at the Abbey *this* year," wrote Harriet Joan Granville on 14 June 1787; but "Miss Port and I went the second day, which was the Messiah, and indeed it fully answered every grand idea I had formed of it."

Meanwhile Dr. Charles Burney had been commissioned by George III to produce a "respectable and faithful record" of the first great Handel Commemoration. Burney's celebrated *Account of the Musical Performances in Westminster-Abbey in Commemoration of Handel* appeared early in 1785. Immediately the London edition was pirated by a Dublin publisher, and a German translation was subsequently issued in Berlin and Stettin. While engaged in composition Dr. Burney exchanged several communications with George III. When the King learned that publication was delayed only by the engravers, he asked to read the unbound pages of the finished work. Upon these he drew up two critical notes, one of which concerned the performance of *Messiah*:

Dr. Burney seems to forget the great merit of the Choral fugue *He trusted in God* by asserting that the words would admit of no particular strokes of passion; now the real truth is that the words contain a manifest *presumption* and *impertinence* which Handel has in the most masterly manner taken advantage of and He was so conscious of the merit of that movement that when ever desired to sit down to the Harpsichord if not instantly inclined to play He used to take this Subject which ever sate His imagination at work and made him produce wonderful fine Capriccios.

At the King's desire old Mrs. Delany supplied numerous particulars for Dr. Burney's volume. Further assistance was provided by the historian's nephew Edward F. Burney, whose two sepia drawings appeared in the published work to illustrate the interior of Westminster Abbey as it appeared during the Commemoration of 1784. Quite appropriately Dr. Burney inscribed his volume to the King, and Dr. Johnson's draft of the royal dedication proved to be the great Samuel's final contribution to English literature. "When Your Majesty is pleased to be present at Musical performances," Johnson wrote, "the artists may congratulate themselves upon the attention of a judge in whom all requisites concur, who hears them not merely with instinctive emotion, but with rational approbation, and whose praise of HANDEL is not the effusion of credulity, but the emanation of Science." Throughout Burney's pages *The Monthly Review* observed his "usual industry, accuracy, good sense, and sentiment." One reviewer lauded the "judicious and elegant author" who, "to a great deal of music in himself, adds a great deal of knowledge of his subject, a great deal of industry, a great deal of modesty, and a great deal of chaste, unaffected humor."

When a nation's intellectual atmosphere is suddenly charged with electricity, its poetical activity is generally stimulated to a corresponding degree. Following the great Commemoration of 1784 London was engulfed in a torrent of versified prose dedicated to the memory of the composer and his works. Apparently nothing could discourage the Hanoverian bard in his journey to Parnassus. Early in the summer of 1784 one Pollingrove Robinson ventured a grotesque poem entitled *Handel's Ghost: An Ode on the Power of His Messiah as Performed at Westminster Abbey: Addressed to Her Majesty*. In a former essay *The Monthly Review* had drily remarked that Robinson's "blank verse differs very little from prose," and the same magazine dismissed *Handel's Ghost* with an equally blunt rebuke: "As this ode is not of the class that will be admired by the few, we shall say nothing more of it." *The English Review* found Robinson's "highly indecent and profane" performance "a kind of travesty" of Dryden's *Alexander's Feast*:

> See him in the fated garden!
> Bleeding, suing for our pardon!
> See the *Saviour all forlorn!*
> See his sacred body torn!
> Hark the stroke!—Ah see the nail!
> See how they pierce!—Hark how they rail!
> Stretch'd on the cross the great **Redeemer** hangs
> In agonizing pangs!

In somewhat higher strain Thomas Maurice signaled the Commemoration with his *Ode Sacred to the Genius of Handel* (1784). A year later Dr. Thomas Scott's *Ode to Handel* was set to music by Benjamin Cooke and performed by a double choir of eight voices at the Commemoration Dinner on 26 May 1785. In 1786 John Ring produced no less than forty-two octavo pages of verse entitled *The Commemoration of Handel*. "The process of the Commemoration is here described," explained *The Monthly Review*, "and the subject of the Messiah represented, in harmonious and elegant verse, which, amidst the triumphs of Music, in some measure maintains the honours of Poesy." In 1787 Edward Jones published

A Poem to the Memory of Handel. During the following year an anonymous ode entitled *The Progress of Music: Occasioned by the Grand Celebration at the Abbey* provoked the caustic censure of *The European Magazine:* "If this gentleman knows as little of the harmony of music as he manifestly does of the harmony of poetry, he knows *nothing.*" Finally the Reverend James Hurdis rose in some measure to the dignity of his subject in *The Village Curate* (1788):

> Sweet music wakes, and with transporting air
> Handel begins. What mortal is not rapt
> To hear his tender wildly-warbled song
> Where'er he strays; but chiefly when he sings
> Messiah come, and with amazing shout
> Proclaim him King of Kings, and Lord of Lords,
> For ever and for ever, Hallelujah.
> Great soul, O say from what immortal fount
> Thou hast deriv'd such never-failing power
> To win the soul, and bear it on the wings
> Of purest extacy, beyond the reach
> Of ev'ry human care. From whence thine art
> To lift us from the earth, and fix us there
> Where pure devotion with unsparing hand
> Pours on the altar of the living God
> The hallow'd incence of the grateful heart.
> O mighty Handel, what seraphic power
> Gave inspiration to thy sacred song?
> Thyself perchance was some supernal spirit,
> Permitted to reside on earth awhile,
> To teach us here what Music is in Heaven.
> If ev'ry Angel that attends the throne
> Of clouded Deity, such song inspire,
> Let but our mortal ears one chorus hear,
> And all the world were gather'd into Heaven.
> The very Devils surely were drawn up
> To listen at the golden doors of light,
> And Hell left wasteful, wide, and desolate.

Considerable astonishment was expressed in London when no Handel Commemoration was scheduled for the late spring of 1788. On April 9 Anna Seward lamented that the trial of

Warren Hastings "prevents the Abbey music this year," and when the same trial was resumed in April 1789, the Handel Commemoration was, to the regret of numerous Londoners, suspended for a second time. In a curious pamphlet entitled *Sense Against Sound; or, A Succedaneum, for Abbey Music* (1788?) one anonymous writer promptly seized his opportunity to satirize the unwieldy Abbey Commemorations, and his sarcastic comments provide amusing evidence that Englishmen were not unanimous in their predilection for mammoth Handelian performances. Alarmed lest "England should wretchedly throw away her Consequence, and her Liberty, by a desperate Attachment to Music," the author complained that "his Country had forgot the Taste of good Writing, and was totally absorpt in her Devotion for Music." Ironically citing the benefits of Handel Commemorations, he observed that the "fair Flowers of our Nobility" now "rush with devout Ardour to this agreeable System of Worship, where they may exercise Repentance and Faith on the Fiddle." Since "Music is infinitely more necessary for England than the Bible," the writer deemed it "a thousand Pities" that "the British Nation should neglect to cultivate on general Plans a supercelestial Science in which (to the stupour of *all* Italy,) her Noblesse is so ecstatically drowned." Failure to repeat the Handel Commemoration in 1788 would, he feared, produce dire consequences throughout London's polite world:

How many beautiful and amiable young Ladies will lose charming Opportunities of sitting some six Hours with their Gallants in the Abbey, and of melting away in musical ecstasies before the Eyes of their melting Lovers! How many exquisite Amateurs of this exquisite Art will miss the unspeakable Gratification of being sometimes petrified,—sometimes dissolved,—sometimes imparadised in the Chorusses of Handel and Haydn!

Later the author provided "many weighty and substantial Reasons" why "the Widows and Orphans of the trusty and well beloved Church cannot too vehemently remonstrate against the Omission of the Abbey Anniversary." Insisting that "all England, both in Town and Country, will suffer materially from the Omission of this charitable Festival," he alluded slily to economic gains to be derived from Handel Commemorations. Every innkeeper along "the great Northern or Western Roads" and "innumerable Swarms of musical Instrument-makers, whose gay Shops are now the chief Embellishment of the Capital," would, he maintained, be "most cruelly out of Pocket" during "the inharmonious Year" of 1788.

For two seasons the Abbey performances were suspended, but at the command of the King they were resumed under royal patronage on 26 May 1790. At this Commemoration Fanny Burney heard *Messiah* as the guest of George III:

The princess Augusta condescended to bring me a most gracious message from the King, desiring to know if I wished to go to Handel's Commemoration, and if I should like the *Messiah*, or prefer any other day? With my humble acknowledgments for his goodness, I fixed instantly on the *Messiah;* and the very amiable Princess came smiling back to me bringing me my ticket from the King.

Miss Burney was much pleased with the rendition of *Messiah* on May 29, but William Johnston Temple confessed that he was "Not so much astonished and delighted" as he "expected." In 1791 the trial of Warren Hastings was postponed in order to facilitate the annual Commemoration in Westminster Abbey. On this occasion the national shrine was a scene of unprecedented splendor. In his *Musical Memoirs* (1830) William Thomas Parke recalled that the spectacle "afforded a gratifying and striking *coup d'oeil*," providing "a dignified display of the British court, united with the brilliant assemblage of the most beautiful and fashionable women of the Island." The band of musicians is said to have totalled 1068, but probably the numbers appearing in any one performance did not much exceed those on former occasions. All four concerts were honored by the presence of a guest no less distinguished than Franz Joseph Haydn. The beauty of Handel's works and the magnificence of their interpretation deeply impressed the Austrian composer. In loving emulation he produced within the next ten years *The Creation* (1798) and *The Seasons* (1801), both of which (though hardly cast in Handel's heroic mold) entitle Haydn to rank as Handel's heir and successor in oratorio. At the performance of *Messiah* in 1791 Haydn sat near the King's box. During the "Hallelujah Chorus" the composer wept like a child, and at its close he was heard to exclaim, "He is the master of us all!" [2]

With the growing taste for prodigious Handelian performances every provincial music-meeting in the kingdom took on fresh spirit and energy. Among those who attended such celebrations none was more ardent or sentimental than Anna Seward.[3] In the years following 1785 Handel Commemorations and three-choir festivals brightened her life with pleasant excursions to Birmingham, Sheffield, Manchester, and London. Her accounts of these musical performances provide concrete evidence that Handel's reputation had not waned during the three decades following his death. In late August of 1785 Miss Seward attended a "brilliant music-meeting" at Manchester, where, "amidst the collected musical strength of the kingdom," she heard "the celebrated Madame Mara" and "all the finest English singers" perform *Messiah* to the accompaniment of "the double drums from the Abbey" and "a band, noble and complete in all its parts." At this "har-

---

[2] After 1791 no Handel celebration took place in London till the first great "Musical Festival" at Westminster Abbey in 1834. In Scotland the First Edinburgh Musical Festival commenced in the Parliament House at Edinburgh on 30 October 1815. *Messiah* was heard on the morning of November 2. According to George Farquhar Graham, *An Account of the First Edinburgh Musical Festival*, Edinburgh, 1816, p. 87, "the number of persons who attended the performance this morning was very great; and consequently the struggle for admission was considerable, and occasioned a good deal of personal inconvenience to the female part of the company, some of whom fainted in consequence of fright and pressure."

[3] See my former study, *Anna Seward: An Eighteenth-Century Handelian*, Williamsburg, 1947.

monic" festival "A mob of several hundred well-dressed people, of both sexes, besieged the door half an hour before it was opened on the morning the Messiah was performed." Miss Seward was "charmed" by "the vollies of the abbey drums" and Mara's "ballooning vocalities," and it gave her "high delight" to hear her intimate friend John Saville "do the noblest justice to the inspirations of Handel." On another "excursion" to hear "the sublime Messiah" at Birmingham she rejoiced that "the dawn of a morning, fortunately cool," enabled her to enjoy "the highest possible intellectual feast, with little alloy from corporal uneasiness." *Messiah* was "finely performed," she reported, "though I never can like to hear it opened by a woman, even when that woman is Mara." So intense was her delight in Handel's oratorios that at one Birmingham Festival she encountered "perilous crowds and Calcutta heat in the morning and evening performance, three days together; eight hours music out of the twenty-four. It was," she added, "hazarding martyrdom to the second favourite science of my life." Back in Lichfield she was "surprised" and "affected" one Sunday to hear the "grand chorus" from *Messiah* at church:

Yesterday morning, Sunday, Mr [William] Inge preached in our choir, a sermon of great learning and ingenuity, composed on the arrival of our new and very fine organ. The discourse was upon church-music, its pleasure and utility; it concluded with— "and in conviction of the benefit devotion receives from sacred music, let us say Halelujah to the God Most High!—and again let us say Halelujah!"—Instantly, by previous appointment, and entirely unexpected by the audience, the organ poured in the grand chorus from the Messiah: "For the Lord God Omnipotent reigneth." Our glorious organ pealed along the aisles, and the choir put forth all her energies in the execution;—her minstrels sung with their heart and soul. Surprised, affected, charmed— almost everybody wept with pleasure.

In choral music Miss Seward considered Handel "pre-eminent, incomparable, transcendent, unrivalled, un-equalled." With pardonable British pride she explained that these "epithets" could be applied "with truth" only "to three men of genius in the known world; to Shakespeare, as a dramatic poet, Newton, as a philosopher, and Handel, as a musician."

In her frank predilection for Handelian oratorio Anna Seward typified those eighteenth-century "ladies of quality" who found in the composer an ineffable force and inspiration. Like most of her contemporaries she firmly believed that musical science "obtained in Handel the *ne plus ultra* of its excellence." During one "grand harmonic festival at Birmingham" she was curious to observe "how Haydn had shot in the strong bow of Handel" and "to compare his emulative powers closely, by listening to the Creation one morning, the Messiah the next." Her account of Haydn's *Creation* and Handel's *Messiah* offers a penetrating comparison of the two composers and reveals the decided musical tastes of English concert-goers in 1802:

By the overture to the Creation I was charmed. The subject is so happy; the imitative harmony so inevitably suggested itself, that a very inferior composer to Haydn must, if possessing any genius, have made a grand affair of it. No wonder then that his genius and science should have produced, in succession, effects so awful, and so exhilarating in this harmonic exordium. First, by that wild and complex dissonance which sublimely represents the tumult of chaos; next, by the low, soft, tremulous, sweet sounds, which arise when that tumult has gradually subsided; instrument after instrument stealing in, and exquisitely picturing on the ear the dawning, expanding, and gradually strengthening light, till suddenly the sun blazes out by the instant fortissimo of the whole orchestra, and by the burst and cannon-exultation of the double drums.

Not one of Handel's overtures suggested, or could properly allow of so picturesque, so dazzling an overture.

But there ended, in this emulative attempt, all approach to the excellence of that peerless master. The recitatives, and their accompaniments, are almost entirely imitative of other sounds, and of motion, and are without sentiment; while to those instrumental imitations all which Handel has given us in that style are infinitely superior. How poor, in the Creation, are the strains which imitate the lark and nightingale, compared to those of similar aim in L'Allegro and Il Penseroso! How inferior Haydn's plumy concert to that given in the prelude and accompaniments to "Hush ye pretty warbling choir," in Acis and Galatea!

We find an attempt in Haydn's oratorio to represent the soaring of the majestic eagle; but the strains more resemble the darting evolutions of the swallow.

The songs are opera-airs, sweet and ornamented; but they breathe no devotion; they excite no sympathy; they have nothing to do with the passions.

The chorusses are all impetuous, swift, and similar; bursts of harmony, skilful as to science, but, compared to Handel's, unmeaning, with little discriminated melody, and no contrast.

It is little wonder that the words translated from the German almost literally into English, should be neither sense nor grammar, nor that they should make wicked work with Milton; yet we meet poetic beauty in two of the lines, thus,

"With softer beams, and milder light, steps on
The silver moon through silent night;"

and the corresponding air is one of the happiest efforts in the composition.

It was with increased veneration for the powers of Handel that we listened, on the ensuing day, to the sublimities of the Messiah; expressing, in turn, every varied passion of the human soul; that we observed the contrasted pathos and energy, sweetnes and dignity, serenity and scorn, supplication and triumph, in the recitatives and songs, in the duet and chorusses of that stupendous work; to the decided air that winds through the fugues of every separate chorus lingering on the ear, and haunting the fancy through successive days; to the hallelujah and amen, that ravish the spirit, and seem to pierce the vault of heaven by their sonorous grandeur. Haydn, great master though he be, sinks eclipsed, like Dryden, when, in his alteration of the play of the Tempest, he puts on the armour of Shakespeare.

When this passage was written Haydn was seventy years old. During the preceding decade he had charmed England on two visits to London and Oxford, and his talents had struck British musicians with new force. But with all his brilliance Haydn could never replace Handel in English hearts. Forty-three years Handel had lain in Westminster Abbey, but the national demigod was not dead. In England he was destined to live another century as "the prince of musicians," "the first and foremost composer of his own or any other age," "the apostle and converter of the universe to the faith of sacred musical art."

V

Following his death in 1759 George Frideric Handel ascended the throne of musical England and there reigned absolute monarch for at least one hundred years. Aesthetic history can scarcely show a parallel to Handel's universal dominance of English music throughout the Georgian period. "All the judicious and unprejudiced Musicians of every country," wrote Dr. Burney in 1785, "upon hearing or perusing his noble, majestic, and frequently sublime FULL ANTHEMS, and ORATORIO CHORUSES, must allow, with readiness and rapture, that they are utterly unacquainted with any thing equal to them, among the works of the greatest masters that have existed since the invention of counterpoint." In 1785 Haydn had not yet visited London, and Mozart was still regarded in England chiefly as a youthful prodigy. Beethoven was fifteen years old, and Sebastian Bach (who had never been known in England) was now all but forgotten even in his own country. To eighteenth-century Englishmen Handel therefore represented the height of musical achievement. Till the time of Mendelssohn English composers revered Handel's oratorios as the matchless ideal of "sacred" choral art, and against the thundering chords of *Israel in Egypt* and *Messiah* all minor lyric strains proved futile. By 1850 "the Divine *Messiah*" had attained broader fame and more enduring popularity than any other choral composition in the Anglo-Saxon world. In molding English musical taste *Messiah* has exerted an influence beyond all power of estimation. How does Handel make this striking appeal to the plain Englishman? And why, after more than two centuries of change upon change in musical art, should this one oratorio continue to hold its own against every newcomer?

Perhaps Handel's popularity may be ascribed partially to fashion and habit. For generations Englishmen have regarded *Messiah* with a kind of national religious pride. Among Victorians *Messiah* became a sort of pious vogue, and "persons of distinction" heard its performance as regularly as fashionable churchmen attended divine service. But certainly *Messiah* does not rest on fashion alone. Eighteenth-century enthusiasts never tired of pronouncing its music "heavenly" and "sublime." Even at its first performance the oratorio "gave universal Satisfaction" in Dublin, since "in the opinion of the best Judges" it "far surpasses anything of that Nature, which has been performed in this or any other Kingdom." *Faulkner's Journal* declared *Messiah* "the finest Composition of Musick that ever was heard" and found Handel's setting "extremely well adapted" to the Scriptural text. At the first London performance Dr. James Beattie recorded that "the audience were exceedingly struck and affected by the music in general." John Mainwaring lauded the majesty and impeccable form of "this wonderful production of his genius," and William Shenstone considered *Messiah* "the best composer's best composition." Robert Burns confessed his delight in "the pathos of Handel's *Messiah*." Evidently its vivid imagination and deep emotional nature appealed intensely to Handel's contemporaries, for even the clergyman who penned a "Letter to a Friend, on going to hear the MESSIAH at the Play-house" was forced to grant that *Messiah* affords "the most finished exhibition of the composer's art now extant amongst us."

But if *Messiah* evinces masterly art it also possesses wide popular appeal. Handel's skilful counterpoint and inexhaustible melody are extraordinary, but equally remarkable is his power to move modest amateurs at the same time that he impresses cultivated professionals. Herein lies one secret of Handel's enduring position in English music: *Messiah* satisfies the needs of all classes. It speaks with equal force to rich and poor, wise and foolish, washed and unwashed. No other composition finds readier acceptance in the working-class mind, and no other oratorio appeals more widely to musicians of all styles, of all nations, of all ages. With profound simplicity and obvious sincerity *Messiah* expresses the noblest aspirations of mankind in universal musical terms. Its massive strength bespeaks the breadth of the popular mood. For seeking to base his title to immortality on direct appeal Handel deserves credit as the most courageous great composer who ever lived.

Much of Handel's popularity may be attributed to the sacred character of his oratorio texts. His Scriptural themes lie close to the heart of the religious world, and in his oratorios he clothed the finest passages of Hebrew literature in effective, theatrical music. From expressions of early auditors of *Messiah* one readily observes that it was not Handel's music alone that won their admiration, but rather his music as an expression of Jennens' Biblical verses. As early as 1744 *Faulkner's Journal* asserted that "nothing can come up to the choice of the subject," since "the Words are those of the sacred Text." Mrs. Delany confessed that she was "a little afraid" of *Messiah*, because she considered "the music *very affecting*" and "found it so," but she "felt great comfort" from its inspiring theme. In 1750 Mrs. Dewes confided that her heart "was raised almost to heaven" by *Messiah*, and declared that Handel's masterpiece was "calculated to raise our devotion, and make us truly sensible of the power of the divine words he has chose." Miss Talbot felt that there could be no "nobler entertainment" than *Messiah*, since "it is impossible for the most trifling not to be the better for it." John Wesley found a Bristol audience more "serious" at *Messiah* than at a sermon, and William Hanbury reported that during a *Messiah* performance at Church-Langton an "eye without tears" was "scarcely" to be "found in the whole church." To the religious man *Messiah* has always seemed "religious" in character. Even today Handel is regarded more as a preacher than as an artist. Thousands hear *Messiah* not so much because they admire its music as because they experience at its performance something like an act of devotion. Handel's religion is essentially popular, and his oratorios provide a perfect expression of popular "religious" sentiment.

Without its carefully selected and superbly arranged Biblical text *Messiah* could never have maintained its universal appeal for two centuries. Nothing is more pleasant than the familiar, and no literature is so familiar to Englishmen as the Hebrew stories of the King James Bible. Of all Handel's librettos that of *Messiah* treats matters of broadest general significance, for the story of Christ's Nativity, Passion, and Resurrection possesses deep and abiding interest for English-speaking peoples everywhere. With such a theme Handel might have been tempted to set to music a controversial theological system, proclaiming in admirable counterpoint his private views on baptismal regeneration and justification by faith. But he and Jennens committed no such error. History and doctrine are so perfectly balanced in *Messiah* that the text, though definitely Christian, leans neither to ardent evangelicalism on the one hand nor to mystical Catholicism or High Anglicanism on the other. In scrupulously avoiding any attempt at exegetical interpretation Jennens presented the Messianic theme from a purely nonsectarian angle, and he thereby expressed the broad Protestantism of a latitudinarian period during which men finally learned the lesson of toleration. Thus Handel's *Messiah* stands far above the fickle winds of taste and fashion, and so long as Christian faith endures it will maintain its position in the English-speaking world.

To a singular degree Handel's Scriptural settings have become the musical expression of the English people. His Biblical theme and forceful strains have invested his oratorios with peculiar charm in the eyes of earnest, Bible-loving

Britons. If the English people are fundamentally a religious race, they are also fundamentally a pragmatic race, and they seldom object to a bit of worldly pomp mingled with their sublime. Handel's oratorios thoroughly gratified their taste for public demonstrations of religious and patriotic fervor. His music was "religious" and solemn; his *simplex sanctaque melodia* made a permanent national impression; his massive choruses and powerful solos drove home to every English heart the essential truths of Anglican religion. In *Messiah* England found full satisfaction for her demands upon "sacred" musical art. Its confident spirit and its monotheistic purity express the religious ideal of a Protestant people more adequately than does its form of worship. To this day the "Hallelujah Chorus" remains a kind of national anthem of the British race. With dry humor Samuel Butler observed that "When we exclaim so triumphantly 'Hallelujah! for the Lord God omnipotent reigneth' we only mean that we think no small beer of ourselves, that our God is a much greater God than any one else's God, that he was our father's God before us, and that it is all right, respectable, and as it should be." Handel is popular in England chiefly because Englishmen are Protestants and Handel set the Protestant Bible to brilliantly "effective" music. Perhaps it was no mere coincidence that *Messiah* began winning immense favor throughout England just as John Wesley's Methodist Revival swept the country with a fresh wave of religious fervor. Persons whom Wesley and Whitefield guided to higher thought were better equipped to comprehend *Messiah*, for Handel gave musical expression to the very doctrines which those evangelists rescued from neglect. It was John Wesley who discovered a public prepared to support Handelian oratorio, and the early vogue of *Messiah* may thus be linked with England's unparalleled evangelical revival of the eighteenth century.

Nowhere is Wesley's doctrine of *assurance* more cogently expressed than in the ringing confidence of *Messiah*. Handel is unrivalled master of direct and simple sentiment, of virile patriotism untroubled by scruples, of energetic religion that knows no doubts. In music of resolute force and authority he fused the national fervor of English Protestantism with the positive assertions of an active people secure in their being chosen of the Lord. His pomp and grandeur suggest an era of absolutism; his triumphant choruses celebrate a strong and mighty God whose immense power bursts with unshakable confidence. Eighteenth-century deism rested upon firm faith in the stability and regularity of Nature's universal frame. Could Handel express that faith more appropriately than in superbly confident music? From the beginning of one of his great choruses he betrays no doubt or hesitation regarding his intentions, and the whole develops so inevitably that the slightest alteration would appear injudicious and any other treatment would seem impossible. Handel constantly punctuates his music with commas, semicolons, and even periods, but he never resorts to question marks. At the cadential point he repeatedly drops into the same formula, regardless of his preceding theme, and this formal conclusion more than all else contributes to that comfortable certainty of knowing exactly where one stands with his music. Like Shakespeare, Handel gives his audience expectation rather than surprise. If he had composed *Messiah* in a spirit of pious introspection, perhaps his music would lack that very quality of robust confidence which ultimately sent his masterpiece into every English-speaking land.

In *Messiah* Handel expressed the "religious" spirit of his adopted country as surely as folksong ever voiced national sentiment. From the beginning his bluff, masterful choruses appealed directly to England's sound and receptive bourgeoisie. "The English," wrote Dr. Burney, "a manly, military race, were instantly captivated by the grave, bold, and nervous style of Handel, which is congenial with their manners and sentiments." Popular British taste was always true to Handel. Oratorio inevitably delighted true-born Englishmen because it revived and developed that art of choral singing which has always constituted the normal expression of English musical art. Here was music for the lungs and feet, music of a healthy, reasonable, politely formal cast, music neither too delicate nor too subtle to gratify those whose taste demanded sturdy rhythm and engaging melody. "His is the muse for the English character," wrote *The European Magazine* in May 1784; "he writes to the masculine genius of a free people," and "while the soul and the genius of music has existence, it will be our pride that Handel composed his works in England." *Messiah* in France or Italy is inconceivable. Even in Germany Handelian oratorio could never have flourished as it flourished in Georgian England. Had Handel settled in Paris or Hamburg his greatest work would perhaps never have been produced, for the oratorios which brought him permanent glory sprang from the peculiar bias of British musical taste. "Though Mr. *Handel* is not an *Englishman*," declared *Gray's Inn Journal* as early as 9 February 1754, "it is however a convincing Proof of our national Taste, that we have made it worth his while to fix his Residence among us." Certainly the voice of a great nation speaks through Handel's majestic strains. His *Messiah* is as English as roast beef, Shakespeare, or Dr. Johnson. Through its touching arias and gigantic choruses one hears the authentic voice of that heroic people for whom it was composed. It will stand forever near the peak of Georgian art as one of those imperishable monuments which mark a period of great genius.

VI

Opus Optimum

> Of all dead men Handel has had the largest place in my thoughts. In fact I should say that he and his music have been the central fact in my life ever since I was old enough to know of the existence of either life or music. All day long —whether I am writing or painting or walking, but always— I have his music in my head; and if I lose sight of it and of him for an hour or two, as of course I sometimes do, this is as much as I do. I believe I am not exaggerating when I say that I have never been a day since I was thirteen without having Handel in my mind many times over.
>
> —SAMUEL BUTLER, *Notebooks*

I

WHEN SAMUEL BUTLER PENNED this striking confession in 1883 the Victorian Age had already reached its peak. For half a century England had indulged in noisy superlatives upon George Frideric Handel, and most Englishmen had decided that the German composer was "the greatest tone-poet of all the ages," "the musical text-book of the English people," and "the sublimest imagination which has ever appeared among the sons of men." A writer in *The Leisure Hour* for 4 February 1865 boldly declared that "A name like that of Shakespeare in Poetry, and Michael Angelo in Art, is the name of Handel in Music—a recognized giant, before whose greatness all lesser men yield, without a thought of comparison." On 5 February 1859 Henry John Gauntlett informed the readers of *Notes and Queries* that Handel "could do in a few bars that which neither Bach, nor Mozart, nor Beethoven could do at any time, or in any number of bars." With insular British pride the "Programme of Arrangements" for the Triennial Handel Festival of 1868 insisted that "the most liberal encouragement of music is to be found in our sea-girt isle," since England's musical taste "springs" from the "deeply-rooted germ" of Handelian oratorio:

To George Frederick Handel we owe our prestige as a musical nation; to his inimitable genius and mighty intellect we are indebted for the chastening influence and elevating tendency of English Oratorios, and with one voice Great Britain's sons and daughters combine to render him homage. Handel's masterpieces—composed to English words without exception—have served as a model for the formation of our national style; his individual idiosyncrasies have become the accepted *formulæ* of sacred musical utterance, and the purity of his themes and majestic proportions of his style have given at once the example, and the spirit of emulation to succeeding generations of native musicians. The works of Handel are monumental records of one of the greatest intellects that ever brought its vast influence to bear upon the glorification of a noble art in its devout application to holy praise; but bright as is the niche of fame which the composer occupies in the temple of the muses, the records of Handel's truest majesty are enshrined in the hearts of the English people.

To nineteenth-century England Handel was a veritable household word. "Were it not profane," wrote Frederick J. Crowest in *Blackwood's Magazine* for June 1894, "men would bow the knee to his name." British musicians firmly believed that "this colossal son of Apollo" was unapproachable and omnipotent, an artistic absolute, "the Shakespeare of music and a poet for all time." China busts of the "divine Saxon" graced the finest Victorian parlors. His likeness appeared in every print-shop window in England, and few collectors failed to secure a lithograph, woodcut, or line-engraving of the national demigod. Impressively bound biographies repeated threadbare anecdotes of Handel's fiery temper and gargantuan appetite, while fulsome articles in domestic magazines faithfully excused his profanity and piously defended every "plagiarism" of "the sublime copyist." In 1843 the English Handel Society was organized "for the production of a superior and standard edition of the works of Handel." Mammoth Triennial Handel Festivals in the Crystal Palace at Sydenham ultimately assumed the character of a national institution, and vast audiences flocked from every corner of the United Kingdom for inspiration from Handel's "sacred" strains. Victorians loved their hero not wisely but too well. Their rhetorical effusions upon Handel as a musical Milton were neither temperate nor discreet. But Handel was their musical king, and the king can do no wrong.[1]

Of all nineteenth-century Handelians none was more typical than Samuel Butler in his boundless devotion to England's chosen god. Never indeed was another man so positively fanatical in his exclusive affection for one composer. From early youth to the grave Butler pondered his special deity several times each day, and he read all musical history in the light of Handel's compositions and personality. He consulted Handel with reverence, as others consult the Bible or Shakespeare. He composed music as nearly as possible in the Handelian mode, and just before his death he addressed his hero in verse. Always it was Handel that he played and adored. "With me," he once declared, "everything in the last century (and a good deal in this) groups itself round Handel." When William Smith Rockstro scolded him for referring to Handel as "one of the greatest of all musicians" in

---

[1] It is a curious fact that the music of Sebastian Bach was practically unknown in England till after 1850. *The Saint Matthew Passion* (1729) was first heard in London on 6 April 1854, when Sterndale Bennett conducted the Bach Society in a performance at Hanover Square Rooms. Repetitions were heard on 28 November 1854 and 23 March 1858. The same organization sang Bach's *Christmas Oratorio* (1733) for the first time in England on 13 June 1861. Fifteen years later the Bach Choir, directed by Hugo Goldschmidt, introduced Bach's *Mass in B Minor* (c. 1738) at St. James's Hall on 26 April 1876.

VIEW OF THE CRYSTAL PALACE DURING THE GREAT HANDEL FESTIVAL (1859)
From an Engraving in *The Illustrated London News* (2 July 1859)

Erewhon (1872), Butler assured his friend with playful indignation that he had called Handel not "one of the greatest" but rather "the greatest of all musicians." Even in his dreams he met his hero: "I dreamt last night," he wrote in 1878, "that Handel played me, for a whole hour, from two new operas which he had just composed, and which were called *Andratina* and *Passina*." Years later he admitted that "Handel, like Homer and Shakespeare, grips me with ever tighter hold." In order to clear a space about his solitary divinity he showered Sebastian Bach with contempt and damned Haydn, Mozart, and Beethoven with faint praise. Scarcely a composer since Handel escaped the ruthless stroke of his pen. "I only want Handel's Oratorios," he stipulated in 1871; "I would have added 'and things of that sort,' but there are no 'things of that sort' but Handel's." His deliberate aversions are nowhere more distinctly stated than in his frankly autobiographical *Way of All Flesh* (1903). "It cost me a great deal to make Ernest [Pontifex] play Beethoven and Mendelssohn," he confessed. "As a matter of fact he played only the music of Handel and of the early Italian and old English composers—but Handel most of all." [2]

In his maniacal passion for Handel's music Samuel Butler was thoroughly characteristic of the musical tastes of his age. Victorian England's persistent devotion to Handelian oratorio sprang less from critical appreciation than from nationalistic pride and militant (if misguided) religious faith. Everyone was supposed to know that Handel had composed his greatest works in England for Englishmen, and that in addition he was (as Horatio Townsend declared) a "Colossus without an equal" in "the highest walks of sacred music." In his celebrated *History of England in the Eighteenth Century* (1878–1890) William Edward Lecky grossly misrepresented the nature of Handel's "sacred" mission by asserting that Handel "was indeed one of those whose lips the Seraphim

---

[2] See my article, "Samuel Butler: Handelian," *The Musical Quarterly*, XXXIV (April 1948).

had touched and purified with the hallowed fire from the altar," and that "it was only when interpreting the highest religious emotions that his transcendent genius was fully felt." During Victoria's long reign the German composer was universally appropriated as the grand musical prophet of the Anglican Church. Heroic, magnanimous Handel was planted on a lofty pedestal and paraded before the multitude as a smug pulpiteer whose art was consecrated exclusively to the service of a Protestant evangelical bourgeoisie. His embarrassing profanities were scrupulously silenced as "mere specks on the sun, scarcely detracting from the noontide glory of the luminary." In plagiarizing the works of other composers he simply practiced (as Rockstro explained) "an Alchemy unknown to other composers" by "picking up pebbles and turning them into gold." His brilliant instrumental music was branded as "slight and experimental," while his exquisite secular cantatas were ignored as "by nature ephemeral." His forty-one Italian operas (built upon the usual operatic themes of sexual passion and intrigue) were dismissed as one long series of unfortunate accidents, and whenever possible his secular arias were adapted to sacred texts and thus redeemed for the Church. "Dove sei amato bene" from *Rodelinda* became "Holy, holy, Lord God Almighty"; "Rendi'l sereno al ciglio" from *Sosarme* became "Lord, Remember David"; "Veni, o figlio" from *Ottone* became "Bow down thine ear, O Lord"; and the familiar "Ombra mai fù" from *Serse* (addressed by the wife-ridden hero to the refreshing shade of his garden plane-tree) became, ironically enough, the "Celebrated Largo" now so highly regarded as an exalted instance of Handel's religious devotion. In 1862 Dean Edward B. Ramsay declared with perfect conviction that "Lascia ch'io pianga" from *Rinaldo* was, "like all Handel's fine Italian airs, essentially of a sacred character." Few Englishmen could recognize the true Handel beneath the black gown and white tie in which his sanctimonious devotees had disguised him. By systematically overlooking his magnificent

Italian operas, by steadily eliminating the bulk of his dramatic oratorios, by deliberately placing an exaggerated emphasis upon the salutary powers of *Messiah,* and by interpreting his oratorios in a stolid, pompous manner, Victorians eventually stifled all the poetry, verve, and wit in Handel's music and ultimately established the widespread misconception that Handel is a solemn church composer *par excellence.*

For such an age *Messiah* quite naturally constituted "the greatest monument of musical genius in the world." To nineteenth-century England Handel's masterpiece was not simply "the crown of oratorial music"; it represented also "the most profoundly religious music which the world has yet known," "the fixed star shining at the very pinnacle of the universal tone-cathedral," and even "the finest adaptation of sound to sense that has ever been produced by the mind of man." If Georgian England regarded *Messiah* as a "fine Entertainment" designed for the playhouse, Victorian England esteemed its "majestic strains" a religious function proper only to the cathedral. A characteristic mid-Victorian estimate of the spiritual truths inherent in Handel's masterpiece appeared in *The Edinburgh Review* for July 1857:

> It is not exaggeration, so much as history, to point to "The Messiah" as almost the only work of art in being, which for one hundred years has steadily gone on rising higher and higher in fame, drawing myriad after myriad to wonder and to tears,—untouched by time, unrivalled by progress;—to characterise it as a heritage derived from our fathers, which will go down, by its own intrinsic and increasing value, to our children's children,—a creation of mortal imagining, which has almost won the reality of an article of belief and the solemnity of an object of worship, by its power to adapt itself to all intelligences, to touch the lowliest, to raise the loftiest, to content the most fastidious.

Late in 1857 the "standard" nineteenth-century biography of Handel issued from the pen of Victor Schoelcher, a verbose political refugee who proved himself too much of a mid-Victorian Mendelssohnian to comprehend Handel's true significance in the growth of musical form. Throughout his ponderous tome Schoelcher seized several opportunities to deplore the solitary fate of Handel's autograph score of *Messiah*:

Buried in a sort of private office, and still kept in its poor original binding, it is concealed from all the world; and, I may say (using the figurative expression of an old nursery tale), that *if I were the queen*, I should have those precious volumes bound in crimson velvet, mounted with gold, and I should have a beautiful cabinet to hold them, which should be surmounted by Roubiliac's fine bust, and supported by four statues of white marble, representing Sacred and Profane Music, Moral Courage and Honesty. This I should place in the throne-room of my palace, proclaiming by this means to every one that it is one of the most invaluable jewels of the English crown.

To nineteenth-century Handelians London's original rejection of *Messiah* in 1743 seemed nothing short of a "national stain." Handel's masterpiece was no mere combination of quavers and crotchets; it was a moral corrective, a divine revelation, a "Christian epic in tones" which ultimately became a religious fetish. In 1857 Ann Eliza Bray assured her readers that "There is not one air, not one chorus, throughout the whole, but is in itself perfect." Speaking of "the spiritual power" which *Messiah* "has exercised over thousands upon thousands in all civilized lands," Frederick J. Crowest asserted in 1894 that Handel's masterpiece is "the most powerful of all civilizing agencies," since its music "has probably done more to convince thousands of mankind that there is a God about us than all the theological works ever written." To criticize *Messiah* was, of course, little short of sacrilege. "Anything like criticism of a work so well-known as the *Messiah* would be both unnecessary and impertinent," wrote J. Cuthbert Hadden in 1888. "Besides, we do not criticise the *Messiah*: a hearing of it is always felt to be something like an act of worship, and its adequate rendering converts even a holiday audience into a devout congregation."

Amid such blind idolatry it is scarcely surprising to observe that Handel's *Messiah* invariably occupied the place of honor not only in London's leading concert halls but also at every provincial music festival throughout the kingdom. Few British choral societies failed to perform *Messiah* at least every other year, and with most organizations annual performances proved essential, not only to fulfill their duty to the public but also to replenish exhausted exchequers against losses incurred by ambitious performances of less popular works. From 1791 to 1861 the Caecilian Society of London performed *Messiah* regularly each year on Christmas Eve. On 20 December 1836 the Sacred Harmonic Society rendered *Messiah* for the first time at Exeter Hall, and thenceforth its performance became a standard feature of London's Yuletide celebration till the Society's dissolution in 1882. On a visit to London in 1852 Lowell Mason was astounded at the number of performances of *Messiah* heard during Christmas week in the metropolitan area alone. "It is said to be the only paying oratorio," he wrote, "and never fails to draw a full house. All the singers know it by heart, so that a rehearsal for it is not needed." Such was its popularity that in 1857 Vincent Novello issued a "beautifully and clearly printed" vocal score which sold for only two shillings. A typical nineteenth-century performance of *Messiah* was vividly described by "Corno di Bassetto" (George Bernard Shaw) in the London *Star* on 3 January 1889:

On New Year's night at the Albert Hall, Messiah is the affair of the shilling gallery, and not of the seven-and-sixpenny stalls. Up there you find every chair occupied, and people standing two or three deep behind the chairs. These sitters and standers are the gallery vanguard, consisting of *prima donna* worshippers who are bent on obtaining a bird's-eye view of Madame Albani for their money. At the back are those who are content to hear

Handel's music. They sit on the floor against the wall, with their legs converging straight towards the centre of the dome, and terminating in an inner circumference of boot soles in various stages of wear and tear. Between the circle of boots and the circle of sightseers moves a ceaseless procession of promenaders to whom the performance is as the sounding brass and tinkling cymbals of a military band on a pier. The police take this view, and deal with the gallery as with a thoroughfare included in the Trafalgar Square proclamation, calling out, "Pass along, pass along," and even going the length of a decisive shove when the promenade is at all narrowed by too many unreasonable persons stopping to listen to the music. The crowd is a motley one, including many mechanics, who have bought Novello's vocal score of the oratorio and are following it diligently; professional men who cannot afford that luxury and are fain to peep enviously over the mechanics' shoulders; musicians in the Bohemian phase of artistic life; masses of "shilling people" of the ordinary type; the inevitable man with the opera-glass and campstool; and one enthusiast with a blanket on his shoulder, who has apparently been ordered by the police to take up his bed and walk.

At a time when industrialism was spreading throughout the provinces and pauperism was creeping into villages and towns, hardworking millhands and palefaced miners faithfully trudged miles each week to practice and perform the three routine choral favorites of Victorian England: Handel's *Messiah,* Haydn's *Creation,* and Mendelssohn's *Elijah.* For more than a century *Messiah* remained the bulwark of England's three-choir festivals and the recurrent delight of her northern choral societies. At the Birmingham Festival of 1852 Lowell Mason was struck by the "astonishing rage" for *Messiah* among the British populace:

Whatever may be the reason, the *fact* is certain, that in England the *Messiah* is vastly more popular than any other oratorio. The best judges of music, professors and amateurs, the learned and the unlearned, the noble and the ignoble, the great and the little, those who ride in proud carriages with servants liveried with buff and scarlet, and those who walk through the rain with a cotton umbrella, the old and grave, and the young and gay, those who love music, and those who do not know whether they have any love for it or not;—all do homage to this mighty production of Handel. Handel is the Shakespeare of music; there has never been but one Handel, and it is not at all probable that there will ever be another. Handel has written but one *Messiah,* nor could he, had he lived until this time, have written another. He might have improved upon this, but another of equal merit, he could not have produced. This oratorio has been heard for a century, and it is as fresh and new now as ever; indeed the more it is heard the better it is appreciated. This oratorio, too, has done much for charity; it has succored the orphan, comforted the widow, and relieved the distressed. . . . The amount received at the performance of the *Messiah,* this morning, was somewhat more than THIRTEEN THOUSAND AND FIVE HUNDRED DOLLARS.

In its enormous vogue among nineteenth-century Englishmen Handel's *Messiah* inaugurated a new era in choral culture and inspired the English Handel cult which persists to the present day.

Following the Handel Commemoration of 1791 no great musical performance took place in London until 1834, when 644 musicians assembled in Westminster Abbey to perform a "Musical Festival" in the presence of William IV and Queen Adelaide late in June. On June 26 Charles Greville reported that "the spectacle is very fine, and it is all admirably managed —no crowd or inconvenience, and easy egress and ingress— but the 'Messiah' is not so effective as I expected, not so fine as in York Minster; the choruses are admirably performed, but the single voices are miserable—singers of extreme mediocrity, or whose powers are gone." This musical celebration ultimately prepared the way for the First Great Handel Festival in 1859. On 1 September 1856 the Crystal Palace Company addressed a letter to the Sacred Harmonic Society, suggesting a rehearsal of several of Handel's oratorios on a hitherto unprecedented scale of magnificence, in preparation for a centenary celebration of his death to be held in the central transept of the Crystal Palace at Sydenham in 1859. This project was warmly endorsed by the Sacred Harmonic Society, and plans at once moved forward to test the capabilities of the Crystal Palace by means of a preliminary Festival in June 1857. Accordingly Handel's *Messiah* was heard on June 15, *Judas Maccabeus* on June 17, and *Israel in Egypt* on June 19. Charles Greville found the performance of *Messiah* and *Israel in Egypt* "amazingly good," and recorded on June 20 that "the beauty of the locale, with the vast crowds assembled in it, made an imposing spectacle." He felt, however, that "the wonderful assembly of 2000 vocal and 500 instrumental performers did not produce musical effects so agreeable and so perfect as the smaller number in the smaller space of Exeter Hall." As a result of acoustical imperfections, "The volume of sound was dispersed and lost in the prodigious space," and he confessed that, "fine as it undoubtedly was, I much prefer the concerts of the Harmonic Society." At the First Great Handel Festival in 1859 conditions were decidedly improved. *Messiah* was heard on June 20, a program of miscellaneous selections on June 22, and *Israel in Egypt* on June 24. At each performance Sir Michael Costa conducted a band of 2,765 vocal and 460 instrumental performers. For the three concerts and one public rehearsal the total attendance was 81,319, as opposed to 48,414 in 1857. Thenceforth Handel Festivals were repeated triennially till 1883; a special Festival was held in 1885 to celebrate the bicentenary of Handel's birth, after which the triennial repetition was resumed. For years the program remained practically the same: a public rehearsal on Friday, *Messiah* on Monday, a miscellaneous selection on Wednesday, and *Israel in Egypt* on Friday. In 1906 *Judas Maccabeus* replaced *Israel in Egypt* as the feature of the final day. A "Programme of Arrangements" for the Triennial Festival of 1871 insisted that "a Handel Festival without the *Messiah* would be as intolerable as *Hamlet* with 'Hamlet' left out, or as an orchestral symphony performed minus its first Allegro." Sir Michael Costa conducted from 1857 to 1880; Sir August Manns from 1883 to 1900; Sir Frederic Cowen from 1903 to 1923; and Sir Henry J. Wood in 1926.[3] Attendance reached a climax in 1882, when 87,769 persons heard an orchestra of some five hundred instrumentalists compete with a chorus of some four thousand voices in a performance which Victorian enthusiasts styled "in every way worthy of that great Master of Song, whose genius it cannot fail to demonstrate, and whose meaning it is intended to honour."

In these "monster" performances of Handel's grandiose works Victorian England displayed a curious misconception of her idol. Prominent conductors dragged his tempi, perverted his schemes of tonality, vulgarized his subtle effects by inordinate multiplication, and made him a pretext for "pious orgies" that would have set Handel's full-bottomed wig fairly bristling with outraged fury. Ostentatious sopranos whose vocal acrobatics would scarcely have been tolerated by London audiences thrilled thousands of undiscriminating churchmen, who thronged the Crystal Palace to experience the pious emotions of divine service without the inconvenience of a sermon or a collection. Incompetent orchestras and unwieldy choruses rudely inverted the relative proportions of Handel's original ensemble, while ignorant public taste demanded sharp contrasts of tone which reduced each movement to a dead level and corroborated the popular notion that Handel was the typical composer for mass effects. If the "Saxon giant" could have left his grave to hear a nineteenth-century Festival performance of *Messiah*, reinforced by Mozart's "additional accompaniments" and shouted by an army of four thousand poorly rehearsed voices, he would

---

[3] To enumerate the soloists who sang in the Triennial Handel Festivals at the Crystal Palace is to list some of the most distinguished singers of the latter half of the nineteenth century. *Sopranos:* Emma Albani, Clara L. Kellogg, Hellen Lemmens-Sherrington, Nellie Melba, Christine Nilsson, Lillian Nordica, Clara Novello, Euphrosyne Parepa-Rosa, Adelina Patti, Hermine Rudersdoff, Therese Titiens, Anna Williams, Edith Wynne. *Contraltos:* Clara Butt, Charlotte Dolby, Janet Patey, Zelia Trebelli. *Tenors:* William H. Cummings, Ben Davies, Edward Lloyd, Joseph Maas, Barton McGuckin, Sims Reeves, Vernon Rigby. *Basses:* Luigi Agnesi, Giovanni Belletti, Andrew Black, Allan Foli, Carl Formes, Charles Santley.

scarcely have recognized the oratorio as his own. But Victorians took self-righteous delight in performing *Messiah* on a Herculean scale. At such demonstrations, declared one unthinking rhapsodist, "We are shown, not a diminished copy, but the natural proportions of the great musician; and only by their help can the most ardent Handelian comprehend how gigantic he is."

To such violent distortion unfavorable reaction was inevitable. As early as 1823 Charles Lamb derided oratorio as a "profanation of the purposes of the cheerful playhouse." During a performance of *Messiah* at Exeter Hall on 16 May 1856 Jane Welsh Carlyle remained "calm and critical" on her "rather hard bench"; later she confessed that she had "felt stifled by the real heat of the place," despite the enthusiasm of her more "emotional" companion:

Geraldine [Jewsbury] said her sister, the "religious Miss Jewsbury," in contradistinction to Geraldine,—wouldn't let her go to the *Messiah* when a girl, because "people," she thought, "who really believed in their Saviour, would not go to hear *singing* about him." I am quite of the religious Miss Jewsbury's mind. Singing about him, with *shakes* and white gloves and all that sort of thing, quite shocked my religious feelings,—tho' I have no religion. Geraldine did a good deal of *emotional weeping* at my side; and it was all I could do to keep myself from shaking her and saying, "come out of *that*!". . . Such a set of ugly creatures as the Chorus women I never did see! I grew so sorry for them, reflecting that each had a life of her own; that perhaps "somebody loved that pig"; that, if I had had any tears in me at the moment, I should have cried for them all packed there like herrings in a barrel, into one mass of sound!

Mrs. Carlyle would have heartily endorsed Edward FitzGerald's note to W. B. Donne on 4 October 1863: "I pitied you undergoing those dreadful Oratorios: I never heard one that was not tiresome, and in part ludicrous. Such subjects are scarce fitted for Catgut. Even Magnus Handel—even Messiah." Later Dr. Friedrich Chrysander lamented in more serious terms the burial of Handel's art beneath ponderous

Handel Festivals at the Crystal Palace. In an article first published in the London *World* on 21 January 1891 George Bernard Shaw, confessing his "view of the Handel Festival" to be "fundamentally" that of "a convinced and ardent admirer of Handel," deplored the current English interpretation of his "favorite oratorio" *Messiah*:

> I have long since recognized the impossibility of obtaining justice for that work in a Christian country. Import a choir of heathens, restrained by no considerations of propriety from attacking the choruses with unembarrassed sincerity of dramatic expression, and I would hasten to the performance if only to witness the delight of the public and the discomfiture of the critics. That is, if anything so indecent would be allowed here. We have all had our Handelian training in church, and the perfect church-going mood is one of pure abstract reverence. A mood of active intelligence would be scandalous. Thus we get broken in to the custom of singing Handel as if he meant nothing; and as it happens that he meant a great deal, and was tremendously in earnest about it, we know rather less about him in England than they do in the Andaman Islands, since the Andamans are only unconscious of him, whereas we are misconscious. To hear a thousand respectable young English persons jogging through For He shall purify the sons of Levi as if every group of semiquavers were a whole bar of four crotchets *a capella*, or repeating Let Him deliver Him if He delight in Him with exactly the same subdued and uncovered air as in For with His stripes we are healed, or lumbering along with the Hallelujah as if it were a superior sort of family coach: all this is ludicrous enough; but when the nation proceeds to brag of these unwieldy choral impostures, these attempts to make the brute force of a thousand throats do what can only be done by artistic insight and skill, then I really lose patience. Why, instead of wasting huge sums on the multitudinous dullness of a Handel Festival does not somebody set up a thoroughly rehearsed and exhaustively studied performance of the Messiah in St James's Hall with a chorus of twenty capable artists? Most of us would be glad to hear the work seriously performed once before we die.

By 1900 Englishmen had begun to express a certain impatience with Britain's exaggerated idolatry of Handel. Connoisseurs scoffed at the Handel Festival as an overgrown giant, while "modernists" sneered at Handel's oratorios as "antiquated," "rococo," and "perruque." Shortly before his death Sir John Stainer declared that his countrymen's slavish adulation of *Messiah* had done much to retard the natural growth of music throughout England. In his *History of Music in England* (1907) Ernest Walker insisted that "We can indeed no longer speak of [Handel's] music, even at its highest, as the supreme crown of the art; the day for that sort of adoration is gone for ever, and we can now see that, secure as is his place among the immortals, he is far from being one of their kings." Steadily the reaction grew more perceptible, till by World War I hostile criticism of *Messiah* had all but dethroned Handel from the exalted position he had occupied for almost two hundred years.[4]

Such adverse reaction was scarcely reflected in the subject-matter of contemporary prose and verse. After reading nineteenth-century British musical history one is hardly astonished to discover that Victorian literature abounds with references to Handel's *Messiah*. To Samuel Butler, of course, Handel's oratorios constituted "the finest musical poems the world knows anything about," and *Messiah* was one of "the crowning glories of the world," to be ranked alongside the *Iliad*, the *Odyssey*, and *Hamlet*. In a characteristic passage from *The Way of All Flesh* Theobald Pontifex complains of twelve-year-old Ernest's undue affection for Handel's masterpiece:

I wish he was not so fond of music, it will interfere with his Latin and Greek. I will stop it as much as I can. Why, when he was translating Livy the other day he slipped out Handel's name in mistake for Hannibal's, and his mother tells me he knows half the tunes in the *Messiah* by heart. What should a

---

[4] For typical expressions of anti-Handelian sentiment consult: D. E. Hervey, "Handel in the Nineteenth Century," *Music*, V, 653–664 (April 1894); J. Cuthbert Hadden, "Handel and the Handel Fetish," *Music*, XVIII, 361–367 (August 1900); Humphrey J. Stewart, "The *Messiah* Fallacy," *The American Organist*, II, 100–101 (March 1919).

boy of his age know about the *Messiah*? If I had shown half as many dangerous tendencies when I was a boy, my father would have apprenticed me to a greengrocer, of that I'm very sure.

In a memorable chapter from George Eliot's *Scenes from Clerical Life* (1857) the heroine, overcome with intense emotion, seeks refuge in Handel's *Messiah*:

Caterina, thinking she was not wanted, went away and sat down to the harpsichord in the sitting-room. It seemed as if playing massive chords, bringing out volumes of sound, would be the easiest way of passing the long feverish moments before twelve o'clock. Handel's "Messiah" stood open on the desk, at the chorus, "All we like sheep," and Caterina threw herself at once into the impetuous intricacies of that magnificent fugue. In her happiest moments she could never have played it so well; for now all the passion that made her misery was hurled by a convulsive effort into her music, just as pain gives new force to the clutch of the sinking wrestler, and as terror gives far-sounding intensity to the shriek of the feeble.

A more serious mood pervades the Reverend John East's *Christmas Eve: A Dream; or, A Review of the Oratorio of "The Messiah"* (1836). In this thirty-six-page diatribe against "the sons and daughters of pleasure" the author laments repeatedly that "the delight taken in the grand Oratorio of the Messiah has no necessary connection with the love of Him whose sublime history it celebrates." A similar spirit permeates the Reverend Thomas Grinfield's *Poetic Rehearsal of Handel's Sacred Oratorio "The Messiah"* (1856). Seeking to "represent the glorious themes of this inspired composition in Miltonic verse," Grinfield proposed "at once to commend and illustrate this masterpiece of Sacred Music" by "preparing the mind for an expected performance, and afterwards reviving the remembrance and impression of the successive parts." For several decades Grinfield's cumbrous effort enjoyed widespread vogue among England's more devout Handelians, until in 1893 his son, Charles Theodore Grinfield, reissued in revised form his *Critical and Poetical Re-*

hearsals of Handel's Oratorio The Messiah. Seven years later in New York one Elizabeth Cheney produced a plebeian rhapsody entitled *Aunt Deborah Hears "The Messiah"* (1900). In this crude caricature a country girl named Amelia receives an illiterate letter from her "lovin' aunt," Deborah Brownlow Lewis, describing the "glimpse of glory" she has recently enjoyed at a Christmas performance of the "orrytoreo" of *Messiah* in Carnegie Hall. During the "Hallelujah Chorus" Aunt Deborah experienced unspeakable rapture:

By an' by Jesus has come out of the grave, an' all heven is rejoicin' over his victory. They call that part the "Halleluyer Chorus," an' ev'rybody stands up. It made me think of the jedgment day to see the faces, rows upon rows of 'em way up to the seelin'. There was one halleluyer arter anuther. It was airth an' heven ans'erin' back an' forth, saints an' angels gathered together an' we with 'em. We ware goin' up a broad gold starecase, fer they sang over an' over, "King of kings, an' Lord of lords," an' each time on a hire note hire an' hire still, till my poor soul could hardly bear to stay into this old body, an' I held onto the back of the seat ahead, me to keep from risin' rite up into the air.

There was more arter that, but my cup was runnin' over an' I didn't take in the rest. Seemed as if I'd risen with my Lord, an' deth an' the grave an' even the trumpet of the angel didn't consarn me. I've made poor work a-tryin' to tell you how it all sounded, but you must hear it fer yourself. I fully expect it will be sung into the next world, an' I shall hev a part into it there, an' sing as high an' as sweet as any of 'em.

In 1741 Handel composed *Messiah* for ladies who wore hoops and gentlemen who carried swords. Fifty years later his masterpiece was heard in Westminster Abbey before a fashionable throng of royalty, nobility, and gentry. During the nineteenth century, however, Handelian oratorio appealed chiefly to England's bourgeoisie. From Aunt Deborah's tortuous orthography it is clear that by 1900 Handel's *Messiah* had become finally and unmistakably the property of the **common man.**

II

"I only ever met one American," wrote Samuel Butler, "who seemed to like and understand Handel. How far he did so in reality I do not know, but *inter alia* he said that Handel 'struck ile with the *Messiah*,' and that 'it panned out well, the *Messiah* did.'" A landmark in the history of American music was passed when "an Extract" from Handel's *Messiah* was heard for the first time west of the Atlantic on Tuesday, 16 January 1770, in George Burns' Music Room in the New York City Tavern, situated on the west side of Broadway between the present Cedar and Thames Streets. A little less than twenty-eight years after Handel's initial production of *Messiah* in Dublin, *The New York Journal* for 4 January 1770 advertised a "Concert of Church Music" to be performed for the benefit of William Tuckey, former choirmaster of Trinity Church, on January 9. At this concert the "First Part" was scheduled to include "Some select instrumental Pieces, chosen by the Gentlemen who are performers: Particularly a CONCERTO on the French horn" rendered by "a Gentleman just arrived from Dublin." Details of the "Second Part" hold special interest for students of Handel's reputation among eighteenth-century Americans:

A SACRED ORATORIO, on the Prophecies concerning CHRIST, and his Coming; being an Extract from the late Mr. HANDEL'S GRAND ORATORIO, called the MESSIAH, consisting of the Overture, and sixteen other Pieces, viz. Airs, Recitatives, and Choruses. Never performed in America. The Words of the ORATORIO will be delivered *gratis* (to the Ladies and Gentlemen) who are pleased to patronize and encourage this CONCERT, or may be purchased of Mr. *Tuckey,* by others for six Pence. As it is impossible that a Performance of this Sort can be carried on without the kind Assistance of Gentlemen, who are Lovers of MUSIC and Performers on Instruments; Mr. Tuckey will always gratefully acknowledge the Favour of the Gentlemen who assist him. TICKETS to be had of Mr. *Tuckey,* at eight Shillings each. To begin precisely at 6 o'Clock.

An advertisement in *The New York Journal* for January 11 postponed Tuckey's concert to January 16 and added that the director had succeeded in securing the "kind Assistance" of "a considerable number of Ladies and Gentlemen" for the performance of *Messiah*. Some seventeen years earlier Tuckey had left his position as Vical Choral of Bristol Cathedral to become "singing Master" to the boys of the Charity School connected with Trinity Church. Perhaps his chorus at *Messiah* was composed chiefly of men and boys drawn from the Trinity Church choir. No part of the words or music has survived, but it is probable that the same selections were heard at Trinity Church on 3 October 1770, when an "excellent" sermon by the rector, Dr. Samuel Auchmuty, for the benefit of "The Corporation for the Relief of the Widows and Children of Clergymen in the Communion of the Church of England in America," was followed by "several pieces of Church Musick, by the most eminent Composers; among others, part of the celebrated *Mr. Handel's Sacred Oratorio of the* MESSIAH." According to *The New York Journal* for October 4, portions of *Messiah* were performed on this occasion by "a considerable number of male and female voices, accompanied with the organ, very much to the general satisfaction" of "a numerous audience, consisting of most of the principal inhabitants, &c. and at which about twenty eight clergymen of the church of England of this and the neighboring colonies attended." In April 1772 New Yorkers again heard "part of Mr. Handle's [!] sacred Oratorio, called the MESSIAH, on the *Passion, Crucifixion, Resurrection,* and triumphant Ascension of JESUS CHRIST," performed "by a select Company" at Trinity Church.

These three performances of *Messiah* undoubtedly attracted considerable attention to an oratorio which had already exerted phenomenal influence upon the choral culture of contemporary England. Musical taste in eighteenth-century America was decidedly English, and Handel's *Messiah* naturally became the pivot about which choral music revolved. From the first performance of selections from *Messiah* at Burns' Room in 1770 its airs and choruses became steady features of weekly subscription concerts, public and private, during the early years of the new republic. On 25 March 1780 a "Concerto Spirituale" at the New York theatre concluded with "the Grand Chorus of the Messiah." At Alexander Reinagle's "Grand Concert" on 20 July 1786 Maria Storer, fresh from triumphs at Handel festivals in Bath and Salisbury, rendered "Comfort ye," "Every valley," and "I know that my Redeemer liveth" in avowed imitation of "Handel's Sacred Music, as performed in Westminster Abbey." A proposed concert at Corré's Hotel on 6 April 1793 was scheduled to include the same selections. In *The Daily Advertiser* for 12 February 1798 John Christopher Moller announced a program which was to close with "And the glory of the Lord shall be revealed." In 1803 Sage & Clough of New York produced the earliest known complete vocal score of *Messiah* published in America. This momentous edition appeared in a large volume containing also selections by William Boyce, Samuel Arnold, Henri Madin, and James Kent. On 8 March 1814 a "grand oratorio" at the French Church in Pine Street featured "extracts" from Haydn's *Creation* and Handel's *Messiah*. Two years later 150 "amateurs" rendered selections from *Messiah* and *Israel in Egypt* at St. Paul's Church on 28 May 1816. By 1820 *Messiah* had become an established favorite among "lovers of musick" in New York City.

Meanwhile the oratorio had spread through several of the Middle Atlantic and Southern states. On 21 March 1796 *The City Gazette* of Charleston, South Carolina, announced a "Spiritual concert, consisting chiefly of overtures, songs and duets, selected from the most celebrated of Handel's oratorios: the Messiah, Judas Maccabeus, Esther, etc." At the performance on March 24 the overture to *Messiah* was followed by "Comfort ye," "Every valley," "He was despised," "But Thou didst not leave," "Rejoice greatly," and "He shall feed His flock," all sung by Mrs. A. M. Pownall. On 13 April 1797 "a selection of *Sacred Music* from the oratorio of the Messiah" was performed at the theatre in Norfolk, Virginia, under the direction of Robert Shaw. A concert by John Henry Schmidt in Baltimore on 16 August 1796 included a "Song from Handel's Messiah on two new piano fortes of Hanston." At Bethlehem, Pennsylvania, a Collegium Musicum, founded by the Moravians upon European models in 1748, performed choruses from Handel's oratorios as early as 1780. Two well-worn manuscript scores of *Messiah*, one copied from Handel's original about 1780, and the other copied from Mozart's adaptation in 1790, are still treasured at Bethlehem as evidence that sundry portions of the oratorio were known to Pennsylvanians shortly after Handel's first introduction to New York in 1770.

In Philadelphia the "grand Chorus from the celebrated *Messiah* of *Handel*" was performed for the first time on 7 October 1772 in Christ Church before a meeting of "The Corporation for the Relief of the Widows and Children of Clergymen in the Communion of the Church of England in America." Fourteen years later "a *Grand Concert* of Vocal and Instrumental Music," inspired by the Commemoration of Handel in London, was rendered at the Reformed German Church in Race Street on 4 May 1786. At this notable performance a "band" of 230 vocal and 50 instrumental performers comprised an ensemble which *The Pennsylvania Packet* on May 30 felt "fully justified" in pronouncing "the most complete, both with respect to number and accuracy of execution, ever, on any occasion, combined in this city, and, perhaps, throughout America." This "feast of harmony" concluded "with the exertions of the full band in the performance of that most sublime of all musical compositions, the grand chorus in the Messiah, by the celebrated Handel." On the evening of 7 June 1786 the "Hallelujah Chorus" climaxed a concert of "vocal and instrumental music" performed under the auspices of the Uranian Society in the hall of the University of Pennsylvania. Apparently this "justly celebrated" chorus provided a standard conclusion for eighteenth-century American musical celebrations of all types, for on 12 April 1787 the First Uranian Concert, courting popular taste, also closed an extremely miscellaneous program at the Reformed German Church with "The Hallelujah Chorus: on the extent and duration of Christ's Government." At this concert each ticket-holder received "a Syllabus, containing the order and words of the pieces to be performed," as well as some "Remarks" upon the performance which probably constitute the earliest annotated programs in the history of American music. To Handel the author of these "Remarks" paid a naive but genuine tribute of respect:

The HALLELUJAH CHORUS from the Messiah. By Handel.
(Introduced by three bars of Instrumental Music)

	Remarks
Hallelujah: For the Lord God omnipotent reigneth:	(Repeated often) [*Here the voices unite*]

Hallelujah: (several times)
    For the Lord God, etc.
 Hallelujah: (several times)
    For the Lord God, etc.
	[*By the Counter,* Tenor and Bass]
	
	 [1*st, by the treble; 2d by the tenor and bass, and then by the counter and tenor, whilst the other parts, through the whole of this passage, are repeating Hall. in every variety.*

The kingdom of this world, is become the kingdom of our Lord, and of his Christ And he shall reign for ever, etc. King of king, and Lord of lords:	[Chorus] [A beautiful fugue] [By the Treble and Counter in long notes; whilst the tenor and Bass repeat 'for ever and ever, Hal.' in quick notes with intervals]

King of king, and Lord of lords:	[Two or three times in very low notes; by the Treble: whilst the Counter, Tenor and Bass are repeating, 'for ever and ever, Hal.' often, in quick notes, with intervals: *The effect is wonderful.*
And he shall reign for ever and ever (often)	
King of King, and Lord of lords:	[Several times: the harmony very full]
And he shall reign, for ever and ever, Hal.	[often: the last Hal. very slow]

On April 23 *The Pennsylvania Packet* declared the First Uranian Concert "more complete and perfect in its execution, and the effect more decidedly pleasing than anything of the kind, ever exhibited in this city." At a "Grand Concert of Sacred Music" heard in the hall of the University of Pennsylvania on 14 July 1790 Maria Storer sang "Comfort ye," "Rejoice greatly," and "I know that my Redeemer liveth" from *Messiah,* and Andrew Adgate's choir rendered the "Grand Hallelujah chorus" in a manner which contemporary periodicals pronounced "truly sublime." On July 15 *The Federal Gazette* and *The Pennsylvania Packet* published identical "reviews" of this "exquisite feast" of music:

In vain might we attempt to express the pleasing emotions which we experienced on this delightful occasion. The most glowing language would but debate the subject. The refined feelings of a large and respectable audience can alone do justice to the merits of the performers. Never were the charms of vocal and instrumental music more happily united. The soul, attuned to harmony, forgot for a moment its earthly fetters, and soared upon the wings of melody to its kindred skies. The "heaven struck" imagination was transported far beyond the limits of mortality, by the *Grand Overture* with which the oratorio commenced: nor was it suffered to flag during the evening; on the contrary, it received fresh inspiration from every succeeding part of the performance, and winged its way to regions still more exalted till the sublime *Hallelujah Chorus* closed the enchantment.

An "Oratorio of Sacred Music" heard in the College Hall on 22 September 1790 included "Worthy is the Lamb" from *Messiah,* sung by a choir under the "conduct" of one Mr. Heim. At a subsequent concert on November 19 the same choir varied its usual repertoire by singing "Glory to God" and "Lift up your heads." A milestone in the annals of Philadelphia music was passed when recruits from the Chestnut Street Theatre sang portions of *Messiah* in the hall of the University of Pennsylvania on 9 April 1801. Nine years later "a Grand Selection of Sacred Music" was heard at St. Augustine's Church, when a "band" of 53 instrumental and 34 vocal performers rendered fifteen selections from *Messiah* on 20 June 1810..

In Boston the name of "the late celebrated Mr. Handel" first appeared on concert bills in 1770. Three years later Boston's first known performance of music from *Messiah* took place on 22 September 1773, when a choral concert for the benefit of the violinist William Selby observed the thirteenth anniversary of George III's coronation with a rendition of the "Grand Chorus in Mr. Handel's oratorio of the Messiah," sung at Concert Hall by the choir of King's Chapel under the direction of W. S. Morgan. On October 28 an unspecified "Chorus in the Messiah" was rendered by "upwards of 50 performers" at Fanueil Hall as part of the final concert in Josiah Flagg's subscription series. During the next decade Handel's name appeared with increasing frequency on Boston concert programs and playbills. Various amateur choral societies sought to promote his oratorios, while local soloists furthered the Handel cult by singing the simpler arias from *Messiah* even before adequate performances of the choruses were possible. On 10 January 1786 William Selby produced a most ambitious "Concert of sacred Musick" at Stone Chapel "for the benefit and relief of the poor prisoners confined in the jail of this town." Selby's remarkable program featured "the first, famous and justly celebrated Recitative, in the Oratorio of the *Messiah,* composed by the inspired Handel," along with "the first Song in the same most sacred Oratorio," both "accompanied by the first and second violin, the tenor and bass instruments." According to *The Pennsylvania Herald* of January 28, "The whole was conducted with the greatest order and decorum, saving a theatrical clap at the conclusion, which can only be imputed to the pitch of enthusiasm to which the excellent overture of Mr. [Johann Christian] Bach wound up the enraptured auditors." In 1786 the first American imprint of the "Hallelujah Chorus" appeared in Isaiah Thomas' *Laus Deo: The Worcester Collection of Sacred Harmony,* extremely significant as the first volume of music to be printed in the United States from movable type. Early in 1787 William Selby and the managers of the Musical Society proposed a second *"Spiritual Concert* for the benefit of those among us who have known better days." On January 15 *The Boston Gazette* announced that Selby's "Charitable Concert" would be heard at Stone Chapel on the following day, and indicated that the "several musical performances" would include "Comfort ye," "Every valley," and the "Hallelujah Chorus" from *Messiah*:

At the performance of this Divine Chorus, called by way of eminence the *Thunder Chorus,* it is usual for the whole audience to rise from their seats, and be upon their feet the whole time of the Chorus, in testimony of the humble adoration of the Supreme Governor of the Universe, our great and universal Parent, and in honor of our blessed Redeemer.

On January 22 *The Boston Gazette* reported that "The overpowering pathos of *Handel* in the first recitative of his *Messiah,* was excellently sung, and forcibly felt by every musical ear present." Other selections the "reviewer" found "beautifully affecting but *Handel! Handel! Handel!"* Like most contemporary periodicals *The Boston Gazette* was usually more enthusiastic than discriminating. "Let the bright Seraphim" from *Samson* could be "excelled" only by the "Hallelujah Chorus" from *Messiah,* and this "vast effort of genius" revealed "perfect illumination—the surprise and astonishment of the audience, at the performance of this divine Chorus, cannot well be described, especially at those parts where the *drums* so unexpectedly thundered in and joined in the glorious Hallelujahs to the 'King of Kings and Lord of Lords.'" A "Concert of Sacred Musick" on 4 October 1787 presented the Musical Society in a performance of "Handel's grand Hallelujah Chorus from the sacred oratorio, Messiah, accompanied with kettledrums." A similar concert of "Sacred Musick Vocal and Instrumental" at Christ Church on 21 May 1788 included a "Song in the Messiah, sung by Mr. Rea." When George Washington visited Boston in October 1789 he was honored by "An *Oratorio,* or, Concert of Sacred Musick" at Stone Chapel, where Mr. Rea sang "Comfort ye," the "favourite air in the Messiah."

On Boston concert bills of the 1790's the familiar name of "the late celebrated Mr. Handel" gradually yielded place to those of Gluck, Grétry, and "the celebrated Haydn." Any choral group, however, could "put over" the "celebrated *Hallelujah* chorus" by sheer force of numbers, and this selection accordingly occupied a permanent place in the repertoire of all musical societies with any pretensions to cosmopolitan taste. In June 1807 fifteen gentlemen, having subscribed two dollars each for the purchase of *Messiah, Judas Maccabeus,* and *Acis and Galatea* as a foundation for a musical library, organized the Massachusetts Musical Society for the practice and performance of choral works by Handel and Haydn. Five years later Dr. G. K. Jackson, a "celebrated Organist and Composer" from New York, conducted "A Grand Sacred Oratorio" at Stone Chapel on 29 October 1812, when nine numbers from *Messiah* were heard on a program including also selections from *Samson* and

Judas Maccabeus. A tribute to the "beatified composer Handel" appeared in *The Boston Gazette* on October 29:

> As there has not been an Oratorio performed in this town, since the year 1783, it may not be improper to observe, that all the musical virtuosos, both in Europe and America, look upon Handel as one of the most sublime composers of sacred harmony. . . . What-ever passion in the heart of man, he wished to excite, he has done. Heroes may be forgotten; nations may become extinct; but the fame of Handel is IMMORTAL! ! !

On 2 February 1813 a program composed of selections from "the oratorios of the most favourite authors of Europe" was performed at Stone Chapel under the direction of Dr. Jackson, "assisted by many respectable Vocal and Instrumental Amateurs and Professors." On this occasion four numbers from *Messiah* were climaxed by the "Grand Hallelujah Chorus, with Trumpet and Kettle Drums." Finally on 14 September 1816 *The Columbian Centinel* first advertised among its notices of "Music for Singing Choirs" James Loring's vocal score of Handel's *Messiah,* published under the "patronage and inspection" of the Handel and Haydn Society and sold to the public at a cost of three dollars per copy.

Of all musical organizations in the United States none has enjoyed a more glorious history than the Handel and Haydn Society of Boston. On 30 March 1815 sixteen gentlemen met, at the invitation of Gottlieb Graupner, Thomas Smith Webb, and Asa Peabody, to organize a musical society "for the purpose of improving the style of performing sacred music, and introducing into more general use the works of Handel and Haydn and other eminent composers." A board of government was established at once, and Thomas Smith Webb became first president on 20 April 1815. Since the Society possessed no music of its own, a subscription was opened among its members on 3 September 1815 for the purchase of copies of the Old Colony Collection, in which later appeared, at the instance of the board of trustees, such choruses as

"Lift up your heads," "Behold the Lamb of God," and "His yoke is easy" from *Messiah*. During the first year two English soloists, Thomas Phillips and Charles Benjamin Incledon, drilled members in the true Handelian interpretation of *Messiah*, and on Christmas Eve of 1815 the Society presented its opening concert in Stone Chapel. A most ambitious program commenced with seven numbers from Haydn's *Creation*, followed by "He shall feed His flock," "I know that my Redeemer liveth," and the "Hallelujah Chorus" from *Messiah*. "Some of the parts electrified the whole auditory," declared *The Columbian Centinel* on December 27, "and notwithstanding the sanctity of the place and day, the excitements to loud applause were frequently irresistible." On 19 March 1816 the president of the Society was authorized to purchase 150 leather-bound copies of Handel's *Messiah* from James Loring at two dollars per copy. Doubtless these books were used at the Society's third concert, when selections from *Messiah* were performed at King's Chapel on 30 May 1816.

Throughout the following season urgent appeals for regular and punctual attendance of members at rehearsals appeared in *The Columbian Centinel*, which announced on 19 March 1817 that the Handel and Haydn Society was planning "to perform the whole of those two celebrated oratorios, the Messiah and the Creation, which have never before been heard in this country." On March 20 the same periodical proceeded to explain that since "there is a diversity of opinion" regarding the "comparative merits" of Handel and Haydn, the Society proposed "to give an opportunity of judging between them" by performing on April 1, 4, and 6 "one of the three sections into which each oratorio is divided upon each evening, which will give specimens of both before the other is forgotten." Unfortunately no record of Boston's decision concerning the relative merits of Haydn's *Creation* and Handel's *Messiah* has survived, but from subsequent programs it is clear that both works enjoyed steady popularity throughout the nineteenth century. For several years, however, *Messiah* was heard only in selections. A lengthy program performed on 5 July 1817 before President James Monroe closed with the "Hallelujah Chorus," and during the following season programs included such familiar arias as "Comfort ye," "Every valley," "O thou that tellest," "He shall feed His flock," and "I know that my Redeemer liveth" (all sung by men). After skirmishing about *Messiah* in this manner for several years directors finally resolved to produce the oratorio in its entirety. On 25 December 1818 the Handel and Haydn Society ventured to offer a full performance of *Messiah* in Boylston Hall—the first complete rendition of an oratorio in America. Thenceforth *Messiah* became the oratorio of oratorios to gratify public taste. Its performance has remained an inviolable Christmas tradition among Bostonians to the present day.

Since its first performance in Boston on 25 December 1818 Handel's *Messiah* has become the foundation of virtually every choral society throughout the United States. As early as 1800 a Handel Society at Dartmouth College was sponsoring lectures on music and performing selections from the oratorios of Handel and Haydn. By 1820 New York City boasted a Philharmonic Society, a Euterpean Society, a Handel and Haydn Society, and a New York Choral Society—all devoted to promoting "sacred" works in the field of oratorio. Finally on 18 November 1831 the Sacred Music Society of New York performed the first complete oratorio ever heard on Manhattan Island, when Uriah C. Hill, father of the New York Philharmonic Society, conducted a chorus of 74 voices and an orchestra of 38 instruments in an uncut version of *Messiah* before an enthusiastic audience in St. Paul's Chapel. Subsequent renditions were heard on January 31 and February 2. Eighteen years later the custom of annual performances of *Messiah* at Christmastide commenced with the first concert of the Harmonic Society of New York in December 1850, when Jenny Lind rendered the soprano solos of *Mes-*

siah with a dignity and pathos not soon to be forgotten.⁵ Throughout the latter half of the century several prominent singers of Europe and America appeared in New York performances of *Messiah*. In 1871 and again in 1884 the celebrated actress, Christine Nilsson, sang "I know that my Redeemer liveth" with memorable skill and brilliance. "She had a peculiar grace of manner," George Upton recalled in 1908, "and seemed to sing with her expressive eyes and every motion of her supple figure." Meanwhile the Oratorio Society of New York had commenced its unbroken tradition of annual Christmas performances of *Messiah* on 25 December 1874. Perhaps the largest chorus ever to sing *Messiah* in the United States was one of two thousand voices, conducted by Dr. Leopold Damrosch in New York City on 7 May 1881.

As Handel's *Messiah* found its way into church choirs, singing schools, and musical societies, its rendition became a familiar and inevitable feature of Christmas and Easter celebrations all over the country. On 29 April 1859 the Chicago Musical Union celebrated the centenary of Handel's death with Chicago's first performance of *Messiah*. Local newspapers hailed the "sublime" oratorio with ecstatic expressions of delight, but *The New York Musical Review and Gazette* was probably nearer truth when it reported that "the choruses were from fair to middling" and that "the orchestra lacked precision to a lamentable degree." In its musical tastes nineteenth-century America was as ardently Handelian as Victorian England. About 1830 Lowell Mason based his familiar Christmas hymn, "Joy to the World," upon a theme from "Glory to God" in *Messiah*. During his visit to Great Britain in 1852 he was struck by London's passionate devotion to Handel's masterpiece, and in his *Musical Letters from Abroad* (1854) he proved that he had absorbed a considerable share of England's enthusiasm:

---

⁵ Today visitors to Westminster Abbey are still reminded of Jenny Lind's love of Handel's music by the quotation from *Messiah* over the tomb in which she was laid in 1871: "I know that my Redeemer liveth."

Great is Handel's oratorio of the *Messiah*! Great in its wonderful and soul-stirring themes! Great in musical inspiration! Great in its moral power! Ye choirs who seek for music of a high order in the oratorio form, purchase Handel's *Messiah*! There is nothing on earth like it! Be not satisfied with anything short of this! Study the sublime choruses; take the easier first, as, *And the glory of the Lord, The Lord gave the Word,* and *For unto us a child is born.* Then the *Hallelujah, Worthy is the Lamb,* and *Amen,* will soon follow; and also those which are still more difficult, as, *And he shall purify, Surely he hath borne our griefs, Behold the Lamb of God,* and others. The music is indeed difficult, it cannot be performed without labor, but the labor bestowed will be productive of rich reward.

On 25 December 1843 Ralph Waldo Emerson heard the "delicious strains" of Handel's *Messiah* in Boston, and though he "understood" only "a very little of all that was told" him, he confessed in his *Journal* that he had delighted in the "solitary" pleasure of its "wonderful" music:

I walked in the bright paths of sound, and liked it best when the long continuance of a chorus had made the ear insensible to the music, made it as if there was none; then I was quite solitary and at ease in the melodious uproar. Once or twice in the solos, when well sung, I could play tricks, as I like to do, with my eyes,— darken the whole house and brighten and transfigure the central singer, and enjoy the enchantment.

This wonderful piece of music carried us back into the rich, historical past. It is full of the Roman Church and its hierarchy and its architecture. Then, further, it rests on and requires so deep a faith in Christianity that it seems bereft of half and more than half its power when sung to-day in this unbelieving city.

In his essay on "Nominalist and Realist" Emerson continued his philosophical musings upon Handel's *Messiah*:

As the master overpowered the littleness and incapableness of the performers and made them conductors of his electricity, so it was easy to observe what efforts nature was making, through so many hoarse, wooden and imperfect persons, to produce beautiful voices, fluid and soul-guided men and women. The genius of nature was paramount at the oratorio.

OPUS OPTIMUM 263

At a performance of *Messiah* on 24 December 1882 Julia Ward Howe "Felt more than ever that no music so beautiful as this has ever been written." To the end of her life she insisted that Handel composed parts of *Messiah* in heaven itself. "Where else," she asked, "could he have got 'Comfort ye,' 'Thy rebuke,' 'Thou shalt break them,' and much besides?"

At the turn of the century the most conspicuous of American musical traditions was the annual production of *Messiah* at Eastertide by the midwestern town of Lindsborg, Kansas. In 1880 Dr. Carl Swensson brought his bride, Alma, to this unique Swedish-American community to help him found Bethany College, a small Lutheran institution designed to serve students drawn from farms throughout the surrounding countryside. Dr. Swensson was a man of ideals and vision; in his youthful enthusiasm he determined to help Lindsborg discover its social unity in music, especially in the music of *Messiah*. Before a college was firmly established his wife had ordered vocal scores of Handel's oratorio from New York, and when the music arrived she distributed it among the farmers and commenced rehearsals. Few townspeople could read music, but gradually the singers learned their parts, and on Easter Sunday of 1882 a band of two-score pioneer farm folk rendered *Messiah* for the first time in Lindsborg. Its success was instantaneous. Storekeepers and shopgirls, farm boys and milkmaids laid aside their duties, climbed into lumberwagons, and drove miles with their families to hear the only great music they had ever known. Year after year the oratorio was repeated with increasing success, till by 1900 its annual Easter performance had become something of a national institution. Almost everyone in Lindsborg could sing *Messiah*. Plowmen sang it in the fields, housewives sang it in the kitchen, children lisped it at play. At one church service it became necessary to take out a little girl who persisted in humming the spirited figurations of "And He shall purify." A list of Lindsborg townsfolk who have sung in

Messiah since 1881 would include teachers, professors, newspaper reporters, school superintendents, music directors, merchants, grocery clerks, postal carriers, bank cashiers, city employees, students from high school and college, justices of the peace, oil inspectors, shoemakers, telephone operators, ministers, nurses, physicians, jewelers, insurance salesmen, millers, and lumbermen. When the annual festival became financially secure, prominent New York artists were engaged to render the solos in *Messiah*. Among those who have sung at Lindsborg one finds such celebrated names as Frances Alda, Sophia Breslau, Olive Fremstad, Johanna Gadski, Amelita Galli-Curci, Signe Lund, Margaret Matzenauer, Arthur Middleton, Lillian Nordica, and Ernestine Schumann-Heink. To bring Madame Schumann-Heink to Lindsborg for the first time it cost every man, woman, and child in this town of approximately two thousand persons an average of seventy-five cents. Several years later the noted German singer donated her voice (and paid her own way to Lindsborg) when the town needed money to erect a new auditorium. To this day the farmers, businessmen, and college students of Lindsborg gather faithfully for rehearsals of *Messiah* twice each week from January to April. For the Easter performance soloists are imported, but the orchestra is composed entirely of students from Bethany College. Five hundred voices—virtually one-fourth of the total population—comprise the chorus. Many townsfolk have been singing *Messiah* annually for thirty years or more, and it is not uncommon for three generations to be represented in the same performance. Housewives who cannot sing bake barrels of doughnuts to feed the thousands who journey from all parts of the nation to attend "America's Oberammergau" on the plains of Kansas. On the night of Good Friday the rendition of *Messiah* is usually broadcast over a national network. To the public its performance represents a single concert; to the local community it constitutes an expression of its very life. As the last note is struck and the final "Amen" fades upon the night, the citizens of Lindsborg stream from the hall in silence, their spirits hushed and reverent, their hearts warmed with the fervor of religious exaltation."

III

Throughout the English-speaking world Handel's *Messiah* has flourished for two hundred years, but on the continent, especially in southern Europe, the oratorio has always proved a feeble and unhealthy exotic. From the beginning Handel's distinctly Protestant choral works have held little appeal for nations thoroughly steeped in the traditions of Roman Catholicism.[6] In France his oratorios were little known for a century after his death. As late as 1844 Henry F. Chorley's praise of *Israel in Egypt* was greeted by Parisians with a confident "Oui, *Le Messie*—c'est son chef-d'œuvre," but even *Le Messie* remained unfamiliar to most Frenchmen till after 1900. "On le connaît partout," complained Ernest David in 1884; "en Angleterre, en Allemagne, en Amérique, et même en Australie! mais pas en France!!" It is hardly too much to say that Handel's oratorios are beyond the comprehension of true-born Frenchmen, so completely does his choral music express a phase of "religious" emotion with which the Latin temperament holds little affinity. Hector Berlioz probably spoke for his age and nation when he derided the fugal "Amen" from *Messiah* as ludicrous and blasphemous, and openly ridiculed "la lourde face emperruqué de ce tonneau

---

[6] Spain, Portugal, Italy, Austria, Hungary, and Belgium have all proved incredibly slow to appreciate the genius of Handelian oratorio. During the past century isolated performances of *Messiah* have been heard from time to time in Madrid, Lisbon, Rome, Vienna, Budapest, and Utrecht, but in none of these capitals has Handel's masterpiece won half the recognition it has enjoyed in London for almost two centuries. Domenico Mustafà, conductor of La Società Musicale Romana, produced *Israel in Egypt* for the first time in Rome on 30 May 1879. Encouraged by its favorable reception, he ventured to introduce *Messiah* a few months later, when four hundred musicians united in a performance which local journals predicted would "mark an epoch in the musical history of the nation."

de porc et de bière qu'on appelle Haendel." [7] In the midst of a *Messiah* performance at the Trocadéro in 1889 Julien Torchet was astonished to observe his friend Edouard Lalo rising to leave the hall. "C'est très beau, solennel, colossal," Lalo whispered, "mais cela me fait baîller atrocement, et, comme je tiens à garder mes mâchoires, je m'en vais." [8]

Till 1873 oratorio in France was confined to a restricted circle of connoisseurs. Apparently all previous efforts to acclimatize Handel in Paris were doomed to failure. As early as 1784 the celebrated Mara sang "I know that my Redeemer liveth" in the old theatre of the Tuileries—"Musique de Haendel, paroles de Milton [!]"—but Richard Mount-Edgcumbe recorded that "the French had not the taste to like it." Throughout the first half of the nineteenth century fragments of *Messiah* were feebly executed on several occasions by amateur choral societies before subscription audiences, but the oratorio was slow to win favor in the French metropolis, and popular taste for Handel's choral works soon became limited on the one hand by the "Alleluia" from *Messiah* and on the other by the "Hymne Triomphale" from *Judas Maccabeus*. On 27 January 1827 Alexandre Choron conducted the first part of *Messiah* (with Latin texts and Mozart's "additional accompaniments") before a small but enthusiastic audience in the theatre of L'Opéra Comique. An essay by François Fétis in *La Revue Musicale* for February 1827 recorded the "enthousiasme" which "les admirables compositions de Haendel" had aroused "aux séances de M. Choron" during the preceding month:

Quoique dépouillé de son orchestre et accompagné seulement par le piano et des basses, ce bel ouvrage a produit sur l'auditoire l'effet le plus vif. Il y a quelque chose de si grand, de si supérieur dans cette œuvre immortelle, qu'on est subjugué, entraîné même

---

[7] "The heavy, bewigged face of this barrel of pork and beer called Handel."
[8] "It is very beautiful, solemn, colossal, but it makes me yawn atrociously, and, since I insist on saving my jaws, I am leaving."

VIEW OF HANDEL'S MONUMENT IN WESTMINSTER ABBEY (1762)

From an Engraving by Edward F. Burney
in Charles Burney's *Account of the Commemoration* (1785)

par ces fugues, objet ordinaire d'effroi pour les amateurs médiocres.[9]

At Choron's *concert spirituel* on 1 June 1827 François Castil-Blaze lauded the "étonnante précision de l'exécution du *Messie*" and reported that "l'*Alleluia* de Haendel a réveillé les auditeurs." Similar performances of excerpts from *Messiah* took place on 24 January 1828 and 17 December 1828, when Fétis recorded that the choral work "ne laisse rien à désirer," though Choron had given "en géneral aux mouvements vifs trop de célérité." La Société des Concerts du Conservatoire rendered selections from *Messiah,* including the "Hallelujah Chorus," on 29 March 1829. Ten years later a series of six "Fragments" from the first part of *Messiah* were published in *Sainte Cécile*. French interest in Handel's masterpiece was further demonstrated in 1840 by the publication of *Le Messie: Grand Oratorio avec Paroles Françaises,* "Réduit pour Piano et Chant" by Ferdinand Gasse.

Not until 1873, however, did Paris hear its first complete performance of Handel's oratorio. On December 19 of that year Charles Lamoureux, determined to give Handel's works a fair trial in France, conducted La Société de l'Harmonée Sacrée in an admirable performance of *Messiah* in the Cirque des Champs-Élysées. Repetitions were heard on December 22 and January 9. In his account of the concert Arthur Pougin lamented that throughout France "nous ne connaissons presque rien des productions gigantesques de Haendel." He declared *Messiah* "le chef-d'œuvre des chefs-d'œuvre, et la manifestation la plus éclantante de cet incomparable génie." Near the close of his essay he pleaded for more frequent Handelian performances in the future. "Tâchons des moins de rattraper le temps perdu, et prouvons au monde

---

[9] "Although performed without orchestra and accompanied only by the piano and bass instruments, this beautiful work produced the most vivid impression on the audience. There is something so grand, so transcendent, in this immortal composition that one is overcome, even transported by these fugues, commonly a source of dismay to ordinary amateurs."

musical que la France est prête à tout aimer, à tout comprendre, à tout admirer." At the first concert *Messiah* was not only heard with respect but applauded with enthusiasm. To an English ear the French words must have sounded strangely unsuited to the character of Handel's music, but Victor Wilder's translation of Charles Jennens' text was hailed by contemporaries as an excellent performance of a difficult task. Inspired by Lamoureux's enthusiasm, La Société des Concerts du Conservatoire performed selections from *Messiah* on 9 February 1874. A repetition on February 16 was followed by similar performances in Paris throughout the succeeding year. Lamoureux conducted *Messiah* again on 14 January 1875, and thereafter the oratorio seemed firmly established in its new environment. If French composers dismissed *Messiah* as bourgeois and monotonous, French critics and musical historians interpreted its music in more favorable terms. In his *Histoire de la Musique* (1885) Henri Lavoix found "la pastorale du *Messie*" a "page d'une exquise pureté," and proceeded to praise "cette colossale composition de l'*Alleluia*, où les voix, disposées avec une extraordinaire puissance, se répondent comme un éternel hosanna." On 16 January 1900 Eugène d'Harcourt celebrated the opening of the Paris Exposition with a performance of *Messiah* in the French capital. Eight years later La Société G. F. Haendel was organized by two young conductors, Eugène Borrel and Félix Raugel, who introduced La Société in renditions of *Messiah* at Besançon on 21 December 1909 and 22 February 1910. These efforts were crowned with triumphant success late in the spring, when *Messiah* was heard in the vast space of the Trocadéro on 23 April 1910. For this memorable performance a chorus of 257 voices was drawn from the Schola Cantorum, Les Chanteurs de la Renaissance, La Société G. F. Haendel, and Les Chanteurs de St. Pierre de Besançon. An orchestra of one hundred musicians included Eugène Borrel as first violinist, Isidore Philipp as pianist, and Vincent d'Indy as kettledrummer. Alexandre Guilmant presided at the organ and performed Handel concertos between the parts of the oratorio. For many musicians this rendition of *Messiah* proved a revelation of Handel's art. Never before had Frenchmen heard the formidable "Hallelujah Chorus"—"cette Voûte de la Sixtine en musique"—sung with such intelligence, precision, and force. A repetition was sung on May 11. Thenceforth Paris heard annual performances of *Messiah* at Christmas and Easter until the beginning of World War I.

If Handel's *Messiah* has always endured a somewhat precarious existence in France, its reputation among Germans has remained solidly established since its first performance in Hamburg in 1772. Till Handel's death his choral works were practically unknown outside of the British Isles. Even in Protestant Germany Handelian oratorio was slow to gain favor till Michael Arne, son of Dr. Thomas Augustine Arne, introduced parts of *Messiah* (with English text) at a private concert in Hamburg on 15 April 1772. The oratorio was repeated on 21 May 1772. Further renditions took place in Hamburg in April and May 1773, and on 31 December 1775 Carl Philipp Emanuel Bach conducted a remarkable performance for which Klopstock prepared the German text. Less than two years later the celebrated Abbé Vogler produced selections from *Messiah* at Mannheim on 1 November 1777. At the rehearsal on October 30 young Mozart, little suspecting that twelve years later he would compose "additional accompaniments" for that very oratorio, found himself so bored with Vogler's own *Psalm Magnificat,* which "lasted a good hour," that he refused to remain for the rehearsal of *Messiah.* At Herder's suggestion Kapellmeister E. W. Wolf conducted a private rendition of *Messiah* in the theatre at Weimar on 13 May 1780. During the performance thirty-one-year-old Goethe became entranced by Handel's music, and in his *Tägebuch* he confided that *Messiah* "gab mir neue Ideen von Deklamation." He was thrilled anew by a repetition of *Messiah* on 25 May 1780. A third performance was given on 7 January 1781, when Herder's excellent German translation of the text was employed for the first time. Later in the same year Herder included a short critical appreciation of Handel's "wahre christliche Epopee in Tönen" in his *Briefe das Studium Theologie Betreffend*. In one passage he examined particular numbers from *Messiah,* praising the sublimity and universality of Handel's theme. "Und doch ist alles so einfach!" he exclaimed; "und Worte aus der Bibel—ja Gottlob! nur Worte aus der Bibel; keine schön-gereimte Cantate." In 1783 *Messiah* was sung at a concert for the Crown Prince at Potsdam. Years later Carl Friedrich Zelter confessed in his autobiography that this performance had determined him at the age of twenty-five to shift from stone-masonry to music:

> Niemals hatte ich bei der Musik etwas Ähnliches empfunden. Da ich von Jugend an von meiner Mutter war zum Bibellesen angehalten worden, so ward mir der Text wie mit einem Schlage gegenwärtig und Händels Musik eine erschöpfende Paraphrase jedes Worts; alles zusammen aber meiner Empfindung des lutherischen Christentums so aufgepasst, so damit zusammenfliessend, dass meine Freude in lauten, ja in schmerzlichen Äusserungen ausbrach und Aufmerksamkeit erregte. Man glaubte, mir sei nicht wohl, und der Kronprinz liess fragen, was mir fehle. Nach Endigung der Musik, welche bis neun Uhr gewärt hatte, schlich ich mich schamhaft fort, lief in der Nacht zu Fusse nach Berlin und benetzte den einsamen Weg mit Tränen der Rührung.[10]

Three years later Zelter served as first violinist at Johann Adam Hiller's celebrated *Massenaufführung* of *Messiah* (with Italian text) in the Domkirche of Berlin on 19 May 1786. Extravagant reports of the magnificence of *Messiah* at West-

---

[10] "Never had I felt the like in the presence of music. Since from youth I had been kept to Bible-reading by my mother, the text was present to me in a flash and Handel's music was an exhaustive paraphrase of each word; but the whole together so fitted my perception of Lutheran Christianity, so fused with it, that my joy broke forth in loud, indeed in painful, utterances and attracted attention. People thought I was not well, and the Crown Prince sent to ask what was the matter with me. At the conclusion of the music, which had lasted until nine o'clock, I slipped out shamefaced, went in the night to Berlin on foot, and moistened the lonely road with tears of emotion."

minster Abbey during the Handel Commemorations of 1784 and 1785 had aroused in German musicians a spirit of emulation, and when Charles Burney's *Account of the Commemoration* was translated into German by J. J. Eschenburg in 1785, Hiller met the challenge by performing *Messiah* on a scale hitherto unknown in the German metropolis.[11] His orchestra (excluding organ and harpsichord) consisted of 38 first violins, 39 second violins, 18 violas, 23 violoncellos, 15 contrabasses, 12 flutes, 12 oboes, 10 bassoons, 8 horns, 6 trumpets, 2 trombones, and 1 drum. His chorus (including all principals) numbered 37 sopranos, 24 altos, 26 tenors, and 31 basses, making a total ensemble of 302 vocal and instrumental performers. For the first performance Hiller did not scruple to court public favor by rescoring *Messiah* according to recent orchestral developments. In his *Nachricht von der Aufführung des Händelschen Messias, in der Domkirche zu Berlin, den 19 Mai 1786* he explained that "many improvements may be made in Handel's compositions by the employment of the wind instruments according to the fashion of the present day." Finding no evidence of oboes, flutes, trombones, or French horns in Handel's original score of *Messiah,* he resolved to add such instruments to his orchestra, thereby boldly violating the subtle balance of Handel's original ensemble. Thenceforth *Messiah* became the typical oratorio for mass effects. On 3 November 1786 Hiller conducted a group of two hundred musicians in a performance of *Messiah* at the University Church in Leipzig, and when the oratorio was repeated with great *éclat* on 11 May 1787, a native of Breslau expressed the hope that Hiller would also introduce *Messiah* to the connoisseurs of that city. Delighted at his success in Berlin and Leipzig, Hiller rendered *Messiah* in the old Maria Magdalena Church of Breslau on 30 May 1788. For this performance his chorus numbered 259 voices,

---

[11] In consequence of London's Handel Commemoration of 1784 *Messiah* was first performed in Copenhagen in March 1786 and in Stockholm during the following month.

and his orchestra included 52 violins, 11 violas, 12 violoncellos, 12 contrabasses, 10 bassoons, 11 oboes, 8 flutes, 8 horns, 4 clarinets, 4 trombones, 7 trumpets, kettledrum, clavicembalo, and organ. Two years later Hiller was appointed cantor of the Leipzig Thomasschule, where his elaborate performances of *Messiah* created a profound impression until his death in 1804.

Meanwhile Baron Gottfried van Swieten, a wealthy amateur with strong Handelian predilections, had engaged Mozart to rescore *Messiah* for a private subscription concert in the Court Library of Vienna in March 1789. Mozart had probably heard Handel's *Messiah* at Covent Garden Theatre during his memorable visit to London in 1764 and 1765. Since that time he had regarded Handel with sincere admiration and respect. But when Baron van Swieten proposed a performance of *Messiah* in a hall which contained no organ, Mozart felt it expedient to replace the missing *continuo* with additional accompaniments designed to strengthen and enrich his orchestra. Unfortunately he was forced in his adaptation to depend entirely upon the defective full-score edition published by Randall & Abell in 1767. His additions proved graceful and brilliant but highly superfluous and scarcely Handelian. Sometimes he merely doubled Handel's parts with additional instruments; more often he proceeded to introduce new woodwinds and strings according to his own taste; in many cases he actually refurbished *Messiah* with ornaments that violated the unity of the oratorio as a whole. In seeking to modernize *Messiah* Mozart displayed an almost total disregard for Handel's purpose. His delicious clarinet passages in "The people that walked in darkness" transformed Handel's blackness into a dreary golden twilight. Two arias, "The trumpet shall sound" and "If God be for us," were considerably reduced in length, while the chorus, "Let all the angels," and its succeeding aria, "Thou art gone up," were omitted entirely. It should be remembered, of course, that Mozart executed these changes solely to meet the exigencies of van Swieten's private performance. He little suspected that within fourteen years his adaptations would be imperfectly published and thereafter accepted throughout the world as the standard edition of Handel's oratorio. And certainly he should not be held responsible for all that stands in the score printed by Breitkopf & Härtel in 1803. From internal evidence it is clear that before publication this score was revised and enlarged by Johann Adam Hiller. Since Mozart's original manuscript of *Messiah* has disappeared, it is almost impossible to determine accurately the share of each composer in the published score, but it is probably safe to assume that the worst features of Mozart's *Messiah* should be ascribed to the less gifted hand of his contemporary.

One strong test of a composer's genius is his power to transcend his own age and to delight the masters of succeeding generations. Mozart was profoundly affected by the music of *Messiah,* and he often extolled the merits of its composer. "Handel," he once told Rochlitz, "knows better than any of us what will make an effect; when he chooses he strikes like a thunderbolt." Other composers shared Mozart's enthusiasm. On one occasion Gluck confessed to Michael Kelly that Handel was to him "the inspired master of our art," whom, "all my life, I have made my study, and endeavoured to imitate." Without Handel's influence Haydn would perhaps never have turned to oratorio. Of all composers, however, none has proved more sincerely devoted to Handel's genius than Beethoven. As early as 1797 his publications included Twelve Variations for Pianoforte and Violoncello on a theme from Handel's *Judas Maccabeus.* In 1811 he sketched several instrumental arrangements of "And the glory of the Lord" and "He shall feed His flock" from *Messiah.* At the climax of the "Agnus Dei" in his *Missa Solennis* (1823) stands Handel's majestic fugal theme from the "Hallelujah Chorus" adapted to the words "Dona nobis pacem." Beethoven habitually pointed to his predecessor as a model for students: "Handel is the unequalled master of all masters," he once said. "Go to him and learn, with small means, how to produce such grand effects." To an English lady he confessed that he "loved Handel" and never tired of praising his music. After playing through Heinrich Graun's *Der Tod Jesu* (1755) for the first time, he picked up Handel's *Messiah* with the words, "Here is a different fellow!" On 28 September 1823 a young Englishman named Edward Schulz visited Beethoven at Baden, and later Schulz recalled that his "repeated" attempts "to turn the conversation to Mozart" had proved vain:

> In the whole course of our table-talk there was nothing so interesting as what he said about Handel. I sat close by him and heard him assert very distinctly in German, "Händel ist der grösste componist der je gelebt hat." I cannot describe to you with what pathos, and I am inclined to say, with what sublimity of language, he spoke of the *Messiah* of this immortal genius. Every one of us was moved when he said, "Ich würde mein Haupt entblössen und auf seinem Grabe niederknien!"

Toward the end of 1824 Johann A. Stumpff, learning that Beethoven did not possess Handel's principal scores, resolved to remedy the situation as soon as he returned to London. In December 1826 he commissioned Andreas Streicher to bring the composer Samuel Arnold's voluminous edition of Handel's works. Beethoven was almost beside himself with joy. On 8 February 1827, less than three months before his death, he wrote to thank Stumpff for his "glorious gift," confessing that his pen could not "describe" the "joy" which he had derived from such a "royal present." Confined to his bed, he often requested his faithful young friend, Gerhard von Breuning, to bring him Handel's scores from the pianoforte where they rested. Leaning the books against the wall, he slowly turned their pages, occasionally pausing to murmur: "Das ist das Wahre!"

For Herder and Goethe, as for Beethoven, Handel represented the peak of musical attainment. In *Adrastea* (1802)

Herder reviewed the life and works of several prominent eighteenth-century figures, and in his special chapter on Handel he glorified *Messiah* as the greatest single feat of the century. "Es kommt wie von Himmel," he wrote, "ohne zerstreunden, das Auge fesselnden Theaterschmuck." In its arias he found "Ausdruck reiner Empfindung"; in its choruses he sensed "die Ethik and Metaphysik seines menschlichen Daseins." Herder considered *Messiah* the archetype of the species:

Im Messias also, in Worten der Propheten und Apostel that sich Händels Geist am mächtigsten hervor. Von der ersten Stimme . . . bis zur letzten . . . herrscht, beinahe bildlos der starke und sanfte Geist aller Empfindungen, die das weite Feld der Religion einhauchet. Kaum berührt wird die Erzählung, allenthalben vom tiefsten Gefühl hervorgedrungen. . . . In prophetischen und apokalyptischen Verkündigungen hebt sich das ganze Chor der Kirche, eine Gemeine der Seelen, eine Geisterversammlung; kein Theater.[12]

To Goethe, too, Handel's *Messiah* constituted a landmark in Christian music. His famous correspondence with Zelter, which commenced in 1799 and ended only with the poet's death in 1832, comprises six volumes, every page of which sparkles with animated remarks upon the merits of Handel and Bach. From 1816 *Messiah* played a conspicuous rôle in Goethe's letters to his friend. In November 1816 Zelter wrote to request a poem which might be set to music for the tercentenary celebration of Luther's Reformation on 31 October 1817. Immediately Goethe projected a grand oratorio modelled on Handel's *Messiah*, based on a series of Scriptural texts which recorded the progress of Hebrew faith from

---

[12] "In *Messiah*, therefore, in the words of the prophets and apostles, Handel's genius was shown at its mightiest. From the first to the last there triumphs almost without images the strong and gentle spirit of all feelings inspired by the broad field of religion. The narrative is scarcely related; everything wells up from the deepest feeling. In prophetic and apocalyptic proclamations the whole choir of the church rises, a unit of souls, a gathering of spirits, not a theatre."

Moses' legislation at Sinai to Christ's Resurrection and Ascension. Had Goethe's plan been executed, his "oratorio" might have proved a worthy German counterpart of *Messiah*, but Zelter responded evasively and the work was abandoned. Possibly a trace of its inspiration is to be observed in Goethe's celestial dialogue in the Second Part of *Faust*. In any case, the proposed oratorio reaffirmed Goethe's enduring faith in Handel's *Messiah* and returned the would-be librettist to his great original with renewed affection. When Johann Friedrich Rochlitz published the first volume of *Für Freunde der Tonkunst* early in 1824, Goethe was so moved by his essay on *Messiah* that he persuaded Traugott Maximilian Eberwein to conduct the musicians of Weimar in a special performance of Handel's oratorio on 16 March 1824. Two weeks later Goethe wrote to congratulate Rochlitz on April 2:

Ihre herzlich eindringende Darstellung des Messias erregte den unwiderstehlischen Wunsch, die alten verklungenen Gefühle in mir zu erneuen, und nun unter Anleitung des wackern Eberweins durch freundliche Teilnahme von Künstlern und Liebhabern vernehme soviel von dem köstlichen Werk, dass ich aufs neue darüber entzückt sein und Ihnen für diesen Genuss aufs verblindlichste danken muss.[13]

In a subsequent review of *Für Freunde der Tonkunst* Goethe expanded his praise of Rochlitz and confessed his desire to be permeated anew with the "Geistesgewalt" of Handel's *Messiah*:

Zwar will ich zuvörderst der gemütlich-ausführlichen Darstellung des Messias von Händel gedenken; sie erregte in mir die unwiderstehliche Sehnsucht, von dem Werke, das mich früher an die ernsteste Tonkunst herangeführt, so viel abermals zu

---

[13] "Your deeply moving description of *Messiah* aroused an irresistible desire to renew in myself the old vanished feelings; and now under the guidance of the worthy Eberwein, through the friendly cooperation of artists and amateurs, I perceive so much in the excellent work, that I am enraptured by it anew and must acknowledge my very great debt to you for this pleasure."

vernehmen, dass die alten, halb verklungenen Gefühle sich wieder entwickelten und die jugendlichen Genüsse in Geist und Seele sich nochmals erneuerten.

Dazu gelange ich denn jetzt unter der Anleitung eines wackern Musikdirektors, durch Teilnahme von Tonkünstlern und Liebhabern. Ich folge nunmehr dem Gange des unschätzbaren Werkes nach vorliegender Anleitung, man schreitet vor, man wiederholt, und so hoffe ich in einiger Zeit ganz wieder von Händelscher Geistesgewalt durchdrungen zu sein.[14]

During his latter years Goethe rejoiced particularly in the architectural construction of Handel's oratorios. His minute analyses of *Messiah, Samson,* and *Judas Maccabeus* served only to corroborate his former respect for Handel's energy, clarity, and moral confidence. For Goethe the composer of *Messiah* represented an ideal of serenity and amplitude— qualities which fascinated the German poet chiefly because he felt that he had failed to realize them fully in his own works.

Despite the praise of poets and musicians, however, Handel's *Messiah* was not swift to win the favor of the German public. During the Napoleonic wars civic organizations produced the oratorios treating Israel's liberation from captivity, but the purpose of such performances was frankly political. As late as 1824 Rochlitz complained that Germans had not yet accepted *Messiah* as an independent work of art deserving a place beside Mozart's *Requiem* and Haydn's *Creation.* He deplored the fact that frequent performances of favorite selections from *Messiah* had violated the essential unity of Handel's work and had done little to further the

---

[14] "Indeed I wish first of all to mention the pleasantly detailed description of Handel's *Messiah;* it aroused in me an irresistible longing to perceive as much once more in that work which earlier led me to the most serious in musical art, so that half-vanished feelings flourished again and youthful pleasures were renewed once more in my spirit and heart.

"This I have now attained under the guidance of a worthy conductor, through the cooperation of musicians and amateurs. I now follow the course of the inestimable work according to the guidance available—I advance, I repeat—and so I hope in time to be entirely saturated again with the Handelian spiritual power."

composer's fame as an epic poet in music. By 1824, of course, the scene was not totally dark. Following the publication of Mozart's "additional accompaniments" in 1803, a vocal score of *Messiah,* edited by Christian Friedrich Schwenke and provided with German text by Christoph Daniel Ebeling, had been published in 1809 by Johann August Böhme. As early as 1791 the Berlin Singakademie had been organized to promote Handel's oratorios, and by 1810 dozens of similar organizations were holding ambitious musical festivals throughout the provinces. At the great Rhenish Festival, established in 1818, thirty-four choral works of Handel were heard during the course of its first forty-four concerts. In 1824 the Frankfort Cäcilienverein performed *Messiah* for the first time. Slowly Protestant Germany yielded to the charm of Handelian oratorio, till by 1850 prominent conductors were performing *Messiah* on a grand scale all over the country. In 1857 Franz Liszt was able to speak of *Messiah* as "a *chef-d'œuvre* which has been for years the 'daily bread,' so to speak, of great and small vocal societies both in England and Germany." [15] During the following year Dr. Friedrich Chrysander issued the first in his monumental series of ninety-seven volumes of *Georg Friedrich Händels Werke,* edited in full score for Die Deutsche Händel-Gesellschaft and issued at irregular intervals between 1858 and 1903 by Breitkopf & Härtel of Leipzig. As a result of Chrysander's patient and laborious efforts Handelian oratorio steadily rose in public esteem. By 1900 his choral works were almost as widely appreciated in Germany as in England. Among the composer's own countrymen, however, *Messiah* has never enjoyed quite the popularity of *Samson, Judas Maccabeus,* and *Israel in*

---

[15] Like Berlioz and Wagner, Liszt found the "Hallelujah-perruque of a Handel" tedious and old-fashioned. At a London performance of *Messiah* in April 1855 Richard Wagner confessed that he "nearly died of ennui" and took pleasure only in the "painful precision" with which British Handelians piously rose at the "Hallelujah Chorus." Wagner had little patience for a nation that persistently heard its *Messiah* each Christmas but waited thirty years to perform *Tristan und Isolde.*

Egypt. Following World War I the great German revival of Handel's music resulted in successful productions of his oratorios in dramatic form with scenery, costume, and action. Ten years later Chancellor Adolf Hitler, seeking to reclaim Handel's music as one of the bulwarks of Nazi culture, provided several of his oratorios with German titles and original texts drawn from Prussian history. By this process of "Aryanization" *Israel in Egypt* became, ironically enough, a celebration of German militarism known as *Mongolenstrum,* while *Judas Maccabeus,* Handel's magnificent tribute to a Jewish patriot, was converted into an oratorio glorifying the Prussian hero *Wilhelm von Nassau!*

IV

Since the publication of Mozart's "additional accompaniments" to Handel's *Messiah* in 1803 the much-vexed question of their propriety has persisted among professionals and amateurs to the present day. Few musicians have denied the exquisite beauty and skill of Mozart's adaptation, but numerous conductors and critics have resented its wholesale acceptance as "an integral part of Handel's work," without which (as Sir George A. Macfarren wrote) "a performance of the *Messiah* must always be regarded as inadequate to fulfill the intentions of Handel." From the beginning Mozart's *Messiah* aroused both praise and censure. In its rich but un-Handelian score Rochlitz and Zelter found much to applaud and also much to condemn. As late as 1856 Moritz Hauptmann observed to Franz Hauser that the additional instrumentation "resembles elegant stucco-work upon an old marble temple, which might easily be chipped off again by the weather." At its first performance in England Mozart's adaptation was severely and judiciously criticized. "We learn," wrote *The Morning Chronicle* for 21 March 1805, "that the celebrated Mozarti [!] has made some additions to this favourite Oratorio, which are spoken of as highly creditable to his genius, and respectful to the memory of Handel. We would recommend their being introduced that the Public might judge whether they are *really improvements*." On March 28 the same journal announced "with great pleasure" a concert scheduled for the following evening, "when the *Messiah,* the master-piece of Handel, is to be produced, with the additional parts, as added by the celebrated Mozart; we are anxious to hear the superior effort produced by this harmonious combination of the great masters of the ancient and modern school of music." Mozart's *Messiah* was accordingly introduced to England on 29 March 1805 as one of General Charles Ashley's "Lenten Oratorios" at Covent Garden Theatre. A penetrating review of the performance appeared in *The Sun* for March 30:

> The *Messiah* was last night performed at Covent Garden Theatre, with new accompaniments composed by Mozart. We entertain a very high respect for the genius of Mozart, but we also hold the unrivalled powers of Handel in due reverence, and therefore must enter our protest against any such alterations in works that have obtained the sanction of time and of the best musical judges. There is an *integrity* in the productions of this great Master, the result of the most powerful talents in his art. His harmonies have a firm and united character. The accompaniments of last night, though manifesting taste and feeling, did not assimilate with the grandeur and energy of the original subject. We trust, therefore, that when the *Messiah* or any other work of Handel is performed it will appear without change or interpolation. Handel is an Englishman by adoption; he produced all his works in this Country, and is still very little regarded in his own. We should therefore guard him in Music, as well as Shakespeare in the Drama, from daring innovation.

From their first performance in England Mozart's "additional accompaniments" raised a storm of disapprobation among singers and concert-goers alike. James Bartleman, the popular baritone, actually declined to participate in performances at which they were used. For a rendition of *Messiah* at Covent Garden Theatre on 30 January 1813 Sir George Smart omitted some of the additions as "not suitable to the accustomed *English* ear, and because Mozart would *not* allow (at the ends of his songs) the singers to make cadences, which many of them would not have agreed to." Following this performance *The Times* and *The Morning Post* were both silent regarding Mozart's additions, but *The Gentleman's Magazine* for March 1813 published a lengthy series of "Thoughts on the Musick of Handel, and on the Mode of Performing it at the Present Day." In this somewhat sarcastic essay one J. Carter deplored Mozart's "improvements" of Handel's *Messiah,* an oratorio which "has always been a favourite" and which, till the present "age of innovation." has been "esteemed his most perfect work." Formerly, he wrote, *Messiah* was held "in such high estimation" that "it was deemed a musical crime to make any deviation from it," but lately its music "has been discovered to be extremely *faulty* in most of its prominent features," and "to *remedy* these alleged errors" various improvements "have been lavished with an unsparing hand" and conducted in London theatres by Sir George Smart. "Since Handel's compositions in these *enlightened* times are found to be *incorrect* and *puerile*," Carter concluded, "why condescend to meliorate and bestow on them a modern polish? Rather throw his *disorganized* masses on the shelf, and let oblivion be their fate, than thus violate the memory of an exalted name, whose soul anticipated in his blissful strains, that eternity of joy, known only in the realms of above!" Similar sentiments were expressed in *The Quarterly Musical Magazine and Review* for 1822: "If [Handel's] music does not contain within itself the seeds of immortality, let it sink into obscurity and be forgotten. It will acquire no additional fame by being tricked out in modern dress." In the same journal "A Querist," conceding that Handel "has been prodigiously overrated" and that his music "has suffered excessively by the monopolizing feeling of his partizans," confessed his frank disapproval of Mozart's "arrangement" of *Messiah*:

That the accompaniments alluded to present, in many points, magnificent displays of instrumental knowledge and effect is certain, but as similar instances are innumerable in MOZART's own original works, I can readily dispense with those in HANDEL. Were I promised a sight of the Grecian warriors before Troy, at a mess dinner, I should ill brook the introduction of snow white napery, or even the Duke of Wellington's Spanish votive plate, and however superior in comfort or cleanliness I may admit the fashion of forks and finger glasses, I should prefer seeing Nestor broiling his beef bone on the wood ashes, and Ulysses, sword in hand, over a "savory chine." Just so, I am content when I hear HANDEL, to hear him display so well the means then within his reach, and feel satisfied with my own admission to the merits of the man who with so little has done so much.

Unfortunately such dissident voices were soon silenced. The ease and grace of Mozart's version, together with the celebrity attached to the composer's name, served to propagate his "additional accompaniments" throughout England shortly after their first introduction in London. In October 1805 they were heard with enthusiasm at the Birmingham Festival, and during the nineteenth century they came to be regarded as an essential feature of Handel's oratorio. British acceptance of Mozart's arrangement testified, of course, to the loss of baroque traditions in England.

Through the breach opened by Mozart a host of misguided but well-intentioned editors, arrangers, and adapters soon rushed in to disfigure the score of *Messiah* almost beyond recognition. Sundry nineteenth-century musicians, following Mozart's dangerous precedent but hardly evincing his superior genius, sought to "modernize" Handel's original intentions by abbreviating, supplementing, arranging, and rearranging his orchestra in ruthless fashion, excusing their adornments with the remarkable explanation that "if Handel had heard them, he would have pardoned the liberties taken because of the charming effects obtained." As early as 1789 Thomas Pitt, chorister of Worcester Cathedral, published two folio volumes of *Church Music, Consisting of Ten Anthems from the*

Sacred Works of Handel, "selected and adapted for the use of choirs." In the preface to this brazen work Pitt explained that "where the beauties of the Music would allow, I have endeavoured to obviate any objection which might arise from prolixity." With shameless effrontery he dared to boast that "In this volume there are fifteen hundred and forty-two bars short of the original." Pitt's mutilation of *Messiah* may be regarded as characteristic of his handiwork in general. "Rejoice greatly" was cut from 108 bars to 52; "O thou that tellest" from 106 bars to 40; "For unto us a Child is born" from 99 bars to 70; "His yoke is easy" from 59 bars to 35; "Every valley" (in the key of D) from 85 bars to 63. Similar prunings and emendations reduced *Messiah* to a grotesque caricature of Handel's original. Early in the nineteenth century the score was arranged for concertina by William Henry Birch, and for pianoforte or harp (with *ad libitum* parts for violoncello and flute) by John Freckleton Burrowes. Among other freaks appeared a lively set of *Messiah Quadrilles* by Augustus Lechmere Tamplin, an arrangement of the "Hallelujah Chorus" as duet for two flutes, and a complete edition of *Messiah* arranged for solo German flute. Throughout the century numerous German conductors adapted *Messiah* to the limits of their private chapels and singing societies: Friedrich Wilhelm Berner, Carl Heinrich Breidenstein, Karl Klage, Philipp Jacob Riotte, J. O. H. Schaum, Christian Friedrich Schwenke, and Daniel Frederic Wilsing. In 1843 Mendelssohn wrote organ accompaniments for two choruses in *Messiah*: the "Hallelujah Chorus" and "For unto us a Child is born." Later Ignaz von Mosel undertook to "revise" eight of Handel's oratorios, including *Messiah,* in adaptations which must stand forever as monuments of arrogant presumption and incompetence. In England Sir Michael Costa designed "additional accompaniments" for a complete "romantic" orchestra (including contra-fagot and ophicleide), while Sir George A. Macfarren proceeded to out-Mozart Mozart with a "performing edition" which exploited the full weight of a military band. Further additions were provided by Edward F. Rimbault and Sir Arthur Sullivan.

In 1885 Robert Franz, observing "imperfections and deficiencies" in Mozart's adaptation, proceeded to publish in Leipzig a new full-score edition of *Messiah,* critically revised on the basis of original manuscripts and considerably augmented by instrumental additions from his own pen. Franz failed, however, to consult the so-called "Dublin score," from which Handel had conducted the first performance, and his additions, though rich and skilfully executed, accordingly reveal slight sympathy for Handel's original. In his review of Franz's score in *The Musical Times* for December 1885 Dr. William H. Cummings pronounced the additions "a great misfortune," particularly because "many earnest musicians, who have no opportunity of thoroughly investigating the matter, will be ready to accept his version as a sure and reliable guide." Seventeen years later Dr. Friedrich Chrysander's scholarly version of *Messiah* was published posthumously by Dr. Max Seiffert for Die Deutsche Händel-Gesellschaft. In this monumental edition Chrysander proved himself a painstaking antiquarian rather than a practical musician. His score was designed not as a model for performance but as an exact reproduction of Handel's autograph manuscripts. Dr. William H. Cummings found the work "ill-advised" and frankly declared that "A great wrong to Art and to the reputation of a great musician has been perpetrated in this mutilation of a masterpiece." Despite some obviously weak spots, however, Chrysander corrected the worst mistakes of previous editions and helped to rescue *Messiah* from the tasteless spectacle of "mammoth" nineteenth-century performances at the Crystal Palace. Meanwhile Dr. Ebenezer Prout, Professor of Music in the University of Dublin, had issued another full-score edition of *Messiah* in 1902. Prout's erudite and exhaustive preface appeared in *The Musical Times* from May to October 1902 as a veritable manifesto of editorial policy. In rescoring

Messiah his "first and most important rule" was that "the most absolute respect must be shown to Handel's text, and to his intentions, whether written or implied, so far as these can be gathered from the indications in his score." Unfortunately Prout's technical competence far exceeded his native musical gifts. His edition proved to be a somewhat academic compromise between truth and current practice. Though he sincerely regarded his work as "an honest effort to reproduce, as nearly as possible, both the letter and the spirit of Handel's greatest oratorio," he conceded in his preface that "No attempt has been made to preserve his orchestral colouring," and thus his wealth of reference material and his intimate acquaintance with Handel's style failed to bring his labors to a successful issue. His newly edited score was first performed at Queen's Hall, London, on 12 November 1902. W. Frye Parker led the orchestra; William H. Cummings accompanied the recitatives on the pianoforte; Prout himself conducted the performance. A chorus of one hundred carefully-selected voices and an orchestra of sixty-five musicians approximated the balance of Handel's original ensemble. With all its authenticity and precision, however, Prout's edition was felt to be somewhat featureless and dull in performance, and astute critics observed that a truly satisfactory edition of *Messiah* had yet to make its appearance.

To the multitude of churchgoers who still delight in Handel's *Messiah* it may appear curious that few contemporaries have ever heard the oratorio as it was performed in Handel's day. For more than a century choral conductors and concert-goers have tacitly agreed to accept the accretions of Mozart and his less inspired successors as indispensable features of Handel's initial design, until today *Messiah* has become a grandiose anachronism, its true splendor almost unrecognizable beneath its outrageous embellishments—at once the best known and least known work in the field of oratorio. As A. Hargreaves Ashworth recently observed, "What we know as 'Messiah' is an accumulation of misconception, corrupt tradition, vulgar emendation and unthinking repetition, lying like rubble over the original music." Perhaps the text of no other musical composition is even approximately so corrupt as that of *Messiah*. Today its music exists in almost fifty different versions, but not one of these "translations" fully reflects the magic and elegance of Handel's original work. Isolated attempts to render *Messiah* in strict accord with the autograph score have revealed an unsuspected transparence and radiance in Handel's music, but until *Messiah* is frequently performed as it was intended to be performed, laymen will continue to regard its composer as grave, stolid, and ponderous. Actually the score of *Messiah* is remarkably thin. Its orchestration is notably deficient in those picturesque details which brighten the pages of *Saul* and *Samson* and *Israel in Egypt*. With the reticence of a consummate artist Handel deliberately shunned elaborate instrumentation in *Messiah*, seldom employing his full powers and skilfully contrasting simplicity with orchestral brilliance. Those who persist in gazing at Handel through Wagnerian spectacles may find the original score of *Messiah* meagre and unrewarding, but those who pause to look more closely discover in its sparing use of color a sharp clarity and a subtle variation of texture achieved within a carefully organized scheme. Handel's orchestration is an integral part of his basic conception, and editors cannot tamper with such an individual feature of his art without serious detriment to his intentions. For many years Handelians have awaited an accurate version of *Messiah* that would preserve the composer's exact notation and at the same time incorporate authentic Handel traditions in a score suitable for public performance. It is gratifying to observe that this complex task has finally been accomplished by Dr. Jacob Maurice Coopersmith, one of the most distinguished Handel scholars now living, whose thorough and sympathetic knowledge of eighteenth-century musical practice has enabled him to eradicate the stereotyped errors of two hundred years, and to overhaul the musical text of

Messiah in such a way as to insure its proper interpretation by contemporary conductors, soloists, and choruses.

With the publication of Dr. Coopersmith's critical edition the future of Handel's *Messiah* should be secure. Few works have been subjected to the editorial indignities endured by *Messiah* since its first performance in 1742, but few works have braved such indignities with equal grace, and certainly few works have enjoyed such enormous vogue throughout the English-speaking world for two hundred years. The vitality of *Messiah* is phenomenal. Year after year its score is mercilessly butchered in performance, its spirited tempi dragged and distorted by conductors whose ignorance of genuine Handelian practice is appalling, its graceful outlines blurred by soloists whose barbarous "traditions" dictate grotesque top notes and trills, its grandeur ruthlessly violated by the insufferable lumbering jog-trot of choristers who proceed with the monotonous rhythmic beat of a machine. But through such misinterpretation *Messiah* somehow manages to retain at least a measure of its original fire and charm. Today a first-rate performance seldom fails to kindle general enthusiasm. In countless cities and towns throughout England and America its annual rendition at Christmas has become a civic institution as well as an indispensable religious rite.[16]

---

[16] An experimental gramophone recording of familiar selections from *Messiah* was made as early as 1906 by the London Welsh Choir, the Queen's Hall Players, and four prominent soloists: Perceval Allen (soprano), Elizabeth Dews (contralto), John Harrison (tenor), and Charles Knowles (bass). An almost complete recording of *Messiah* (36 sides) was released in December 1936 by the Columbia Recording Corporation (Set M-MM-271), featuring the B.B.C. Choir and the London Philharmonic Orchestra under the direction of Sir Thomas Beecham, with the following soloists: Dora Labbette (soprano), Muriel Brunskill (contralto), Nellie Walker (contralto), Hubert Eisdell (tenor), and Harold Williams (baritone). A second and more complete recording (38 sides) was issued in the autumn of 1946 by the Columbia Recording Corporation (Set M-MM-666), featuring the Huddersfield Choral Society and the Liverpool Philharmonic Orchestra under the direction of Dr. Malcolm Sargent, with the following soloists: Isobel Baillie (soprano), Gladys Ripley (contralto), James Johnston (tenor), and Norman Walker (bass). Since 1900 countless miscellaneous recordings of single arias and

It is most unfortunate, however, that those who sincerely delight in Handel's *Messiah* seldom trouble themselves to investigate the wealth of forgotten treasures buried among the composer's less familiar works. Apparently Fate has fixed on *Messiah* as the one composition by which Handel is to be known to posterity, and his name is accordingly reverenced by thousands whose knowledge of his music is bound on the one hand by endless repetitions of the "Dead March" from *Saul* and on the other by hackneyed adaptations of the "Celebrated Largo" from *Serse*. Handelians worship an almost unknown god. Of Handel's thirty-two oratorios and forty-one Italian operas the musical masses seem content to listen year after year to the one unapproachable favorite, while portions of the composer's finest music—his brilliant operatic arias, his secular oratorios and cantatas, his vigorous *concerti grossi*—are shamefully neglected when not altogether lost in oblivion. A knowledge of *Messiah* is far from a knowledge of Handel. Incomparable as it is, *Messiah* is in no sense completely representative of Handel's art, for it fails to illustrate his inexhaustible variety and versatility, his fondness for the playful and the merry, his passionate devotion to the English countryside, and his almost Shakespearean power to delineate human emotion. Perhaps *Messiah* is on the whole the most even of Handel's oratorios, but *Alexander's Feast* and *L'Allegro* and *Samson* and *Semele* contain inspirations to rank with the most distinguished music he ever composed. It is to be hoped that concert-goers of the future will break the bonds of custom and patronize Handel's lesser known but equally meritorious compositions. As the Reverend William Hughes remarked in 1758, "We live in an Age of great Delicacy and Refinement, ever improving, and it is greatly to be hop'd, ever going on to improve. We are not to be enslav'd by Prejudice and Custom, two of the

---

choruses from *Messiah* have been released both in England and in the United States.

most ridiculous and tyrannical Things in Nature, but on the contrary we are to consider it as our immediate Duty, to search to the very bottom of Things, and to make the utmost Use of our reasonable Faculties—The GLORY of HUMAN NATURE."

Appendix A

TEXT OF HANDEL'S *MESSIAH*

[It should be noted that Handel's text frequently involves slight alterations from the Biblical source.]

Majora Canamus
[Virgil, *Eclogue* IV]

And without controversy, great is the mystery of godliness: God was manifested in the flesh, justified by the Spirit, seen of angels, preached among the Gentiles, believed on in the world, received up into glory. In whom are hid all the treasures of wisdom and knowledge [*I Timothy* 3:16; *Colossians* 2:3].

PART I

I. OVERTURE

II. RECITATIVE *Accompanied* (Tenor)
Comfort ye, comfort ye my people, saith your God. Speak ye comfortably to Jerusalem, and cry unto her that her warfare is accomplished, that her iniquity is pardoned. The voice of him that crieth in the wilderness, Prepare ye the way of the Lord, make straight in the desert a highway for our God [*Isaiah* 40:1-3].

III. AIR (Tenor)
Every valley shall be exalted, and every mountain and hill made low; the crooked straight, and the rough places plain [*Isaiah* 40:4].

IV. CHORUS
And the glory of the Lord shall be revealed, and all flesh shall see it together: for the mouth of the Lord hath spoken it [*Isaiah* 40:5].

V. RECITATIVE *Accompanied* (Bass)

Thus saith the Lord of Hosts: Yet once a little while and I will shake the heavens, and the earth, the sea, and the dry land. And I will shake all nations, and the desire of all nations shall come. The Lord, whom ye seek, shall suddenly come to his temple, even the messenger of the covenant, whom ye delight in. Behold, He shall come, saith the Lord of Hosts [*Haggai* 2:6–7; *Malachi* 3:1].

VI. AIR (Bass)

But who may abide the day of His coming? And who shall stand when He appeareth? For He is like a refiner's fire [*Malachi* 3:2].

VII. CHORUS

And He shall purify the sons of Levi, that they may offer unto the Lord an offering in righteousness [*Malachi* 3:3].

VIII. RECITATIVE (Alto)

Behold, a virgin shall conceive, and bear a Son, and shall call His name Immanuel: God with us [*Isaiah* 7:14].

IX. AIR (Alto) and CHORUS

O thou that tellest good tidings to Zion, get thee up into the high mountain. O thou that tellest good tidings to Jerusalem, lift up thy voice with strength. Lift it up, be not afraid; say unto the cities of Judah, Behold your God! Arise, shine, for thy light is come, and the glory of the Lord is risen upon thee [*Isaiah* 40:9; 60:1].

X. RECITATIVE *Accompanied* (Bass)

For, behold, darkness shall cover the earth, and gross darkness the people. But the Lord shall arise upon thee, and His glory shall be seen upon thee. And the Gentiles shall come to thy light, and kings to the brightness of thy rising [*Isaiah* 60:2–3].

XI. AIR (Bass)

The people that walked in darkness have seen a great light; and they that dwell in the land of the shadow of death, upon them hath the light shined [*Isaiah* 9:2].

XII. CHORUS

For unto us a Child is born, unto us a Son is given. And the government shall be upon His shoulder. And His name shall be called Wonderful, Counsellor, The Mighty God, The Everlasting Father, The Prince of Peace [*Isaiah* 9:6].

XIII. PASTORAL SYMPHONY

XIV. RECITATIVE (Soprano)
There were shepherds abiding in the field, keeping watch over their flocks by night [*Luke* 2:8].

XV. RECITATIVE *Accompanied* (Soprano)
And, lo! the angel of the Lord came upon them, and the glory of the Lord shone round about them, and they were sore afraid [*Luke* 2:9].

XVI. RECITATIVE (Soprano)
And the angel said unto them, Fear not: for, behold, I bring you good tidings of great joy, which shall be to all people. For unto you is born this day in the city of David a Saviour, which is Christ the Lord [*Luke* 2:10–11].

XVII. RECITATIVE *Accompanied* (Soprano)
And suddenly there was with the angel a multitude of the heavenly host praising God, and saying [*Luke* 2:13]:

XVIII. CHORUS
Glory to God in the highest, and peace on earth, good will towards men [*Luke* 2:14].

XIX. AIR (Soprano)
Rejoice greatly, O daughter of Zion; shout, O daughter of Jerusalem. Behold, thy King cometh unto thee. He is the righteous Saviour, and He shall speak peace unto the heathen [*Zechariah* 9:9–10].

XX. RECITATIVE (Alto)
Then shall the eyes of the blind be opened, and the ears of the deaf unstopped. Then shall the lame man leap as an hart, and the tongue of the dumb shall sing [*Isaiah* 35:5–6].

XXI. AIR (Alto)
He shall feed His flock like a shepherd; and He shall gather the

lambs with His arm, and carry them in His bosom, and gently lead those that are with young [*Isaiah* 40:11].

XXII. AIR (Soprano)

Come unto Him, all ye that labour and are heavy laden, and He will give you rest. Take His yoke upon you, and learn of Him; for He is meek and lowly of heart; and ye shall find rest unto your souls [*Matthew* 11:28–29].

XXIII. CHORUS

His yoke is easy and His burthen is light [*Matthew* 11:30].

PART II

XXIV. CHORUS

Behold the Lamb of God, that taketh away the sins of the world [*John* 1:29].

XXV. AIR (Alto)

He was despised and rejected of men: a man of sorrows, and acquainted with grief. He gave His back to the smiters, and His cheeks to them that plucked off the hair. He hid not His face from shame and spitting [*Isaiah* 53:3; 50:6].

XXVI. CHORUS

Surely He hath borne our griefs, and carried our sorrows. He was wounded for our transgressions; He was bruised for our iniquities. The chastisement of our peace was upon Him [*Isaiah* 53:4–5].

XXVII. CHORUS

And with His stripes we are healed [*Isaiah* 53:5].

XXVIII. CHORUS

All we like sheep have gone astray; we have turned every one to his own way; and the Lord hath laid on Him the iniquity of us all [*Isaiah* 53:6].

XXIX. RECITATIVE *Accompanied* (Tenor)

All they that see Him laugh Him to scorn. They shoot out their lips, and shake their heads, saying [*Psalm* 22:7]:

XXX. Chorus
He trusted in God that He would deliver Him. Let Him deliver Him, if He delight in Him [*Psalm* 22:8].

XXXI. Recitative *Accompanied* (Tenor)
Thy rebuke hath broken His heart; He is full of heaviness. He looked for some to have pity on Him, but there was no man; neither found He any to comfort Him [*Psalm* 69:20].

XXXII. Air (Tenor)
Behold, and see if there be any sorrow like unto His sorrow [*Lamentations* 1:12].

XXXIII. Recitative *Accompanied* (Tenor)
He was cut off out of the land of the living; for the transgressions of Thy people was He stricken [*Isaiah* 53:8].

XXXIV. Air (Tenor)
But Thou didst not leave His soul in hell; nor didst Thou suffer Thy Holy One to see corruption [*Psalm* 16:10].

XXXV. Chorus
Lift up your heads, O ye gates; and be ye lift up, ye everlasting doors; and the King of glory shall come in. Who is this King of glory? The Lord strong and mighty, the Lord mighty in battle. Lift up your heads, O ye gates; and be ye lift up, ye everlasting doors; and the King of glory shall come in. Who is this King of glory? The Lord of Hosts, He is the King of glory [*Psalm* 24:7–10].

XXXVI. Recitative (Tenor)
Unto which of the angels said He at any time, Thou art my Son; this day have I begotten Thee [*Hebrews* 1:5]?

XXXVII. Chorus
Let all the angels of God worship Him [*Hebrews* 1:6].

XXXVIII. Air (Bass)
Thou art gone up on high; Thou hast led captivity captive, and received gifts for men; yea, even for Thine enemies, that the Lord God might dwell among them [*Psalm* 68:18].

XXXIX. Chorus
The Lord gave the word; great was the company of the preachers [*Psalm* 68:11].

XL. Air (Soprano)
How beautiful are the feet of them that preach the gospel of peace, and bring glad tidings of good things [*Romans* 10:15].

XLI. Chorus
Their sound is gone out into all lands, and their words unto the ends of the world [*Romans* 10:18].

XLII. Air (Bass)
Why do the nations so furiously rage together? And why do the people imagine a vain thing? The kings of the earth rise up, and the rulers take counsel together against the Lord and against His Anointed [*Psalm* 2:1–2].

XLIII. Chorus
Let us break their bonds asunder, and cast away their yokes from us [*Psalm* 2:3].

XLIV. Recitative (Tenor)
He that dwelleth in heaven shall laugh them to scorn; the Lord shall have them in derision [*Psalm* 2:4].

XLV. Air (Tenor)
Thou shalt break them with a rod of iron; Thou shalt dash them in pieces like a potter's vessel [*Psalm* 2:9].

XLVI. Chorus
Hallelujah! for the Lord God omnipotent reigneth. The Kingdom of this world is become the kingdom of our Lord, and of His Christ; and He shall reign for ever and ever. King of Kings, and Lord of Lords, Hallelujah! [*Revelation* 19:6; 11:15; 19:16].

PART III

XLVII. Air (Soprano)
I know that my Redeemer liveth, and that He shall stand at the latter day upon the earth. And though worms destroy this body,

yet in my flesh shall I see God. For now is Christ risen from the dead, the first-fruits of them that sleep [*Job* 19:25–26; *I Corinthians* 15:20].

XLVIII. Chorus

Since by man came death, by man came also the resurrection of the dead. For as in Adam all die, even so in Christ shall all be made alive [*I Corinthians* 15:21–22].

XLIX. Recitative *Accompanied* (Bass)

Behold, I tell you a mystery: we shall not all sleep; but we shall all be changed, in a moment, in the twinkling of an eye, at the last trumpet [*I Corinthians* 15:51–52].

L. Air (Bass)

The trumpet shall sound, and the dead shall be raised incorruptible, and we shall all be changed. For this corruptible must put on incorruption, and this mortal must put on immortality [*I Corinthians* 15:52–53].

LI. Recitative (Alto)

Then shall be brought to pass the saying that is written: Death is swallowed up in victory [*I Corinthians* 15:54].

LII. Duet (Alto and Tenor)

O death, where is thy sting? O grave, where is thy victory? The sting of death is sin, and the strength of sin is the law [*I Corinthians* 15:55–56].

LIII. Chorus

But thanks be to God, who giveth us the victory through our Lord Jesus Christ [*I Corinthians* 15:57].

LIV. Air (Soprano)

If God be for us, who can be against us? Who shall lay any thing to the charge of God's elect? It is God that justifieth. Who is he that condemneth? It is Christ that died, yea rather, that is risen again, who is at the right hand of God, who makes intercession for us [*Romans* 8:31, 33–34].

LV. Chorus

Worthy is the Lamb that was slain, and hath redeemed us to

God by His blood, to receive power, and riches, and wisdom, and strength, and honour, and glory, and blessing [*Revelation* 5:12].

LVI. CHORUS

Blessing and honour, glory and power, be unto Him that sitteth upon the throne, and unto the Lamb for ever and ever. Amen [*Revelation* 5:13].

Appendix B

A LIST OF SUBSCRIBERS TO THE ORIGINAL FULL-SCORE EDITION OF HANDEL'S *MESSIAH* (1767)

The King [George III]
The Queen [Charlotte]
His Royal Highness the Duke of York
His Royal Highness the Duke of Gloucester
His Royal Highness the Duke of Cumberland

A

The Rev. Mr. [Thomas] Ashcroft, Fellow of St. John's College, Cambridge
Mr. John Anderson, of Cambridge
Mr. [Thomas] Atwood, of Bath
Mr. Aldred, of Wakefield
Mr. Samuel Arnold
Mr. Theodore Aylward, Organist of Oxford Chapel, and St. Lawrence, Guildhall
Mr. James Abington

B

Miss Butler
The Rev. Mr. [Henry] Bates, A.M. Fellow of St. Peter's College, Cambridge
The Rev. Mr. [John] Bostick, of King's College, Cambridge
Mr. [Joah] Bates, A.M. Fellow of King's College, Cambridge
Mr. John Burton
Mr. C[harles] R. Burney
Mr. [Samuel] Brookes
Mr. George Berg, Organist of St. Mary at Hill

C

William Cowper, Esq;
James Craney, Esq;
Mr. William Cock, Tallowchandlers-hall, 2 Books
Mr. [John] Chapman
Mr. [Benjamin] Cooke, Organist of St. Peter's Westminster, and Master of the Boys

D

The Right Hon. Earl Donnegall
Edward Dodwell, Esq;
The Rev. Mr. [William] Davison, A.M. of St. Peter's College, Cambridge
The Rev. Dr. [William] Dechair
Samuel Dyer, Esq;
Mr. Maurice Dreyer
Mr. John Dechamps
Mr. Peter Dechamps

F

The Hon. Mr. Fitzwilliam
James Ford, M.D.

G

[Joseph] Girdler; A.M. of Pembrooke [!] Hall, Cambridge
Mr. [Steady] Grinfield, L.L.B. of Trinity Hall, Cambridge

H

Isaac Heaton, jun. Esq;
The Rev. Mr. [Edward] Howkins, A.M. Fellow of Trinity College, Cambridge
Mr. William Holden, of Birmingham
Mr. Samuel Howard
Mr. [Joseph] Hague
Mr. [Robert] Hudson, Gentleman of his Majesty's Chapel Royal, and of St. Paul's Cathedral
The Rev. Dr. [Thomas] Hurdis, Canon of Windsor

J

Charles Jennens, Esq; 3 Books
John Jacob, Esq;
John Johnstone, Esq;
Mr. Samuel Johnson
Mrs. [John] Johnson, of Cheapside, 12 Books

K

Mr. Kenleside

L

The Rev. Mr. [Henry] Land
Mr. Charles Lindegrene, 3 Books
Mr. Thomas Linley, of Bath
Mr. [Nicholas] Ladd, Gentleman of his Majesty's Chapel Royal, and of St. Peter's Westminster

M

Charles Morris, Esq;
Mr. George Malme
Mess. Millgrove and Brooks, of Bath, 6 Books
The Madrigal Society, at the Queen's Arms, Newgate-street

N

Mr. [James] Newsham, of Dewsbury

O

Mrs. Osgood
Mr[s. Elizabeth] Orpin, of Bath
The Singers at Osset

P

Miss Powys, of Lilford in Northamptonshire
The Rev. Mr. [Robert] Pindar, A.M. Fellow of King's College, Cambrige [!]

Mr. [Samuel] Prime, of St. John's College, Cambridge
Mr. William Plattel
Mr. Francis Pemberton
Mr. John Perkins, Organist of Findon in Northamptonshire

R

Dr. John Randall, Organist of King's College, and Professor of Music in the University of Cambridge
Mr. Francis Roome, of Derby
Mr. Richard Randall, Organist of Dulwich College

S

Miss Sophia Shard
John Smith, Esq; of Sydling, Dorsetshire
The Rev. Mr. [John] Sharp, Fellow of Trinity College, Cambridge
Mess. Sharps, in Mincing-lane
Mr. [Richard] Stevens, of Cambridge
Mr. Thomas Sikes
Mr. John Steigler
Mr. Solinus
Mr. Simpson
Mr. William Salmon
Mr. Sheureux
Mr. Samuel Spragg

T

Miss Tomkinson, of Dorfold
Mess. [Charles and Samuel] Thompson, of St. Paul's Church-yard, 12 Books

W

The Right Hon. Earl of Warwick
Sir Edward Walpole, Bart.
Christopher Whichcote, Esq;
Mr. [Thomas] Wyatt, of Wells
Mr. C[harles] F[rederick] Weideman
Mr. [John] Wynne, of Cambridge, 6 Books

Y

Lady [Sarah] Yonge

Select Bibliography

INCIDENTAL WORKS ARE cited in the text and notes of this volume. Only titles of peculiar interest to students of Handel's *Messiah* appear in the bibliography provided below. Although the list is by no means complete, it should prove suggestive to those who wish to investigate further Handel's rôle in the history of taste. On problems concerning the relation of poetry and music in eighteenth-century England one should consult John W. Draper's *Eighteenth-Century Aesthetics: A Bibliography*, Heidelberg, 1931. An exhaustive general guide to Handelian studies may be found in Kurt Taut's *Verzeichnis des Schrifttums über Georg Friedrich Händel*, Leipzig, 1933.

"An Account of the Life of George-Frederick Handel: with a Description of the Intended Celebrity at Westminster-Abbey and the Pantheon in Commemoration of his Memory," *The European Magazine*, V, 163–166 (March 1784).
Aikin, John, *Essays on Song-Writing*, London, [1772].
Alison, Archibald, *Essays on the Nature and Principles of Taste*, Edinburgh, 1790.
Anson, Elizabeth and Florence, *Mary Hamilton, Afterwards Mrs. John Dickenson, at Court and at Home, from Letters and Diaries, 1756 to 1816*, London, 1925.
Armstrong, Thomas, "The *Messiah* Accompaniments," *Music and Letters*, IX, 18–28 (January 1928).
Ashworth, A. Hargreaves, "Handel's *Messiah*: Sixty Yorkshire Performances Reviewed," *Musical Opinion*, LXIII, 437–438 (July 1940); 479–480 (August 1940); 522–523 (September 1940).
———"*Messiah* According to Handel," *Musical Opinion*, LXVI, 43–44 (November 1942).
Avison, Charles, *An Essay on Musical Expression*, London, 1752.
———*A Reply to the Author of Remarks on the Essay on Musical Expression*, London, 1753.
Bache, Alfred, "A Heretical Criticism on Handel's *Messiah*," *Organist and Choirmaster*, XIV, 242–243 (15 February 1907).

Bairstow, Edward C., *Handel's Oratorio "The Messiah,"* London, 1928.
Baker, John, *Diary,* edited by Philip C. Yorke, London, 1931.
Balfour, Arthur James, "The Works of Handel," *The Edinburgh Review,* CLXV, 214–247 (January 1887).
Bayly, Anselm, *The Alliance of Musick, Poetry, and Oratory,* London, 1789.
———— *A Practical Treatise on Singing and Playing,* London, 1771.
Beattie, James, *Essays on Poetry and Music, as They Affect the Mind,* Edinburgh, 1776.
Bedford, Arthur, *The Great Abuse of Musick,* London, 1711.
Benson, John Allanson, *Handel's Messiah: The Oratorio & Its History,* London, [1923].
Bernhardt, Reinhold, "Die 'kalte arie' in Mozarts Messiasbearbeitung," *Die Musik,* XXII, 435–440 (March 1930).
———— "W. A. Mozarts Messias-bearbeitung und ihre Drucklegung in Leipzig 1802–03," *Zeitschrift für Musikwissenschaft,* XII, 21–45 (October 1929).
Bitter, Karl Hermann, *Ueber Gervinus' Händel und Shakespeare,* Berlin, 1869.
Boughton, Rutland, "*Messiah* or Multiplication Table?" *The Musical Standard,* XXXVI, 401–402 (23 December 1911).
Bramston, James, *The Man of Taste,* London, 1733.
Bray, Ann Eliza, *Handel: His Life, Personal and Professional,* London, 1857.
Bredenförder, Elizabeth, *Die Texte der Händel-Oratorien,* Leipzig, 1934.
Brenet, Michel, *Haendel: Biographie Critique,* Paris, 1912.
———— "Le Vrai *Messie* de Haendel," *Le Guide Musical,* LVI, 363–366 (8 May 1910).
Brown, John ("Estimate"), *A Dissertation on the Rise, Union, and Power, the Progressions, Separations, and Corruptions, of Poetry and Music,* London, 1763.
Brownlow, John, *Memoranda; or, Chronicles of the Foundling Hospital,* London, 1847.
Bumpus, John S., *A History of English Cathedral Music, 1549–1889,* 2 vols., London, [1908].
Burgh, Allatson, *Anecdotes of Music, Historical and Biographical,* 3 vols., London, 1814.
Burney, Charles, *An Account of the Musical Performances in Westminster-Abbey, and the Pantheon, May 26th, 27th, 29th;*

and June the 3d, and 5th, 1784, in Commemoration of Handel, London, 1785.

——————— *A General History of Music from the Earliest Ages to the Present Period*, 4 vols., London, 1776–1789.

Burney, Frances (Madame D'Arblay), *Diary & Letters (1778–1840)*, edited by Charlotte Barrett, with preface and notes by Austin Dobson, 6 vols., London, 1905.

——————— *Early Diary (1768–1778)*, edited by Annie Raine Ellis, 2 vols., London, 1889.

——————— *Memoirs of Doctor Burney*, 3 vols., London, 1832.

Busby, Thomas, *A Complete Dictionary of Music*, London, 1786.

——————— *Concert Room and Orchestra Anecdotes of Music and Musicians*, 3 vols., London, 1825.

Butler, Samuel, *Works* (Shrewsbury Edition), edited by Henry Festing Jones and A. T. Bartholomew, 20 vols., New York, 1926.

Carter, J., "Thoughts on the Musick of Handel, and on the Mode of Performing it at the Present Day; Conceived on Hearing the Sacred Oratorio of the *Messiah* at Drury Lane Theatre," *The Gentlemen's Magazine*, LXXXIII, 220–222 (March 1813).

Cartwright, James J., *The Wentworth Papers, 1705–1739*, London, 1883.

Cheney, Elizabeth, *Aunt Deborah Hears "The Messiah"*, New York and Cincinnati, 1900.

Chorley, Henry F., "The Messiah," in *Handel Studies*, London, 1859, pp. 3–47.

——————— *Thirty Years' Musical Recollections*, edited by Ernest Newman, New York, 1926.

Chrysander, Friedrich, *G. F. Händel*, 3 vols., Leipzig, 1858–1867.

Clarke, Eliza, *Handel*, London, 1885.

Colles, H. C., *Voice and Verse: A Study in English Song*, London, 1928.

Cooke, Benjamin, *An Ode on Handel Performed at the Commemoration Dinner May 26th 1785*, [London, 1785].

Cowper, William, *Correspondence*, 4 vols., edited by Thomas Wright, New York, 1904.

——————— *Poems*, edited by J. C. Bailey, London, 1905.

——————— *Unpublished and Uncollected Poems*, edited by Thomas Wright, London, 1900.

Coxe, William, *Anecdotes of George Frederick Handel and John Christopher Smith*, London, 1799.

Cradock, James, *Literary and Miscellaneous Memoirs*, 4 vols., London, 1828.
Crosse, John, *An Account of the Grand Musical Festival, Held in September, 1823, in the Cathedral Church of York*, York, 1825.
Crotch, William, *Substance of Several Courses of Lectures on Music*, London, 1831.
Crowdy, John, *A Short Commentary for the Use of Audiences on Handel's Oratorio "The Messiah"*, London, [1875].
Crowest, Frederick J., *A Book of Musical Anecdote*, 2 vols., London, 1878.
——— "Handel and English Music," in Traill, H. D., and Mann, J. S. (editors), *Social England*, New York, 1909, V, 118–130.
——— "Handel: Man and Musician," *Blackwood's Magazine*, CLV, 825–846 (June 1894).
——— *Musicians' Wit, Humor, and Anecdote*, London, 1902.
——— *The Great Tone-Poets*, London, 1878.
Culwick, James C., *Handel's Messiah: Discovery of the Original Word-Book Used at the First Performance in Dublin, April 13, 1742*, Dublin, 1891.
Cummings, William H., *Handel*, London, 1904.
——— "Handel's *Messiah*," *The Musical Times*, XXVI, 705–706 (December 1885).
——— "Handel's *Messiah*," *The Musical Times*, XLIV, 16–18 (January 1903).
——— "The Mutilation of a Masterpiece," *Proceedings of the Musical Association*, Thirtieth Session, London, 1904, pp. 113–127.
"Curious Arrangements of the Hallelujah Chorus," *The Musical Times*, XLII, 458–459 (July 1901).
Cusins, William G., *Handel's Messiah: An Examination of the Original and of Some Contemporary MSS*, London, 1874.
Davey, Henry, *History of English Music*, London, 1895.
David, Ernest, *G. -F. Händel, Sa Vie, Ses Travaux, et Son Temps*, Paris, 1884.
Delany, Mary Granville, *Autobiography and Correspondence*, 6 vols., edited by Lady Llanover, London, 1861–1862.
Dent, Edward J., "English Influences on Handel," *Monthly Musical Record*, LXI, 225–228 (August 1931).
——— *Foundations of English Opera*, Cambridge, 1928.
——— *Handel*, London, 1934.

Dent, Edward J., *Handel in England,* Halle, 1936.
Dickins, Lilian, and Stanton, Mary (editors), *An Eighteenth-Century Correspondence,* London, 1910.
Dickinson, A. E. F., "The Revival of Handel's *Messiah,*" *The Musical Times,* LXXVI, 217–218 (March 1935).
Dix, Morgan, *A History of the Parish of Trinity Church in the City of New York,* 4 vols., New York, 1898–1906.
"Dublin Handeliana and a Hospital: A Holiday Note," *The Musical Times,* XLIV, 661–662 (October 1903).
Du Bos, Abbé Jean Baptiste, *Critical Reflections on Poetry, Painting, and Music,* 2 vols., translated by Thomas Nugent, London, 1748.
Dwight, John S., "George Frederick Handel," *The Atlantic Monthly,* LV, 495–507 (April 1885).
———— "Handel and His *Messiah,*" *Dwight's Journal of Music,* II, 89–93 (25 December 1852); 97–98 (1 January 1853).
East, John, *Christmas Eve: A Dream; or, A Review of the Oratorio of "The Messiah,"* London, 1836.
Eastcott, Richard, *Sketches of the Origin, Progress, and Effects of Music, with an Account of the Ancient Bards and Minstrels,* Bath, 1793.
Edwards, F. G., "Handel's *Messiah*: Some Notes on its History and First Performance," *The Musical Times,* XLIII, 713–718 (November 1902).
———— "The Foundling Hospital and its Music," *The Musical Times,* XLIII, 304–311 (May 1902); 377–379 (June 1902).
Escombe, Neville, "*The Messiah*: A Protest and a Plea," *The Musical Times,* LXXX, 177–178 (March 1939).
An Examination of the Oratorios which have been Performed this Season at Covent-Garden Theatre, London, 1763.
FitzGerald, Edward, *Letters & Literary Remains,* edited by William Aldis Wright, 7 vols., London, 1902.
Flower, Newman, *George Frideric Handel: His Personality and His Times,* London, 1923.
Forbes, William, *An Account of the Life and Writings of James Beattie, LL.D.,* 2 vols., London, 1824.
Gardner, Hugh, "The Pre-Mozartian *Messiah,*" *The Musical Times,* LXXVI, 597–601 (July 1935).
Gerson, Robert A., *Music in Philadelphia,* Philadelphia, 1940.
Gervinus, G. G., *Händel und Shakespeare,* Leipzig, 1868.

Ginder, C. Richard, "The Wonderful Saxon," *The Catholic World*, CXLII, 316–323 (December 1935).
Goethe, Wolfgang von, *Sämtliche Werke*, 45 vols., Berlin, 1909.
—————— *Goethes Tagebücher (1776–1782)*, edited by Heinrich Dünker, Leipzig, 1889.
Goldsmith, Oliver, "On the Different Schools of Music," *The British Magazine*, I, 74–76 (February 1760); 181–184 (April 1760).
Graham, George Farquhar, *An Account of the First Edinburgh Musical Festival, Held between the 30th of October and 5th of November, 1815*, Edinburgh, 1816.
Greville, Charles, *The Greville Memoirs*, edited by Lytton Strachey and Roger Fulford, 8 vols., London, 1938.
Grinfield, Thomas, *Critical and Poetical Rehearsals of Handel's Oratorio The Messiah*, edited by Charles Theodore Grinfield, London, 1893.
—————— *Poetic Rehearsal of Handel's Sacred Oratorio "The Messiah*," London, 1856.
Günther, Hans, *Johann Gottfried Herders Stellung zur Musik*, Leipzig, 1903.
Hadden, J. Cuthbert, "Charles Jennens and *The Messiah*," *Musical Opinion*, XXXIII, 763–764 (August 1910).
—————— *George Frederick Handel*, London, 1888.
—————— "Handel and the Handel Fetish," *Music*, XVIII, 361–367 (August 1900).
—————— "Handel, the Man," *The Argosy*, LXXI, 141–149 (June 1900).
Hadland, F. A., "The Handel Festival—A Retrospect," *The Monthly Musical Record*, L, 148–150 (July 1920).
Hadow, W. H., "Music," in Turberville, A. S. (editor), *Johnson's England*, Oxford, 1933, II, 190–208.
Hampden, John, *An Eighteenth-Century Journal*, London, 1940.
Hanbury, William, *The History of the Rise and Progress of the Charitable Foundations at Church-Langton*, London, 1767.
Handel, George Frideric, *Letters and Writings*, edited by Erich H. Müller, London, 1935.
—————— *Messiah* [Facsimile of the autograph score, executed in photolithography for the Sacred Harmonic Society], London, 1868.
—————— *Messiah* [Facsimile of the autograph score, executed in photolithography for Die Deutsche Händel-Gesellschaft], 3 vols., edited by Friedrich Chrysander, Hamburg, 1889–1892.

SELECT BIBLIOGRAPHY

Handel, George Frideric, *Messiah* [Original full-score edition], London, [1767].

——— *Messiah*, edited in full score by Samuel Arnold, London, [1789]. (In *The Works of G. F. Handel*, 180 Numbers, edited by Samuel Arnold, London, [1785–1797]).

——— *Messiah* [Full-score edition, incorporating "additional accompaniments" by W. A. Mozart and further "alterations" by Johann Adam Hiller], Leipzig, 1803.

——— *Messiah*, edited in full score by Edward F. Rimbault, London, 1850. (Vol. IX in *The Works of Handel*, 13 vols. in 15, edited for the Handel Society by various hands, London, [1844–1858]).

——— *Messiah*, edited in full score by Robert Franz, Leipzig, 1885.

——— *Messiah*, edited in full score by Friedrich Chrysander, Leipzig, 1902. (Vol. XLV in *Georg Friedrich Händels Werke*, 96 vols. in 70, edited for Die Deutsche Händel-Gesellschaft by Friedrich Chrysander, Leipzig, [1858–1903]).

——— *Messiah*, edited in full score by Ebenezer Prout, London, 1902.

——— *Messiah*, edited in vocal score by Jacob Maurice Coopersmith, New York, 1947.

Harris, James, *Three Treatises*, London, 1744.

Hastings, George Everett, *The Life and Works of Francis Hopkinson*, Chicago, 1926.

Hastings, Thomas, *Dissertation on Musical Taste*, New York, 1853.

Haweis, H. R., "Handel," *The Contemporary Review*, X, 503–529 (April 1869); XI, 60–78 (May 1869).

——— *Music and Morals*, London, 1871.

Hawkins, John, *A General History of the Science and Practice of Music*, 5 vols., London, 1776.

Hayes, William, *Anecdotes of the Five Music-Meetings at Church Langton*, Oxford, 1768.

——— *The Art of Composing Music by a Method Entirely New, Suited to the Meanest Capacity*, London, 1751.

——— *Remarks on Mr. Avison's Essay on Musical Expression*, London, 1753.

Hearne, Thomas, *Reliquiae Hearnianae: The Remains of Thomas Hearne*, edited by Philip Bliss, Oxford, 1867.

Herder, Johann Gottfried, *Sammtliche Werke*, 33 vols., edited by Bernhard Suphan, Berlin, 1913.

Hervey, D. E., "Handel in the Nineteenth Century," *Music*, V. 653–664 (April 1894).

Heywood, Eliza, *Epistles for the Ladies*, 2 vols., London, 1749.

Higginson, J. Vincent, "Handel's Messiah," *The Catholic Choirmaster*, XXVIII, 158–161, 167 (20 December 1942).

Hiller, Johann Adam, *Nachricht von der Aufführung des Händelschen Messias, in der Domkirche zu Berlin, den 19 Mai 1786*, Berlin, [1786].

Hitzlg, Wilhelm, *Georg Friedrich Händel, 1685–1759; Sein Leben in Bildern*, Leipzig, [1935].

Hogarth, George, *The Birmingham Festival of 1852*, Birmingham, 1852.

——————— *Musical History, Biography, and Criticism*, London, 1835.

Holden, John, *An Essay Toward a Rational System of Music*, Glasgow, 1770.

Holt, Edward, *The Public and Domestic Life of George the Third*, 2 vols., London, 1820.

Hoyle, John, *A Complete Dictionary of Music*, London, 1791.

Hueffer, Francis, and Tovey, Duncan F., "Handel," in *Encyclopædia Britannica*.

Hughes, Helen Sard, *The Gentle Hertford: Her Life and Letters*, New York, 1940.

Hughes, John, *Poems on Several Occasions*, 2 vols., edited by William Duncombe, London, 1735.

Hughes, William, *The Efficacy and Importance of Musick*, London, [1749].

——————— *Remarks upon Church Musick; to which are added Several Observations upon Some of Mr. Handel's Oratorio's, and Other Parts of His Works*, Worcester, [1758].

Hurdis, James, *The Village Curate*, London, 1788.

Jackson, Robert Wyse, *Jonathan Swift, Dean and Pastor*, London, 1939.

Jackson, William, *The Four Ages; Together with Essays on Various Subjects*, London, 1798.

——————— "Remarks on the Peculiar Excellencies in Handel's Music," *The Universal Magazine*, CI, 170–172 (September 1797).

——————— *Thirty Letters on Various Subjects*, 2 vols., London, 1783.

Jacob, Hildebrand, *Of the Sister Arts*, London, 1734.

Jahn, Otto, *Life of Mozart*, 3 vols., translated by Pauline O. Townsend, London, 1891.

Jebb, John, *Three Lectures on the Cathedral Service of the Church of England*, London, 1843.

Johnson, H. Earle, *Musical Interludes in Boston, 1795–1830*, New York, 1943.

Johnstone, J. Alfred, "Dr. Coward's Sheffield Choir and Handel's *Messiah*," *The Musical Standard*, XXXVI, 145 (2 September 1911).

Jones, Edward, *A Poem to the Memory of Handel*, London, 1787.

Jones, Henry Festing, *Samuel Butler, Author of Erewhon*, 2 vols., London, 1919.

Jones, William, *A Treatise on the Art of Music*, Colchester, 1784.

——— *Physiological Disquisitions; or, Discourses on the Natural Philosophy of the Elements*, London, 1781.

Kelly, John Alexander, *German Visitors to English Theaters in the Eighteenth Century*, Princeton, 1936.

Kelly, Michael, *Reminiscences*, 2 vols., London, 1826.

Kidson, Frank, "Handel's Publisher, John Walsh, His Successors and Contemporaries," *The Musical Quarterly*, VI, 430–450 (July 1920).

Kirkman, James Thomas, *Memoirs of the Life of Charles Macklin, Esq.*, 2 vols., London, 1799.

Knox, Vicesimus, *Essays Moral and Literary*, 2 vols., London, 1778.

Kollmann, Augustus Frederic Christopher, *An Essay on Musical Harmony*, London, 1796.

——— *An Essay on Practical Musical Composition*, London, 1799.

Lang, Paul Henry, *Music in Western Civilization*, New York, 1941.

Langhorne, John, *The Tears of Music; A Poem to the Memory of Mr. Handel*, London, 1760.

Lawrence, W. J., "Eighteenth-Century Magazine Music," *The Musical Antiquary*, III, 18–39 (October 1911).

——— "Handeliana: Some Memorials of the Dublin Charitable Musical Society," *The Musical Antiquary*, III, 107–109 (January 1912).

Lecky, W. E. H., *A History of England in the Eighteenth Century*, 2 vols., London, 1878–1890.

Lefanu, Alicia, *Memoirs of the Life and Writings of Mrs. Frances Sheridan*, London, 1824.

Leichtentritt, Hugo, *Handel*, Stuttgart and Berlin, 1924.

——————— "Handel's Harmonic Art," *The Musical Quarterly*, XXI, 208–219 (April 1935).

"Letter to a Friend, on going to hear the MESSIAH at the Playhouse," *The Gospel Magazine; or, Treasury of Divine Knowledge*, II, 67–72 (February 1775).

Lockman, John, *Rosalinda, A Musical Drama: To which is Prefixed an Enquiry into the Rise and Progress of Operas and Oratorios*, London, 1740.

——————— "To the Manes of Mr. Handel," *The London Magazine*, XXVIII, 447 (August 1759).

Lunn, Henry C., "The Handel Festival," *The Musical Times*, XIII, 442–443 (July 1868).

Luxborough, Lady, *Letters Written by the Late Right Honourable Lady Luxborough to William Shenstone, Esq.*, London, 1775.

Lysons, Daniel, *History of the Origin and Progress of the Meeting of the Three Choirs of Gloucester, Worcester, and Hereford, and of the Charity Connected with It*, Gloucester, 1812. [Subsequently revised and enlarged by John Amott (1864), Charles Lee Williams (1894), Harry Godwin Chance (1922), and Theodore Hannam-Clark (1931)].

Macfarren, George A., "Handel and His *Messiah*," *The American Whig Review*, IX, 135–147 (February 1849).

——————— *Messiah: An Analysis of the Oratorio*, London, 1857 [Wordbook, preface, and analysis published for the Handel Festival of 15 June 1857].

Mainwaring, John, *Memoirs of the Life of the Late George Frederic Handel*, London, 1760.

Maitland, J. A. Fuller, *The Age of Bach and Handel*, Oxford, 1902 [Vol. IV in *The Oxford History of Music*].

——————— and Squire, William Barclay, "Handel," in *Dictionary of National Biography*.

Malcolm, Alexander, *A Treatise of Musick, Speculative, Practical and Historical*, Edinburgh, 1721.

Malcolm, James Peller, *Anecdotes of the Manners and Customs of London during the Eighteenth Century*, 2 vols., London, 1808.

Malmesbury, Earl of (editor), *A Series of Letters of the First Earl of Malmesbury, His Family and Friends, from 1745 to 1820*, 2 vols., London, 1870.

Mann, A. H., "An Account of the Handel MSS. in the Fitzwilliam Museum at Cambridge," *The Musical Times* (Special Handel Supplement), XXXIV, 16–19 (14 December 1893).
———————"Handel's *Messiah*," *The Musical Times*, XLIV, 28 (January 1903).
———————[Handel's *Messiah* at Cambridge: Reproduction of Eighteenth-Century Performances,] *The Musical Times*, XLVII, 608–609 (September 1906).
The Manners of the Age: In Thirteen Moral Satirs [!], London, 1733.
Mansfield, Orlando A., "The Minuet in Handel's *Messiah*," *The Musical Quarterly*, V, 90–99 (January 1919).
Marshall, Mrs. Julian, *Handel*, London, 1883.
Mason, John, *An Essay on the Power of Numbers and the Principles of Harmony in Poetical Composition*, London, 1749.
Mason, Lowell, *Musical Letters from Abroad*, New York, 1854.
Mason, William, *Essays, Historical and Critical, on English Church Music*, York, 1795.
Maurice, Thomas, "Ode Sacred to the Genius of Handel," *The European Magazine*, V, May 1784 (Supplement).
McCrillis, Herbert O., "Handel and *The Messiah*," *The New England Magazine*, New Series, XXXIV, 169–178 (April 1906).
Melody, the Soul of Music: An Essay towards the Improvement of the Musical Art, Glasgow, 1798.
Merlin, Countess de, *Memoirs of Madame Malibran*, 2 vols., London, 1844.
Messiter, Arthur Henry, *A History of the Choir and Music of Trinity Church, New York*, New York, 1906.
Miller, James, *Harlequin-Horace; or, The Art of Modern Poetry*, London, 1731.
Mount-Edgcumbe, Richard, *Musical Reminiscences of an Old Amateur*, London, 1827.
"Mr. Charles Jennens: The Compiler of Handel's *Messiah*," *The Musical Times*, XLIII, 726–727 (November 1902).
Müller-Blattau, Joseph, "Händel und Goethe," in *Händel-Jahrbuch*, edited by Rudolf Steglich, Leipzig, 1932, pp. 25–37.
Myers, Robert Manson, *Anna Seward: An Eighteenth-Century Handelian*, Williamsburg, 1947.
———————*Early Moral Criticism of Handelian Oratorio*, Williamsburg, 1947.
———————"Fifty Sermons on Handel's *Messiah*," *The Harvard Theological Review*, XXXIX, 217–241 (October 1946).

Myers, Robert Manson, "Mrs. Delany: An Eighteenth-Century Handelian," *The Musical Quarterly*, XXXII, 12–36 (January 1946).

———— "Neo-Classical Criticism of the Ode for Music," *Publications of the Modern Language Association*, LXII, 399–421 (June 1947).

———— "Samuel Butler: Handelian," *The Musical Quarterly*, XXXIV (April 1948).

Nettel, Reginald, *Music in the Five Towns, 1840–1914*, Oxford, 1944.

Newton, John, *Messiah: Fifty Expository Discourses, on the Series of Scriptural Passages, which form the Subject of the Celebrated Oratorio of Handel*, 2 vols., London, 1786.

Nichols, John, *Literary Anecdotes of the Eighteenth Century*, 9 vols., London, 1812–1816.

An Ode to Mr. Handel, London, 1745.

Odell, George C. D., *Annals of the New York Stage*, New York, 1927—

"On the Works of Handel," *The Quarterly Musical Magazine and Review*, I, 280–284 (1818).

Overton, John H., and Relton, Frederic, *The English Church from the Accession of George I to the End of the Eighteenth Century, 1714–1800*, London, 1906.

The Oxford Act, London, 1735.

The Oxford Act: A New Ballad-Opera, London, 1733.

Papendiek, Charlotte Louise Henrietta, *Court and Private Life in the Time of Queen Charlotte: Being the Journals of Mrs. Papendiek*, 2 vols., edited by Mrs. Vernon Delves Broughton, London, 1887.

Parke, William Thomas, *Musical Memoirs*, 2 vols., London, 1830.

Parry, John, *An Account of the Royal Musical Festival, Held in Westminster Abbey, 1834*, London, 1834.

Pearce, C. W., "The ΣΥΜΜΕΤΡΙΑ of Handel's *Messiah*," *Musical Opinion*, XLIX, 929–931 (June 1926).

Pennington, Montagu (editor), *A Series of Letters between Mrs. Elizabeth Carter and Miss Catherine Talbot, from the Year 1741 to 1770*, 4 vols., London, 1809.

Perkins, Charles C., and Dwight, John S., *History of the Handel and Haydn Society*, Boston, 1883–1893.

Piozzi, Hester Lynch, *Anecdotes of the Late Samuel Johnson, LL.D.*, London, 1786.

Pohl, C. F., *Mozart und Haydn in London*, Vienna, 1867.

Polymnia; or, The Charms of Musick, by a Gentleman of Cambridge, London, 1733.

Potter, John, *Observations on the Present State of Music and Musicians,* London, 1762.

Pougin, Arthur, *À propos de l'exécution du Messie de Haendel au Cirque des Champs-Élysées, le 19 décembre 1873,* Paris, 1873.

Prod'homme, J. -G., "Haendel, Bach et leurs Œuvres en France," *Mercure de France,* CCLVIII, 260–277 (1 March 1935).

The Progress of Music: Occasioned by the Grand Celebration at the Abbey, London, 1788.

Prout, Ebenezer, "The German Handel Society's Edition of the *Messiah,*" *The Monthly Musical Record,* XXXII, 201–203 (November 1902).

——— "Handel's *Messiah*: Preface to the New Edition," *The Musical Times,* XLIII, 311–313 (May 1902); 380–383 (June 1902); 460–463 (July 1902); 528–531 (August 1902); 592–594 (September 1902); 655–659 (October 1902).

——— "Handel's Orchestration," *The Musical Times,* XXV, 12–13 (January 1884); 69–70 (February 1884); 138–141 (March 1884); 193–196 (April 1884); 256–260 (May 1884); 326–329 (June 1884).

——— "Handel's Wind Parts to the *Messiah,*" *The Monthly Musical Record,* XXIV, 73–76 (April 1894).

Ramsay, Dean Edward B., *Two Lectures on the Genius of Handel and the Distinctive Character of His Sacred Compositions,* Edinburgh, 1862.

Raugel, Félix, "Note sur l'instrumentation du *Messie* de Haendel," *La Tribune de Saint Gervais,* XVI, 265–269 (December 1910).

——— "Plan de l'oratorio [du *Messie*]," *La Tribune de Saint Gervais,* XVIII, 300–303 (December 1912); XIX, 14–17 (January 1913); XIX, 42–45 (February 1913).

Redway, Virginia Larkin, "Handel in Colonial and Post-Colonial America," *The Musical Quarterly,* XXI, 190–207 (April 1935).

Remarks upon the Use and Abuse of Musical Festivals, by an English Churchman, Bristol, 1843.

"Review [of *Messiah*]," *The Quarterly Musical Magazine and Review,* X, 234–246 (1828).

Ring, John, *The Commemoration of Handel: A Poem,* London, 1786.

Robertson, Thomas, *An Inquiry into the Fine Arts,* London, 1784.

Robinson, Percy, *Handel and His Orbit,* London, 1908.
Robinson, Pollingrove, *Handel's Ghost: An Ode on the Power of His Messiah,* London, 1784.
Rochlitz, Friedrich, "Händels Messias," in *Für Freunde der Tonkunst,* 4 vols., Leipzig, 1824–1832, I, 227–280.
Rockstro, William Smith, *The Life of George Frederick Handel,* London, 1883.
Rolland, Romain, *Haendel,* Paris, 1910.
——————— "Haendel et le *Messie,*" *La Tribune de Saint Gervais,* XVIII, 297–299 (December 1912).
——————— "Le *Messie* de Haendel au Trocadéro," *Revue Musicale,* VI, 191–193 (15 May 1910).
Runciman, J. F., "The Handel Festival," *The Saturday Review,* LXXXIX, 775–776 (23 June 1900).
The Sacred Oratorios as Set to Music, London, 1799.
Salter, Sumner, "Appoggiaturas in the Solos of Handel's *Messiah,*" *The New Music Review,* XXX, 5–9 (December 1930); 49–53 (January 1931).
Sargeaunt, John, "Dr. Johnson and Music," in *Johnson Club Papers,* London, 1899, pp. 171–189.
Schering, Arnold, *Geschichte des Oratoriums,* Leipzig, 1911.
Schoelcher, Victor, *The Life of Handel,* translated by J. Lowe, London, 1857.
Schrader, Bruno, "The Handel Revival in Germany," *The Forum,* XXV, 191–202 (April 1898).
Scott, Cyril, "The Influence of Handel on Victorian Morals," *The Sackbut,* IV, 350–355 (July 1924).
——————— *The Influence of Music on History and Morals,* London, 1928.
See and Seem Blind; or, A Critical Dissertation on the Publick Diversions, London, [1732].
Sense Against Sound; or, A Succedaneum, for Abbey Music, London, [1788].
A Series of Reflections on the Sacred Oratorio of the Messiah, by a Lady, London, 1812.
Seward, Anna, *Letters (1784–1807),* 6 vols., edited by A. Constable, Edinburgh, 1811.
——————— *Poetical Works,* 3 vols., edited by Sir Walter Scott, Edinburgh, 1810.
Shaw, George Bernard, "Haendel et l'Angleterre," *Revue Musicale,* IX, 1–4 (15 April 1913).

Shaw, George Bernard, *London Music in 1888–89 as Heard by Corno di Bassetto (Later Known as Bernard Shaw)*, London, 1937.

────── *Music in London, 1890–94*, 3 vols., London, 1932.

Shedlock, J. S., "Handel's *Messiah* (An Old Vocal Score)," *The Monthly Musical Record*, XXXIX, 221–222 (October 1909).

────── "Mozart and the *Messiah*," *The Monthly Musical Record*, XXV, 266–267 (December 1895).

────── "Mozart, Handel, and Johann Adam Hiller," *The Musical Times*, LIX, 370–371 (August 1918).

Shenstone, William, *Letters*, edited by Marjorie Williams, Oxford, 1939.

Sheridan, Thomas, *British Education; or, The Source of the Disorders of Great Britain*, London, 1756.

Shield, William, *Introduction to Harmony*, London, 1800.

"Singing the *Messiah* in Kansas," *The Literary Digest*, LXXIII, 37–38 (15 April 1922).

Smith, Robert, *Harmonics; or, The Philosophy of Musical Sounds*, Cambridge, 1749.

Smith, William C., "The Earliest Editions of Handel's *Messiah*," *The Musical Times*, LXVI, 985–990 (November 1925).

────── "George III, Handel, and Mainwaring," *The Musical Times*, LXV, 789–795 (September 1924).

────── "Handel's Failure in 1745: New Letters of the Composer," *The Musical Times*, LXXVII, 593–598 (July 1936).

────── "Handel's *Messiah*: Recent Discoveries of Early Editions," *The Musical Times*, LXXXII, 427–428 (December 1941).

Sonneck, O. G., *Early Concert-Life in America (1731–1800)*, Leipzig, 1907.

Spitta, Philipp, *Johann Sebastian Bach*, 3 vols., translated by Clara Bell and J. A. Fuller Maitland, London, 1899.

Squire, William Barclay, "Handel in 1745," *Riemann-Festschrift, Gesammelte Studien*, Leipzig, 1909, pp. 423–433.

Statham, Henry Heathcote, "Handel," *Fortnightly Review*, XXXIII, 53–75 (1 January 1880).

────── *My Thoughts on Music and Musicians*, London, 1892.

Steglich, Rudolf, "Betrachtung des Händelschen *Messias*," in *Händel-Jahrbuch*, edited by Rudolf Steglich, Leipzig, 1931, pp. 15–78.

Stewart, Humphrey J., "The *Messiah* Fallacy," *The American Organist*, II, 100–101 (March 1919).

Stillingfleet, Benjamin, *The Principles and Power of Harmony*, London, 1771.
Streatfeild, R. A., "The Granville Collection of Handel Manuscripts," *The Musical Antiquary*, II, 208–224 (July 1911).
——————— *Handel*, London, 1909.
——————— *Handel Autographs at the British Museum*, London, 1912.
——————— *Modern Music and Musicians*, New York, 1906.
Stukeley, William, *Family Memoirs*, 3 vols., London, 1880–1885.
Taylor, Sedley, *The Indebtedness of Handel to Works of Other Composers*, Cambridge, 1906.
Temple, William Johnston, *Diaries*, edited by Lewis Bettany, Oxford, 1929.
Thayer, Alexander Wheelock, *The Life of Ludwig van Beethoven*, 3 vols., edited by H. E. Krehbiel, New York, 1921.
Townsend, Horatio, *An Account of the Visit of Handel to Dublin*, Dublin, 1852.
Turnbull, Robert, "Handel and His *Messiah*," in *Musical Genius and Religion*, London, 1907, pp. 24–35.
Twining, Thomas, *Aristotle's Treatise on Poetry Translated with Two Dissertations on Poetical and Musical Imitation*, London, 1789.
——————— *Recreations and Studies of a Country Clergyman of the Eighteenth Century*, London, 1882.
Vernier, G., *L'Oratorio Biblique de Haendel*, Cahors, 1901.
Victor, Benjamin, *Original Letters, Dramatic Pieces, and Poems*, 3 vols., London, 1776.
Vincent, William, *Considerations on Parochial Music*, London, 1787.
Walker, Ernest, *A History of Music in England*, Oxford, 1907.
Walpole, Horace, *Letters*, 16 vols., edited by Mrs. Paget Toynbee, Oxford, 1905.
Webb, Daniel, *Observations on the Correspondence between Poetry and Music*, London, 1762.
Webb, William, "Handel," *The Musical World*, IX, 152–154 (27 June 1838).
Weinstock, Herbert, *Handel*, New York, 1946.
Weld, Arthur Cyril Gordon, "Is Haendel's *Messiah* Inspired or Sacred?" *Music*, XI, 469–472 (February 1897).
Wesley, John, *Journal*, 8 vols., edited by Nehemiah Curnoch, London, 1909–1916.

Wesley, John, *Letters,* 8 vols., edited by John Telford, London, 1931.
Westrup, Jack Allan, *Handel,* London, 1938.
────── "Interpretation in *Messiah,*" *Musical Opinion,* LXIII, 247–248 (March 1940); 294–295 (April 1940).
Wilder, Victor, *Le Messie . . . Exécuté au Cirque des Champs-Élysées sous la Direction de Charles Lamoureux, le Jeudi 14 Janvier 1875,* Paris, 1910.
Williams, C. F. Abdy, *Handel: His Life and Works,* London, 1901.
The Woman of Taste: Occasioned by a Late Poem, entitled The Man of Taste, by a Friend of the Author's, London, 1733.
Woodeforde, James, *The Diary of a Country Parson,* edited by John Beresford, 5 vols., Oxford, 1924–1931.
Words of All the Favourite Oratorios Set to Music by Mr. Handel, London, 1790.
Words of Such Pieces as are most usually Performed by the Academy of the Ancient Music, London, [1761].
Wyndham, Henry Saxe, *The Annals of Covent Garden Theatre from 1732 to 1897,* 2 vols., London, 1906.
Zweig, Stefan, "Le Messie de Haendel," *Les Annales Politiques et Littéraires,* CXIII, 12–15 (10 January 1939).

Index

Abington, James, 299
Academy of Ancient Music, 23
Account of the Commemoration, An (Burney), 190–191, 193, 195, 215–216, 271
Account of Corsica, An (Boswell), 197
Acis and Galatea, 34, 45, 53, 85, 93, 103, 166, 173, 182, 184, 224, 257
Adaptations of *Messiah,* 282–286; Mozart's "additional accompaniments," 272–273, 279–282
Addison, Joseph, 2, 4, 6–14, 17–18, 19, 30, 47, 49
Adelaide, Queen, 24
Adgate, Andrew, 254
Admeto, 20
Adrastea (Herder), 274–275
Advice (Smollett), 52
Agnesi, Luigi, 243 (note)
Albani, Emma, 239, 243 (note)
Albert, Prince, xxi
Albert Hall, *Messiah* in, 239–240
Alda, Frances, 264
Aldred, Mr., 299
Alessandro, 20
Alexander's Feast (Dryden), 217
Alexander's Feast (Handel), 34, 53, 84, 85, 93, 119, 173, 180, 182, 184, 288
"All they that see Him," 107 (note), 176
"All we like sheep," 71–73, 176, 247
Allen, Perceval, 287 (note)
Almahide, 12
Alsop, Antony, 58
Alterations in *Messiah,* 77–78, 116
Amelia, Princess, 215
Amelia (Fielding), 147–148
"Amen" Chorus, 117 (note), 160, 178, 262, 264–265
Amott, John, 166 (note)
Anacreontic Society, 91

"And He shall purify," 69–70, 174, 245, 262, 263
"And, lo!" 182
"And the glory of the Lord," 75, 173–174, 251, 262, 273
"And with His stripes," 74, 176, 245
Anderson, John, 299
Andratina, 235
Anecdotes: concerning Handel, 63, 78–80, 89–90, 131, 142, 187; concerning *Messiah,* 89–90, 162–164, 165, 167–168, 169, 170–171, 244, 270, 274
Anglicanism, *Messiah* and, 59, 75–76, 82–83, 228–230, 235–239
Anne, Princess, 23
Arblay, Madame d', *see* FANNY BURNEY
Arbuthnot, John, 49, 94, 113
Argyll, Duke of, 47
aria cantabile, 15
aria d' agilità, 15
aria di bravura, 15
aria di mezzo carattère, 15
aria di portamento, 15
aria parlante, 15
Ariosti, Attilio, *see* ATTILIO
Armstrong, John, 48
Arne, Michael, 269
Arne, Thomas Augustine, 152 (note), 269
Arnold, Samuel, 170–171, 185, 187–188, 251, 274, 299
Arsinoe (Clayton), 9, 11
Art of Composing Music, The (Hayes), 48, 151
Ashcroft, Thomas, 299
Ashley, General Charles, 280
Ashworth, A. Hargreaves, 285–286
Athaliah, 37, 44, 45, 46, 50
Attilio (Ariosti), 16
Atwood, Thomas, 299

321

Auchmuty, Samuel, 250
Augusta, Princess, 190, 192, 193, 197, 220
Aunt Deborah Hears "The Messiah" (Cheney), 248
Australia, *Messiah* in, xix, 265
Austria, *Messiah* in, 265 (note), 272–273
Avison, Charles, 146
Avolio, Signora, 90, 93, 99, 101, 105, 106, 107 (note), 116
Aylward, Theodore, 299

B.B.C. Choir, 287 (note)
Bach, Carl Philipp Emanuel, 269
Bach, Johann Christian, 256
Bach, Johann Sebastian, 36, 37, 38, 74, 75, 85, 225, 234 (note), 235, 275; compared with Handel, 81–84
Bach Choir, 234 (note)
Bach Society, 234 (note)
Bailey, James, 106, 107 (note)
Baillie, Isobel, 287 (note)
Baker, Edmund, 89
Baker, John, 155
Baldwin, Richard, 94
Baltimore (Maryland), *Messiah* in, 252
Bartleman, James, 280
Bates, Henry, 299
Bates, Joah, 188, 190, 193, 299
Bath, 161, 168, 251; *Messiah* in, 161, 162
Beard, John, 114? 116
Beattie, James, 79, 116–117, 226
Beecham, Sir Thomas, 287 (note)
Beethoven, Ludwig van, xx, 70, 85, 150, 225, 235, 273–274
Beggar's Opera, The (Gay), 5, 21–23, 133
"Behold and see," 107 (note), 176
"Behold, a virgin shall conceive," 107 (note)
"Behold, I tell you a mystery," 107 (note)
"Behold the Lamb of God," 122, 175, 259, 262
Belgium, *Messiah* in, 265 (note)
Belletti, Giovanni, 243 (note)
Bennett, Sterndale, 234 (note)
Berg, George, 299
Berlin, *Messiah* in, 270–271, 278

Berlin Singakademie, 278
Berlioz, Hector, 265–266, 278 (note)
Bermingham, William, 58 (note)
Bernard, Mrs., 112
Berner, Friedrich Wilhelm, 283
Bertolli, 26
Besançon, *Messiah* in, 268
Bethany College, 263–264
Bethlehem (Pennsylvania), *Messiah* in, 252
Birch, William Henry, 283
Birmingham Festival, *Messiah* at, 152 (note), 165, 221, 222, 223, 240–241, 282
Black, Andrew, 243 (note)
Blackwood's Magazine, 233
Bland, John, 185
"Blessing and honour," 160, 178
Boccage, Anne Marie du, 149
Boddeley's Bath Journal, 162
Böhme, Johann August, 278
Bolingbroke, Henry St. John, Viscount, 42
Bononcini, Giovanni Battista, 11, 16, 74, 119
Bononcini, Marc Antonio, 11, 13
Book of Musical Anecdote, A (Crowest), 165
Booth, Barton, 29
Borrel, Eugène, 268
Boschi, Giuseppe, 4–5
Bostick, John, 299
Boston, *Messiah* in, xix, 255–260, 262–263; *see also* HANDEL AND HAYDN SOCIETY OF BOSTON
Boston Gazette, The, 256–257, 258
Boswell, James, 66–67, 172, 196, 197
Boyce, William, 166, 251
Boylston Hall (Boston), *Messiah* in, 153 (note), 260
Bramston, James, 27
Bray, Ann Eliza, 238
"Break forth into joy," 107 (note)
Breidenstein, Carl Heinrich, 283
Breitkopf & Härtel, 58 (note), 273, 278
Breslau, Sophia, 264
Breslau, *Messiah* in, 271–272
Breuning, Gerhard von, 274
Briefe das Studium Theologie Betreffend (Herder), 270

INDEX

Bristol, 162, 250; *Messiah* in, 128, 161, 165, 227
British Museum, 65 (note), 105
Broderip, Robert, 161
Brookes, Samuel, 299
Broughton, Thomas, 53
Brown, John ("Estimate"), 60, 172–173
Brown, Lady, 129–130
Brownlow-Street Lying-in Hospital, 143
Brunskill, Muriel, 287 (note)
Budapest, *Messiah* in, 265 (note)
Burnet, Thomas, 27
Burney, Charles, 67, 89–90, 99, 128–129, 143, 145, 150–151, 155, 160, 168, 185, 190, 193, 195, 196–197, 198, 225, 230, 299; *Account of the Commemoration*, 190–191, 193, 195, 215–216, 271
Burney, Edward F., 216
Burney, Fanny (Frances), Madame d'Arblay, 188, 220
Burns, George, 249, 251
Burns, Robert, 226
Burrowes, John Freckleton, 283
Burton, John, 299
Busby, Thomas, 170–171
"But Thou didst not leave," 107 (note), 176, 251
"But who may abide," 107 (note), 174, 181, 182
Butler, Samuel, 86, 229, 232, 234–235, 246–247, 249
Butler, Miss, 299
Butt, Clara, 243 (note)

Caecilian Society (London), 153 (note), 239
Calypso and Telemachus (Hughes), 18
Cambridge University, 49, 185; *Messiah* at, 164–165
Camilla (Bononcini), 10, 11
Carlyle, Jane Welsh, 244
Carnegie Hall (New York), *Messiah* in, xix, 248
Caroline, Princess, 68
Caroline, Queen, 40, 50, 51, 133
Carter, Elizabeth, 145
Carter, J., 281
Castil-Blaze, François, 267

Catholicism, *Messiah* and, 228, 265
Cavendish, William, Duke of Devonshire, 88, 93
"Celebrated Largo, The" *(Serse)*, 236, 288
Chance, Harry Godwin, 166 (note)
Chandos, Duke of, 23, 24
Chandos Anthems, 190
Chanteurs de la Renaissance, Les, 268
Chanteurs de St. Pierre de Besançon, Les, 268
Chapman, John, 300
Charitable Infirmary, 89, 97, 101
Charitable Musical Society, 89, 91, 97, 98, 101, 108–109, 110, 111, 112, 179
Charleston (South Carolina), *Messiah* in, 251
Charlotte, Queen, 65 (note), 185, 190, 191, 193, 194, 195, 197, 217, 299
Cheney, Elizabeth, 248
Chesterfield, Lady, 131
Chesterfield, Philip Dormer Stanhope, Earl of, 14, 131
Chestnut Street Theatre (Philadelphia), 255
Chicago, *Messiah* in, xix, 261
Chicago Musical Union, 261
Choice of Hercules, The (Bach), 75
Chorley, Henry F., 265
Choron, Alexandre, 266–267
Chorus, The (Hogarth), 27, 28
Christ Church (Dublin), 94
Christ Church (Boston), *Messiah* in, 257
Christ Church (Philadelphia), *Messiah* in, 252
Christian Remembrancer, The, 212
Christmas, *Messiah* at, xix–xx, 153 and note, 239–240, 248, 259, 260, 260–261, 269, 287
Christmas Eve: A Dream (East), 247
Christmas Oratorio, The (Bach), 75, 234 (note)
Chrysander, Friedrich, 66 (note), 244–245, 278, 284
Church Music (Pitt), 282–283
Church-Langton, *Messiah* in, 162–164, 227–228
Cibber, Colley, 29, 41
Cibber, Susannah Maria Arne, 89, 90, 99–100, 101, 105, 106, 107 (note), 114, 116

324 INDEX

Cirque des Champs-Élysées, *Messiah* in, 267
City Gazette, The (Charleston), 251
Clayton, Thomas, 9, 11
Clive, Catherine (Kitty), 114, 116, 182
Cobham, Lady, 131
Cobham, Lord, 21–22
Cock, William, 300
Collins, William, 167
Columbia Recording Corporation, 287 (note)
Columbian Centinel, The, 258, 259
"Come unto Him," 75, 106, 107 (note), 175
"Comfort ye," 66, 75, 107 (note), 173, 251, 254, 256, 257, 260, 263
Commemoration of Handel, The (Ring), 217
Common Sense, 41
Composition of *Messiah*, xix, 63–78
concerti grossi (Handel), 288
Confessions (Rousseau), 80
Congreve, William, 52, 53, 121
Conscious Lovers, The (Steele), 90
Continuation of the Complete History of England (Smollett), 158
Cooke, Benjamin, 185, 217, 300
Coopersmith, Jacob Maurice, 286–287
Copenhagen, *Messiah* in, 271 (note)
Coram, Thomas, 135, 136
Corelli, Arcangelo, 111
"Corno di Bassetto," see GEORGE BERNARD SHAW
Coronation Anthems, 85, 190
Costa, Sir Michael, 242, 283
Covent Garden Theatre, 33, 114–115, 131, 173; *Messiah* in, 115–118, 119, 122, 124–125, 127, 144, 147–157, 170–171, 272, 280–281
Cowen, Sir Frederic, 242
Cowper, William, 185, 199–200, 206–211, 300
Coxe, William, 150, 168
Cradock, James, 117 (note)
Craftsman, The, 22, 42–43
Craney, James, 300
Creation, The (Haydn), 221, 240, 251, 277; compared with *Messiah*, 223–224, 259–260
Critic, The (Sheridan), 48

Critical observations upon *Messiah*, xxi, 76, 86, 100, 114, 146–147, 160, 172–179, 199–214, 215–216, 223–224, 239–240, 244–245
Critical and Poetical Rehearsals of Handel's Oratorio The Messiah (Grinfield), 247–248
Crow-Street Music Hall, 91
Crowest, Frederick J., 165, 233, 238
Crystal Palace (London), *Messiah* in, xxi, 234, 241–246, 284
Culwick, James C., 105 and note
Cummings, William H., 243 (note), 284, 285
Cusins, W. G., 78 (note)
Cuzzoni, Francesca, 16, 155

Daily Advertiser, The (London), 114, 124–125, 138, 156–157, 180
Daily Advertiser, The (New York), 252
Daily Journal, The, 24, 26, 40
Damrosch, Leopold, 261
Dartmouth College, 260
David, 27, 158
David, Ernest, 265
David and Bathsheba (Porpora), 120
Davies, Ben, 243 (note)
Davison, William, 300
"Dead March" *(Saul)*, 288
Deborah, 37, 40–44, 46, 47, 50, 111
Deborah; or, A Wife for You All (Fielding), 43–44
Dechair, William, 300
Dechamps, John, 300
Dechamps, Peter, 300
Deidamia, 20, 67, 118 (note), 180
Delany, Mary Granville Pendarves, 21, 22, 26, 41, 51, 111–112, 118 (note), 120, 131, 139, 141, 157, 197, 214–215, 216, 227
Delany, Patrick, 100, 120
Denmark, *Messiah* in, 271 (note)
Dennis, John, 12, 19
Dettingen Te Deum, 119, 190
Deutsche Händel-Gesellschaft, Die, 278, 284
Dewes, Ann Granville, 127–128, 227
Dewes, Court, 214–215
Dews, Elizabeth, 287 (note)

Dissertation on the Rise, Union, and Power of Poetry and Music, A (Brown), 172–173
Dod, B., 154
Dodwell, Edward, 300
Dolby, Charlotte, 243 (note)
Domkirche (Berlin), *Messiah* in, 270–271
Donne, W. B., 244
Donnegall, Earl of, 300
"Dove sei amato bene" *(Rodelinda)*, 236
Dowden, Edward, 103–104
Drake, Thomas, 58 (note)
Dreyer, Maurice, 300
Drury Lane Theatre, 5, 9; *Messiah* in, 170
Dryden, John, 52, 53, 217, 224; *see also* ALEXANDER'S FEAST; AN ODE FOR ST. CECILIA'S DAY
Dublin, 26; in mid-eighteenth century, 90–92, 110–113; *Messiah* in, 84, 88–89, 95–113, 114, 226, 227
Dublin, University of, 284
Dublin News-Letter, The, 97, 103
Dubourg, Matthew, 88–89, 91, 93, 99, 101, 108, 110, 115, 116
duetti di camera (Handel), 68–73
Dunciad, The (Pope), 47, 85, 88, 113, 131, 151
Dyer, Samuel, 300

East, John, 247
Easter, *Messiah* at, 261, 263–265, 269; *see also* LENT
Ebeling, Christoph Daniel, 278
Eberwein, Traugott Maxmilian, 276
Edinburgh, *Messiah* in, 221 (note)
Edinburgh Review, The, 237
Editions of *Messiah:* facsimile, 65–66 (note); Randall & Abell, 77, 183–185, 187, 272; subscribers to, 183–185, 299–302; Samuel Arnold, 187–188, 274; Mozart-Hiller, 272–273, 279–282; English Handel Society (Rimbault), 234; Robert Franz, 284; Die Deutsche Händel-Gesellschaft (Chrysander), 278, 284; Ebenezer Prout, 284–285; Jacob Maurice Coopersmith, 286–287
Edward, Prince, 190, 192, 193, 197

Efficacy and Importance of Musick, The (Hughes), xxi–xxii, 40
Egmont, Earl of, 23
Eisdell, Hubert, 287 (note)
Elijah, 157
Elijah (Mendelssohn), 240
Eliot, George, 247
Elizabeth, Princess, 190, 192, 193, 197
Emerson, Ralph Waldo, 262
England, *Messiah* in, xix–xxi, 113–248, 265, 279–285; during eighteenth century, 113–231, 237; during nineteenth century, xxi, 74, 86–87, 116, 117 (note), 143, 152, 166 (note), 211–214, 225–231, 232–248, 261, 278 (note), 279–285; reaction against *Messiah,* 244–246; *Messiah* in Victorian literature, 246–248; during twentieth century, xix, xxi, 285–289; *see also* names of individual cities and towns
English Handel Society, 234
English Review, The, 217
Epistles for the Ladies (Heywood), 125–126
Erba, 74
Erewhon (Butler), 234–235
Eschenburg, J. J., 271
Essay on the Genius and Writings of Pope (Warton), 52
Essay on Musical Expression, An (Avison), 146
Essay on the Operas, An (Dennis), 19
Esther, 23–29, 31, 32, 33, 36, 40, 44, 45, 46, 50, 93, 111, 147, 251
Etearco (Bononcini), 13
European Magazine, The, 189, 191–192, 193, 194, 198, 218, 231
"Every valley," 107 (note), 173, 251, 256, 260, 283
Examination of the Oratorios, An, 33–34, 173–179
Exeter, *Messiah* in, 128
Exeter Hall (London), *Messiah* in, 153 (note), 239, 242, 244

Fairies, The (Smith), 145–146
Faneuil Hall (Boston), *Messiah* in, 255
Farinelli, 16
Faulkner, George, 104, 114

Faulkner's Journal, 91 (note), 92, 95, 96–97, 98, 99, 100–102, 103, 106, 108–110, 226–227
Faust (Goethe), 276
Faustina, 16, 28
Federal Gazette, The, 254–255
Fétis, François, 266
Fielding, Henry, 43–44, 130, 147–148
First performance of *Messiah:* in Dublin, xx, 84, 95–107; in London, 114–118
FitzGerald, Edward, 53, 85–86, 244
Fitzwilliam, Viscount, 188, 300
Flagg, Josiah, 255
Floridante, 20
Flower, Sir Newman, 56 (note)
Foli, Allen, 243 (note)
Foote, Samuel, *The Minor,* 122
"For behold, darkness," 107 (note), 174
"For unto us a Child is born," 70–71, 75, 132, 160, 174–175, 213, 262, 283
Forbes, Sir William, 117 (note)
Ford, James, 300
Formes, Carl, 243 (note)
Foundling Anthem, 136, 143, 190
Foundling Hospital (London), 135–144; *Messiah* in, 127, 138–144, 151, 153, 156, 163, 179
France, *Messiah* in, 231, 265–269
Frankfort Cäcilienverein, 278
Franz, Robert, 284
Frasi, 52
Fremstad, Olive, 264
French Church (New York), *Messiah* in, 251
Für Freunde der Tonkunst (Rochlitz), 276–277

Gadski, Johanna, 264
Gahagan, Usher, 58 (note)
Gainsborough, Thomas, 136, 168
Galli-Curci, Amelita, 264
Garrick, David, 90, 107, 123, 145–146, 168
Gasse, Ferdinand, 267
Gates, Bernard, 23
Gauntlett, Henry John, 232–233
Gay, John, 3, 5, 16, 21–23, 52, 53; see also ACIS AND GALATEA; THE BEGGAR'S OPERA
Gazetteer, The, 138

Geminiani, Francesco, 91, 146
General Advertiser, The, 118 (note), 131, 138, 139
Gentleman's Magazine, The, 58, 137, 139, 140, 157, 159, 281
George I, 132, 187
George II, 24, 40, 44, 50, 56, 93, 116–117, 131, 132, 133, 136, 187
George III, 65 (note), 172, 183, 187–196, 212–213, 215–216, 220, 221, 255, 299
George V, 65 (note)
Georgian England, *Messiah* in, 113–231, 237
Germany, *Messiah* in, 231, 265, 269–279
Giardini, Signor, 122–123, 165
Gibson, Edmund, Bishop of London, 23–24, 29, 33, 56
Gilbert, William Schwenck, 72
Girardeau, Isabella, 5
Girdler, Joseph, 300
"Glory to God," 175, 255, 261
Gloucester, 161, 162, 167; *Messiah* in, 123, 152 (note), 166, 167–168, 169
Gluck, Christoph Willibald, 257, 273
Godolphin, Lady, 129
Goethe, Wolfgang von, 269, 274–277
Goldschmidt, Hugo, 234 (note)
Goldsmith, Oliver, 38, 90
Gospel Magazine, The, 120–124
Granville, Bernard, 127, 139
Granville, Bernard II, 215
Granville, Harriet Joan, 215
Graun, Heinrich, 274
Graupner, Gottlieb, 258
Gray's Inn Journal, 231
Green, Samuel, 190
Green, Thomas, 156
Grétry, André Ernest Modeste, 257
Greville, Charles, 241–242
Grimaldi, Nicolini, *see* NICOLINI
Grimm, Johann Friedrich Karl, 171
Grinfield, Charles Theodore, 247–248
Grinfield, Steady, 300
Grinfield, Thomas, 247–248
Grub-Street Journal, 16–17
Guilio Cesare, 20
Guilmant, Alexandre, 268–269

Hadden, J. Cuthbert, 238–239, 246 (note)

INDEX 327

Hague, Joseph, 300
Halifax, *Messiah* in, 165
Hall, Robert, 212–213
"Hallelujah Chorus," xix, 62, 63, 66, 68, 74, 79, 81, 85–86, 107 (note), 117 (note), 127, 132, 144, 147, 160, 161, 177, 194, 196, 205, 212–213, 218, 221, 222, 229, 245, 248, 251, 252, 253, 254, 255, 256, 257, 258, 259, 260, 262, 266, 267, 268, 269, 273, 278 (note), 283; custom of standing during performance of, 116–117, 123, 256
Haman, 28
Haman and Mordecai (Pope), 23–24, 53, 115
Hamburg, *Messiah* in, 231, 269
Hamilton, Mary, 196–197
Hamilton, Newburgh, 35, 52
Hamlet, xx, 107, 242, 246
Hanbury, William, 119, 162–164, 227–228
Handel, George Frideric: *Life and Character:* xxi, 64–65, 149–150, 233–234, 236; his blindness, 141, 150, 155; his death and burial, 156–157; his generosity, 143–144; his harpsichord performance, 3, 5, 216; his independence, 129; his materialism, 31–33; his organ performance, 90, 95–96, 99, 138, 140, 141, 149–150; his religion, 31, 78–83; anecdotes concerning, 63, 78–80, 89–90, 131, 142, 187; compared with Sebastian Bach, 81–84; monuments to, 160–161; in Dublin, 88–108; in London, 3–44, 63–87, 113–157; in Oxford, 44–47; not a church composer, 84–87, 235–237
Reputation: his phenomenal vogue in England, xx–xxi, 144–147, 157–161, 224–231, 232–248; his place in English fiction, 130, 147–148, 246–247; satires upon (poetical), 27–29, 50; (prose), 25–26, 41–48, 114–115, 218–220; tributes to (poetical), xxi, 26, 48–50, 101–102, 124–125, 131–132, 146, 157, 158–160, 210–211, 216–218, 247–248; (prose), 3–4, 35, 38, 39, 40, 48–49, 79, 85, 100–101, 113, 125–128, 130, 144–147, 149, 150, 156–158, 160, 166–167

Handel, George Frideric (*Cont.*): 172–179, 211–214, 222, 223–225, 231, 232–238, 240–241, 246–248, 253–255, 256, 258, 261–263, 266–269, 270, 273–277; *see also* UNIVERSALITY
Works: his Italian operas, 3–9, 15, 16, 17, 19, 20, 21–23, 30–33, 236–237, 288; his shift from opera to oratorio, 23–33, 40–51; his oratorios: general characteristics, 33–40; his faulty declamation, 75–76; his librettists, 52–57; his peculiar powers in, 35–40; his "plagiarisms," 68–75, 234, 236; *see also* ITALIAN OPERA; ORATORIO; names of individual arias, choruses, operas, and oratorios
Handel and Haydn Society (Boston), xix, 153 (note), 258–260
Handel and Haydn Society (New York), 260
Handel Commemorations: of 1784, 152–153, 188–211, 212–213, 215–218, 252, 271 and note; subsequent commemorations, 214–215, 218–221, 241, 271
Handel Festivals, xxi, 110, 213, 233, 234, 241–246, 251
Handel's Ghost (Robinson), 217
Handel's Songs Selected from His Oratorios, 181, 186
Hannam-Clark, Theodore, 166 (note)
Hannibal, 246
Hanston, Mr., 252
Harcourt, Eugène d', 268
Hardingham, Mr., 165
Harlequin-Horace (Miller), 19
Harmonic Society of New York, 153 (note), 260
Harrington, Henry, 169 (note)
Harris, James, 145
Harris, Mrs. James, 165, 171
Harrison, James, 185
Harrison, John, 287 (note)
Hastings, Warren, 218–219, 220
Hauptmann, Moritz, 279
Hauser, Franz, 279
Hawkins, Sir John, 31, 79–80, 119, 145, 150
Haydn, Franz Joseph, 219, 220–221, 223–224, 225, 235, 240, 251, 257, 258,

INDEX

Haydn, Franz Joseph (*Cont.*): 259–260, 273, 277; *Creation* versus *Messiah*, 223–224
Hayes, William, 48, 144, 146, 151, 161, 162, 165, 166, 167
"He shall feed His flock," 75, 107 (note), 132, 175, 251–252, 259, 260, 273
"He that dwelleth," 107 (note)
"He trusted in God," 176, 216, 245
"He was cut off," 107 (note), 176
"He was despised," 63, 68, 75, 100, 107 (note), 127, 128, 132, 147, 175–176, 180, 182, 213–214, 251
Hearne, Thomas, 44
Heaton, Isaac, 300
Heidegger, John James, 27, 48
Heim, Mr., 255
Herder, Johann Gottfried, 269–270, 274–275
Hereford, *Messiah* in, 167, 169
Hertford, Lady, 114
Hervey, D. E., 246 (note)
Heseltine, James, 58 (note)
Heywood, Eliza, 125–126
Hill, Aaron, 3–4, 29–30
Hill, John, 106, 107 (note)
Hill, Uriah C., 260
Hiller, Johann Adam, 270–272, 273
"His yoke is easy," 69, 175, 259, 283
Histoire de la Musique (Lavoix), 268
History of England in the Eighteenth Century (Lecky), 235–236
History of Music in England (Walker), 246
History of the Origin and Progress of the Meeting of the Three Choirs (Lysons), 152 (note), 166 (note)
Hitler, Adolf, 279
Hogarth, George, 118
Hogarth, William, 27, 28, 136
Holden, William, 300
Holinshed, Raphael, 74
Holmes, Vice-Chancellor, 44, 47
Homer, 30, 86, 172, 187, 208, 209, 235, 246
Hone, William, 56 (note)
Hopkinson, Francis, 167–168
"How beautiful are the feet," 106, 107 (note), 177
Howard, Samuel, 300
Howe, Julia Ward, 263

Howkins, Edward, 300
Huddersfield Choral Society, 287 (note)
Hudson, Robert, 300
Hudson, Thomas, 82
Hughes, John, 18, 20
Hughes, William, xxi–xxii, 40, 146–147, 288
Humphreys, Samuel, 24–25, 29, 44, 53
Hungary, *Messiah* in, 265 (note)
Hurdis, James, 218
Hurdis, Thomas, 300
Hydaspes (Mancini), 12–13
Hymen, 93, 118 (note), 180
"Hymne Triomphale" (*Judas Maccabeus*), 266

"I know that my Redeemer liveth," 75, 107 (note), 161, 169, 177, 194, 205, 251, 254, 259, 260, 261, 266
"If God be for us," 75, 107 (note), 272
Il Moderato (Jennens), 54, 57, 62, 93
Il Penseroso (Milton), 52, 54
Iliad, The, 172, 246
Incledon, Charles Benjamin, 259
Indy, Vincent d', 268
Inge, William, 222
Ireland, *Messiah* in, 47, 84, 88–89, 95–113, 114, 226, 227
Irwin, Lady A., 41, 47
Israel in Egypt, 35, 36, 37, 51, 56, 60, 74, 78, 119, 125, 167, 213, 225, 242, 251, 265 and note, 278–279, 286
Italian opera in England, 3–23, 29–33, 113, 130, 236–237, 288; operatic conventions, 14–15; vain singers, 16–17; Italian texts, 17–18; anti-British implications, 18–19; influence of *The Beggar's Opera*, 21–23; oratorio an extension of, 35
Italy, *Messiah* in, 231, 265 (note)

Jackson, G. K., 257–258
Jacob, John, 301
Jacobson, Theodore, 136
Janson, Mr., 89–90
Jebb, John, 213
Jennens, Charles, 54–57, 92–93, 103, 105 and note, 113–114, 125, 148–149, 185, 227, 301; his libretto of

Jennens, Charles (*Cont.*):
    Messiah, 58–63, 227–229, 268, 291–298; his dissatisfaction with *Messiah*, 76–78
Jephtha, 159, 188
Jerusalem Delivered (Tasso), 3
Jewsbury, Geraldine, 244
John, St., 59
Johnson, Mr., 91
Johnson, E., 148–149
Johnson, John, Mrs., 301
Johnson, Samuel, 20, 58 and note, 171–172, 185, 216, 301
Johnston, James, 287 (note)
Johnstone, John, 201
Jones, Edward, 217–218
Joseph, 118 (note), 120
Joshua, 111, 125–126
Journal of a Tour to the Hebrides (Boswell), 172
"Joy to the World," 261
Jubilate (Handel), 90
Judas Maccabeus, 33, 47, 53, 111, 126, 153, 155, 159, 164, 166, 170, 173, 182, 242, 251, 257, 258, 266, 273, 277, 278, 279
Judith (Arne), 152 (note)

Keats, John, 66
Kellogg, Clara L., 243 (note)
Kelly, George, 57
Kelly, Michael, 273
Kenleside, Mr., 301
Kent, James, 251
King Lear, 123
King's Chapel (Boston), *Messiah* in, 255, 256, 257, 259
King's Theatre in the Haymarket, 23–29, 40–43
Kinnoul, Lord, 79
Kirkpatrick, James, 58 (note)
Kitson, C. H., 58 (note)
Klage, Karl, 283
Klopstock, Friedrich Gottlieb, 58–59, 269
Kneller, Sir Godfrey, 136
Knowles, Charles, 287 (note)

Labbette, Dora, 287 (note)
Ladd, Nicholas, 301
L'Allegro (Milton), 52, 54

L'Allegro, Il Penseroso, ed Il Moderato, 60, 85, 92, 93, 115, 159, 224, 288
Lalo, Edouard, 266
Lamb, Charles, 244
Lambe, William, 106, 107 (note)
Lamoureux, Charles, 267–268
Land, Henry, 301
Langhorne, John, 159–160
"Lascia ch'io pianga" *(Rinaldo)*, 236
Laus Deo: The Worcester Collection of Sacred Harmony (Thomas), 256
Lavoix, Henri, 268
Lecky, William Edward, 235–236
Lectures on *Messiah*, xxi, 213–214
Lefanu, Alicia, 169 (note)
Leicester, *Messiah* in, 164
Leipzig, 82, 272, 278, 284; *Messiah* in, 271
Leipzig Thomasschule, 272
Leisure Hour, The, 232
Lemmens-Sherrington, Hellen, 243 (note)
Lent, *Messiah* during, 27, 32, 34, 84, 112, 153 and note, 280
"Let all the angels of God," 176–177, 272
"Let the bright Seraphim" *(Samson)*, 257
"Let us break," 107 (note), 177
"Letter to a Friend," 120–124, 226
Library of Congress, 184
Libretto of *Messiah*, 54, 56–57, 58–63, 227–229, 291–298
Lichfield, *Messiah* in, 222
Life of Hughes (Johnson), 20
Life of Watts (Johnson), 58
"Lift up your heads," 160, 176, 195–196, 255, 259
Lind, Jenny, 260–261
Lindegrene, Charles, 301
Lindsborg (Kansas), *Messiah* in, 263–265
Linley, Elizabeth Ann, 168–170
Linley, George Frederick, 168
Linley, Maria, 169 and note, 170
Linley, Thomas, 168, 185, 301
Lisbon, *Messiah* in, 265 (note)
Liszt, Franz, 278 and note
Liverpool, *Messiah* in, 165
Liverpool Philharmonic Orchestra, 287 (note)

Livy, 246
Lloyd, Edward, 243 (note)
Lockman, 119, 158–159
London, George, 7
London, *Messiah* in, xix, 113, 114–144, 145, 147–157, 160–161, 170–172, 188–189, 192–221, 226, 227, 238, 239–240, 241–245, 279–282
London Chronicle, The, 194–195
London Daily Post, The, 115, 118 (note), 125, 129, 180
London Magazine, The, 140, 141
London Philharmonic Orchestra, 287 (note)
London Welsh Choir, 287 (note)
"Lord gave the word, The," 177, 262
Loring, James, 258, 259
Love-à-la-Mode (Macklin), 123
Lowe, Thomas, 116
Lund, Signe, 264
Luther, Martin, 275–276
Lysons, Daniel, 152 (note), 166 (note), 169–170

Maas, Joseph, 243 (note)
Macbeth, xx
Macfarren, Sir George A., 279, 283–284
Macklin, Charles, *Love-à-la-Mode*, 123
Maclaine, Mr., 96, 99, 106
Maclaine, Mrs., 106, 107 (note)
Madin, Henri, 251
Madrid, *Messiah* in, 265 (note)
Madrigal Society, 301
Mainwaring, John, 102, 119, 130, 160, 226
Malme, George, 301
Man of Taste, The (Bramston), 27
Manchester, *Messiah* in, 221–222
Mancini, Francesco, 12–13
Manners of the Age, The, 19, 27
Mannheim, *Messiah* in, 269
Manns, Sir August, 242
Manuscripts of *Messiah*, 78 (note), 108, 110, 112, 179, 180, 252; autograph score, 63–66, 117 (note), 185, 238; preliminary sketches, 67; Dublin score, 106, 284; Foundling score, 141–142 and note, 179
Mara, Gertrude Elisabeth, 194, 221, 222, 266

Maria Magdalena Church (Breslau), *Messiah* in, 271–272
Mason, John, 106, 107 (note)
Mason, Lowell, 239, 240–241, 261–262
Mass in B Minor (Bach), 75, 234 (note)
Massachusetts Musical Society, 257
Matzenauer, Margaret, 264
Maurice, Thomas, 217
McGuckin, Barton, 243 (note)
Melba, Nellie, 243 (note)
Melbourne, *Messiah* in, xix
Memoirs of the Life of the Late George Frederic Handel (Mainwaring), 160
Mendelssohn, Felix, 64, 66, 225, 235, 238, 240, 283
Mercer's Hospital, 89, 90, 94, 95, 96, 97, 101, 110
Messiah, 29, 33, 35–36, 51, 54 (note); adaptations of, 282–286; Mozart's, 272–273, 279–282; alterations in, 77–78, 116; anecdotes concerning, 89–90, 162–164, 165, 167–168, 169, 170–171, 244, 270, 274; Anglicanism and, 59, 75–76, 82–83, 228–230, 235–239; Bach's *Saint Matthew Passion* and, 83–84; Christmas performances of, xix–xx, 153 and note, 239–240, 248, 259, 260–261, 269, 287; correct title of, 54 (note); composition of, xix, 63–78; critical observations upon, xxi, 76, 86, 100, 114, 146–147, 160, 172–179, 199–214, 215–216, 223–224, 239–240, 244–245; Easter performances of, 261, 263–265, 269; editions of: facsimile, 65–66 (note); Randall & Abell, 77, 183–185, 187, 272; subscribers to, 183–185, 299–302; Samuel Arnold, 187–188, 274; Mozart-Hiller, 272–273, 279–282; English Handel Society (Rimbault), 234; Robert Franz, 284; Die Deutsche Händel-Gesellschaft (Chrysander), 278, 284; Ebenezer Prout, 284–285; Jacob Maurice Coopersmith, 286–287; first Dublin performance, xx, 84, 95–107; first London performance, 114–118; first New York performance, 249–250; Haydn's *Creation*

Messiah (*Cont.*):
and, 223–224, 259–260; lectures on, xxi, 213–214; Lent performances of, 27, 32, 34, 84, 112, 153 and note, 280; libretto of, 54, 56–57, 58–63, 227–229, 291–298; manuscripts of, 78 (note), 108, 110, 112, 179, 180, 252; autograph score, 63–66, 117 (note), 185, 238; preliminary sketches, 67; Dublin score, 106, 284; Foundling score, 141–142 and note, 179; moral criticism of, 115–116, 117–118, 119–128, 132–134, 186, 198–214; in motion pictures, xix; in novels, 246–247; phonograph records of, xix, 287–288 (note); "plagiarisms" in, 68–75; poetical tributes to, xxi, 101–102, 124–125, 131–132, 157, 158–160, 210–211, 216–218, 247–248, 251; prose tributes to, 57, 79–80, 86, 100–101, 108–113, 116–117, 127–128, 143–144, 146–147, 160, 166–167, 167–168, 172–179, 211–216, 221, 222, 223–225, 226–228, 232–243, 246–248, 253–255, 256, 261–263, 266–269, 270, 273–277, 280–282; Protestantism and, xix, 78–87, 228–230, 235–239, 265, 269, 278; publication of, 118, 179–186, 187–188, 234, 239, 251, 256, 259, 267, 273, 278, 279, 282–287; radio performances of, xix; Roman Catholicism and, 228, 265; sacred or secular? 78–87; sermons on, xxi, 199–207; translations of: French, 268; German, 269–270, 278; Latin, 266; universality of, xix–xxi, 144–147, 157–161, 170, 172, 225–231, 237–241, 287; wordbooks of, 103–107, 112, 124, 148–149, 154, 196.

In Australia, xix, 265; in Austria, 265 (note), 272–273; in Belgium, 265 (note); in Denmark, 271 (note); in England, xix–xxi, 113–248, 265, 279–285; during eighteenth century, 113–231, 237; during nineteenth century, xxi, 74, 86–87, 116, 117 (note), 143, 152, 166 (note), 211–214, 225–231, 232–248, 261, 278 (note), 279–285; reaction against, 244–246; in Victorian literature, 246–248; during twentieth century,

Messiah (*Cont.*):
xix, xxi, 285–289; in France, 231, 265–269; in Germany, 231, 265, 269–279; in Hungary, 265 (note); in Ireland, 47, 84, 88–89, 95–113, 114, 226, 227; in Italy, 231, 265 (note); in Portugal, 265 (note); in Scotland, 221 (note); in Spain, 265 (note); in Sweden, 271 (note); in United States, xix–xx, 249–265, 285–289; during eighteenth century, 249–258; during nineteenth century, 255, 257–264; during twentieth century, xix–xx, 264–265, 285–289; *see also* individual arias and choruses; individual cities and towns.
Messiah (Alsop), 58
Messiah (Pope), 58
Messiah Quadrilles (Tamplin), 283
Messias, see MESSIAH IN GERMANY
Messias (Klopstock), 58–59
Messie, see MESSIAH IN FRANCE
Methodism, 31, 167, 200, 229–230
Michael Angelo, 232
Middleton, Arthur, 264
Miller, James, 19, 53
Millgrove & Brooks, 301
Milton, John, 51, 52–53, 54, 58, 85, 92, 134, 209, 224, 234, 247, 266; *see also* SAMSON; SAMSON AGONISTES; L'ALLEGRO, IL PENSEROSO, ED IL MODERATO
Minor, The (Foote), 122
Miser, The (Fielding), 43
Missa Solennis (Beethoven), 273
Moller, John Christopher, 251
Mongolenstrum, 279
Monroe, James, 260
Monthly Review, The, 58, 207, 216, 217
Moral criticism of Handelian oratorio, 23–24, 26–29; of *Messiah,* 115–128, 132–134, 186, 198–214
Morell, Thomas, 53
Morella, 111
Morgan, W. S., 255
Morning Chronicle, The, 279–280
Morning Post, The, 281
Mornington, Lord, 90–91
Morris, Charles, 301
Mosel, Ignaz von, 283

332 INDEX

Moses, 27, 276
Motion pictures, *Messiah* in, xix
Mount-Edgcumbe, Richard, 266
Mozart, Wolfgang Amadeus, xx, 32, 38, 64, 66, 74, 166 (note), 225, 235, 269, 273, 274, 277, 283–284; "additional accompaniments" to *Messiah*, 243, 252, 266, 269, 272–273; reception in England, 279–282
Musical Letters from Abroad (Mason), 261–262
Musical Memoirs (Parke), 220
Musical Society, 256, 257
Musical Times, The, 284–285
Mustafà, Domenico, 265 (note)
Muzio Scevola, 20

Nachricht von der Aufführung des Händelschen Messias (Hiller), 271
Napoleon, 277
Neal, Mr., 91, 95, 96, 103
Neal's Musick Hall, 91–92, 93, 95, 96, 97, 98, 99, 101, 103, 104, 108, 110
Netterville, Lord, 109, 110
New York, *Messiah* in, xix, 249–251, 260–261; see also ORATORIO SOCIETY OF NEW YORK
New York Choral Society, 260
New York City Tavern, *Messiah* in, 249
New York Musical Review and Gazette, The, 261
New York Journal, The, 249, 250
New York Philharmonic Society, 260
Newsham, James, 301
Newton, Sir Isaac, 223
Newton, John, 200–207, 211–214
Nicolini (Grimaldi), 4–5, 11, 12, 13
Nilsson, Christine, 243 (note), 261
"Ninth Symphony" (Beethoven), 85
"Nominalist and Realist" (Emerson), 262
Nordica, Lillian, 243 (note), 264
Norfolk (Virginia), *Messiah* in, 252
Norwich, *Messiah* in, 165
Notes and Queries, 149 (note), 232–233
Nottingham, *Messiah* in, 164
Novello, Clara, 243 (note)
Novello, Vincent, 239, 240
Novels, English, Handel in, 130, 147–148, 246–247; *Messiah* in, 246–247

"O death, where is thy sting?" 73, 107 (note), 132, 178
"O sacred Head now wounded," 75
"O thou that tellest," 107 (note), 174, 182, 260, 283
Observations on the Present State of Music and Musicians (Potter), 39, 158
Occasional Oratorio, The, 173, 182
Ode for St. Cecilia's Day, An (Handel), 53, 93, 115
Ode on the Passions (Collins), 167
Ode to Handel, An (Scott), 217
Ode to the Memory of Mr. Handel, An (Hayes), 167
Ode to Mr. Handel, An, 118 (note), 131–132
Ode Sacred to the Genius of Handel (Maurice), 217
Odyssey, The, 246
Of Taste (Pope), 135
Old Colony Collection, 258–259
Olney Hymns (Cowper), 208
"Ombra mai fu" *(Serse)*, 236; see also "THE CELEBRATED LARGO"
Onely, Richard, 58 (note)
Opéra Comique, L', 266
Oratorio in England, 23–51; birth of concert oratorio, 23–25; early reaction to, 25–29; eighteenth-century definitions of, 33–35; general characteristics of, 35–40; mode of eighteenth-century performance, 41, 147–153, 170–171, 193–194, 197–198, 214–215; mode of nineteenth-century performance, xxi, 234, 237, 239–240, 241–244, 245, 279–285; mode of twentieth-century performance, 285–287; moral criticism of, 23–24, 26–29, 115–128, 132–134, 186, 198–214; prohibitive prices of, 41–43, 170
Oratorio Society of New York, xix, 153 (note), 261
Orpin, Elizabeth, 301
Osgood, Mrs., 301
Ottone, 236
Overture to *Messiah*, 74, 76, 78, 98, 105 (note), 162, 173, 251, 254
Oxford, 161; *Messiah* in, 126, 163
Oxford Act, The, 45–46

INDEX

Oxford Act: A New Ballad-Opera, The, 46–47
Oxford University, 44–47; *Messiah* at, 164

Palmer, Mary, 196–197
Pantheon, 189, 192
Paradise Lost (Milton), 58, 134, 209
Parepa-Rosa, Euphrosyne, 243 (note)
Paris, *Messiah* in, 231, 265–269
Parke, William Thomas, 220
Parker, Richard, 136
Parker, W. Frye, 285
Parnasso, 118 (note), 180
Passina, 235
"Pastoral Symphony," 74, 105 (note), 147, 175, 268
Patey, Janet, 243 (note)
Patti, Adelina, 243 (note)
Paul, St., 27, 59, 63
Peabody, Asa, 258
Pemberton, Francis, 302
Pennsylvania, University of, *Messiah* at, 253, 254, 255
Pennsylvania Herald, The, 256
Pennsylvania Packet, The, 252, 254–255
"People that walked in darkness, The," 107 (note), 174, 272
Pepusch, John Christopher, 21
Pepys, Samuel, 66–67
Pergolesi, Giovanni, 38
Perkins, John, 301
Philadelphia, *Messiah* in, 252–255
Philharmonic Society (New York), 260
Philharmonick Society (Dublin), 94, 95
Philipp, Isidore, 268
Philips, Ambrose, 12
Phillips, Thomas, 259
Phonograph records, *Messiah* on, xix, 287–288 (note)
pifferari, 74
Pilkington, Letitia, 26, 107–108
Pindar, Robert, 301
Pitt, Thomas, 282–283
"Plagiarisms" in *Messiah,* 68–75
Plattel, William, 302
Plutarch, 74
Poem to the Memory of Handel, A (Jones), 217–218

Poetic Rehearsal of Handel's Sacred Oratorio "The Messiah" (Grinfield), 247–248
Poetical satires upon Handel, *see* SATIRES
Poetical tributes to Handel, *see* TRIBUTES
Poetical tributes to *Messiah, see* TRIBUTES
Polymnia; or, The Charms of Musick, 49–50
Pooley, Reverend, 56 (note)
Pope, Alexander, 23, 24, 26, 44, 47, 52, 53, 58, 85, 88, 113, 131, 134, 135, 151
Porpora, Nicola, 120
Port, Miss, 215
Portugal, *Messiah* in, 265 (note)
Potter, John, 39, 74, 158
Pougin, Arthur, 267–268
Pownall, Mrs. A. M., 252
Powys, Miss, 301
Prime, Samuel, 302
Progress of Music, The, 218
Prose satires upon Handel, *see* SATIRES
Prose tributes to Handel, *see* TRIBUTES
Prose tributes to *Messiah, see* TRIBUTES
Protestantism, *Messiah* and, xix, 78–87, 228–230, 235–239, 265, 269, 278
Prout, Ebenezer, 284–285
Psalm Magnificat (Vogler), 269
Psalmanazar, George, 8–9
Public Advertiser, The, 148, 152 (note), 155–156, 182, 183
Publication of *Messiah,* 118, 179–186, 187–188, 234, 239, 251, 256, 259, 267, 273, 278, 279, 282–287; *see also* EDITIONS OF *Messiah*
Purcell, Henry, 21, 38, 75, 178
Putland, John, 94
Pyrrhus and Demetrius (Scarlatti), 11

Quarterly Musical Magazine and Review, 281–282
Queen's Hall (London), *Messiah* in, 285
Queen's Hall Players, 287 (note)
Queen's Theatre in the Haymarket, 3–9

Racine, Jean Baptiste, 23, 24, 44
Radamisto, 20
Radio, *Messiah* on, xix
Ramsay, Allan, 136
Ramsay, Edward B., 213–214, 236
Randall, John, 165, 185, 302
Randall, Richard, 302
Randall & Abell, 77, 183–185, 272
Raugel, Félix, 268
Rea, Mr., 257
Reeves, Joseph, 58 (note)
Reeves, Sims, 243 (note)
Reformed German Church (Philadelphia), *Messiah* in, 252
Reinagle, Alexander, 251
Reinhold, Thomas, 116
"Rejoice greatly," 106, 107 (note), 175, 251, 254, 283
Relapse; or, Virtue in Danger, The (Vanbrugh), 122
Remarks on Mr. Avison's Essay on Musical Expression (Hayes), 146
Remarks upon Church Musick (Hughes), 146–147
Remarks upon the Use and Abuse of Musical Festivals, 213
"Remonstrance addressed to William Cowper, Esq. in 1788" (Seward), 210–211
"Rendi'l sereno al ciglio" *(Sosarme)*, 236
Rentfree, Toby, 12–13
Reply to the Author of Remarks on the Essay on Musical Expression, A (Hayes), 146
Requiem (Mozart), 74, 166 (note), 277
Revue Musicale, La, 266–267
Reynolds, Sir Joshua, 136, 168, 196–197
Rhenish Festival, 278
Riccardo Primo, 20
Rich, John, 21, 29
Rigby, Vernon, 243 (note)
Rimbault, Edward F., 284
Rinaldo, 3–9, 20, 21, 31, 47, 84, 236
Ring, John, 217
Riotte, Philipp Jacob, 283
Ripley, Gladys, 287 (note)
Robinson, Percy, 69 (note)
Robinson, Pollingrove, 217
Robinson, Turner, 26
Rochfort, John, 94

Rochlitz, Johann Friedrich, 273, 276–277, 279
Rockstro, William Smith, 234–235, 236
Rodelinda, 20, 236
Rolli, Paoli, 42
Roman Catholicism, *Messiah* and, 228, 265
Rome, *Messiah* in, 265 (note)
Roome, Francis, 302
Rosalinda (Lockman), 119
Rosamond (Clayton), 6, 11
Rossi, Giacomo, 3–4
Rothery, William, 112
Roubiliac, Louis François, 160–161, 238
Rousseau, Jean Jacques, 80
Royal Academy of Music, 16, 21, 22
Rubens, Peter Paul, 146
Rudersdoff, Hermine, 243 (note)
Russel, W., 148–149
Russell, Mr., 130

Sacred Harmonic Society, 66 (note), 143, 153 (note), 239, 241, 242
Sacred Music Society of New York, 260
Sacred Oratorio, A, 115–118, 131, 134, 180, 186
Sage & Clough, 251
Saint Cécile, 267
Saint Matthew Passion (Bach), 234 (note); compared with *Messiah*, 83–84
Salisbury, 161, 162, 251
Salisbury Festival, *Messiah* at, 161, 165, 169
Salmon, William, 302
Samson, 35, 52, 60, 67, 111, 114–115, 118 (note), 120, 126–127, 146, 147, 155, 159, 170, 173, 178–179, 180, 182, 184, 188, 257, 277, 278, 286, 288
Samson Agonistes (Milton), 52
Sandwich, Earl of, 196
Santley, Charles, 243 (note)
Sargent, Malcolm, 287 (note)
Satires upon Handel (poetical), 27–29, 50; (prose), 25–26, 41–48, 114–115, 218–220
Saul, 37, 47, 51, 54, 55–56, 57, 61, 62, 102, 111, 118 (note), 146, 180, 286, 288

INDEX

Saville, John, 222
Scarlatti, Alessandro, 11
Scenes from Clerical Life (Eliot), 247
Schaum, J. O. H., 283
Schiavonetti, Elisabetta Pilotti, 5
Schmidt, John Henry, 252
Schoelcher, Victor, 237–238
Schola Cantorum, 268
Schubert, Franz, 32, 66
Schulz, Edward, 274
Schumann-Heink, Ernestine, 264
Schwenke, Christian Friedrich, 278, 283
Scipione, 20
Scotland, *Messiah* in, 221 (note)
Scots Magazine, 190, 193, 198
Scott, Thomas, 217
Scott, Sir Walter, 32, 211
Seasons, The (Haydn), 221
See and Seem Blind, 25–26, 50
Seiffert, Max, 284
Selby, William, 255–256
Semele, 53, 81, 120, 131, 288
Senesino, 16, 26, 27, 50, 128
Sense Against Sound, 219
Series of Reflections on the Sacred Oratorio of the Messiah, A, 211–212
Sermons on *Messiah*, xxi, 199–207
Serse, 236, 288
Seward, Anna, 52, 209–211, 218–219, 221–224
Shaftesbury, Lord, 118
Shakespeare, William, xx, 4, 32, 62, 74, 76, 123, 168, 178–179, 189, 223, 224, 230, 231, 233, 234, 235, 241, 242, 246, 280, 288
Shard, Sophia, 302
Sharp, John, 302
Sharps, Messrs., 302
Shaw, George Bernard, 172, 239–240, 245
Shaw, Robert, 252
Sheffield, *Messiah* in, 221
Shelley, Percy Bysshe, 66
Shenstone, William, 166–167, 226
Sheridan, Richard Brinsley, 48, 90, 168, 169
Sheridan, Mrs. Richard Brinsley, *see* Elizabeth Ann Linley
Sheridan, Thomas, 100
Sheureux, Mr., 302
Sikes, Thomas, 302

Simpson, Mr., 302
"Since by man came death," 177–178
Siroe, 22
Smart, Sir George, 280–281
Smith, John, 302
Smith, John Christopher, 65 (note), 113, 141, 142 and note, 143, 145, 150, 151, 156
Smith, William C., 179 (note)
Smock-Alley Theatre, 107
Smollett, Tobias, 52, 158
Société des Concerts du Conservatoire, 267, 268
Société G. F. Haendel, 268
Société de l'Harmonée Sacrée, 267
Società Musicale Romana, 265 (note)
Solinus, Mr., 302
Solomon, 155
Sonatas or Chamber Aires for a German Flute, Violin, or Harpsichord, 180
Songs in *Messiah*, 181–183, 185, 186
Sophia, Princess, 190, 192, 193, 197
Sosarme, 236
Spain, *Messiah* in, 265 (note)
Spectator, The, 2, 4, 6–14, 17–18, 30
Spragg, Samuel, 302
St. Andrew's Church (Dublin), 90
St. Augustine's Church (Philadelphia), *Messiah* in, 255
St. James's Hall (London), *Messiah* in, 245
St. Patrick's Cathedral (Dublin), 94, 95, 108
St. Paul's Chapel (New York), 260
St. Paul's Church (New York), 251
St. Werburgh Church (Dublin), 95
Stainer, Sir John, 246
Stanley, John, 122–123, 143
Star, The (London), 239–240
Steele, Richard, 4, 5–6, 90
Steigler, John, 302
Stevens, Richard, 302
Stewart, Humphrey J., 246 (note)
Stockholm, *Messiah* in, 271 (note)
Stone Chapel (Boston), *see* King's Chapel
Storer, Maria, 251, 254
Strada, 26
Stradella, Alessandro, 74
Strafford, Lady, 47

Streicher, Andreas, 274
Stukeley, William, 138
Stumpff, Johann A., 274
Subscribers to *Messiah* (first edition), 183–185, 299–302
Sullivan, Sir Arthur, 72, 284
"Surely He hath borne our griefs," 75, 176, 262
Susanna, 155
Sweden, *Messiah* in, 271 (note)
Swensson, Alma, 263
Swensson, Carl, 263
Swieten, Baron Gottfried van, 272
Swift, Jonathan, 12, 16, 21, 90, 94–95, 107–108, 134
Symphony Hall (Boston), *Messiah* in, xix
Synge, Edward, Bishop of Elphin, 114

Talbot, Catherine, 47–48, 119, 126–127, 140, 141, 227
Tamerlano, 20
Tamplin, Augustus Lechmere, 283
Task, The (Cowper), 208–211
Tasso, 3, 30
Tatler, The, 6
Taylor, Sedley, 69 (note)
Tears of Music, The (Langhorne), 158–159
Te Deum (Handel), 90
Tempest, The, 224
Temple, William Johnston, 220
Teseo, 20
Theatre Royal (Lincoln's Inn Fields), 21
Theatrical Register, The, 170
"Their sound is gone out," 107 (note), 177
"Then shall be brought to pass," 107 (note)
"Then shall the eyes of the blind," 107 (note), 175
Theocritus, 53
"There were shepherds," 107 (note)
Thomas, Isaiah, 256
Thompson, Charles, 302
Thompson, Samuel, 302
Thomyris (Bononcini), 11
"Thou art gone up," 107 (note), 177, 272
"Thou shalt break them," 107 (note), 177, 263

Thrale, Hester Lynch, Mrs., 171, 172
Three Choirs, 163, 165–168; *see also* GLOUCESTER; WORCESTER; HEREFORD
Three Lectures on the Cathedral Service of the Church of England (Jebb), 213
"Thus saith the Lord," 107 (note), 174
"Thy rebuke," 107 (note), 176, 263
Times, The (London), 281
Titian (Tiziano Vicellio), 146
Titiens, Therese, 243 (note)
"To the Manes of Mr. Handel" (Lockman), 158–159
Tod Jesu, Der (Graum), 274
Tom Jones (Fielding), 130
Tomkinson, Miss, 302
Torchet, Julien, 266
Town and Country Magazine, The, 215
Townsend, Horatio, 91 (note), 97 (note), 105, 235
Translations of *Messiah:* French, 268; German, 269–270, 278; Latin, 266
Trebelli, Zelia, 243 (note)
Tributes: to Handel (poetical), xxi, 26, 48–50, 101–102, 124–125, 131–132, 146, 157, 158–160, 210–211, 216–218, 247–248; (prose), 3–4, 35, 38, 39, 40, 48–49, 79, 85, 100–101, 113, 125–128, 130, 144–147, 149, 150, 156–158, 160, 166–167, 172–179, 211–214, 222, 223–225, 231, 232–238, 240–241, 246–248, 253–255, 256, 258, 261–263, 266–269, 270, 273–277
To *Messiah* (poetical), xxi, 101–102, 124–125, 131–132, 157, 158–160, 210–211, 216–218, 247–248, 251; (prose), 57, 79–80, 86, 100–101, 108–113, 116–117, 127–128, 143–144, 146–147, 160, 166–167, 167–168, 172–179, 211–216, 221, 222, 223–225, 226–228, 232–243, 246–248, 253–255, 256, 261–263, 266–269, 270, 273–277, 280–282
Trinity Church (New York), 249, 250
Trinity College (Dublin), 93, 98, 105 (note)
Tristan und Isolde (Wagner), 278 (note)
Trivia (Gay), 3
Trocadéro (Paris), *Messiah* in, 266, 268–269

"Trumpet shall sound, The," 75, 107 (note), 128, 147, 178, 272
Tuckey, William, 249–250
Turner, Sir Edward, 150
Two Lectures on the Genius of Handel (Ramsay), 213–214
Tyrwhitt, Thomas, 58 (note)

United States, *Messiah* in, xix–xx, 249–265, 285–289
Universal Magazine, The, 194, 198, 207
Universal Spectator, The, 124
Universality of *Messiah,* xix–xxi, 144–147, 157–161, 170, 172, 225–231, 237–241, 287
University Church (Leipzig), *Messiah* in, 27
"Unto which of the angels," 106, 107 (note)
Unwin, William, 199
Upton, George, 261
Uranian Society, 252–254
Urbani, Valentini, *see* VALENTINI
Urio, 74
Utrecht, *Messiah* in, 265 (note)

Valentini (Urbani), 5, 11–12
Vanbrugh, John, 121; *The Relapse,* 122
Vanini, Francesca, 5
"Veni, o figlio" *(Ottone),* 236
Victor, Benjamin, 112–113, 151
Victoria, Queen, xxi, 238
Victorian England, *Messiah* in, xxi, 74, 86–87, 116, 117 (note), 143, 152, 166 (note), 211–214, 225–231, 232–248, 261, 278 (note), 279–285; reaction against, 244–246; in Victorian literature, 246–247
Vienna, *Messiah* in, 265 (note), 272–273
Village Curate, The (Hurdis), 218
Virgil, 30, 291
Vogler, Abbé, 269
Voltaire, François Marie Arouet, 134

Wagner, Richard, 197, 278 (note), 286
Wake, William, Archbishop of Canterbury, 29
Walker, Ernest, 246
Walker, Nellie, 287 (note)
Walker, Norman, 287 (note)
Walpole, Sir Edward, 302
Walpole, Horace, 33, 49, 99, 114–115, 130–131, 215
Walpole, Robert, 21, 22, 42, 133
Walsh, John, 118, 180–185, 186
Ward, Joseph, 106, 107 (note)
Warton, Joseph, 52
Warwick, Earl of, 302
Washington, George, 257
Water Musick, The, 159
Watts, Isaac, 58
Watts, J., 154
Way of All Flesh, The (Butler), 235, 246–247
Webb, Thomas Smith, 258
Weideman, Charles Frederick, 302
Weimar, *Messiah* in, 269–270, 276
Weinstock, Herbert, 56 (note)
Wellington, Duke of, 283
Wells, *Messiah* in, 161
Well-Tempered Clavier, The (Bach), 74
Wentworth, Lady Lucy, 47
Wesley, Charles (the Younger), 165
Wesley, John, 31, 128, 133, 134, 167, 200, 227, 229–230
Wesley, Samuel, 166 (note)
Westminster Abbey, 261 (note); *Messiah* in, 143, 188–211, 214–221, 241, 248, 251, 270–271; Handel buried in, xx, 157, 224; his monument in, 160–161
Westminster Infirmary, 143
Westmoreland, Lady, 131
Wetton, H. Davan, 142
Whichcote, Christopher, 302
Whitefield, George, 133, 229
Whitehall Evening Post, The, 156, 157
"Why do the nations," 107 (note), 147, 177
Whyte, Laurence, 101–102
Wilder, Victor, 268
Wilhelm von Nassau, 279
William IV, 241
Williams, Anna, 243 (note)
Williams, Charles Lee, 166 (note)
Williams, Harold, 287 (note)
Wilsing, Daniel Frederic, 283
Wise, Henry, 7
Wolf, E. W., 269

Woman of Taste, The, 27–29, 50
Wood, Sir Henry J., 242–243
Worcester, 162, 282; *Messiah* in, 166–167, 168, 169
Wordbooks of *Messiah,* 103–107, 112, 124, 148–149, 154, 196
World, The (London), 245
"Worthy is the Lamb," 160, 178, 196, 255, 262
Wren, Sir Christopher, 74
Wright & Wilkinson, 185
Wyatt, James, 189, 190

Wyatt, Thomas, 302
Wynne, Edith, 243 (note)
Wynne, John (of Cambridge), 302
Wynne, John (of Dublin), 95
Wynne, Sir Watkin Williams, 188

Yale University, 154
Yonge, Lady Sarah, 302
York, *Messiah* in, 241

Zelter, Carl Friedrich, 270, 275–276, 279

L4